"*Trauma-Focused ACT* is going to go down as one of the [informed care. Written in a highly accessible, practical style, Harris provides the acceptance and commitment therapy (ACT) therapist with a comprehensive, step-by-step approach to working with traumatized clients. The book is chock-full of tidbits of clinical advice that could only come from a highly skilled therapist with loads of experience working with trauma. If you read this book from cover to cover (and maybe read it again), you will have a complete sense of how to roll out, manage, and complete a high-potency treatment with a traumatized client. There aren't many books out there that achieve this high ground, and this is one of them! Highly recommended."

> —**Kirk Strosahl, PhD**, cofounder of ACT, and coauthor of *Brief Interventions for Radical Change*

"This beautifully written and intensely practical book offers a rich array of clinical insights and strategies covering the many nuances and concerns that show up when working with various forms of trauma from an ACT point of view. I consider it *the* ACT book for trauma, and a must-read for mental health practitioners who are looking for a compassionate and transformative approach to helping their clients heal old wounds and engage their lives now in ways that matter to them."

> —**John P. Forsyth, PhD**, coauthor of *The Mindfulness and Acceptance Workbook for Anxiety* and *Acceptance and Commitment Therapy for Anxiety Disorders*

"Nobody writes with greater clarity and offers more concrete, useful, and innovative suggestions and strategies than Russ Harris. This is *the* definitive book for treating trauma-related difficulties with compassion, courage, and cutting-edge scientific tools."

> —**Todd B. Kashdan, PhD**, professor of psychology, and author of *Curious?* and *The Upside of Your Dark Side*

"This book is a major milestone in understanding how ACT can support recovery from trauma. In this comprehensive manual, Russ Harris provides rationales, exercises, and transcripts to give therapists clear guidance on working effectively with the full range of problems associated with trauma. From hypervigilance, reexperiencing, avoidance, freezing, and dissociation to responses of shame and guilt—*Trauma-Focused ACT* provides numerous sensitive, respectful, and progressive ways to work with clients. Written with warmth and compassion, this is the indispensable guide for using ACT to help people with trauma."

> —**Eric Morris, PhD**, senior lecturer and psychology clinic director at La Trobe University, and coauthor of *Acceptance and Commitment Therapy for Psychosis Recovery*

"Russ Harris's ACT publications are renowned for being incredibly accessible and clinically useful. I can honestly say that with *Trauma-Focused ACT*, Russ has outdone himself. At every step along the journey, Russ generously offers modifications and practical tips to help us when things don't go according to plan, while keeping us grounded in the science of ACT. *Trauma-Focused ACT* is an important clinical resource that truly honors the complexity of human suffering and the interpersonal therapeutic endeavor."

> —**Sheri Turrell, CPsych**, peer-reviewed ACT trainer; coauthor of *ACT for Adolescents* and *The Mindfulness and Acceptance Workbook for Teen Anxiety*; psychoanalyst; and adjunct lecturer at the University of Toronto

"This is an excellent, comprehensive, contemporary, and instructive guide on how to conduct TFACT. Importantly, consistent with the ACT framework, the TFACT approach is sensitively person-focused, holistic, and open to incorporating empirically supported strategies from different therapy models. Russ describes TFACT in a very accessible and practical way, with lots of illustrative therapist-client transcripts, worksheets, and other useful clinical tools. This book will serve as an excellent resource for clinicians at any level and from any theoretical orientation in their delivery of empowering support to people whose lives are constrained by the pain of trauma."

> —**Kenneth Pakenham, PhD**, emeritus professor of clinical and health psychology at The University of Queensland, and author of *The Trauma Banquet*

"ACT is a powerful therapeutic approach to working with trauma and its complex associated issues, such as complicated grief, identity issues, and shame. Russ Harris has pulled together all the latest cutting-edge research and practice into a manual that is broad and deep in its theoretical and practical application. If you work with clients who experience trauma, then this is a must-buy for your bookshelf, that you will find yourself constantly reaching for."

> —**Joe Oliver**, founder of Contextual Consulting, and coauthor of *The Mindfulness and Acceptance Workbook for Self-Esteem*

"I am profoundly grateful for this book. Russ Harris has applied his masterful ability to make complex ACT concepts highly accessible to the vitally important and often enigmatic treatment of trauma. Filled with exercises, metaphors, and handouts, this book offers dozens of fresh tools for your practice. The addition of the essential physiological factors which often accompany trauma is critical to the understanding of its treatment and is sure to enrich your clinical conversations. Russ walks us through dialogues with clients demonstrating a brilliant clinician's understanding of the importance of weaving compassion and dignity into sessions. He will leave you with little doubt that you can hold challenging sessions with trauma survivors. If you work with clients with trauma, this is a must-read text."

> —**M. Joann Wright, PhD**, fellow of the Association of Contextual Behavioral Science, peer-reviewed ACT trainer, and coauthor of *Learning ACT for Group Treatment* and *Experiencing ACT from the Inside Out*

"As a psychotherapist, whether you work with traumatized patients or not, this book is for you. With his usual simple but precise language, Russ Harris leads you through applying your ACT skills to simple or complex trauma. This well-designed model—based on four flexible stages of intervention—encourages therapists to apply ACT according to personal style, experience, and creativity."

> —**Nanni Presti**, professor at Kore University of Enna, Sicily

"Russ Harris did it again—gifting us a guide about a complex clinical issue, written in a simple yet comprehensive way that distills the latest insights about trauma-focused clinical work. *Trauma-Focused ACT* is unique in its wide applicability: It will give you a firm framework for your clinical work while also leaving—and emphasizing—space and opportunities to flexibly adapt the framework to each of your individual clients. For experienced ACT therapists, it will be a source of inspiration how to further tweak and refine their trauma-focused work."

> —**Valerie Kiel**, psychologist, and peer-reviewed ACT trainer

"Russ Harris excels in making complicated stuff comprehensible. If you have experience with ACT for some time and now want to start working with people who have experienced trauma, this book is for you. If you have worked treating people who have experienced trauma and now want to start using ACT, this book is for you. In a very structured yet flexible way, Russ Harris guides you through the important aspects of trauma and the six core processes of ACT. The work comes to life with the many case examples and dialogues that help you understand how to address important issues."

> —**Jacqueline A-Tjak, PhD**, clinical psychologist, and peer-reviewed ACT trainer

"This manuscript is an invaluable resource for clients wrestling with any form of traumatic experience—guiding them to get back into their life, move beyond trauma, and find themselves again. It's written with so much compassion and knowledge, and it's full of resources that demonstrate—page by page—how ACT can make a difference when working with trauma-related matters. If you're a clinician working with trauma, passionate about third-wave therapies, this is a must-read book!"

—**Patricia E. Zurita Ona, PsyD**, author of *The ACT Workbook for Teens with OCD* and *Acceptance and Commitment Therapy for Borderline Personality Disorder*

"In the spirit of his go-to clinical text, *ACT Made Simple*, Russ Harris has produced another vital and practical resource for clinicians working with trauma. *Trauma-Focused ACT* presents a user-friendly, yet sophisticated, model of case conceptualization, treatment planning, and cutting-edge interventions derived from ACT and informed by the latest science on trauma. Russ walks the reader through countless case examples and clinical exchanges to help translate principles into practice, emphasizing the safety and willingness of the client throughout the stages of therapy. Given the high prevalence and varied manifestations of trauma across cultures and populations, this book is sure to be of great value to clinicians."

—**Lou Lasprugato**, marriage and family therapist, and peer-reviewed ACT trainer

"Russ Harris has an unusual ability to describe the work of ACT in a way that is both simple, clear, and profound. He has shown this in his earlier books, and this one on treatment of trauma is yet another example. The fact that he gives the concept of trauma a wide definition makes the book highly relevant for most, if not all, therapists working with psychological suffering."

—**Niklas Törneke, MD**, coauthor of *Learning RFT* and *The ABCs of Human Behavior*

Trauma-Focused

ACT

A Practitioner's Guide to
Working with Mind, Body & Emotion Using
Acceptance & Commitment Therapy

RUSS HARRIS

CONTEXT PRESS

An Imprint of New Harbinger Publications, Inc.

Publisher's Note

This publication is designed to provide accurate and authoritative information in regard to the subject matter covered. It is sold with the understanding that the publisher is not engaged in rendering psychological, financial, legal, or other professional services. If expert assistance or counseling is needed, the services of a competent professional should be sought.

Distributed in Canada by Raincoast Books

NEW HARBINGER PUBLICATIONS is a registered trademark of
New Harbinger Publications, Inc.

Context Press
An imprint of New Harbinger Publications, Inc.
5674 Shattuck Avenue
Oakland, CA 94609
www.newharbinger.com

Cover design by Amy Daniel; Acquired by Catharine Meyers;
Edited by Rona Bernstein; Indexed by James Minkin

FSC
www.fsc.org
MIX
Paper from
responsible sources
FSC® C011935

Library of Congress Cataloging-in-Publication Data

Names: Harris, Russ, 1938- author.
Title: Trauma-focused ACT : a practitioner's guide to working with mind, body, and emotion using
  acceptance and commitment therapy / Russ Harris.
Description: Oakland, CA : New Harbinger Publications, [2021] | Includes bibliographical references and
  index.
Identifiers: LCCN 2021029333 | ISBN 9781684038213 (trade paperback)
Subjects: LCSH: Acceptance and commitment therapy. | Psychotherapist and patient. | Post-traumatic
  stress disorder--Treatment.
Classification: LCC RC489.A32 H375 2021 | DDC 616.89/1425--dc23
LC record available at https://lccn.loc.gov/2021029333

Printed in the United States of America

23   22   21

10   9   8   7   6   5   4   3   2   1   First Printing

To my beloved Natasha: my friend, my companion, my advisor, my supporter, my teacher, my mentor, my guide…and the absolute love of my life. So many times, I wanted to give up—but you kept me going. So many times, I was stuck—and you helped me out. Volim te zauvek.

Contents

PART FOUR: Healing the Past

PART FIVE: Building the Future

What Is "Trauma-Focused ACT"?

CHAPTER ONE

The Many Masks of Trauma

"Trauma" is the Greek word for "wound," and "psyche" is the Latin word for "soul." From these ancient words, we get both the clinical term "psychological trauma" and the poetic term "soul wound." The latter term seems to convey much better the deep anguish and suffering so commonly involved in trauma. The pain from these wounds—physical, emotional, psychological, or spiritual—can impact every area of human life, and the fallout is often devastating: shattered world views; a fractured sense of self; loss of trust, security, or meaning; and the list goes on.

Soul wounds may occur at any age. For some, the trauma starts in childhood, at the hands of abusive caregivers. For others, it's not until adulthood that something tears their world apart. And when these life-shattering events happen, they can affect anything and everything: relationships, work, leisure, finances, physical health, mental health—even the very structure of the brain.

In acceptance and commitment therapy (ACT), we work intensively with every aspect of these soul wounds: cognitions, emotions, memories, sensations, urges, physiological reactions, and the physical body itself. And at times we will find this work intensely challenging. Inevitably, it triggers our own painful thoughts and feelings: perhaps anxiety, sadness, or guilt; perhaps frustration or disappointment; perhaps worry, self-doubt, or self-judgment. But when we make room for our own discomfort, dig deep into our compassion, and create a sacred therapeutic space—a place where we stand side-by-side with our clients, to help them heal their pasts, reclaim their lives, and build new futures—then our work, though often stressful, is deeply rewarding.

What Is Trauma?

Somewhat surprisingly, while it's easy to find a definition of posttraumatic stress disorder (PTSD), it's hard to find a clear definition of trauma. So to ensure we're on the same page, I'm going to share my own. (This isn't the "right" or "best" definition; it's just one that I trust works for our purposes.)

A "traumatic event" is one that involves a significant degree of actual or threatened physical or psychological harm—to oneself or others. This can include everything from miscarriage to murder; from divorce, death, and disaster to violence, rape, and torture; from accidents, injuries, and illnesses to the medical or surgical treatments for those things. It may also include incidents where people instigate, perpetrate, fail to prevent, or witness actions that violate or contradict their own moral code.

A "trauma-related disorder" involves:

1. direct or indirect experience of traumatic events

2. distressing emotional, cognitive, and physiological reactions to that experience

3. the inability to cope effectively with one's own distressing reactions

In this book, whenever I use the word "trauma," it's short for "trauma-related disorder," an umbrella term for a vast number of problems resulting from trauma, including PTSD, drug and alcohol problems, relationship issues, depression, anxiety disorders, personality disorders, sleep disorders, moral injury, chronic pain syndrome, sexual problems, aggression and violence, self-harming, suicidality, complicated grief, attachment disorders, impulsivity, and more. (Indeed, a clear diagnosis of PTSD is rare in comparison to the many other presentations of trauma.)

Many of these problems mask the trauma history that underpins them, leaving it deeply buried and long forgotten. And although we talk of "simple" trauma (a reaction to one major traumatic event) or "complex" trauma (relating to many traumatic events over a long period, often starting in childhood), there are many shades of gray between these extremes. However, no matter how simple or complex trauma may be, it always involves three streams of symptoms, which continually flow in and out of each other:

- **Reexperiencing traumatic events:** People reexperience traumatic events in a variety of ways, including nightmares, flashbacks, rumination, and intrusive cognitions and emotions.

- **Extremes of hyperarousal and hypoarousal:** Later, we'll explore these terms in depth; for now, let's keep it simple. With clients, rather than "hyperarousal," we talk about "fight or flight mode," which gives rise to anger, irritability, fear, anxiety, hypervigilance, difficulty sleeping, and poor concentration. Likewise, rather than "hypoarousal," we talk about "freeze or flop mode": the immobilization and shutting down of the body, which fosters apathy, lethargy, disengagement, emotional numbing, and dissociative states.

- **Psychological inflexibility:** The overarching aim of ACT is to develop psychological flexibility: the ability to be present, focused on and engaged in what we're doing; to open fully to our experience, allowing our cognitions and emotions to be as they are in this moment; and to act effectively, guided by our values. More simply: "be present, open up, and do what matters."

The flipside of this is psychological inflexibility, which boils down to:

  - cognitive fusion (our cognitions—including thoughts, images, memories, schemas, and core beliefs—dominate our awareness and our actions)

  - experiential avoidance (the ongoing attempt to avoid or get rid of unwanted cognitions, emotions, sensations, and memories—even when doing so is problematic)

  - remoteness from values (lack of clarity about or disconnection from our core values)

- unworkable action (ineffective patterns of behavior that tend to make life worse in the long term, such as social withdrawal, self-harm, and excessive use of drugs)

- loss of contact with the present moment (distractibility, disengagement, and disconnection from thoughts and feelings)

These three streams of symptoms—reexperiencing trauma, extremes of arousal, and psychological inflexibility—overlap and reinforce each other in a myriad of complex ways, giving rise to a truly vast range of clinical issues.

What Is Trauma-Focused ACT?

Trauma-focused ACT (TFACT) is neither a protocol nor a treatment for one specific disorder, such as PTSD. It is a compassion-based, exposure-centered approach to doing ACT, which is (a) trauma-informed: drawing upon relevant fields, such as evolutionary science, polyvagal theory, attachment theory, and inhibitory learning theory; (b) trauma-aware: attuned to the possible role of trauma in a wide range of clinical issues; and (c) trauma-sensitive: alert to the risks of experiential work, especially mindfulness meditation.

TFACT has three interweaving strands that apply to all trauma-related issues: living in the present, healing the past, and building the future.

Living in the present. This is the lion's share of our work in TFACT. It includes helping clients learn how to ground and center themselves; catch themselves disengaging or dissociating and bring their attention back to the here and now; connect with and be "at home" in their body; overcome debilitating hyperarousal and paralyzing hypoarousal; unhook from difficult cognitions and emotions; practice self-compassion in response to their pain; focus on and engage in what they're doing; interrupt dwelling on the past and worrying about the future; access a flexible, integrated sense of self; narrow, broaden, sustain, or shift attention as required; practice ACT-congruent emotion regulation; savor and appreciate pleasurable experiences; and connect with, live by, and act on their values. And it also includes skills training as required (e.g., assertiveness and communication skills) to enable values-based living.

Healing the past. Here we explore with clients how their past has shaped their present thoughts, feelings, and behaviors and actively work with past-oriented cognitions and the emotions that go with them. This includes "inner child" work, exposure to traumatic memories, forgiveness, and grieving.

Building the future. Here we use values-based goal setting, including relapse-prevention plans, to help clients plan and prepare for the future. Ideally, we're aiming for "posttraumatic growth": growing and changing in positive ways through the ordeals of the past, and applying the strengths, insights, and wisdom gained along the way, to build a better future.

Why Use Trauma-Focused ACT?

Acceptance and commitment therapy was created in the mid-eighties by Steven C. Hayes, Professor of Psychology at the University of Reno, Nevada, and further developed by his two cofounders, Kirk Strosahl and Kelly Wilson. Since that time, over 3,000 published studies—including more than 600 randomized controlled trials—have shown ACT's effectiveness with a wide range of clinical issues, from PTSD, depression, and anxiety disorders to substance use, shame, and chronic pain (Boals & Murrell, 2016; Lang et al., 2017; Gloster et al., 2020; Luoma et al., 2012).

Of particular note is some recent research by the World Health Organization (WHO). Since 2016, the WHO has been rolling out ACT programs in refugee camps around the world, and in 2020 its first randomized controlled trial was published in *The Lancet* (Tol et al., 2020). The results were impressive. The participants were South Sudanese women in a Ugandan refugee camp. Most of them had experienced repeated gender-based violence, as well as the horrors of warfare and the ongoing stress of living in a camp of 250,000 refugees. Yet just ten hours of ACT, delivered in a group program run by lay facilitators, resulted in significant reductions in both PTSD and depression.

However, aside from the evidence base, there are several other good reasons to use ACT for trauma-related issues.

A transdiagnostic approach. TFACT is a transdiagnostic model based on a small number of core processes that we can flexibly use with all diagnoses in the *Diagnostic and Statistical Manual of Mental Disorders* (DSM), including co-occurring disorders. For example, we could work with a client experiencing chronic pain, PTSD, and alcohol problems—and simultaneously target all those issues using the same few core ACT processes. Given that trauma presents in so many ways and comorbidity is common, such versatility is handy.

An exposure-based approach. TFACT includes exposure as a core element. In layperson's terms, exposure basically means deliberately making contact with "difficult stuff" to learn new, more helpful ways of responding to it. Inside our body, "difficult stuff" may include memories, thoughts, images, feelings, impulses, sensations, urges, emotions, numbness, and physiological reactions. Outside our body, "difficult stuff" may include people, places, objects, events, or activities. Prior to exposure, this "difficult stuff" triggers self-defeating patterns of behavior, but during exposure, clients learn new, more flexible, life-enhancing ways of responding.

An interpersonal approach. TFACT offers many ways to work at an interpersonal level—including an explicit focus on what is happening in the therapeutic relationship. This is good news, given that interpersonal problems are so common in trauma.

An integrative approach. As we travel through the world of TFACT, we'll explore a number of different theories that integrate well with it, including polyvagal theory, attachment theory, and inhibitory learning theory. (But don't worry—we won't get bogged down in the minutiae; we'll explore these theories from a practical perspective: light on technical jargon, heavy on clinical application.)

A compassion-based approach. Self-compassion is an integral part of TFACT—an essential aspect of all work with trauma. This ability to acknowledge our own pain and suffering and respond to ourselves with genuine kindness is fundamental for healing and recovery and a powerful antidote to shame.

A combined "bottom-up" and "top-down" approach. Early sessions of TFACT are typically "bottom up" in their emphasis: working with the physical body, emotions, feelings, sensations, somatic awareness, autonomic arousal, and so on. Later sessions are typically more "top-down": focusing more on cognitive flexibility, values, goal setting, action planning, and problem solving. However, most sessions include both approaches; the proportion of each varies from session to session, flexibly tailored to the needs and responses of each unique client.

A comprehensive approach. TFACT is a rich, multilayered, holistic approach for working comprehensively with all aspects of simple or complex trauma. Within this book you'll learn principles and processes for working with addiction, interpersonal problems, insomnia, self-harm, suicidality, emotion dysregulation, flashbacks, traumatic memories, dissociative states, a fractured sense of self...and a whole lot more. However, you don't have to be an ACT purist; if you wish to include resources from other models, such as eye-movement desensitization and reprocessing (EMDR) or prolonged exposure, *you can!* As we'll explore later, TFACT blends well with other models.

A brief approach. The demand for brief therapy is rapidly growing, and practitioners face the ever-growing challenge of how to optimize outcomes with as few treatment sessions as possible. Fortunately, TFACT works well as a brief therapy. Most of the book assumes standard therapy sessions of fifty minutes, with an average of ten to twelve per client. Of course, some clients do need long-term therapy, extending over years, but the majority respond well in shorter time frames. Chapter thirty-three, "TFACT as a Brief Intervention," covers how to do TFACT in settings where you only have a few sessions, which may even be as short as thirty minutes.

How to Use This Book

In writing this book, I assume you already know something about ACT: that you've done at least a beginners' level training or read an introductory textbook. Therefore, I have not included accounts of how ACT was developed or in-depth descriptions of basic theory. So if you're brand new to ACT, you *will* be able to pick it up as you go—but I recommend you first read the whole book, cover to cover, before using it. (This is because the core ACT processes are interdependent, so if you don't have a grasp of the whole model and the way these processes interact, you'll likely get stuck.) And then, if you like the approach, immediately work through an introductory level ACT textbook to build up the essential foundational knowledge that isn't covered here.

(On that note, I assume many readers have already read my own introductory level textbook, *ACT Made Simple* (Harris, 2019), so I've done my best to minimize overlap. Inevitably, there is some, but there's also a whole lot of brand-new stuff: many new topics, tools, techniques, and methods for working flexibly with function and process. And where I've revisited a favorite practice, such as "dropping anchor," I've taken it in a new direction with a clear trauma focus.)

EXTRA BIT

I've written a free e-book called *Trauma-Focused ACT—The Extra Bits*, which you can download from the "Free Resources" page on http://www.ImLearningACT. com. There you'll find links to all the worksheets and handouts featured in this book, as well as scripts for exercises and metaphors, YouTube videos, and MP3 audio recordings. In most chapters, you'll find an "Extra Bits" box like this one, which lists all the free materials in the corresponding chapter of the e-book. For example, in chapter one of Extra Bits, you'll find a PDF on "ACT and Telehealth," which shows you how to adapt everything in this textbook for both audiovisual and audio-only telehealth.

Structure

There are five parts to the book. Part one, "What Is 'Trauma-Focused ACT'?" explores what trauma is and how to conceptualize and work with it from an ACT perspective. Part two, "Beginning Therapy," covers the first two sessions, with an emphasis on setting up for maximal effectiveness and safety. Parts three, four, and five cover the three interweaving strands of TFACT: "Living in the Present," "Healing the Past," and "Building the Future."

Adapt Everything

As you go through this book, please adapt and modify everything to suit your way of working. That includes metaphors, scripts, worksheets, exercises, tools, techniques—everything! If you can think of a different way to say or do something that would work better for you and your clients, then go for it. Tap into your creativity; draw upon your experience; make it your own.

Curiosity and Openness

The TFACT approach has many commonalities with other models of trauma therapy—but also significant differences. So please bring an attitude of curiosity and openness to your learning. If you read something here that goes against your previous training, don't automatically dismiss it, but don't automatically take it on board, either. Instead, open to it; consider it; question it. Maybe it has a place in your way of working—or maybe it doesn't. No model is perfect; all have strengths and weaknesses; so take what's useful from this one, and leave anything that's not. And keep in mind the words of Carl Jung: "Learn your theories as well as you can, but put them aside when you touch the miracle of the living soul."

CHAPTER TWO

An ACT Model of Trauma

Are you ready to dive into the deep and icy waters of case conceptualization? In TFACT we conceptualize trauma somewhat differently than in many other models, so it's important to understand this perspective, as it's the foundation for all that follows. (A word of caution for ACT newbies: this chapter introduces a slew of technical terms, so if you find it daunting, don't worry; it will all come together later as we get into the clinical applications. And for experienced ACT practitioners, a quick refresher never hurts, right?) Before we get into the ACT model of trauma, I'll give a quick summary of ACT and some useful exercises to illustrate key concepts to your clients.

A Brief Summary of ACT

Acceptance and commitment therapy is an existential, humanistic, mindfulness-based, cognitive behavioral therapy. In everyday language, the aim of ACT is to help people reduce psychological suffering and build rich, meaningful lives. It does this through helping us to:

- learn new psychological skills to reduce the impact of difficult emotions and cognitions—so they can't push us around, hold us back, or get in the way of life

- clarify our values (how we want to treat ourselves, others, and the world around us) and use them to guide our actions and enhance our life

- focus attention on what is important and engage fully in whatever activity we do

The Six Core Processes of ACT

Based on a philosophy of science known as *functional contextualism* and a theory of language known as *relational frame theory*, the ACT model rests on six core processes, illustrated in the diagram below. (This is often playfully called "the hexaflex.")

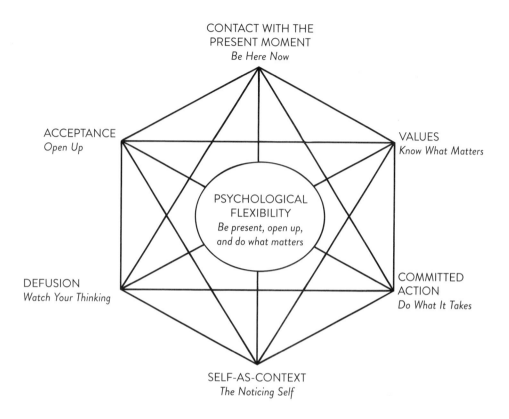

CONTACT WITH THE
PRESENT MOMENT
Be Here Now

ACCEPTANCE
Open Up

VALUES
Know What Matters

PSYCHOLOGICAL
FLEXIBILITY
*Be present, open up,
and do what matters*

DEFUSION
Watch Your Thinking

COMMITTED
ACTION
Do What It Takes

SELF-AS-CONTEXT
The Noticing Self

The ACT Hexaflex

CONTACT WITH THE PRESENT MOMENT (BE HERE NOW)

Contacting the present moment means flexibly paying attention to our here-and-now experience: narrowing, broadening, sustaining, or shifting our attention, as desired. This involves consciously paying attention to the physical world around us or the psychological world within us, connecting with and engaging fully in our experience.

ACCEPTANCE (OPEN UP)

Acceptance means willingly making room for unwanted private experiences, such as cognitions, emotions, memories, urges, and sensations. (The term "private experience" refers to any aspect of our inner psychological world.) Instead of fighting, resisting, or running from these unwanted experiences, we open up and give them space; allow them to freely flow through us.

Note that acceptance does not mean passively accepting a difficult situation; ACT advocates committed action to improve difficult situations, or to leave them—whichever is the better option. Acceptance means "experiential acceptance": accepting private experiences.

DEFUSION (WATCH YOUR THINKING)

Defusion (short for "cognitive defusion") involves learning to notice, acknowledge, and separate from our cognitions; to "step back" and observe them, instead of being dominated by them. We see our cognitions for what they are—constructions of words or pictures or both—and allow them to be present. We don't challenge them, distract from them, or push them away; instead, we hold them lightly. We allow them to guide us when useful, but we don't allow them to dominate us. (Defusion and acceptance are interwoven: we make room for our cognitions, and allow them to freely come and stay and go, in their own good time. And we defuse from cognitions, which pull us into a struggle with our inner experience—*This feeling is terrible! I have to get rid of it!*)

SELF-AS-CONTEXT (THE NOTICING SELF)

In everyday language, we talk about two parts of the mind. There's a part that thinks—generating thoughts, beliefs, memories, fantasies, and so on. And there's another part that silently notices, focuses, pays attention; that's aware of what we're thinking, feeling, sensing, or doing in any moment. Technically, we call this "self-as-context," but clinically, we use terms like the "noticing self," "observer self," or "the part of you that notices."

To confuse matters, there's a second meaning of self-as-context. It's a synonym for "flexible perspective taking"—the cognitive process that underpins defusion, acceptance, contacting the present moment, self-awareness, self-reflection, compassion, theory of mind, empathy, the noticing self, imagining yourself in the future or the past, seeing things from other people's viewpoints, and a whole lot more. In this book, we'll use both meanings at different times.

Practical Tip

In the ACT model, there are four core mindfulness processes: contact with the present moment, defusion, acceptance, and self-as-context. So the term "mindfulness" may refer to any one of (or a combination of) these processes.

VALUES (KNOW WHAT MATTERS)

Values are desired qualities of behavior: how you want to treat yourself, others, and the world around you. They describe how you want to behave in your relationships with anyone or anything—now, and ongoing. We can use our values for inspiration, motivation, and guidance. Like a compass, they give us direction and help us find our way when we are lost.

COMMITTED ACTION (DO WHAT IT TAKES)

Committed action means taking effective action, guided by our values, to build a life that's rich, full, and meaningful. This includes goal setting, action planning, problem solving, and exposure. It also includes learning and applying any skill that enhances life—from self-soothing and relaxation to interpersonal skills such as assertiveness, communication, and conflict resolution.

Psychological Flexibility

As you can see in the figure above, the core processes are interconnected elements of "psychological flexibility": the ability to act effectively, mindfully guided by values. The greater our psychological flexibility—our ability to be fully conscious, open to our experience, acting in line with our values—the greater our quality of life. Psychological flexibility enables us to respond effectively to our problems, develop a deep sense of meaning and purpose, and engage fully in life here and now.

Self-compassion, a fundamental, intrinsic aspect of ACT, doesn't get listed on the hexaflex because it actually involves *all six processes*; we'll explore this in chapter fourteen.

The ACT Triflex

We can lump the six core processes into three larger units, as shown in the figure below, which is playfully known as "the triflex" (Harris, 2009a).

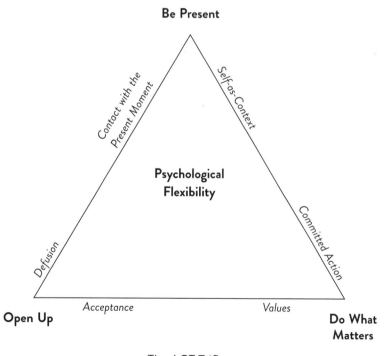

The ACT Triflex

Self-as-context and contact with the present moment both involve flexibly paying attention to and engaging in your here-and-now experience (in other words, "Be present").

Defusion and acceptance both involve noticing thoughts and feelings, seeing them for what they truly are, making space for them, and allowing them to freely come and go of their own accord (in other words, "Open up").

Values and committed action both involve initiating and sustaining life-enhancing action (in other words, "Do what matters").

So we can describe psychological flexibility as the ability to "be present, open up, and do what matters."

Two Useful Exercises

The following exercises are extremely useful for introducing key ACT concepts, and we'll refer back to them in later chapters. (Both work well in telehealth; see the PDF "ACT and Telehealth" in chapter one of Extra Bits.) As you read them, I encourage you to act them out, speaking the words aloud; this will be a much richer learning experience than simply reading them. The scripts are "bare bones"; in session, we flesh them out with specific examples drawn from the client's life. For example, after the line "…the difficult problems and challenges you need to deal with…," we would mention one or two of the client's problems (e.g., "the conflict with your kids" or "the ongoing treatment for your injuries").

Hands as Thoughts

The Hands as Thoughts exercise (Harris, 2009a) demonstrates the costs of fusion ("getting hooked" by thoughts) and benefits of defusion ("unhooking"). We do all the actions mentioned in the script, inviting the client to copy us.

Therapist: Would you be willing to do a quick exercise with me, to give you a sense of what we're aiming to do next?

Client: Sure.

Therapist: Okay, (points to an area of the room in front of the client) well, imagine that in front of you is everything that's truly important to you. All the pleasant stuff that's important—like the people, and places, and activities you love; your favorite food, music, sports, and movies; and so on (gives some examples specific to the client). And, also, all the painful stuff: the difficult problems and challenges you need to deal with, and all the difficult tasks you need to do (gives some examples specific to the client). And put your hands together like this (therapist puts hands together, palms upward, as if an open book; client copies) and imagine that these hands are your thoughts and feelings.

Client:	Okay.
Therapist:	So copy me, and let's see what happens when we get hooked by our thoughts and feelings. (*Therapist slowly raises their hands toward their face; client copies.*) That's it, and bring them right up so they're covering your eyes. (*Both continue the motion, until both have their hands touching their faces—covering up their cheeks, eyes, and foreheads.*) So this is what it's like when we're hooked by our thoughts and feelings. And notice three things. (*Both therapist and client keep their hands over their eyes.*) One. Look around the room, and notice: How much are you missing out on? How cut off and disconnected are you from all the important stuff out there?
Client:	A lot!
Therapist:	You're not kidding. Now two—notice: How difficult is it to focus on things? Imagine the task you need to do, or the person you love, is in front of you right now; how hard is it to give them your full attention?
Client:	Bloody hard!
Therapist:	For sure. And three—notice: How difficult is it to take action, to do the things that make your life work? How hard to drive a car or cook dinner or type on a computer (*gives a few mores examples specific to the client*)?
Client:	Yeah, you can't do it.
Therapist:	Okay. So that's what happens when we get hooked. Now once again, copy me, and let's see what happens when we unhook from our thoughts and feelings. (*Therapist, ever so slowly, lowers their hands from their face and rests them in their lap; client copies.*)
Therapist:	So notice: How much more can you take in? How much easier is it to engage and connect; to keep your attention focused on the task at hand? (*Client nods, agrees.*) And move your arms around. (*Therapist waves their arms around; client copies*) How much easier is it now to do the things that make your life work; to drive a car, or type on a computer, or cook dinner (*therapist mimes these activities while mentioning them*)?
Client:	A lot!
Therapist:	And notice these things (*therapist moves their hands around*) haven't disappeared. They're still here. So if you can use them, do so. Because even really difficult thoughts and feelings can give us valuable information about things we need to deal with or do differently. But if you can't make any good use of them, you just let them sit there.

Pushing Away Paper

The Pushing Away Paper exercise (Harris, 2011) illustrates the costs of experiential avoidance and the benefits of acceptance. (This exercise involves strenuous effort with the arms, so it is unsuitable for any client or practitioner with neck, shoulder, or arm problems. A good nonphysical alternative is the Struggle Switch metaphor in chapter twelve.)

In this exercise, the client and therapist each have a sheet of paper.

Therapist: Imagine that in front of you is everything that's truly important to you. All the pleasant stuff that's important—like the people, and places, and activities you love; your favorite food, music, sports, and movies, and so on (*gives some examples specific to the client*). And, also, all the painful stuff: the difficult problems and challenges you need to deal with, and all the difficult tasks you need to do (*gives some specific examples*). And imagine this sheet of paper is all your difficult, unwanted thoughts, feelings, urges, and memories.

Client: Okay.

Therapist: So let's see what happens when we struggle with this stuff. Are you okay to copy me? (*Therapist grips the paper tightly with both hands, one on either side; client copies.*) Great. Now keeping a tight hold, push it away from you, as hard as you can. (*Both client and therapist extend their arms.*) This is what everyone tells you to do, right? Friends, doctors, therapists? Get these thoughts and feelings away from you!!

But you know—it doesn't look like we're trying very hard here (*therapist says this humorously and playfully*). How about we push a bit harder. (*Both client and therapist push harder.*) That's it—straighten those elbows; get those thoughts and feelings as far away as you possibly can. (*Client and therapist maintain this posture for the next section of the exercise: holding the paper tightly by the edges, arms straight, as far from the chest as possible.*)

Now notice three things. First, how tiring is this? We've only been going for less than a minute, and already it's tiring. Imagine doing this all day; how much energy would it consume?

Second, notice how distracting it is. If the person you love were right there in front of you, how hard would it be to give them your full attention? If your favorite movie were playing on a screen over there, how much would you miss out on? If there's an important task in front of you right now or a problem you need to address or a challenge you need to tackle, how hard is it to focus on it?

Third, notice while all your effort and energy is going into doing this, how hard it is to take action, to do the things that make your life work, such as (*therapist gives some examples based on the client's history*). So notice how difficult life is when we're struggling with our thoughts and feelings like this. We're distracted, we're missing out on life, it's hard to focus, we're exhausted, and it's so hard to do the things that make life work.

Now, let's see what happens when we drop the struggle with our thoughts and feelings. (*Therapist relaxes their arms, drops the paper into their lap. The client copies the therapist and expresses a loud sigh of relief.*) Big difference, huh? How much less tiring is this? How much more energy do you have now? How much easier is it to engage with and focus on what's in front of you? If your favorite person were in front of you right now, how much more connected would you be? If your favorite movie were playing, how much more would you enjoy it? If there were a task you needed to do or a problem you needed to address, how much easier would it be to focus on it?

Now move your arms and hands about—(*therapist gently shakes their arms and hands around; client copies*). How much easier is it now to take action: to cuddle a baby, play tennis, hug the person you love?

And notice these things (*therapist indicates the paper in their lap*) haven't disappeared. We haven't gotten rid of them. They're still here. But we've got a whole different way of responding to them. We're handling them differently. They're no longer holding us back, or bringing us down, or jerking us around. And if there's something useful we can do with them, we can use them. Because even really painful thoughts and feelings often have information that can help us—even if it's just pointing us toward problems we need to address or things we need to do differently. And if there's nothing useful we can do with them, we just let them sit there.

Note that in both of the above exercises, there *is no intention to get rid of thoughts and feelings*; at the end, the hands remain, as does the paper. Similarly, in both exercises we point out that even the most painful thoughts and feelings are often useful; provided we respond to them mindfully, we can often use them constructively to improve our lives. But this will not be possible if we are fused with or trying to avoid them. Finally, both exercises also clarify that there are two main purposes for learning these new skills: (a) to enable effective values-based action, and (b) to help your client focus attention on what's important.

Practical Tip

Clients won't learn defusion or acceptance simply from doing these exercises. These are psychoeducational metaphors. We always need to follow them with active training in defusion or acceptance skills.

Now that we've covered the ACT basics , let's explore how to conceptualize cases.

Case Conceptualization in TFACT

The eight-part case conceptualization that follows is suitable for clients with any type of trauma-related disorder. First, an important note: When gathering information, we don't work through a case conceptualization form, completing each section sequentially; we complete these forms *outside of session*, to organize our thoughts or create treatment plans. Taking a history is a nonlinear process, gathering bits and pieces here and there, compiling it over time. So we'd rarely obtain *all* of the below information at intake; usually it spills over into session two. But the excellent news is, we *don't have to know* all this information before we start doing TFACT. We can get the broad strokes at intake and gather more details later, as relevant.

As you read through this, keep in mind a client you're currently seeing, and at the end of each section, pause for a few moments and reflect on how this applies. (Better still, download the case conceptualization worksheet from Extra Bits, and fill it in as you go.)

Part 1: Client's Therapy Goals

In chapter seven, we'll explore how to establish goals for therapy—and why they are so important. They fall into three broad classes:

A. emotional goals (how the client wants to *feel* different, for example, to feel happy, to feel less anxious, to get rid of unwanted thoughts and feelings)

B. behavioral goals (what the client wants to *do* differently, for example, to exercise more, to be more supportive to their family)

C. outcome goals (what the client wants to *have*, *get*, or *achieve*, for example, find a partner, get a job, leave a relationship, recover from an illness or injury)

What are your client's goals in each of these categories?

Part 2: Past History

Although TFACT has a strong here-and-now focus, working with the past is also important. What traumatic events have played a significant role in current issues? Was there any childhood trauma? Have other major life events—not necessarily traumatic, but disruptive and stressful—precipitated the current presentation?

Part 3: Physical Barriers

Are there physical barriers (as opposed to psychological) holding the client back from a rich and meaningful life? For example, are they in a dangerous environment, such as a prison or crime-ridden neighborhood? Or exposed to racism, victimization, prejudice, social injustice, harassment, sexual discrimination, religious persecution, bullying, rejection, or violence? Or involved in dysfunctional relationships? Or doing a job (e.g., emergency services) that regularly exposes them to traumatic events? Or social, medical, financial, legal, occupational, or domestic problems?

Part 4: Reexperiencing Trauma and Abnormal Arousal

Clients reexperience traumatic events in a variety of ways, including flashbacks, nightmares, intrusive emotions, and cognitions, dwelling on painful memories and ruminating on past events. These private experiences are unpleasant and distressing, and they trigger the threat response systems of the autonomic nervous system.

The best known of these systems is the "fight or flight" response: the sympathetic nervous system perceives a threat and kicks us into a state of high alert, preparing us to flee or attack. This state of *hyperarousal* gives rise to symptoms such as excessive sweating, muscle tension, rapid heart rate, palpitations, hypervigilance, exaggerated startle response, irritability, difficulties concentrating or sleeping, and emotions related to fleeing (such as fear, anxiety, panic) or to fighting (frustration, anger, rage).

If a stimulus is perceived as life threatening, and the person's attempts to attack or flee appear futile, then the parasympathetic nervous system activates the "freeze"—or "emergency shutdown"—response; this prepares the person to lie down, stay quiet and still, and give up any attempt at escape. This state of *hypoarousal* gives rise to symptoms such as numbness, lethargy, apathy, boredom, disengagement, and dissociation.

All of these private experiences are unpleasant and distressing in themselves. But what makes their negative impact so much greater is the myriad of inflexible ways that humans respond to them collectively, known as *psychological inflexibility*. This constitutes the third stream of symptoms in trauma-related disorders, and the next few parts of the case conceptualization explore its key elements: cognitive fusion, experiential avoidance, loss of contact with the present moment, remoteness from values, and unworkable action.

Part 5: Cognitive Fusion

Cognitive fusion means that cognitions dominate our awareness or actions (or both). When we fuse with cognitions, they seem like:

- commands we need to obey

- something important, requiring our full attention

- threats to our health and well-being

- advice we should follow

- statements of absolute truth

Fusion is usually problematic because it tends to interfere with living one's values, acting effectively, and engaging in life. Six categories of fusion show up repeatedly: past, future, self, judgments, rules, and reasons.

FUSION WITH THE PAST AND FUTURE

Fusion with past-oriented cognition includes dwelling on painful memories, going over old hurts and mistakes, grieving for what has been lost, feeling resentment or regret, ruminating, blaming oneself or others, or dwelling on how good life was before the trauma.

Fusion with future-oriented cognition includes worrying, catastrophizing, and predicting the worst. The future seems scary or bleak: bad things will happen; people will hurt you, abandon you, or let you down; life will be empty and miserable.

And often past and future overlap: what happened in the past will happen again in the future.

FUSION WITH SELF-CONCEPT

"Self-concept," or "the conceptualized self," are terms that refer to all the thoughts, beliefs, and ideas we have about who we are and how we got that way. In the case of trauma, clients typically fuse with a negative self-concept: *I'm not good enough, I'm broken, I'm damaged, I'm disgusting, I'm unworthy, I'm hopeless, I'm useless, I deserved it, I'm to blame,* and so forth.

When past traumatic events become central to a person's identity and life story, this is technically termed "event centrality"; clients believe they have been irreparably damaged or tainted by their trauma; it defines who they are: worthless, unlovable, defective, and so on.

Some clients fuse with an impoverished self-concept: *I have no idea who I am, I'm nothing, I'm no one.* Others avoid a threatening negative self-concept through fusion with an excessively positive self-concept: narcissism. And occasionally people fuse with multiple conceptualized selves: the different "personalities," "identities," or "alters" of dissociative identity disorder.

FUSION WITH JUDGMENTS

Clients often fuse with judgments about life (*it sucks, it's pointless*), the world (*it's unsafe, dangerous, evil*), other people (*they don't care, you can't trust them*), themselves (*I'm to blame, it's my fault*). They also fuse with judgments about their own cognitions, emotions, and memories (*they are awful, horrible, unbearable; I can't stand them*), which in turn feeds negative self-concept (*these awful thoughts and feelings show how damaged I am*).

FUSION WITH RULES AND REASONS

Rules are often useful; it's good to know which side of the road we have to drive on. But when we fuse with rules, our behavior becomes rigid and inflexible. Our cognitive rules often contain words like "should," "have to," "must," "need," "ought," or terms and conditions like "only if," "can't unless," "shouldn't because," "won't until." Some common examples: "I must do it perfectly—and if I can't, there's no point in doing it," "I have to drink to cope," "You can't trust men," "I shouldn't let people get close because they'll hurt me." The greater the fusion with rules, the stronger the compulsion to follow them—and the greater the anxiety when bending or disobeying them.

Rules overlap with reasons: all those cognitions about why we can't change, shouldn't change, or shouldn't even have to change: *I can't do it, it's too hard, I don't have the time, I don't have the energy, it'll go wrong, I've tried before and I always fail, it's too scary, I'm too depressed*, and so on. And of course, if we fuse with these reasons, then we don't change.

FUSION WITH NARRATIVES, SCHEMAS, AND CORE BELIEFS

All the categories of fusion above—past and future, self-concept, judgments, rules and reasons—combine to create complex narratives, schemas, and core beliefs. Here is a trauma-related example: *Because these terrible things happened to me* (past), *I'm damaged goods* (judgment, self-concept), *which is why I keep taking drugs* (reason), *and I can't stop taking them because I need them to cope* (rule), *so life is pretty shitty* (judgment), *and I can't see it getting any better* (future).

In particular, look out for fusion with the following belief system, which underpins experiential avoidance: *These thoughts and feelings are bad, unnatural, and unbearable* (judgment); *they mean that there's something wrong with me* (self-concept); *and I can't get on with my life until they are gone* (reason); *so I have to get rid of them* (rule).

Part 6: Experiential Avoidance

Experiential avoidance (EA) is the ongoing attempt to avoid or get rid of unwanted private experiences (e.g., cognitions, emotions, sensations), even when doing so is harmful. EA is normal, and everybody does it. We only target EA in therapy when it becomes excessive, rigid, or inappropriate to such an extent that it negatively impacts the client's health and well-being or gets in the way of doing things that make life meaningful. (Please remember this; we aren't mindfulness fascists, insisting people must always accept all private experiences.)

Clients have all sorts of painful cognitions and emotions, which they naturally want to avoid or get rid of—and by the time they come to therapy, they've usually discovered many different strategies for doing so, including drugs, alcohol, gambling, social withdrawal, people pleasing, self-harming, suicidality...and the list goes on.

Note that we only label behavior "experientially avoidant" if its *primary aim* is to avoid unwanted inner experiences. If you go to the gym primarily motivated by values around self-care and goals around improving physical health, that is not experientially avoidant. But if your primary motivation is to avoid emotional discomfort (e.g., to avoid feelings of anxiety or thoughts about getting fat), then it *is* experientially avoidant. (Obviously, all behaviors have multiple motivations, so we're talking about which predominates.)

At times, EA is ineffective but harmless. And at other times—used flexibly, moderately, and appropriately—it can be life enhancing. But when EA is *excessive*, *rigid*, or *inappropriate*, it usually makes life worse rather than better. For example, higher levels of EA mediate the relationship between traumatic events and general psychological distress, predict severity of symptoms across a range of disorders, increase the likelihood of substance use relapse, and mediate the relationship between maladaptive coping strategies and psychological distress (Chawla & Ostafin, 2007). Among people experiencing posttraumatic stress, those with higher levels of EA report less posttraumatic growth and meaning in life and attenuated well-being (Kashdan & Kane, 2011). And in veterans both with and without PTSD, the more focused they were on experiential avoidance and emotion regulation, the worse their mental health was (Kashdan et al., 2010).

Part 7: Loss of Contact with the Present Moment

In trauma, we see significant loss of contact with the present moment. We can think of this in terms of the three Ds: Distractibility, Disengagement, and Disconnection from your inner world.

Distractibility. Many clients find it hard to focus. They get easily distracted by their thoughts, feelings, and memories, and their attention wanders away from the task at hand.

Disengagement. This refers to "going through the motions"—being emotionally distant from or uninterested in one's current activity. For example, clients may eat their food without noticing or appreciating the taste, or talk to a loved one without any interest in the conversation, or perform a task on "automatic pilot" with little conscious awareness. Social disengagement is especially common, with many clients reporting feeling cut off or emotionally distant from their loved ones.

Disconnection from the inner world. The third *D* is for disconnection from one's inner world. Some clients are very disconnected from their cognitions, unable to tell us what they are thinking. Others are disconnected from their emotions—unable to tune into them, identify them, or label them accurately. The more disconnected you are from your inner world, the harder it is to "know yourself," meaning the less your self-awareness or insight.

Part 8: Remoteness from Values

As fusion and avoidance consume our clients' lives, they become ever more remote from their values. Common values that get lost are self-care, caring for others, intimacy, courage, trust, assertiveness, independence, playfulness, gratitude, compassion, and responsibility—but of course, this varies hugely from person to person. For some, this remoteness from values is because their life has been so focused on survival and avoiding pain, they've never had the opportunity to reflect on their values. For others, it happens because of fusion with rigid rules; this pulls them away from the lush tropical landscape of values into the harsh barren wasteland of *should*, *must*, and *have to*.

Part 9: Unworkable Action

When actions effectively make life richer and more meaningful, we describe them as "workable." On the other hand, "unworkable actions" (behaviors that often meet short-term needs but worsen life in the long term) commonly result from fusion, experiential avoidance, or both. For example, problematic use of drugs or alcohol is usually maintained by (a) attempts to avoid painful cognitions and emotions, and (b) fusion with several categories of cognition, such as reasons ("I need this to cope"), self-concept ("I've got an addictive personality"), or judgments ("It's not harmful").

"Away moves" is a popular term for unworkable actions because they take you away from the person you want to be and the life you want to build. Away moves are anything the client does that makes life worse, keeps them stuck, worsens problems, inhibits growth, prevents effective solutions, and impairs health and well-being.

The negative long-term consequences of unworkable action give rise to even more painful thoughts and feelings, which fuel even more fusion and avoidance: a chronic vicious cycle.

Practice, Practice, Practice

You don't need me to tell you this—but I'm going to anyway, because that's the kind of annoying person I am. (Did you note the fusion with self-concept there?) If you want to do TFACT well, reading a book won't cut it; you have to practice, practice, practice; and then practice some more. So please download a case conceptualization worksheet from Extra Bits, and fill it in for a current client. Once complete, place it alongside the hexaflex or triflex diagram presented earlier in this chapter, and, looking from one to the other, carefully consider: which ACT processes apply to which aspects of your client's difficulties?

I recommend you fill out at least one of these worksheets every day, because the better you conceptualize trauma from a TFACT perspective, the more effective you'll be in session.

> **EXTRA BIT**   Please download the free e-book *Trauma-Focused ACT: The Extra Bits* from the "Free Resources" page on http://www.ImLearningACT.com. In chapter two, you'll find printable versions of the hexaflex and triflex, a case conceptualization worksheet, and scripts for both Hands as Thoughts and Pushing Away Paper.

Takeaway

ACT is a type of cognitive behavioral therapy that creatively uses values and mindfulness skills to help people reduce psychological suffering and build meaningful lives. It achieves this through developing psychological flexibility: our ability to focus on and engage in what we are doing, to acknowledge and allow our cognitions and emotions to be as they are, and to act effectively, guided by our values. In other words: "be present," "open up," "do what matters."

ACT is a transdiagnostic approach, which enables us to conceptualize any clinical issue in terms of psychological inflexibility: cognitive fusion, experiential avoidance, loss of contact with the present moment, remoteness from values, and unworkable action. This makes it well-suited for the huge range of problems related to trauma, and the best way to understand its versatility is to do lots and lots (and lots) of case conceptualization.

CHAPTER THREE

Fight, Flight, Freeze, Flop

All too often, our clients interpret their difficult cognitions, emotions, and physiological reactions as signs of being weak, defective, or crazy. So if we can help clients make sense of these experiences and reframe them as attempts of the mind, brain, and body to keep us safe and protect us from harm, we can pave the way for acceptance and self-compassion. Ideally, we begin this work on the very first session.

The Science Behind Our Responses

The autonomic nervous system regulates our body's internal organs. It has two parts: the sympathetic nervous system (SNS), which "stirs us and speeds us up," and the parasympathetic nervous system (PNS), which "stills us and slows us down." These systems are the basis for why we respond to threats as we do.

Fight or Flight

When we perceive danger, the SNS activates "fight or flight" mode, preparing us to either resist the threat or flee from it. Among other changes, many large muscles tense up, ready for action; the heart and lungs speed up to pump well-oxygenated blood to the muscles; and the hormone cortisol is released, raising blood glucose levels to provide lots of energy. In fight or flight mode, the SNS gives rise to emotions such as fear, anxiety, panic, irritation, anger, and rage. The SNS gets its name because of these feelings; "sympathetic" is derived from the Greek words *syn* and *pathos*—meaning "with feelings."

Polyvagal Theory

Para is the Greek word for "against"; the PNS gets its name because it "goes against" the SNS. Remember, while the SNS stirs and speeds us, the PNS stills and slows us. The vagus nerve is the largest nerve in the PNS. It gets its name from the Latin word *vagus*, which means "wandering"; it "wanders around" the body, innervating many different organs and areas, especially in the face, chest, and abdomen. To understand the role of the PNS in trauma, we can turn to the hugely influential polyvagal theory (PVT; Porges, 1995). *Poly* is Greek for "many"; PVT gets its name because the vagus nerve has many diverse features and functions.

The vagus nerve has two main branches—dorsal (back) and ventral (front)—and when we are not under threat, the ventral branch fosters a state of "rest and digest," where we can slow down, relax, socialize, connect, and bond with others (and digest our food). I often call it "share/care" mode, because it inclines us to be loving, caring, and considerate; to share with, connect with, and look after others. When in this mode, we experience feelings of warmth, calm, and contentment.

However, the moment we perceive a threat, the SNS takes over, and we instantly switch from share/care to fight/flight: preparing to stand our ground or run away. But what happens if the threat is so extreme that fight or flight is futile, for example, if you're helplessly pinned under a rockslide, or you're a child being savagely beaten by an adult?

When the threat is extreme and attempts to fight or flee are unlikely to be useful, the dorsal branch of the vagus nerve takes the helm and switches us into emergency shutdown mode. To conserve energy, the PNS shuts down many physiological functions. It immobilizes the body, slows down the heart and lungs, drops blood pressure, and pauses nonessential activities such as digestion. In the early stages of shutdown, someone may be "frozen stiff," "rooted to the spot," or "paralyzed with fright." But in more extreme shutdown, their legs may fail and they may flop to the floor or even lose consciousness. We can call this either "freeze/flop" or "emergency shutdown" mode: a state that fosters dissociation, numbness, apathy, despair, and disinterest.

The "Fawn" Response

There's a trend in trauma literature to write about four trauma responses: fight, flight, freeze, and fawn. "Fawning" means working hard to please and appease other people. A child may work hard to be "a good kid" as a protective strategy when caregivers are abusive or neglectful, and an adult may take "people pleasing" to extremes, repeatedly neglecting their own needs, values, and boundaries in relationships to gain approval and fulfill the needs of others. Personally, I prefer not to bundle "fawn" with fight, flight, and freeze because the latter are all automatic, instinctive responses of the autonomic nervous system—whereas fawning is not.

Psychoeducation

Psychoeducation about these responses is important. When clients understand what is going on in their bodies and why, those experiences become less threatening, which facilitates acceptance. However, *too much* psychoeducation can make for an intellectual session and eat up valuable time that could be better spent on experiential work. So we need to strike a balance. Beginning with a metaphor is a useful way to start.

The Bear Metaphor

The Bear Metaphor is a simple and memorable way to convey the key points discussed above. There are two versions: one for hyperarousal and one for hypoarousal.

The Bear Metaphor: Fight/Flight

Therapist: Do you know much about the fight or flight response?

Client: A bit.

Therapist: Would it be okay to talk about it for a couple of minutes, to help make sense of what's going on with your body?

Client: Sure.

Therapist: Cool. Well, if you can, imagine one of your caveman ancestors is out by himself hunting rabbits, and suddenly he comes face to face with this huge mother bear. And she's got these two young bear cubs by her side. So to her, this human is a threat. So what does she do to protect her cubs?

Client: She charges.

Therapist: Right, she charges. Hard and fast. She wants to kill this guy—he's a threat to her cubs. So if he wants to survive, your ancestor's only got two options...

Client: Fight or flight!

Therapist: Right. So instantly his nervous system takes over. And it's not like he thinks, *Uh oh—I'd better switch into fight or flight mode.* Before he can even register a thought, his nervous system switches into fight or flight mode. All those large muscles in his arms and legs, chest and neck—they tense up, ready for action, to fight or to run. His body floods with adrenaline, heart speeds up, pumping blood to his muscles. He's pumped to the max. You ever feel like that?

Client: All the time.

Therapist: Yeah, and it takes a lot out of you, right? And that's because this fight or flight response is supposed to be very short-lived—it's supposed to last just long enough to get you out of danger—and then it's supposed to switch off. But your nervous system's not doing that; the fight or flight response isn't switching off. So all that losing your temper, getting angry about stuff, those tense muscles in your neck and back—that's your fight mode working overtime. And the anxiety, fear, sweating, getting startled—that's your flight mode. Same thing with your insomnia—when a bear's after you, you don't want to be sleeping.

We can readily link any symptoms of hyperarousal to this metaphor. So, for example, for trauma-related sexual problems such as erectile dysfunction, loss of libido and anorgasmia, we can say, "When you're under threat, your nervous system switches off any part of the body that's not essential for survival. When a bear's after you, having sex is not a priority."

Practical Tip

If clients don't believe in evolution, we can change the language: "ancient" ancestors rather than "cavemen"; "designed" rather than "evolved." We don't even need to mention ancient ancestors; we can just say "This is what your body does when under threat."

The Bear Metaphor: Freeze/Flop

If hypoarousal is also an issue, we can extend the Bear Metaphor as follows:

Therapist:	So that's fight or flight, but there's another mode your nervous system goes into, called freeze or flop, or emergency shutdown mode. So let's suppose your ancestor throws his spear at the bear, but misses. What's he gonna do?
Client:	Run for it.
Therapist:	Right—so off he goes, pegs it as fast as he can. But, you know, not even Usain Bolt can outrun a bear.
Client:	(laughs) Right.
Therapist:	So the bear chases—and it's furious—and it catches the guy, throws him to the floor, gets stuck into him—claws, teeth, the works—so at this point, your ancestor's only chance of survival is to be as quiet and still as possible. If he fights back, or tries to escape, the bear will hurt him even more. But if he's still and silent, then maybe, if he's lucky, the bear will lose interest, leave him alone—because he's not a threat anymore. But hey—it's hard to do that when a bear is biting you, right?
Client:	Yeah, pretty much impossible.
Therapist:	Right. It *would* be impossible, if not for our emergency shutdown response. See, there's this big nerve in your body, called the vagus nerve, and in these high-risk situations when fight or flight seems futile, it actually immobilizes you. That's why we say "frozen with fear" or "paralyzed by fright." So your ancestor's vagus nerve actually paralyzes his muscles, so he *literally* can't move, can't talk, can't do anything. And at the same time, it shuts off his feelings—makes him go numb, cuts off the pain, so he won't scream and struggle. So he's lying there, paralyzed by fright, numb with fear, speechless with terror. And if he's lucky, the bear sees he's no longer a threat and leaves him alone. And if the wounds aren't too severe, he survives.

Client: That makes sense.

Therapist: Yeah, so some of your symptoms—numbness, apathy, no energy, zoning out, feel-ings of hopelessness, wanting to just lie down and give up—this is your nervous system in shutdown mode.

Again, we can link all symptoms of hypoarousal to this metaphor. For example, in the case of dissociative states, the last line of dialogue might change to this:

Therapist: So he's trapped there, and it's really horrible; so the nervous system's response is to spare him—it makes him zone out, or split off, or gives him an out-of-body expe-rience. Now, he's got some distance from what's happening to him, and again, this helps him survive.

This knowledge is hugely helpful for clients who froze during traumatic events—especially sexual assault or abuse—who have blamed themselves (or been shamed by others) for not resisting. And we can flesh it out with the well-known examples of the deer frozen in the headlights (freeze) or the mouse going limp in the jaws of the cat (flop). Furthermore, if clients believe in evolution, we can add, "These basic survival responses are ancient—they evolved many millions of years ago, long before humans existed. They first appeared in fish, and we can find them in all mammals, birds, and reptiles." (But if clients don't believe in evolution, we might say, "So basically our nervous systems are 'designed' to react like this—fight, flight, freeze, flop—because these responses help us survive when we're in grave danger. It's the same common design for all mammals, birds, and reptiles.")

Following this, we can raise an important question: "So you may be wondering, why does this keep happening?" To answer this, we discuss the role of the amygdala.

The Amygdala: The Brain's Threat Detector

Although we commonly talk about the amygdala (singular), there are actually two amygdalae, one on each side of the brain, in the temporal lobes. These collections of nuclei (i.e., clusters of neurons that cooperate to perform specific tasks) perform a number of different functions but are best known for their role in processing fear.

Therapist: So there's a part of your brain called the amygdala, and it's basically a threat detec-tor. As soon as it detects any kind of threat, it sets off an alarm, which activates your fight or flight response, or, in some cases, freeze or flop. And because of what you've been through with XYZ (*XYZ = specific details from the client's trauma history, such as the car crash, the war, violent parents*), your amygdala is now in a state of constant red alert—it's seeing threats everywhere, all the time. Anything that even remotely reminds your amygdala of XYZ will set off the alarm, including thoughts, feelings, memories, people, places, objects, situations, and activities. Quite often, we don't even know what's triggering it—it's set off by stuff outside of conscious awareness.

Neuroplasticity

Many clients are doubtful as to whether therapy will work, so a brief discussion about neuroplasticity can help:

Therapist: Have you heard of neuroplasticity?

Client: I'm not sure.

Therapist: Well, it's a big word, but the basic concept is that our brain changes continually. There are over 80 billion neurons in the brain, and they're all interconnected, and we can sort of rewire them—lay down new circuits. We can't pull out the old neural pathways—there's no delete button in the brain—but we can lay down new ones on top of the old ones. And that's what we're aiming to do here.

So if we did an MRI scan of your brain before you start therapy and after you finish, we'd see differences in those two scans. Those skills I mentioned earlier—as you practice them, you rewire your brain. For example, right behind here (*therapist taps a spot on their forehead in the mid-point between their eyebrows*) is the prefrontal cortex, which is like the "mission control" center of the brain. And you're going to lay down new connections between that part and your amygdala, the threat detector—so you can adjust its settings, so the alarms don't keep going off.

Practical Tip

Be wary of simplistic ideas about "cause and effect" in the neuroscience of trauma. We should remember that a trauma reaction involves a whole human being and their ongoing interaction with the environment via all of their biological systems. For example, there are many other aspects of the nervous system—aside from the vagus nerve—involved in freeze responses, and the same goes for the amygdala's role in fear. So we should "hold lightly" any neurobiological explanation for a trauma reaction, remembering it's just one tiny piece of a vast field of science in which many theories compete and continually evolve.

Acceptance and Self-Compassion

To facilitate defusion, acceptance, and self-compassion, ACT explores the evolutionary origins of the mind: how it has evolved in such a way that it naturally creates psychological suffering (Hayes et al., 1999). And for the same purposes, ACT also explores the evolutionary origins and adaptive functions of emotions, drawing upon affective science (Tirch et al., 2014; Harris, 2015; Luoma & LeJeune, 2020). In TFACT, two key points we make with our clients, and visit repeatedly, are:

- "These reactions are occurring through no fault of your own; they are the product of millions of years of evolution." (Or for nonevolutionists: "This is the way your body has been designed.")

- "These are survival responses. This is your body, brain, and mind trying to protect you, keep you safe."

In later chapters, we'll explore these themes repeatedly, and you'll see how we can reframe even intensely painful emotions, like shame, and cognitive processes, such as suicidality, in terms of this protective function. We might say, "The problem is not that there's something wrong with you—it's just that your mind and your body are trying too hard to protect you; they're overly keen, doing these things to excess." Reframing clients' symptoms in this way makes them easier to accept and facilitates defusion from self-judgment.

> **EXTRA BIT**
>
> Download *Trauma-Focused ACT: The Extra Bits* from the "Free Resources" page on http://www.ImLearningACT.com. In chapter three, you'll find links to several YouTube animations I've made about (a) the three "parts" of the brain: reptilian, mammalian, and neocortex; (b) the amygdala, hippocampus, thalamus, and prefrontal cortex; and (c) the different meanings of "freeze" (there's a third meaning I didn't have space to include here!).

Takeaway

The sympathetic nervous system (SNS) stirs and speeds us up (hyperarousal), and the parasympathetic nervous system (PNS) stills and slows us (hypoarousal). When we perceive a threat, the SNS activates fight/flight mode—giving rise to fear and anger. But if fight/flight appears futile, the PNS activates the freeze/flop mode—giving rise to dissociation, apathy, and numbness.

A bit of psychoeducation about fight/flight and freeze/flop helps clients to understand their symptoms, paving the way for acceptance, defusion, and self-compassion.

CHAPTER FOUR

Keeping It Safe

For at least the first few sessions, most clients are highly anxious. This is hardly surprising. It's scary to make yourself vulnerable, allow yourself to "be seen," reveal things you've hidden from many others. It's a huge act of trust, especially if you've been hurt, manipulated, or betrayed in other relationships. So it's completely natural and expected that even though we do all we can to make therapy a safe space, clients will at times feel anxious, insecure, doubtful, distrusting, or fearful. So right from the start, we validate and normalize these reactions as they occur; and as therapy progresses, we help clients respond to them with acceptance, defusion, and self-compassion.

In this chapter, we'll explore what we can do to make therapy safer. We'll start with setting up our sessions, and then we'll look at trauma-sensitive mindfulness.

Setting Up Sessions

To enhance our clients' sense of safety in session, we should carefully consider the physical arrangement of the office, the therapeutic relationship, the use of self-disclosure, informed consent, the "press pause" technique, and making it easy for clients to say no.

Seating Arrangements

Most therapists sit opposite or at an angle to their clients, with no table in between. For many clients this is fine, but for some it's confronting and uncomfortable. Therefore, it's a good idea to have at least one large cushion available so the client can place it over their lap if they want a protective barrier.

We can also ask, "How is this seating arrangement for you? We can move the chairs if you prefer to sit a bit differently." (I once had a client who, for the first few sessions, sat as far away from me as she possibly could, her chair backed against the wall. Over time, she gradually moved closer.)

Therapeutic Relationship

ACT therapists adopt a Rogerian stance of authenticity, congruence, and unconditional positive regard for the client. We take a mindful, compassionate approach to our clients' suffering, and we use

ACT on ourselves when our own reactions interfere with therapy. And we often describe the therapeutic relationship as a form of teamwork:

Therapist: The idea is that you and I work together as a team, to help you build the sort of life you want to live. So it's not going to be me analyzing you or telling you how to live your life—it's a collaboration; we work together. And as we go, please do let me know if there's anything I'm saying or doing that's getting in the way of us being a strong team. I'm always willing to change what I do, if it helps us work together better.

Therapist Self-Disclosure

ACT encourages (but does not demand) therapist self-disclosure for the following purposes:

A. To normalize and validate the client's experience. For example: "Yes. I do that kind of thing too. My mind really beats me up over it" or "Yes, I get really anxious in those situations too."

B. To strengthen rapport through empathy, compassion, and authenticity. For example: "As you're telling me this, I'm noticing a lot of sadness showing up inside me. You can probably see my eyes are tearing a bit. This deeply touches me."

C. To model core ACT processes for the client. For example, to model defusion: "I notice my mind telling me that you seem upset with me. Is my mind way off base, or has it picked up on something important?"

D. To address the therapeutic relationship. For example: "I could have this wrong—so let me know if that's the case. It's just…I don't feel like we're a strong team here. I feel like I'm pushing and you're resisting. What's it like from where you're sitting?"

E. To give safe, compassionate, and authentic feedback to the client in the service of raising awareness of the effects of their behavior in session.

   So let's suppose a client is complaining of disconnection and lack of intimacy. At an appropriate moment, we might share, "Right now, I feel really disconnected from you. You're so caught up in all these thoughts, it's like you've disappeared from the room. I wonder if something like this may be going on at times when you're feeling that disconnection with others?"

   At a later point in the session, where the client is more engaged, we might say, "Now I feel much more connected with you. It's like you're fully back in the room, and you're really engaging in what we're doing here. I feel like we're a team now. Do you notice any difference?"

It goes without saying that therapist self-disclosure needs to be wise, appropriate, compassionate, authentic, and *always for the benefit of the client*—to help them progress toward their therapy goals. And we err on the side of caution. For example, disclosures like A and B above are probably fine in early sessions; but disclosures like D and E are more confronting, so probably better left until later.

Even a light "sprinkle" of self-disclosure can be helpful. For example: "Your mind is a lot like mine. The things your mind says to you are so similar to the things my mind says to me!" In addition to deepening rapport, this establishes a central ACT theme of "common humanity": we are all in the same boat; we all struggle and suffer; we all have minds that naturally create suffering; life is difficult for each and every one of us.

Informed Consent

Informed consent is good ethical practice and establishes trust. It goes something like this:

Therapist: There's a lot of difficult stuff going on for you, and obviously we've only scratched the surface, so I really want to hear more about it. But before we do that, I'm wondering if we can take a few minutes to discuss how we could work together, and what that would involve.

Client: Sure.

Therapist: Great. So I mainly work from a model called ACT—acceptance and commitment therapy. (*playfully*) Yeah, I know it sounds a bit odd, but don't let the name put you off. It's a science-based approach, with over 3,000 published studies showing its effectiveness.

Client: Wow!

Therapist: Yeah, so can I explain a bit about how it works—and make sure you're open to it?

Client: Sure.

Therapist: Great. So, there are a lot of difficult thoughts and feelings and urges and memories you're struggling with—you're suffering *a lot*—and there's also a whole bunch of really difficult situations you're dealing with. And when difficult stuff like this shows up, for any of us, we have two main ways of responding. One way is doing things that take us toward a better life, more like the one we want; I call those "towards moves." The other way is doing things that kind of take us away from the life we want—you know, keep us stuck or hold us back or make things worse—and I like to call those "away moves." (*playfully*) Sorry for the jargon.

Client: (*smiling*) That's okay.

Therapist: And all day long, you and me, and everyone else on the planet, we're always doing this. One moment, we're doing those towards moves—doing things that help us build the sort of life we want, behave like the sort of person we want to be—and the next moment, we're doing away moves, behaving *unlike* the sort of person we want to be, doing things that keep us stuck or create new problems.

Client:	Yeah. That makes sense.
Therapist:	So towards moves are basically things you'll start doing or do more of if therapy is successful. And away moves are things you'll stop doing or do less of. Like, for example, you said that you'd like to stop fighting with your partner all the time.
Client:	Yeah, that's right.
Therapist:	So, that's the basic idea. Now the problem is, when difficult thoughts and feelings show up, we tend to get hooked by them. Sorry, more jargon! What I mean by "hooked" is, they dominate us. They take over. It's like they hook us—and they reel us in, and they jerk us around like a puppet on a string, and they pull us into doing things that are problematic, those away moves.
Client:	Okay.
Therapist:	So basically there are two main parts to ACT. One part is learning new skills to handle all those difficult thoughts and feelings—to take away their power, so they can't jerk you around and keep pulling you into those away moves. And another bit of jargon: we call those "unhooking skills."
Client:	That figures.
Therapist:	The other part is to get better at doing towards moves—which involves finding out what really matters to you, who you care about, how you want to treat yourself and others, and basically doing things that make life better. So it's a very active approach. And the aim is for you to leave each session with an action plan: something you're going to take away and practice or experiment with, to help you deal with these issues.
Client:	(*anxiously*) Hmmmm. That sounds a bit scary.
Therapist:	That's a completely natural reaction. Most people find therapy a bit scary, because hey, you're doing something new, stepping out of your comfort zone. And that *is* scary. But I guarantee you, we are going to play it safe. We'll go slow, and I'm here with you every step of the way. And if you decide that this approach isn't for you, we can try something else.

(Of course, informed consent also includes all the standard items: confidentiality, expected number and frequency of sessions, terms of payment, and so on. And if the client does not wish to do ACT, we can either use a different model or refer to another practitioner.)

Press Pause

"Press pause" is a simple mindfulness intervention to raise awareness of psychologically inflexible behaviors or reinforce psychologically flexible ones. We often introduce it on the first session:

Therapist: Can I have permission to "press pause" from time to time, so if I notice you saying or doing something that looks like it might be helpful in terms of dealing with your problems, I can just slow the session down and get you to notice what you're doing?

   For example, I might ask you to just pause for a moment, take a breath, check in, and notice what you're thinking or feeling—and then we'd look at what you were just saying or doing immediately before I pressed pause. That way, you'll be able to see more clearly what you're doing that's helpful, and we can look at ways you can use that outside of this room. Would that be okay with you?

   And can I also "press pause" if I see you doing something that looks like it may be feeding into your problems or making them worse, so we can address it? And of course, this goes both ways—you can also "press pause," any time you like.

The Freedom to Say No

It goes without saying that we never coerce or push clients into ACT processes. We want them to know they are in full control of what they choose to do:

Therapist: At times I will encourage you to try out new skills to help you handle these difficult thoughts and feelings—and that may pull you out of your comfort zone—so I want to be clear that you never have to do them. Please let me know if I ever suggest anything that you're not sure about, or you don't see the point of, or you don't really want to do, and I will always take that on board, straight away.

We expect that at times in therapy, clients will hesitate or express reluctance to do things they find challenging or uncomfortable, such as various experiential exercises or homework tasks, and it's vitally important that when this happens, we don't cross that line from encouragement to coercion (especially when working with complex trauma, where many clients have been subjected to coercion in previous relationships). So we check in frequently: "Are we okay to keep going here?" "Would you like to slow down or take a break?" "My mind's telling me I'm being a bit pushy here; do I need to step back?"

And when doubts and fears about any aspect of therapy show up, we never discount or dismiss them. We first normalize and validate such reactions and look at the useful purpose they serve: "This is your mind doing its job: trying to keep you safe, protect you from getting hurt." We can then return to the client's therapy goals and compassionately and respectfully explore those doubts and fears from the perspective of workability: will acting on them help or hinder the client's progress toward the life they want to build? (This is a first gentle step in defusion; we'll explore this approach in depth in later chapters.)

It's also useful to agree on a nonverbal safety signal the client can use if they want us to stop, such as making the classic "time out" sign or holding up a brightly colored card. "Press pause" works well for this purpose: the client simply mimes pressing a button on a remote.

Trauma-Sensitive Mindfulness

People often think "mindfulness" is Buddhism, or meditation, or positive thinking, or relaxation, or religion, or distraction, or a way to control your feelings—but (at least, from an ACT perspective) it's none of those things. So what actually is it?

Defining Mindfulness

There are numerous definitions of mindfulness floating around; the following one (Harris, 2018) combines key elements of many others:

"Mindfulness" refers to a set of psychological skills for effective living, which all involve paying attention with flexibility, openness, curiosity, and kindness.

This brief definition highlights three important points:

1. "Mindfulness" refers to a set of diverse skills.

2. The aim is to cultivate *flexible* attention: the ability to consciously broaden, narrow, sustain, or shift our attention to different aspects of our here-and-now experience.

3. Mindful attention is not cold or clinical; it has the qualities of openness, curiosity, and kindness.

Alternative Terms to "Mindfulness"

Some clients report prior bad experiences with mindfulness: they didn't like it, they couldn't do it, or it didn't work. Upon inquiry, we usually discover they are talking about formal mindfulness meditation—as opposed to the flexible, trauma-sensitive mindfulness practices we focus on in this book. And if we ask, "What were you hoping to get out of it?" we usually find they were trying to get rid of unwanted thoughts and feelings. So although it's not "wrong" or "bad" to use the word "mindfulness," it's often better to skip it, and instead use specific names for the skills you teach: "unhooking," "opening up," "dropping anchor," "savoring," "focusing," "engaging," "noticing," and so on.

We also need to be clear about the differences between mindfulness, distraction, and relaxation. The word "distraction" comes from the Latin *distrahere*, meaning "to draw away from." Distraction techniques draw attention away from unwanted cognitions, emotions, and memories in order to reduce emotional pain. They are the very opposite of mindfulness practices, where we deliberately turn toward unwanted private experiences, with openness and curiosity.

Similarly, the primary aim of a relaxation technique is to control our feelings: to get rid of tension and anxiety and replace it with calm and relaxation. But with mindfulness, we do not attempt to control how we feel; we open up and make room for difficult feelings and allow them to be as they are.

We *can* include relaxation and distraction techniques in TFACT, but we need to clearly distinguish them from mindfulness and specify when they are appropriate (see chapter twenty-three) to prevent mixed messages and confusion.

Mindfulness Meditation

In people who have experienced trauma, formal mindfulness meditation can trigger adverse reactions, including anxiety, fear, panic, and the reexperiencing of traumatic memories (Lindahl et al., 2017). This isn't surprising when we consider common elements of trauma-related sequelae: social disengagement, physical immobility, and problematic absorption in one's inner world (rumination, worrying, flashbacks, and so on). If clients with such issues attempt a formal mindfulness meditation practice that involves sitting still (physical immobility), staying silent with their eyes closed (social disengagement), and focusing inward (absorption in their inner world), they are at risk of fusion, dissociation, or reexperiencing trauma.

Trauma-sensitive mindfulness involves tailoring mindfulness interventions to avoid such risks. So, at least for early sessions, it's safer to introduce practices that *increase physical movement* as opposed to encouraging immobility; *maintain or increase social engagement* rather than reducing it; and enable clients to acknowledge their thoughts and feelings without getting lost in them. "Dropping anchor" exercises (chapter eight) are especially useful for these purposes. Below I'll cover some important considerations regarding trauma-sensitive mindfulness.

BREATH AND BODY

Many mindfulness practices—especially formal mindfulness meditations—include a central focus on breathing. This is useful for most people, but a small number of clients, when focusing on the breath, become anxious, dizzy, or lightheaded. For this reason, most of the practices in this book do *not* include a central focus on the breath. It's not "wrong" or "bad" or "unsafe" to have such a focus—it's just wise to be cautious. So, when first introducing a breath-focused exercise, keep it brief; check in with the client regularly; and if they respond adversely, stop and explore their reaction.

If clients respond well to short breath-focused exercises, we can then experiment with longer ones. But if not, there are hundreds of other things to focus on: sounds in the room, what you can see, sensations of stretching, and so on.

Many mindfulness practices focus on the body; this is often called "somatic awareness," "somatic mindfulness," or "bodywork" (see chapter twenty-two). It can be challenging to keep bodywork safe, because often clients are striving hard to avoid particular parts of the body, especially the chest and abdomen (because this is where anxiety sensations are often most intense), areas associated with their trauma history (e.g., parts involved in sexual abuse or parts that have been disfigured through injury), and areas that are the focus of intense dislike or loathing (as may occur in gender dysphoria or body dysmorphic disorders). In such cases, we can initially help clients connect mindfully with "safe zones" of the body—areas unlikely to trigger problematic reactions. (For example, for most people, the hands and feet are safe zones.) Then over time, through a process of graded exposure, we can help them tune in to avoided areas.

EVERYTHING IS AN EXPERIMENT

Every intervention is an experiment, and we never know for sure what will happen. It's often helpful to share this with our clients:

Therapist: I wonder if you'd be willing to try an experiment here—an exercise I think could really help.

Client: Sure.

Therapist: Cool. I call it an experiment because I never know for sure what's going to happen. Most people find it helpful, and that's what I'm hoping for—but I never really know. So let's keep an open mind and see what happens, okay?

This approach models honesty and openness, which contributes to the therapeutic alliance. In addition, we take the pressure off: there is no particular result that must be achieved. An experiment is an opportunity to find out what works and what doesn't. If the results are as hoped, great. If not, we compassionately explore what happened, and work with the client's reaction (see chapter nineteen).

WHAT'S THE AIM?

The more unusual or uncomfortable the exercise, the clearer we need to be about the purpose. What's the point of this exercise? How's it going to help with their therapy goals? For example, depending on the issue, we might explain the aim as:

- to help you be present with your children, or focus on your work

- to help you to open up and make room for difficult feelings and let them flow through you without carrying you away

- to unhook yourself from difficult thoughts so they don't keep pulling you into self-defeating behavior

- to unhook yourself from memories that keep pulling you into the past

- to take control of your body when it's freezing up or shutting down

- to disrupt worrying and ruminating

Without such clarity, many clients erroneously assume that mindfulness practices are intended to get rid of unwanted thoughts and feelings, to make them feel happy or relaxed. But in mindfulness practices, we don't try to control our thoughts and feelings; we allow them to be as they are in this moment—whether pleasant or painful. Nor do we aim to "clear our mind"; with openness and curiosity, we acknowledge the thoughts that are present, and allow them to freely come, stay, and go.

So when clients try to use these new skills to get rid of unwanted thoughts and feelings, they're not practicing mindfulness; they're practicing experiential avoidance. We know this has happened when they say, "It's not working." When we ask what they mean by "not working," they reply, "I'm not feeling any better," or "I'm still anxious," or "The thoughts are still there." We then need to clarify the real aims of the exercise. Four metaphors are useful for doing this quickly: Pushing Away Paper (chapter two), Hands as Thoughts (chapter two), Dropping Anchor (chapter eight), and the Struggle Switch metaphor (chapter twelve).

INVITATIONS VERSUS DEMANDS

Every exercise is an invitation, never a demand. Notice the difference between these instructions:

- "I'd *like* you to push your feet gently into the floor, and notice what that feels like."

- "I *invite* you to push your feet gently into the floor, and notice what that feels like."

Other phrases to consider include: "Could I suggest…?" "Would you be open to…?" "Would you be willing to…?"

Of course, there's more to a genuine invitation than the words we use; much relies on our authenticity, congruence, and compassion. Also, the more clearly an exercise links to the client's therapy goals, the more inviting it is. For example: "I've got in mind an exercise we could do right now that I think could really help with X (*mentions one of the client's therapy goals*). The aim of it is to Y (*clearly states the aim*). Would you be willing to try it?"

BABY STEPS

Clients are often struggling with multiple problems. If they attempt too many changes all at once, they can easily become overwhelmed, resulting in increased anxiety, hopelessness, or giving up. However, if they make no changes at all, they'll remain stuck. So we need to help clients find a balance, while also watching our own tendencies. If we tend to go veeeery slowly, we may need to pick up the pace; but if we habitually charge in full-speed ahead, we may need to slooooow down. Basically, we individualize what we do for each client, carefully track their responses, and adjust what we do accordingly.

We can use the language of "baby steps" and "domino effects" to emphasize that small steps over time have significant effects, and a positive change in one aspect of life often has secondary effects on others. This same sensibility applies to all the exercises we do and skills we teach. If we suspect that an intervention is likely to be too demanding, too overwhelming, too challenging for a client, we scale it down—make it smaller, simpler, easier, or even change it altogether. The challenge for us all is to be flexible; if what we're doing isn't working, we need to modify it.

Six Recommendations

Based on the above considerations, here are six recommendations to make mindfulness exercises safer:

1. Individualize exercises for each unique client; for example, instead of focusing on the breath or body, you may initially focus on sounds in the room or the view out the window.

2. Encourage clients to keep their eyes open and fixed on a spot, rather than closed.

3. Clearly explain the purpose, linking it to the client's therapy goals.

4. Promote social engagement by talking with your clients throughout exercises: ask them what's happening, what's showing up, and so on.

5. Encourage active movement during the exercises—especially changing position, altering body posture, and stretching.

6. Make sure exercises are invitations, not demands—and repeatedly check for willingness: Is the client okay to keep going? Do they need a break?

Takeaway

Tailor what you do so it's safe and appropriate for each unique client. Be cautious about formal meditation practices that involve immobility, silence, and closed eyes. Later, as clients' psychological flexibility increases, you can introduce such practices—but always with caution.

Clearly communicate the aims of your interventions. Set them up as experiments, and be willing to modify or drop what you're doing, as need be. An explicit emphasis on safety and teamwork, along with appropriate self-disclosure, helps build a strong therapeutic alliance.

CHAPTER FIVE

The Choice Point

Have you ever found yourself overwhelmed by a client's initial presentation? So many interconnected problems, you can't figure out where to start? If so, you may appreciate my personal favorite tool in ACT: the "choice point" (Ciarrocchi et al., 2013; Harris, 2018). We can bring in this simple but powerful tool at any stage of therapy to:

- explain the ACT model

- set goals

- do functional analysis of a problematic behavior

- provide a rationale for exposure

- create a safety plan

- set an agenda

- and a whole lot more!

In this chapter, we'll cover using the choice point to establish therapy goals, introduce the ACT model, and conceptualize trauma.

Introducing the Choice Point

Before introducing the choice point to a client, we always listen compassionately to the client's narrative, validate their feelings, and empathize with their difficulties. In the transcript below, all of this has already happened.

The client, Helen, is a thirty-five-year-old flight attendant. Six months earlier she was the victim of a vicious sexual assault. Her issues include symptoms of hyperarousal (insomnia, impaired concentration, palpitations, excessive sweating); reexperiencing the trauma (nightmares and flashbacks); hypoarousal ("freezing up"), worrying, ruminating, and self-judgment; conflict, tension, and avoidance of intimacy with her husband, Mike; poor performance at work; social withdrawal; heavy drinking; and staying up until the early hours of the morning, watching TV.

Therapist: Is it okay if I draw a little diagram to summarize what we've discussed and create a map for what we do next?

Client: (*nodding*) Sure.

On a blank sheet of paper, the therapist draws two diverging arrows and labels them "towards" and "away," as below. (Reminder: to adapt this for telehealth, see the PDF "ACT for Telehealth," in Extra Bits, chapter one). The client already knows the terms "towards moves," "away moves," "hooked," and "unhooking" from the informed consent process—but the therapist briefly describes them again, for clarity.

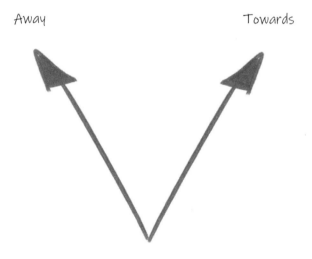

Therapist: So this arrow is your away moves—things you do that take you away from the life you want to build; things you'd like to stop doing or do less of. And this arrow is your towards moves—things you do that take you toward the life you want; things you'll start or do more of if therapy is successful.

Client: (*nodding*) Okay.

Therapist: And what I'm going to jot down here (*points to the blank space below the arrows*) are some of the main thoughts and feelings you're struggling with, and the difficult situations you're facing.

Client: Alright.

Therapist: (*writing while speaking*) So you've got flashbacks, painful memories, nightmares; feelings of anger, anxiety, sadness, and guilt; physical reactions such as freezing up, palpitations, sweating, muscle tension; self-judgmental thoughts like *I'm unworthy, I'm weak, I'm damaged goods.* (*continues writing while speaking*) And difficult situations like tension with Mike, falling behind at work, difficulty sleeping.

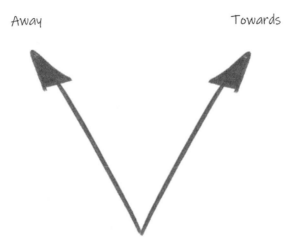

Away   Towards

flashbacks, memories, nightmares, anger,
anxiety, sadness, guilt, freezing up,
palpitations, sweating, muscle tension
I'm unworthy, weak, damaged goods
conflict with Mike, work problems, sleep problems

At this point, a few clarifications. First a quick reminder: "away moves" are values-incongruent, self-defeating behaviors; "towards moves" are values-guided, effective behaviors; and both include *overt* behaviors (physical actions) and *covert* behaviors (cognitive processes). At the bottom of the choice point, we write down the main cognitions and emotions the client is struggling with. This may include physical pain, withdrawal symptoms from drugs, urges, memories, and fight/flight or freeze/flop reactions. We also write down situations that trigger away moves.

Practical Tip

If pushed for time, don't write this information down; simply talk about it while pointing to the diagram.

Mapping Out Away Moves

Next, the therapist explores Helen's away moves:

Client: (*looking at the paper, curious*) Yeah, that's about right.

Therapist: And quite naturally, at times you get hooked by all these thoughts and feelings. (*Therapist writes "hooked" alongside the away arrow.*) They jerk you around like a puppet on a string and pull you into those away moves, taking you away from the life you want.

Client: They sure do.

Therapist: So let's jot down some of your away moves. (*Therapist writes while speaking, listing the "away moves" down the side of the arrow*). There's yelling at Mike, drinking too much, worrying...what else?

Client: I guess, avoiding meetings at work and falling behind on everything...and avoiding my friends...

Therapist: Staying up all hours of the night?

Client: Yes. That too.

Therapist: And those freeze responses—when you lock up and you can't move?

Client: Yes, definitely. I hate that.

Therapist: Naturally. And remember, freezing up is automatic, involuntary. You don't choose it; your vagus nerve does. So one of the aims here is to learn new skills that can help, so if you do start freezing up, you can catch it and override it—and choose to do something different.

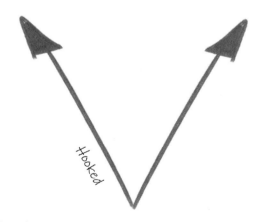

Yelling at Mike
Drinking too much
Worrying
Avoiding meetings
Falling behind
Avoiding friends
Staying up late

Hooked

flashbacks, memories, nightmares, anger,
anxiety, sadness, guilt, freezing up,
palpitations, sweating, muscle tension
I'm unworthy, weak, damaged goods
conflict with Mike, work problems, sleep problems

Before we return to our example of using the choice point with Helen, here are four important points about away moves.

Point one: "Away" doesn't mean away from pain. It means away from values, or away from the life you want to build, or away from the sort of person you want to be. "Hooked" is a synonym for inflexible responding: fusion, experiential avoidance, or any combination thereof. So away moves may result from either *fusion with* or *avoidance of* cognitions and emotions (and often, both).

Point two: The client always defines what is an away move—never the therapist. Early in therapy, a client may see self-destructive behavior (e.g., excessive drug or alcohol use) as a towards move. When this happens, it's useful to recall the transtheoretical "stages of change" model (Prochaska & DiClemente, 1983). Here's a brief recap:

Pre-Contemplation	I don't see this behavior as a problem
Contemplation	I'm thinking about changing this behavior
Preparation	I'm actively preparing to change this behavior
Action	I've started doing the new behavior
Maintenance	I'm continuing to do the new behavior
Relapse	I've fallen back into the old behavior

If a client says a self-defeating or self-destructive behavior is a towards move, that usually indicates "pre-contemplation": they don't yet see it as a problem. We address this as follows:

First, we double-check: does the client understand the meaning of towards moves? We might say, "Can I just check we're using these terms in the same way? Towards moves are things you'll start doing or keep doing if therapy is successful. Is this something you want to keep doing, to the same extent?" If the client answers yes, we don't want to debate it. Clearly, they are in pre-contemplation, so if we start trying to persuade them that this behavior is self-defeating, it could easily create tension and strain the alliance. Instead, we want to find goals that strengthen the alliance: behaviors that the client *does* want to change. So, we flag this in our notes as an issue to address later—and for now, we write it down *from the client's perspective*, as a towards move. (Obviously there are exceptions; for example, for a high-risk behavior such as suicidality, we'd address that immediately.)

We then work with the client on changing behaviors that they *do* see as problematic, using core ACT processes. This builds the alliance and helps the client develop psychological flexibility.

Later in therapy, we revisit the issue. By then, it's usually obvious that this behavior is a barrier to the client's other values-based goals, so we ask, "When you first came to see me, you classed this as a towards move. Do you still see it that way?" If for some reason, the client *hasn't* yet noticed the unworkability of their behavior, we raise their awareness through gentle questioning: "So on the one hand, you want to be doing things differently in your life, such as A, B, and C (*values-based goals and actions*), but on the other hand, you keep doing X (*the problematic behavior*). I'm wondering, do you see any conflict there?"

Point three: Emotions, urges, sensations, memories, and autonomic responses always go at the bottom of the choice point. The towards and away arrows only document behaviors: flexible and inflexible ways of responding to the thoughts and feelings at the bottom.

Similarly, an individual thought (like *I'm stupid* or *Nobody likes me*) always goes at the bottom of the choice point. However, cognitive processes such as ruminating, worrying, or obsessing are covert behaviors, so they go on the away arrow.

Point four: Any activity can be a towards move or an away move, depending on the context. When I stay in bed and keep hitting the snooze button primarily to avoid dealing with important tasks—I consider that an away move. But on holiday, when I hit the snooze to enjoy the well-earned pleasure of a long sleep-in—I consider that a towards move.

So if an activity takes us toward the life we want, then in that context it's a towards move; but if, in a different context, that same activity takes us away from the life we want, then it's an away move. Thus, on my own choice point, beside the away arrow, I'd write "sleeping in to avoid important tasks," and by the towards arrow, "sleeping in to enjoy my holiday."

With the choice point, we can take any DSM disorder, relationship issue, or other clinical problem and rapidly "deconstruct it" into the same four elements:

- difficult situations (including work, relationship, financial, legal, or medical problems)

- difficult private experiences (including all types of cognition and emotion)

- inflexible responding to private experiences ("getting hooked": fusion or avoidance)

- problematic overt or covert behaviors, resulting from fusion or avoidance (away moves)

Unhooking Skills

Let's return to our session with Helen.

Therapist: So here's what basically going on. (*Pointing to the diagram while speaking*) You've got these challenging situations you're dealing with, and you've got lots of difficult thoughts and feelings and memories showing up. And when you get hooked by this difficult stuff inside you, you get pulled into these away moves—drinking too much, yelling at Mike, staying up late even when you're exhausted, and so on.

Client: (*thoughtful*) Yeah.

Therapist:	So our aim here is to work together, as a team, to help you turn this around and build a better life.
Client:	*(laughs sarcastically)* Good luck with that!
Therapist:	If I could listen in to your mind right now, what would I hear it saying?
Client:	This'll never work.
Therapist:	*(playfully)* Is that the polite version?
Client:	*(laughs)* Yeah.
Therapist:	*(laughs)* Thought so. Can I hear the unedited version?
Client:	Well, okay, you asked for it. This is fucking bullshit. There's no fucking way it's going to work!
Therapist:	*(smiles)* Excellent. That's the way my mind speaks too! And it's completely natural to have thoughts like that; almost all my clients do.
Client:	Really?
Therapist:	Absolutely. So your mind is saying this won't work—and even though it's saying that, we can still agree to work together as a team, right?
Client:	Sure.
Therapist:	And we can still agree on our aims here, even though your mind says it won't work?
Client:	Yeah, I guess.
Therapist:	So our aims are twofold. One is to develop some unhooking skills, so when all these difficult thoughts and feelings show up, you can unhook from them *(Draws a ring around all the thoughts and feelings at the bottom of the diagram)*—take all the power out of them, take away their impact—so they can't jerk you around, or hold you back. *(Writes the word "Unhooked" alongside the towards arrow.)*

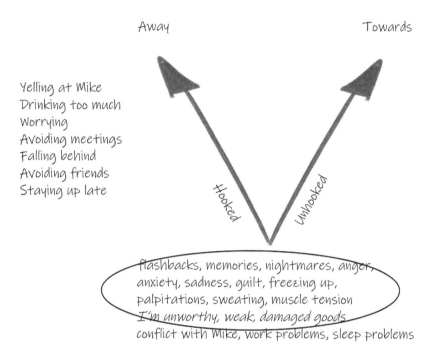

Away   Towards

Yelling at Mike
Drinking too much
Worrying
Avoiding meetings
Falling behind
Avoiding friends
Staying up late

Hooked   *Unhooked*

flashbacks, memories, nightmares, anger,
anxiety, sadness, guilt, freezing up,
palpitations, sweating, muscle tension
I'm unworthy, weak, damaged goods
conflict with Mike, work problems, sleep problems

Client:	You think you can do that?
Therapist:	I think *you* can do that. But I don't expect your mind to agree with me. Is it saying something right now?
Client:	Pretty much the same as before.
Therapist:	Bullshit? Won't work? (*Client nods.*) Yep, I expect it'll keep saying that, over and over.

Defusion involves responding flexibly to our thoughts: noticing them with curiosity, seeing their true nature as constructions of words or pictures, allowing them to freely come and stay and go, and using them for guidance if helpful. Notice how the therapist is already instigating, modeling, and reinforcing defusion through an open and curious attitude toward the client's difficult thoughts: noticing and naming them, normalizing and validating them, and allowing them to be present without challenging them.

Towards Moves

Now we'll see how the therapist prompts Helen to identify towards moves to add to the choice point.

Therapist:	And the other aim of this approach is to get you doing more of these towards moves—things that help you build the life you want.
Client:	I don't quite understand...
Therapist:	Well, basically towards moves are anything you'll start doing or do more of if therapy is successful. For example, you mentioned you want to start jogging again—so would that be taking you toward the sort of life you want to build?
Client:	Yes!
Therapist:	Cool. I'll jot that down. (*writes it alongside the towards arrow*) Anything else?
Client:	I'm not sure.
Therapist:	Well, you said yelling at Mike is an away move, so what would you like to do instead?
Client:	I guess more patience. Staying calm instead of flying off the handle.
Therapist:	Okay, (*writing it down*) so talking calmly, being patient. What about drinking?
Client:	I like drinking!
Therapist:	Don't we all? The thing is, you said "drinking too much" is an away move; so if therapy is successful, what will your drinking habits look like?
Client:	(*heavy sigh*) Honestly—I'm not sure. But less than now.
Therapist:	So for now I'll just put "drinking moderately"?
Client:	Okay.
Therapist:	What about work?
Client:	Yes, I'll be going to meetings, and keeping up with everything.
Therapist:	You said it's hard to focus at work—so just wondering, should we add "focusing on my work"?
Client:	Yes. That'd be a miracle!
Therapist:	Friends?

Client: Yes, yes—seeing friends again.

Therapist: How about establishing good sleep routines?

Client: Yes, that sounds good.

Therapist: Okay, and I'm going to add one more thing here—"learning unhooking skills." I'm assuming that would be a towards move too, learning how to unhook from all this difficult stuff, and "unfreeze" yourself?

Client: Yes, definitely.

Therapist: Okay, well, that's a great start. We can add to this later.

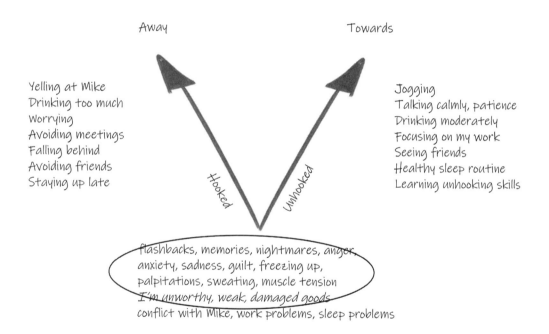

Many clients need prompting to come up with towards moves, and in chapter fifteen we cover several strategies for doing this. But sometimes, despite our best efforts, a client will say, "I don't know," and they may even become distressed about not knowing. If so, we compassionately validate their feelings and normalize this lack of knowledge: "That's really quite common at this stage. Can we flag that as something to explore later?" Then, for the time being, we focus on unhooking skills—and leave towards moves until later, when we formally explore values.

A Note About Action Versus Outcome

Many clients feel disempowered—and one way to empower them is through helping them focus on what is within their control. Let's consider insomnia. Naturally, clients want to have a good night's sleep—but there is no guarantee they will achieve that outcome; it's out of their direct control. What *is* within their control is to implement the principles of sleep hygiene (see chapter twenty-three). Therefore, in the session with Helen, the therapist treats insomnia as a situation (in which sleeping is difficult) and places it at the bottom of the choice point. In away moves, the therapist writes "staying up late" (an ineffective behavioral response to insomnia), and in towards moves, "healthy sleep routine" (an effective behavioral response to insomnia). The therapist deliberately does *not* write "sleeping well" in towards moves, because while that's the desired outcome, it is outside the client's control.

The same applies to a medical condition or injury: cure or recovery is outside of a person's direct control. So we would frame this as a problematic situation (e.g., "chronic pain syndrome," "arm injury," "cancer") and place it at the bottom of the choice point. Away moves would be unworkable responses to that situation (e.g., heavy drinking, avoiding medical advice), and towards moves would be effective ones (e.g., following medical advice, practicing self-compassion, seeking support).

Summarizing

One benefit of the choice point is how well it can summarize the client's situation and give us a helpful visual way to check in with them to see if it seems on target.

> *Therapist:* So, what I've drawn here is just bare bones—but how is it as a snapshot of your main problems?
>
> *Client:* It's interesting. (*looks thoughtful*)
>
> *Therapist:* I'm pleased to hear that. As a general plan for working together...this seems okay?
>
> *Client:* (*nodding*) Yes—it makes sense.

The client's reaction above is quite common. The simple visual representation often makes complex issues seem a lot simpler. (This is partly because the therapist selectively focuses on key aspects of the main issues. If the therapist exhaustively listed every single symptom and problem, the process would take much longer and be counterproductive.)

The exchange above involves "reframing": looking at problems from a new perspective to foster more flexible responses. Most clients believe that their difficult private experiences are the problem and that the aim of therapy is to get rid of them. But ACT offers a radically different perspective: it's not our emotions and cognitions that create our problems; it's fusing with or trying to avoid them, and the ineffective behavior that results.

When we successfully introduce the new perspective that "getting hooked" and doing "away moves" are the problems—and "unhooking skills" and "towards moves" are the antidotes—this reframes both the issue and the aims of therapy. (Of course, things don't always go so smoothly as above. At times, clients may have negative reactions, and we'll look at how to deal with that in chapter nineteen.)

A Simple Homework Task

After running through the above, we can now use the choice point for homework:

Therapist:	I'm wondering if between now and next session you'd be willing to do a couple of things, to build on what we've done today?
Client:	Like what?
Therapist:	Well, as you go through your day, see if you can notice when you're doing towards moves and when you're doing away moves. And when you do towards moves, take a moment to slow down and appreciate it, like "Hey, here I am doing something that matters." Notice what it's like behaving like the sort of person you want to be, doing stuff to build the sort of life you want.
Client:	Okay.
Therapist:	Also, when we do away moves, we often don't realize it straight away. So the moment you realize it, just pause for a moment, acknowledge it—and don't beat yourself up over it, just see if you can identify the thoughts and feelings that are hooking you. Ask yourself, "What just hooked me?"
Client:	Okay, I can do that.

We could flesh out this homework in various ways. We could give the client a blank choice point and ask them to place it somewhere prominent, as a memory aid. Or they could take a photo of the completed choice point and use it as a reminder. Or they could keep a record of towards and away moves, using the worksheets in Extra Bits. It's a quick way to help clients develop self-awareness: to notice when their behavior is workable and when it isn't; and to become more conscious of the thoughts, feelings, and situations that trigger their problematic behaviors.

Fill in a Choice Point

Now it's your turn to fill in a choice point for a current client. You can download a blank diagram from Extra Bits, or draw one on a sheet of paper. (Please do this, even if you never intend to use one with a real client, because it will help you to understand the ACT model. Allow about ten minutes.)

What's Hooking Your Client?

Start at the bottom of the choice point. Use the entire bottom quarter of the page to write down the following:

Situations: What difficult situations is the client struggling with? This includes social, medical, occupational, financial, legal, domestic, and relationship problems.

Thoughts and feelings: What difficult private experiences is the client struggling with? This includes thoughts, feelings, memories, images, urges, sensations, and physiological reactions.

Away Moves

Next write in the client's away moves. What overt and covert behaviors *does the client see* as problematic?

Towards Moves

Finally, write in towards moves. This section is usually the hardest to complete. Clients are often good at describing the difficult situations they face, the thoughts and feelings they struggle with, and the problematic behaviors they are doing. But they often find it hard to identify values, or value-congruent goals and actions. So if you have little or nothing to write here, that's golden information: it highlights important areas for you to explore.

So how did you fare in this exercise? I hope you got a sense of how to approach complex issues with TFACT. (Of course, if you're not keen on the choice point, you don't *have to* use it; there are many alternatives to any tool or technique. But if you do like it, there are many ways to utilize it.)

Might clients perceive the choice point as *too* simplistic—especially those with complex presentation, multiple issues, and comorbidity? Well, it's possible, of course; but it's unlikely as long as we (a) compassionately validate the client's difficulties, and (b) clearly explain: "Obviously there's a lot more complexity to your issues than this. This tool is a way to narrow the focus so we can start doing something practical, right away."

After the Choice Point, What Next?

After completing a choice point, we can give clients a choice: do they want to focus first on towards moves or unhooking skills? If the former, we move into values and committed action. If the latter, we move into any of the four core mindfulness skills (defusion, acceptance, contact with the present moment, self-as-context). Whichever option they choose, our first task is to introduce a practical trauma-sensitive mindfulness skill that they can immediately start using, to help them *both* unhook from thoughts and feelings *and* act in line with their values. (We'll cover this in chapter eight.)

EXTRA BIT

In chapter five of *Trauma-Focused ACT: The Extra Bits*, you'll find printable versions of the choice point, a comparison of the choice point and the matrix (another popular ACT tool), and a towards/away moves worksheet.

Takeaway

We can use the choice point for many purposes, including "quick and dirty" case conceptualization, explaining the ACT model, establishing therapy goals, setting an agenda for a session, and raising self-awareness. It's well worth taking the time to familiarize yourself with this tool, because (as you'll see) it has many other practical applications.

CHAPTER SIX

The Journey Ahead

So, here we are in the final chapter of part one, and the main question now is: how can you best use the rest of the book? Basically, you have two options. Option one is to work through each chapter in sequence, as if following a protocol. Although TFACT is *not* a protocol, if you're an ACT newbie, then option one is wise. However, for those more experienced in ACT, I recommend option two, which is to freely "pick and choose": take what's useful from any chapter and apply it as needed at any point in therapy. Before moving forward, though, let's look at the four flexible stages of TFACT—which coincide with parts two through five of this book—and some common pitfalls to avoid.

Four Flexible Stages

I will now tentatively suggest four stages of therapy. Please hold them loosely and use them flexibly.

Stage one, beginning therapy, usually takes two sessions: the intake session (where we take a history, obtain informed consent, and establish therapy goals) followed by the first session of active therapy.

Stages two, three, and four typically take several sessions. The number varies depending on the extent and severity of the client's trauma history, the number of problems they have, how well they respond to TFACT, how much they practice new skills—and of course, how effectively *we* work.

For most clients, it will take about eight to twelve sessions to cover *everything* in this book—and sometimes, many more. But fortunately, we don't have to cover everything, because individual elements of TFACT are helpful by themselves. For example, we could teach a client a flexible trauma-sensitive mindfulness skill, and this could be of huge benefit, even if we never see them again. Similarly, a session focused solely on defusion, values, or self-compassion can be hugely beneficial by itself, even without the rest of the model. Naturally, we *want* to cover it all—but in the real world, that's not always possible. This is why I've included chapter thirty-three: "TFACT as a Brief Intervention."

The table below summarizes these four flexible stages.

Stages of TFACT

Stage One: Beginning Therapy (One to two sessions)	• Taking a history • Obtaining informed consent • Establishing therapy goals • Psychoeducation on trauma • Dropping anchor
Stage Two: Living in the Present (Four to six sessions)	• Defusion • Acceptance and self-compassion • Clarifying values • Committed action • Breaking destructive patterns • Working with the body • Relaxation, sleep, and self-soothing • Developing a flexible sense of self • Relationship skills • Mindful appreciation
Stage Three: Healing the Past (Two to four sessions)	• "Inner child" work • Grieving • Forgiving • Exposure to traumatic memories
Stage Four: Building the Future (Two to four sessions)	• Long-term goals • Maintenance and prevention plans • Exploring posttraumatic growth • Ending therapy

These stages all overlap, and, aside from stage one, which we always cover first, we can freely weave between them as desired. So, for example, in stage two, if we want a more "bottom-up" approach (working with the body, emotions, sensations) rather than a "top-down" approach (working with cognitions), we can start with the strategies listed in the lower half of that box, then later, bring in the ones in the upper half. Similarly, for some clients, we may want to work first on "healing the past," in which case we'd focus on stage three strategies initially, then introduce stage two later.

At What Stage Do We Begin Exposure to Traumatic Memories?

In TFACT, unlike many other models, we tend to leave formal exposure to traumatic memories until quite late in therapy. There are several reasons for this. One, it's often unnecessary. Many clients make significant improvements in their life, health, and well-being without ever needing to do such work. For example, in the WHO's ACT protocol for refugee camps, participants achieved positive outcomes without any formal exposure to traumatic memories (Tol et al., 2020).

Two, if such work is necessary, it's much easier to do when the client already has skills in defusion, acceptance, dropping anchor, self-as-context, and self-compassion.

And three, clients are usually more willing to do this challenging work when it's clearly linked to values-based goals. For example, suppose a client wants to resume sexual intimacy with their partner but is avoiding such activity because it triggers memories of sexual assault. They may be more motivated later in therapy to undertake formal exposure in the service of achieving this specific values-based goal—as opposed to doing it earlier in therapy on the rationale that "it's necessary to recover from trauma."

Three Common Pitfalls for Practitioners

As the saying goes, "forewarned is forearmed"—so I want to quickly flag three common pitfalls for practitioners. Watch out for these traps; they are sooooo easy to fall into.

1. Fusion with Diagnosis

A diagnostic label is helpful in a context where it gives access to useful knowledge and effective treatment. But it's not helpful in a context where it increases stigma, fosters fusion with a sense of being defective or inadequate, or leads to ineffective treatment. Problems can occur when practitioners fuse with diagnoses and try to treat the DSM disorder rather than the unique human being in front of them.

To avoid this trap, hold diagnostic labels lightly. Look at the issue with ACT eyes; identify the fusion, avoidance, remoteness from values, unworkable action, and loss of contact with the present moment. This will open up many possibilities for intervention.

2. Talking About ACT Instead of Doing It

This is an incredibly common trap for ACT practitioners. We like talking about ACT because there are so many interesting metaphors and fascinating bits of psychoeducation. But just as we can't learn to play piano simply by talking about it, our clients won't develop new ACT skills simply through hearing metaphors or discussing how ACT processes can be helpful. We need to actively help clients learn and practice new ACT skills *in session*—noticing and naming their feelings, mindfully scanning their bodies, practicing self-compassion, and so on—and then encourage them to practice regularly at home. (I can usually tell when therapists have been talking about ACT rather than doing it because they say things like "We talked about acceptance" or "We did the Pushing Away Paper metaphor," or "I asked the client to reflect on it." It's fine to briefly discuss what acceptance is and how it can help, and illustrate it with a metaphor, but you then need to actively practice acceptance skills *in session*.)

3. Practitioner Avoidance

Working with trauma is challenging. Sometimes practitioners undermine the effectiveness of therapy by trying to avoid their own uncomfortable thoughts and feelings. Without realizing it, they may subtly discourage clients from discussing traumatic memories or suicidal thoughts, or avoid challenging experiential exercises, or stay away from exposure even though they know it's warranted. Indeed, therapist avoidance is usually a major factor in the previous pitfall: talking about ACT instead of doing it; for most of us, it's a lot more comfortable to talk and chat and discuss than to do challenging experiential work (especially exposure). So in order to be effective, we need to apply ACT to ourselves: in line with our values as practitioners, commit to effective action in session, making room for all the discomfort that arises.

What Measures Can We Use?

Most practitioners use formal measures to track clients' progress. These may include trauma-specific measures (e.g., PTSD Checklist [PCL-6]), general measures of psychological distress (e.g., Kessler Psychological Distress Scale [K6]), quality of life measures (e.g., General Health Questionnaire [GHQ]), or ACT-specific measures (e.g., Multidimensional Experiential Avoidance Questionnaire [MEAQ-30]; Comprehensive Assessment of Acceptance and Commitment Processes [CompACT]). There are no specific measures recommended for TFACT—so please choose according to your personal preference.

Practical Tip

Completing measures eats up precious session time that could arguably be better spent doing ACT, so consider asking clients to fill them in before or after a session.

Takeaway

There's no one "right" sequence for TFACT. The stages of therapy above offer rough guidelines only; hold them loosely and apply them flexibly. You're going on a journey, and this book is like a guide to interesting places worth exploring—rather than some strictly scheduled itinerary. So take what's useful, leave the rest, and adapt and modify everything to suit your needs.

PART TWO

Beginning Therapy

CHAPTER SEVEN

Firm Foundations

There's a lot to cover in the first session of therapy (the intake session): taking a history, informed consent for TFACT, establishing therapy goals, and psychoeducation about trauma. (If we don't have time to do all that, we can continue it in session two.) We covered informed consent in chapter four, and psychoeducation on trauma in chapter five, so here we'll focus on the other items.

The Untold Story

"There is no greater agony than bearing an untold story inside you," wrote Maya Angelou. So we listen mindfully to our clients as they talk about their hurts and their hopes, their loves and their losses. We create a "sacred space" where they can be seen and heard and understood. We validate and normalize their feelings; witness their stories and respond with understanding and compassion. This is how the healing process begins.

But this is just the start. Supportive, reflective, compassionate listening is nowhere near enough to enable recovery from trauma. We need to use the client's narrative as a doorway to developing psychological flexibility. So when we meet new clients and hear their stories, we watch for anything that can help with this transition.

A large chunk of the intake session involves taking a history, and how you do this will depend upon your previous training. Practitioners trained in brief therapy take a short history, then promptly move into active intervention in the intake session. Practitioners trained more traditionally may spend an entire session or two gathering history before beginning active intervention. One thing to keep in mind: we don't need to gather a client's entire trauma history on intake. It's fine to begin with a snapshot of their main problems and an overview of relevant past events. We can gather more information later, as it becomes relevant to a specific issue we're focusing on.

Do Clients Have to Talk About Their Trauma?

No. Clients do not *have to* talk about their trauma. (Clients do not *have to* do anything!) Indeed, if clients are pressured or coerced into talking about their trauma, against their will, there's a risk of retraumatizing them. So while we like to know about the client's past and how it has impacted them, we don't need to know every detail in order to help them develop psychological flexibility. And we should not push them to talk about it if they're unwilling. Some clients may be incapable of verbalizing their trauma until they have enough defusion, acceptance, and mindful grounding skills to cope with the emotional pain involved. Therefore, if clients are unwilling or unable to talk about their trauma, we start building TFACT skills with whatever issues they *are* willing to discuss.

When clients *are* able and willing to talk about their trauma, we go slowly and cautiously, checking often for willingness: "Is it okay to keep talking about this?" And we carefully observe their reactions while encouraging them often to notice how they're feeling or what they're thinking. And if, at any point, a client seems emotionally overwhelmed or extremely fused, or a flashback occurs, or we see behavior suggestive of dissociation—then we stop taking a history and move into active intervention to help them cope with their reaction (see chapter eight). Then, once the client is no longer over-whelmed but centered and able to engage, we can continue with the history.

Validate, Validate, Validate

There's probably no need to say that we repeatedly validate and normalize the client's reactions—neurobiological, emotional, cognitive, and behavioral—to the traumatic events they've experienced. We wish to explicitly convey that these are normal reactions to traumatic events: your mind, brain, and body working hard to keep you safe. (Sometimes, overenthusiastic practitioners inadvertently invalidate their clients, because they leap into core ACT skills without first doing this important groundwork—forgetting that this is usually the first step in both defusion and acceptance.) Likewise, many clients have done things to cope with trauma that they now feel ashamed of or guilty about. So again, we want to validate, validate, validate. We want to convey, "You did what you needed to do to cope with what you were going through; it served a useful purpose at that time."

Checking In

While taking a history, we can from time to time ask the client to "check in" and notice their feelings. For example, we might say, "Can I press pause for a moment? I want to hear the rest of this, but I can't help noticing you look very upset. Can I ask, what are you feeling right now?" We may follow up by asking, "Where are you feeling that in your body?" and "What would you call this feeling?"

Doing this gives us valuable information. If a client says they feel nothing, or they don't know what they are feeling, this probably indicates experiential avoidance and disconnection from their inner world. On the other hand, suppose a client reports a tight chest and knots in the stomach and labels this "anxiety"; that indicates some useful ability in contacting the present moment and noticing and naming emotions. From there, we may gauge their capacity for acceptance by inviting the client to "sit with the feeling" and see if they can "open up and make room for it." If they can't do this, so be it; but if they can, that's a good start for building acceptance skills.

We may do something similar to assess a client's ability to notice their thoughts: "I'm curious—you've been sharing something very personal here with me; I'm wondering, if I could listen in to your mind right now, what would I hear it telling you about this?"

Strengths and Resources

As the client talks about their problems, we listen compassionately, validate their difficulties, and look out for psychological rigidity. But this is only half of the equation. We also want to discover skills, strengths, and resources they can utilize. To do this we may ask:

- Are there any areas of your life where things are okay or going well?

- What do you enjoy doing? Do you have any hobbies or interests?

- Does anything you do give you a sense of meaning or purpose or a connection with something bigger? Or a sense of pride or achievement? Or a sense of being true to yourself?

- Are there any times when difficult thoughts and feelings show up, but you don't let them hold you back from doing what really matters to you?

Such questions tap into strengths and resources that we can draw upon later, as a springboard to values and committed action.

Establishing Therapy Goals

It's important to establish ACT-congruent therapy goals early on; without them, we may find that the client expects something different from what we are offering. However, this can be challenging. Clients usually have a strong agenda of experiential avoidance; their main aim is to "feel better" and get rid of unwanted cognitions, emotions, and memories. These "emotional goals" will create huge problems if we agree to them, so skillful reframing is required.

How to Reframe Emotional Goals

The following prompt (from Strosahl et al., 2012) is a good way to elicit emotional goals:

Therapist: I'd like to get a sense of what you want from our sessions. So could you please complete this sentence? "I'll know therapy is working for me when I..."

Almost always, clients will reply with emotional goals such as "when I...stop feeling anxious, stop doubting myself, stop feeling depressed, stop losing my temper, stop feeling so angry, stop being so jittery, get rid of these memories and nightmares, stop feeling numb and empty, stop taking things personally, stop being so narky, don't have any pain." These goals all have the same agenda—experiential avoidance: *get rid of my unwanted cognitions, emotions, and sensations.*

Sometimes this is stated as "when I...get over this, get my old self back, be normal, build self-esteem, be like everyone else, put this behind me, feel good about myself, get on with my life." We would then ask, "And how will you know you've achieved that?" The client's next reply then reveals the agenda: "I'd be feeling XYZ; I'd stop feeling ABC."

Other emotional goals include "when I…am happy, feel good, feel normal, have more confidence, feel calm, laugh again, feel joy, feel relaxed, feel positive about life." We may reply, "So you're not feeling the way you really want to. What kind of thoughts and feelings *are* you having?"; this immediately reveals the unwanted thoughts and feelings.

EMOTIONAL GOALS ARE NORMAL!

All the goals listed above are *normal*. We're *all* experientially avoidant; we all want to feel good and avoid feeling bad. The problem is, *excessive* experiential avoidance—and all the problems it fosters—plays a central role in trauma-related disorders; so if we agree to such goals, we reinforce it. Our clients are usually deeply distressed, overwhelmed, or paralyzed by painful thoughts, feelings, and memories, and we want to reduce their psychological suffering as fast as possible. But we don't do that by trying to avoid or get rid of them. So we need to reframe these goals, to make them ACT-congruent— and do so without confrontation. For example, we'd never say, "We don't try to get rid of your difficult thoughts or feelings in ACT. This approach isn't about 'feeling good.'" (Especially when over 3,000 published studies show emotional pain *will* reduce and clients *will* feel better.)

THE "CATCH-ALL" GOAL FOR ACT

Fortunately, there's a "catch-all" ACT-congruent therapy goal that applies to every client, a simple phrase that quickly reframes any goal about emotional control: "Learning new skills to handle difficult thoughts and feelings more effectively." Once we know what difficult private experiences the client wants to avoid, we can say:

Therapist: There are some very difficult thoughts, feelings, and memories showing up for you, such as (*mentions a few*). So one thing we can do is help you learn some new skills to handle that stuff more effectively.

Here are two examples:

Client: I wouldn't take things so personally. I wouldn't get so down about it when Dave teases me.

Therapist: Okay, so at the moment, when you take things personally or get down about it, what kind of thoughts and feelings show up for you? (*elicits answers*) And what do you do when you get hooked by those thoughts and feelings? (*elicits answers*) So one thing we could do here is help you learn how to unhook from those difficult thoughts and feelings—take the power and impact out of them so they don't jerk you around. Would that be useful?

Client:	I want more self-esteem.
Therapist:	What do you mean by self-esteem?
Client:	Oh you know—feeling good about myself.
Therapist:	Okay, so thinking and feeling differently about yourself; more positive; more upbeat?
Client:	Yeah.
Therapist:	So I'm guessing there are thoughts and feelings showing up for you that you don't want; what are they? (*elicits answers*) And what do you do when you get hooked by those thoughts and feelings? (*elicits answers*) So one thing we could do here is help you learn new skills to handle those difficult thoughts and feelings—take their power away so they can't bring you down or hold you back. Does that sound like it would be helpful?

On occasion a client may say that what they want most is to get rid of their awful memories. In this case, the Horror Movie metaphor (Harris, 2015) comes in handy.

The Horror Movie Metaphor

Therapist:	We can't simply eliminate memories—there's no delete button in the brain—but what we can do is transform them. Suppose we compare these memories to a terrifying horror movie—but obviously much, much worse, because horror movies are fictional, whereas this stuff really happened. So what happens is, at the moment, when your memories appear, it's like watching a horror movie on a massive TV screen, all by yourself, late at night, in a huge empty house, in the middle of the countryside, during a thunderstorm. It's terrifying, overwhelming. But we can transform the way you respond to those memories, so that although it's the same horror movie, now it's playing on the screen of a smart phone, and that phone is in the corner of the room, and it's broad daylight, sun streaming in through the windows, and you're hanging out with the people you love, eating delicious food, listening to great music, doing things you really like to do. So would you be interested in learning some skills that will help you to do that?

All of the above reframing makes it easy to introduce new TFACT skills, such as defusion, acceptance, and self-compassion. (And if using a choice point for this process, we'd write unwanted thoughts and feelings at the bottom, and we'd write "unhooking skills" on the towards arrow.)

THE ONE EXCEPTION: NUMBNESS

There is one exception to the "catch-all" goal mentioned above: when clients are trying to get rid of emotional numbness. The client in the transcript that follows was emotionally, physically, and sexually abused throughout her childhood and is prone to dissociation, self-harming, skin picking, and binge eating. She is successful in her career as an artist, but very detached from her two young children. She feels like she will never connect with them and is not even sure she wants to. She says she's never felt happy, never experienced a sense of achievement, fulfilment, or love and affection. Here's how we might address this:

Client: I'm so sick of being like this. I just want to know what it's like to feel some laughter or joy or happiness or love. Something!

Therapist: You're not feeling any of that?

Client: I don't feel anything anymore.

Therapist: You're totally numb?

Client: Pretty much. I mean, sometimes I get down or cranky. But mostly, I just feel dead.

Therapist: That's very common for people who've been through what you have. (*Therapist briefly explains how emotional numbness results from "emergency shutdown" mode, then continues...*) So one useful thing we can do here is help you learn some new skills to tune into your body, so you can access the full range of your feelings. And I say "the full range," because we can't simply pick and choose which feelings we have. It's really about learning how to tune into your body and feel *all* your emotions. So another thing we can do here is learn how to handle the difficult feelings when they show up; how to take the impact out of them, so they can't jerk you around. And when you learn how to connect with your own feelings, that will help you to connect with your children.

How to Establish Overt Behavioral Goals

In addition to the goals above, we want to establish overt behavioral goals: "I'm wondering, if our work here is successful, what you will be *doing* differently?" We may add:

• What will you start or do more of?

• What will you stop or do less of?

• How will you treat yourself differently?

• How will you treat others differently?

- What places, events, or activities will you start or resume?

- Who are the most important people in your life? What will you be doing differently in those relationships?

There are many other questions we could ask, including the classic "magic wand" question:

Therapist:	Suppose I have a magic wand here—a real one, real magic—and I wave it right now... and suddenly all these difficult thoughts and feelings you've been struggling with lose all their impact. They no longer jerk you around; they're like water off a duck's back. Then what would you do differently?

In the transcript that follows, the therapist uses yet another popular strategy: the seven-day documentary.

SESSION WITH SUE: OVERT BEHAVIORAL GOALS

Sue is a forty-year-old woman, married with two young daughters. A few years earlier she was the victim a vicious sexual assault, involving repeated rape over several hours. She has many trauma-related symptoms, including self-hatred, disgust and revulsion around her body, high levels of anxiety, continual worrying, avoidance of sexual and emotional intimacy with her husband, and repeated cutting on her thighs and lower abdomen with a razor blade. She makes no eye contact at all with the therapist, keeps her head downcast the whole time. She has placed a large cushion across her lap, hiding her body from waist to knee.

Therapist:	I just want to get a little clearer about how your life will be different, if our work here is successful. So imagine we follow you around with a camera crew now and we film you for a week—twenty-four/seven, recording all the things you say and do—and we make a documentary about it. And then we do the same at some point in the future, after therapy has finished, and make *another* documentary. What kind of things would we see you doing or hear you saying on that new documentary?
Client:	I could probably look at you.
Therapist:	Okay, so we'd see more eye contact?
Client:	Mmm, yep. Sometimes I can do that but...but yeah.
Therapist:	Are there particular people that we'd see you having more eye contact with?
Client:	People like you, that know what happened.
Therapist:	Is that the hardest, people that know?
Client:	Yeah. Sometimes I can do it but with...you know, people I just met. But not people who know.

Therapist:	Okay. Would there be any other changes we'd see on that video?
Client:	Yeah, I probably wouldn't um, just be so awkward.
Therapist:	Okay. So...what would we see on the video?
Client:	Um well, I'd probably just, I wouldn't kind of just try and hide all the time, have things cover me. (*Client indicates the cushion covering her thighs.*)
Therapist:	Like the cushion?
Client:	Yeah.
Therapist:	So if you were here, you'd be sitting without the cushion?
Client:	Yep. And I could maybe wear different clothes.
Therapist:	What kind of clothes?
Client:	Um, like...tank tops or boots or, you know, just kind of a bit more modern.
Therapist:	Okay. So you'd dress a bit more modern?
Client:	Yeah.
Therapist:	And what would we see or hear differently on the documentary when you're with your husband?
Client:	Oh I'd probably talk to him a bit more, wouldn't lie so much.
Therapist:	Okay. So you'd be more honest with him?
Client:	Yeah, I wouldn't hide so much.
Therapist:	Got it. Are there any things in particular that you wouldn't be hiding?
Client:	Um, oh like you know, like cutting and stuff.
Therapist:	Okay. So would there be less cutting or it would stop completely?
Client:	I wouldn't do it.
Therapist:	So if the urge to cut shows up, what will you do differently—instead of cutting yourself?
Client:	Ummmm. (*shakes head*) I don't know.
Therapist:	No problem—that's something we can look at later. Are there any other things that we'd see on the new documentary that would make us go "Wow! Sue's really made some progress there...therapy really helped!"?

Client: (*faintly chuckling*) Oh I probably wouldn't keep my house so clean.

Therapist: So if you aren't so busy cleaning, what will you do with all that extra time?

Client: Play with the girls.

Therapist: Cool. So we'd see you playing with the girls more. Anything else we'd see?

Client: Um, I wouldn't have to worry about everything. I could just let the girls go to their friends' houses without um, worrying about it.

Therapist: So on the documentary, what would we see or hear that would show us "Wow! Sue's really good at unhooking from her worries"?

Client: They could just go.

Therapist: Just go to their friends' houses?

Client: Yeah, there wouldn't have to be so much planning and I wouldn't be sitting at home worried the whole time.

Therapist: Right. So on the current video, when the girls are at their friends' and you're at home, what would we see or hear that we'd know, "Sue's really been hooked by her worries!"?

Client: Um...oh I'd be cleaning or showering or something.

Therapist: Okay. So in the new video, when the girls are off, and you've unhooked from your worries, what would we see you doing instead of showering or cleaning?

Client: Um. Maybe reading a book or doing some exercise.

Therapist: Right. What kind of exercise would you do?

Client: Um, walking. Maybe ride...ride a bike.

A FEW NOTES

There are several things worth noting about the above transcript.

Note one: It seems long when written down, but in the actual session, it only took a few minutes.

Note two: When the client revisited the emotional goal of "not being worried," the therapist reframed it to the (covert) behavioral goal of "unhooking from worries." There are many ways to use this reframe. For example, if a client says, "I wouldn't be feeling depressed," we may say, "So what would we see or hear on the new documentary that would show us you had unhooked from all those depressing thoughts and feelings?"

Note three: Questions like "What will you stop doing?" identify behaviors that clients see as problematic but do not establish behavioral goals. How so? Well, behavioral goals describe what you want to *do* (as opposed to what you *don't want* to do). So we need to follow up with "What will you do instead?" For example, when Sue said she wouldn't cut any more, the therapist asked, "If the urge to cut shows up, what will you *do* differently?" (If the client doesn't know, we normalize and validate that response, and flag it for later exploration.)

Note four: Some clients react negatively to the word "goals"; it triggers shame or fear of failure. So consider avoiding using it in early sessions. (In the transcript above, it is never mentioned.)

How to "Extract" Values from Goals

Our next step is to "extract" some values from beneath the client's overt behavioral goals. (Some practitioners clarify values *first* before establishing goals; either way is fine.) Usually, the values are right beneath the surface. For example, in the transcript above, what values do you think are likely underneath these goals: *play with the kids, do less planning, stop cutting, ride a bike, read a book, make eye contact, wear modern clothes*? Please generate some answers before reading on.

At this point, the therapist does not know what the client's values are, but it's fine to make an educated guess:

Therapist: So please tell me if I've got this right or wrong. I'm getting the sense that as a mom, you really want to be more playful and easygoing—is that right?

Client: Yeah. And not so serious. I want to be more fun.

Therapist: Okay. So as a mother, being playful, easygoing, and fun-loving. And with your husband, seems like you want to be more open and honest?

Client: Yes.

Therapist: What about with other people? It seems like you're wanting to be more open, more authentic—like, being the real you, instead of hiding away?

Client: Yeah. Yeah. And, you know—more um, like with my husband, talking a bit more, and saying what I really think.

In the above example, the values explicitly named are being playful, easygoing, fun-loving, open, honest, authentic. But note: the therapist never uses the word "values" because this term is commonly misunderstood. Generally, it's better to avoid this term until later in therapy, when values become the central focus. Sometimes therapists protest: "But isn't this putting words into the client's mouth?" To which I reply, "Well, um, sort of, I guess…but not really." What we are doing here is helping clients put their values into words—often for the first time in their life. If we get it wrong, they'll usually correct us: "No, it's not that…" But if we're right, they usually leap on it.

However, if you're not comfortable with this approach, don't do it; wait until you start formal values clarification, as in chapter fifteen. Also keep in mind that some clients—especially those with complex trauma—have such an impoverished sense of self that the very idea of values is utterly alien, and it may be a very slow process to clarify them (see the "Impoverished Self" section, in chapter twenty-one). So if you're not getting anywhere—if the client repeats "I don't know what I want" or "I just want to feel better"—don't turn it into a source of tension; approach it as outlined below.

Barriers to Establishing Therapy Goals

At times, it's fairly easy to establish therapy goals; and at other times, it's fiendishly difficult. Let's take a quick look at the most common barriers, and how to overcome them.

I DON'T CARE ABOUT ANYTHING

Sometimes clients say they don't care about anything at all. However, we know they wouldn't come to therapy unless they cared about *something*. They at least care about reducing their own suffering—and usually they also care about significant others. So we can highlight the value of caring (for self or others) straight off the bat:

Client: I don't care about anything.

Therapist: I hear you say that…and yet, here you are…you turned up to the session. And that wasn't easy, right? You said yourself, it brought up a lot of anxiety, you thought about canceling. And yet, even with all those difficult thoughts and feelings, you made it. So I'm wondering: what do you care about enough that you actually attended?

Clients' replies to the above question fall into one of two categories: caring about self (e.g., *I want to feel happy, I want my life back, I'm just sick of feeling like this*) or caring about others (e.g., *I don't want to be a burden to my kids, I don't want my wife to leave me*). We can then explore:

Therapist: So notice this. There's a part of you that says, "I don't care about anything." And there's another part of you—let's call it "the caring part"—that got you here today, even though you felt anxious and wanted to cancel. So if we can help you access that "caring part" a bit more, it can be a useful resource for motivation.

HOPELESSNESS, NIHILISM, AND SUICIDALITY

Sometimes clients are fused with nihilism or hopelessness: *Life has no purpose. Everything is pointless. Life is suffering and then you die. There's no point in doing anything because life is meaningless. There's no hope. Nothing works. I'm a lost cause.* To work with this, see chapter ten, the section headed "Therapy Session: Defusion from Doubt and Hopelessness." And for suicidal ideation, see chapter twenty-six.

INSIGHT AND UNDERSTANDING

Sometimes a client will say they are coming to therapy because "I want to understand myself" or "I want to know why I'm like this." We may reply, "That's a given. As we do this work you'll get a lot of understanding about your thoughts and feelings, and where they come from, and why you have them, why you do what you do, what really matters to you, and so on. But if that's all you get from our work together—you understand yourself, but nothing in your life changes, things carry on exactly as they are today—would that be a good outcome? Or are there some things you want to be different in your life?

NO GOALS AT ALL

No matter how skillful we get at establishing goals, at times, we will hit a brick wall. The client will respond to every question with "I don't know" or "I've got no idea," or shrug their shoulders and go silent, or express that they don't want anything at all. If this happens, we stop questioning, and instead we compassionately explore the client's reaction. Are they fused with hopelessness? Overwhelmed by the questions? Unable to imagine the future? We can address these barriers as required, then return to the question.

However, we want to avoid tension or conflict. So if a client repeatedly says, "I don't know," we may reply, "I cans see that right now, you really don't know what you want. Actually, that's quite common. How about we put that on the agenda for later: make it part of our work, going forward, to figure it out? The main thing is, right now you're hurting, you're suffering. So let's make that our main goal: learning new skills to handle all those painful thoughts and feelings more effectively."

Takeaway

Reflective, compassionate listening as a client tells their story is of fundamental importance. If clients are able and willing to talk, we find out not only how they have suffered in the past, and the problems they have in the present, but also their strengths and resources. We then set goals for therapy—and, if possible, tease out values. This information streamlines our sessions and ensures we are aligned with our clients; without it, we easily get stuck. Establishing goals also fosters hope and optimism; it gives clients a sense that things can improve, changes can happen, a better life is possible.

CHAPTER EIGHT

Anchors Away

Welcome to the longest chapter in the book—and arguably the most important, because the skill we cover applies to so many facets of trauma. I call this skill "dropping anchor" (Harris, 2007): a collective term for many mindfulness practices, all based on the same three-step formula. Dropping anchor exercises are powerful first-line interventions for emotion dysregulation, flashbacks, dissociation, hyperarousal, hypoarousal, social disengagement, worrying, ruminating, obsessing, panic attacks, extreme fusion, addictive behavior, self-harming, suicidality, aggression…and a whole lot more.

Earlier, I mentioned an ACT protocol that I wrote (helped by many others) for the World Health Organization for use in refugee camps. Dropping anchor is the core mindfulness skill within that protocol; participants learn it early in session one. It's quick and easy to teach, and people from many different countries—including Uganda, Sudan, Syria, and Turkey—respond to it well. Of note, in the first published randomized controlled trial of this protocol (Tol et al., 2020), there was not a single adverse outcome; so it's a good example of trauma-sensitive mindfulness.

I've chunked this mega-chapter into five sections. First is "Dropping Anchor: The Basics." This covers the core components of dropping anchor. Next comes "Working with Extremes of Arousal," which includes transcripts from two different therapy sessions. Sections three and four, "Debriefing" and "Modifying," look at how to debrief these exercises and modify them for different issues. And section five, "Homework," is self-explanatory.

Dropping Anchor: The Basics

In the transcript below, you'll see how dropping anchor gets its name and how to introduce it to clients. This example focuses on anxiety, but the same method applies for all emotions.

Therapist: So what you're experiencing right now, I call this an "emotional storm," because you've got all these thoughts whirling around inside your head, and all these feelings whipping through your body. And when an emotional storm gets hold of us, and sweeps us away, there's nothing effective we can do; we can't deal with the challenge or the problem effectively.

Client: I know! That's why I keep fucking up.

Therapist: Yeah, the storm just jerks you around all over the place.

Client:	Right!
Therapist:	So would you be interested in learning a skill to help you handle these emotional storms?
Client:	Yeah, yeah. That would be good. That would be great.
Therapist:	Cool. Well, let's talk about real storms for a moment. Suppose you're on a boat, sailing into harbor, just as a huge storm blows up. You want to drop anchor as fast as possible, right? Or your boat will get swept out to sea.
Client:	Right.
Therapist:	But dropping anchor doesn't control the storm. It just holds the boat steady—until the storm passes in its own good time. And we're going to do something similar: learn how to "drop anchor" when emotional storms blow up inside you.
Client:	Okay.
Therapist:	So this isn't a way to control your feelings—just like a real anchor doesn't control storms. It's a way to hold yourself steady—even as that storm rages inside you.
Client:	(*hesitant*) Hmmm...soooo...what's the aim?
Therapist:	Well, actually there are three aims. One is to take the impact out of all those difficult thoughts and feelings, so they don't jerk you around so much. Two is to help you stay in control of your actions—so you can control what you're saying and doing, to act more effectively. And three, it's to help you focus attention on what's important.
Client:	Okay. Makes sense.
Therapist:	So okay to give it a go?
Client:	Okay.

(But what if the client says they want to make the storm go away? We'll address that shortly.)

Practical Tip

Always specify that the boat is sailing into harbor (or a shallow cove) when the storm blows up. Why? Because out at sea, boats *do not* drop anchor during storms—and your nautically minded clients will point that out.

Also, if a client is dissociating or overwhelmed, skip the metaphor and go straight into active intervention. Say something like "I can see you're overwhelmed, and I want to help you handle it. Can I take you through an exercise to help you?" If the client can't speak, say, "Nod your head, or tap your foot, if that's okay." Later, once the client is centered, you can introduce the metaphor during the debrief.

The ACE Formula: Acknowledge, Connect, Engage

Using the three core processes of dropping anchor, we can create literally hundreds of different exercises, improvise on the fly, modify what we do based on the client's responses, and vary the duration from ten seconds to twenty or thirty minutes. The acronym "ACE" summarizes these processes:

A—*Acknowledge your inner world*

C—*Connect with your body*

E—*Engage in what you're doing*

Note: as alternatives, A can be "Acknowledge your thoughts and feelings"; C can be "Come back into your body"; and E can be "Engage in the world."

In dropping anchor exercises, we usually run through three to five "ACE cycles," repeatedly acknowledging thoughts and feelings, connecting with the body, and engaging in current activity. In this section, I'll describe each ACE component separately, and in the next section, you'll see how they flow into and overlap with each another when we use them clinically.

A—ACKNOWLEDGE YOUR INNER WORLD

This involves mindfully noticing and naming your inner experience. For example, when anxiety shows up, a client may notice threatening images, scary thoughts, or unpleasant sensations such as a racing heart. Or, when trying to break an addiction, a client may notice urges, cravings, and withdrawal symptoms. The aim is to notice these private experiences with openness and curiosity—and to nonjudgmentally name them, with phrases like *I'm having, Here is,* or *I'm noticing* (e.g., *I'm having thoughts about being worthless, Here is a painful memory,* or *I'm noticing numbness.*)

This is relatively easy when clients are able to tell us what they are thinking and feeling. For example, if we ask the client, "What are you feeling right now?" and they report sadness, we may say:

Therapist: So acknowledge this emotion is present...say to yourself, *I'm noticing sadness.*

The client may say such phrases aloud or silently, according to personal choice. (In early sessions, most clients prefer the silent option.) And if they can't be specific about the cognitions and emotions present, we can use nonspecific terms such as "pain," "discomfort," or "difficult thoughts and feelings":

Therapist: Acknowledge that right now there's something difficult and painful showing up...and if you can't put it into words, that's okay...just say to yourself, *Here's something painful.*

As we cycle repeatedly through the ACE formula, this nonjudgmental noticing and naming of inner experiences—without trying to avoid or get rid of them—usually fosters both defusion and acceptance. This may not happen on the first round, but it's often starting by the second or third.

As therapy progresses, we expand, lengthen, and deepen the *Acknowledge* component in dropping anchor exercises. We spend more time helping clients to connect with and explore the thoughts and feelings present—to open up and make room for them, and respond with self-compassion. Or we work more on the defusion elements, inviting clients to observe the flow of their thoughts for a while, before moving on to the next phase.

Troubleshooting: If Clients Can't or Won't Notice or Name

Sometimes clients are unable to name what they are noticing. This is either because they're so distressed or shut down that it's impossible to think, or because they don't yet have the skill of naming their private experiences. If we know or suspect clients will have such difficulties, then for the first round of acknowledging, we omit the instructions about naming, and instead say something like:

> *Therapist:*   Acknowledge that right now there's something difficult and painful showing up. And just get a sense of what it is: whether it's thoughts or feelings or a memory or something happening in your body.

Then, as we get into the second cycle of ACE, we start encouraging the client to name the experience. We ask, "What's showing up now? What kind of thoughts are going through your head? What kind of feelings can you notice in your body?" If the client is now able to answer us, we include this information in the next round of acknowledging:

> *Therapist:*   Okay, so again, acknowledge what's going on inside you...say to yourself, *I'm noticing feelings of anxiety...and thoughts about "doing it wrong."*

However, if the client still can't tell us what they're thinking or feeling, we again say something like:

> *Therapist:*   Okay, so right now, it's hard to put this into words, and that's oaky. Again, just acknowledge that there is something difficult and painful showing up for you. And again, just see if you can get a sense of what it is: thoughts or feelings or a memory or something happening in your body.

Another problem we may encounter is that sometimes clients *don't want to* acknowledge difficult thoughts and feelings. In this case, they can acknowledge their desire to avoid them:

> *Therapist:*   So acknowledge there's something going on in your inner world that's very difficult...and you don't want to look at it right now...so silently say to yourself, *Here's something painful and I'm not ready to look at it.*

What about clients who report not knowing what they are feeling? Or those who say they are "not thinking anything"? This may be due to experiential avoidance or skill deficits in noticing and naming their cognitions and emotions (often both). In chapter ten (for cognitions) and chapter thirteen (for emotions), we'll cover the skills clients need to overcome such barriers. In early sessions, before these skills are developed, we may say, "Acknowledge there's something uncomfortable" or "Acknowledge an absence of thoughts and feelings."

C—CONNECT WITH YOUR BODY

The idea here is to connect with (or come back into) the body. For example, we may suggest that clients sit up straight, push their feet into the floor, stretch their arms—and notice, with curiosity, the movements involved and the changing physical sensations. And we tailor what we do to suit each unique client. For example, if they have chronic pain exacerbated by stretching their arms, we might instead suggest, "Ever so slowly, shift your position in the chair to a more comfortable one…that's it… ever so slowly…and notice how you're doing that…notice what muscles you're using…"

Connecting with the body can include stretching, walking, yoga, tai chi, changing body posture, hugging oneself, tapping or stroking or massaging various parts of the body, slowly shifting position in the chair, mindful body scans, and so on. And if a client is avoidant of certain aspects of the body (e.g., areas scarred or injured or involved in sexual abuse, or parts disliked and unwanted in body dysmorphic disorder), we initially focus on "safer" areas, unlikely to trigger negative reactions. For example, we may encourage them to slowly wiggle their fingers, tap their feet, or nod their head. (These are also good options for helping a "frozen" client regain mobility; the extremities of hands, feet, and head are usually the easiest body parts to get moving.)

It's important that we always tailor this process to suit each unique client. For example, early on in therapy, one of my clients, who is transgender, did not want to connect with their hands or their feet because this triggered unpleasant thoughts and feelings; they considered their hands and feet to be "too big and masculine." So instead, we focused initially on shrugging their shoulders and stretching their neck.

As the client connects with their body, we encourage them to keep acknowledging their difficult cognitions and emotions. (If we *don't* do this, dropping anchor will function as distraction.)

What About Mindful Breathing?

As mentioned in chapter four, early in therapy, let's be cautious about focusing on the breath. But if clients *are* okay with it (as most are), it can facilitate connection with the body. For example:

Therapist: Notice the breath, flowing in and out of your nostrils… Notice your rib cage, rising and falling, as the lungs inflate and empty… And notice the gentle rise and fall of your abdomen… And the subtle raising and lowering of your shoulders…

With such exercises, we can increase connection with the body by inviting the client to place one hand on their chest, the other on their abdomen:

Therapist: Notice your hand rising as your chest expands…and falling as the breath flows out again… And notice your other hand…gently rising and falling…as your abdomen gently moves in and out…

Another option is to close and open both hands, in time with breathing:

Therapist: As you breathe in, curl your hands into gentle fists...and as you breathe out, let them open...

The next phase of dropping anchor is to *Engage*.

E—ENGAGE IN WHAT YOU'RE DOING

After acknowledging thoughts and feelings, and connecting with the body, the aim is to refocus and engage in current activity. We may ask clients to notice where they are, what they are doing, and what they can see, hear, touch, taste, and smell. (If someone protests, "I can't notice all that!" we modify the exercise to notice only one or two things at a time.) We can really be creative here, drawing attention to anything external, from sounds of distant traffic to cracks in the ceiling.

Therapist: And now taking a moment to really notice where you are and what you are doing... looking around the room, and noticing what you can see...on the floor...and on the ceiling...and to either side of you...noticing the flowers in the vase upon the table... the color of the leaves...and the way the light reflects off the glass...and noticing all the different sounds you can hear...sounds coming from you...and from me...and from the air conditioner...and the traffic outside... And breathing in the air, noticing what that's like...and noticing you and me here, doing this activity...

We can, if desired, ask clients to describe aloud what they are noticing; this is especially useful when they are finding it hard to be present. (However, some people don't like doing this—so always make it optional.) In this phase, we continue to acknowledge thoughts and feelings (again, to prevent this from functioning as distraction). For example, after a client has engaged with the world around them, we might say, "So notice, there are still difficult thoughts and feelings showing up...there's your body around those feelings—can you move or stretch a little, notice it moving?...and notice, there's a whole room around you...and notice you and me here, working together as a team—doing this strange exercise."

When we ask the client to "notice you and me," this utilizes the therapeutic relationship as an anchor in the here and now. At times, we may push this further, asking things like "Can you notice the color of my shoes? The color of my shirt? My position in the chair? Can you notice how I'm stretching my arms, just like you?"

Practical Tip

It's *not* a good idea to tell clients "You are safe," because this may be interpreted as "You are safe; therefore you should not be feeling anxious, fearful, or insecure." While dropping anchor often helps clients access a sense of safety and security, we want to clearly communicate that anxiety and insecurity are normal; it makes perfect sense that the client would have such feelings, given what they've been through.

We then repeat the ACE cycle, at least another two or three times, but each time around we go more slowly, with longer pauses and less instruction (so clients learn how to do it for themselves). At the end of the first cycle, we say:

Therapist: Okay, so that's the basic drill. Can we run through it again? Great. And this time, I'll do less talking. So let's start with the A. Take a moment to notice your inner world...acknowledging your thoughts...acknowledging your feelings...and are they the same as before or different?

Client: Pretty much the same.

Therapist: Feelings of anxiety?

Client: Yeah.

Therapist: And the same scary thoughts?

Client: Yeah.

Therapist: Okay. So acknowledging that those thoughts and feelings are present...and allowing them to be there...and silently saying to yourself, *I'm noticing anxiety*...and at the same time connecting with your body...straightening up your back...pushing your feet into the floor...

There is *no need to follow a script* for these exercises. You can if you wish—there's one in Extra Bits—but it's better (and more enjoyable) to improvise. Give your voice a kind, calm quality, and go slowly, pausing for five to ten seconds (or longer) between instructions. And be sure to model all the actions for your client—for example, press your own feet down and stretch your own arms outward, as you invite the client to do likewise. This makes clients feel less self-conscious and builds that sense of teamwork. Also feel free to vary the order of the components; for example, with some clients, it works better to connect with the body first.

We typically cycle through this process—acknowledging inner experience, connecting with the body, and engaging in the world—for at least three or four minutes, until the aims of the exercise are achieved. This raises an important question...

What Are the Aims of Dropping Anchor?

Dropping anchor exercises have many different aims. The most common ones are:

A. to gain more control over physical actions—so we can act effectively when difficult thoughts and feelings are present. This is a powerful antidote to the physical immobility ("freezing up") associated with hypoarousal, flashbacks, intense shame or hopelessness, and dissociation.

B. to reduce the impact and influence of our cognitions and emotions. Consciously noticing and naming them reduces their influence over our behavior (whereas when we're on automatic pilot, they easily hook us and pull us into away moves). Indeed, we can think of dropping anchor exercises as a form of ACT-congruent "emotion regulation." We are not trying to avoid, get rid of, or control emotions, but we are reducing their impact through responding mindfully. And as the impact lessens, it becomes easier to stay in the present moment and choose effective actions over self-defeating ones.

C. to interrupt problematic *covert* behaviors, such as worrying, ruminating, and obsessing.

D. to interrupt problematic *overt* behaviors, such as aggression, social withdrawal, self-harming, or substance abuse.

E. to help us "wake up," focus on and engage in what we are doing: the antidote to disengagement, distractibility, and dissociation.

We need to be clear in our own mind what the aims are for each unique client in each specific situation—and clearly communicate this. If not, confusion is likely. So it's worth taking the time to practice your spiels. For example, suppose a client says, "I don't get it. Why keep coming back to the body?" You can reply with a quick user-friendly version of points A and C above: "Well, it's to help gain control of your physical actions, so you don't get jerked around by your thoughts and feelings. And it's also to get you out of your head." Likewise, if a client asks, "What's the point of acknowledging?" you want a simple, snappy version of point B: "Well, it's the first step in unhooking from difficult thoughts and feelings. Learning to notice and name them takes some of their power away." (If the client wants to know more, you could explain how this helps with defusion or acceptance, using the rationales in chapters ten and thirteen.)

Practical Tip

If clients are willing to have and open to their emotions, and able to remain engaged in the session, all we need do is hold a safe space for them, where they can "be with their feelings." But if clients are starting to dissociate, avoiding or struggling with their emotions, fusing with helplessness or hopelessness, or so overwhelmed by their feelings that they can't engage in the session—then dropping anchor is called for.

Dropping Anchor Versus Distraction

I hate to be repetitive, but there's so much misunderstanding around this, I'm going to say it again: when dropping anchor, there's no intention to *distract*. Distraction is a form of experiential avoidance. And given that our clients are already high in experiential avoidance, we don't want to reinforce it. (Besides, most clients already have many ways of distracting themselves, so we want to give them something new.)

The aim with dropping anchor is to learn a *new* way of responding to thoughts and feelings, one that is *radically different* from avoidance. The aim is to notice, name, and allow these thoughts and feelings; make room for them; let them freely come, stay, and go in their own good time.

On that note, there's a big difference between most grounding techniques and dropping anchor. In most models, grounding functions as distraction. For example, popular grounding techniques include holding an ice cube and noticing it melt, counting backward from a hundred in sevens, snapping an elastic band around your wrist, silently reciting a poem or mantra or the times tables, and so on. The usual aim of these practices is to distract from difficult thoughts and feelings, to reduce emotional distress.

Some popular grounding exercises at first glance appear to involve mindfulness: using your five senses to notice the world around you, slowly stretching your body, savoring a drink, going for a walk and taking in the sights and the sounds, and so on. But again, the primary aim of these practices is usually to reduce emotional pain. Typically, they use the C or the E of ACE, but not the A; so without that ongoing acknowledgment of inner experience, they function as distraction.

Does Dropping Anchor Reduce Pain?

If a client drops anchor while in intense emotional pain, it's unlikely the pain will disappear. However, usually it loses its impact; its power "drains away." And within a few minutes (sometimes much faster), many clients report a sense of calmness, even as the storm continues. At other times, emotional pain *will* drop rapidly—and as mentioned earlier, clients may misinterpret this as the main purpose and then start misusing this practice to control how they feel. If so, they soon complain, "It's not working" or "It's lost its effectiveness," which we'd address as in chapter four (in the section headed "What's the Aim?").

Practical Tip

Any type of mindfulness exercise may, on occasion, increase pain because clients suddenly become aware of sensations, thoughts, or emotions they usually suppress or distract themselves from. Dropping anchor is no exception. If this ever happens, we segue into work on undermining experiential avoidance (chapter twelve).

Working with Extremes of Arousal

The "window of tolerance" is a popular concept in trauma therapy; it refers to the zone of arousal in which a person can function most effectively. But in TFACT, we prefer to talk about a "window of flexibility," which we help clients to widen as their state of arousal varies. In other words, we develop clients' ability to respond flexibly—to be present, acknowledge inner experience, and take effective control of physical actions—during various degrees of autonomic arousal. If at any point clients are "outside their window of flexibility" (i.e., unable to respond flexibly to their emotions, cognitions, and physiological reactions), we quickly help them "get back into the window" through dropping anchor. The transcripts that follow illustrate this process.

Session with Lottie: Hypoarousal

Lottie is a forty-two-year-old nurse, a single mother of two, with complex trauma. Her history includes repeated childhood sexual abuse and domestic violence and sexual assault in adulthood. The scene in the transcript below takes place about halfway through the intake session. While talking about abuse by her father, Lottie has become overwhelmed and unable to speak. She is shaking and trembling, face pale, tears in her eyes. The therapist has asked her what is happening, but Lottie is either unwilling or unable to reply. The therapist guesses she is either completely overwhelmed by her emotions to the point of shutdown or she is dissociating (or both).

As you read this transcript (and the next), please imagine yourself saying and doing something similar with your own client. (And if you're willing, try reading the words aloud to get a deeper experience.)

> *Therapist:*   Lottie, I can see you're struggling with something very difficult right now, and you can't speak. If you can hear me, please nod your head. (*Lottie does not respond.*) Lottie, please nod your head, even a little bit, if you can hear me. (*Lottie nods her head slightly.*) Great. I want to help you deal with whatever this is that you're struggling with, so I'd like to take you through a little exercise to help you handle it. Just nod your head if that's okay. (*Lottie nods.*) Okay, great.

When clients can't speak, we can ask them to nod their head, tap one foot, or move one finger to indicate they can hear us. Once we've established such communication, we can follow the ACE formula. We could also, if desired, try to ascertain what is showing up for the client: "Nod your head if you're feeling some strong emotions," "Nod your head if there's a painful memory," and so on.

Therapist: (*Acknowledging the inner world*) Okay. So you don't have to speak, but just acknowledge to yourself that there's something very difficult you're struggling with right now...and take a moment to acknowledge whatever it is that's showing up...whether it's thoughts, feelings, memories...

Therapist: (*Connecting with the body*) And these thoughts or feelings or memories are happening inside your physical body, which seems to be all locked up. Just nod if your body seems kind of frozen or locked. (*Client nods.*) Okay, so let's see if you can unlock it a bit, get it moving. Can you tap one of your feet? (*Client taps right foot.*) Great. Can you tap the other one? (*Client taps left foot.*) Great, see if you can tap them both together, like this. (*Therapist taps both feet up and down. Client does the same.*) Very good.

Therapist: Now can you wiggle the fingers on one hand? (*Client wiggles fingers on right hand.*) And can you wiggle the fingers on the other hand? (*Client does so.*) And can you wiggle them all together, like this? (*Therapist wiggles all fingers; client copies.*) That's great. And is it okay if we keep going with this? (*Client nods.*) Okay, so see if you can loosen up your head a bit...try turning from side to side... (*Client does so.*)...that's great...and can you maybe shrug your shoulders a little... (*Client does so.*)... excellent...

Therapist: (*Acknowledging, Connecting*) So notice there are difficult thoughts or feelings or memories showing up, and you have a body around them, which you can move. Can we keep going with this? (*Client nods.*) Okay, see if you can move your legs a little, jostle them up and down, like this. (*Therapist demonstrates, client copies.*) Great. And now see if you can push your feet down really hard, into the floor...and notice how that lifts you up off the chair a bit...and now ease off. (*Therapist demonstrates, client copies.*) Excellent. And see if you can maybe gently shrug your shoulders...and can you stretch your arms out a little? (*Therapist demonstrates, client copies.*) That's good. So there are difficult feelings and memories showing up, and your body is around them, and you can move your body, you have some control over it...

Therapist: (*Connecting, Engaging*) And see if you can keep moving, I know it's a bit odd, but it's important to unlock your body...you can copy me if you like, or just move it how you want (*Therapist and client continue to move their bodies—tapping feet, stretching arms, shrugging shoulders, etc.*)...and at the same time, see if you can also get a sense of the room around you...notice three or four things you can see directly in front of you...and can you turn your head to one side, and notice what you see there...that's great...and can you look up, see what's on the ceiling...and down on the floor...and also notice what you can hear...my voice...and the traffic outside... the air conditioner...so notice where you are...and notice you and me here, doing this weird exercise...

Therapist:	(*Acknowledging, Connecting, Engaging*) So there's a lot of painful stuff showing up inside you, and around that stuff is your body, which you can move—is it okay to keep moving? (*Client and therapist keep moving their bodies—stretching, shrugging, tapping feet, etc.*)...and around your body, there's this room here, and you and me, working together...
Therapist:	And I'm wondering, are you able to talk yet, about what's going on? (*Client shakes her head.*) Okay, you don't have to. Is it getting any easier to tune in to what I'm saying? (*Client nods.*) And you're starting to unlock a bit in your body? (*Client nods.*) Is it okay to run through this again? (*Client nods.*)

The therapist runs through the ACE cycle another three times, varying the instructions. This takes about five minutes. By the end of the fourth cycle, the client is present and able to talk, and the therapist debriefs the exercise. We'll cover debriefing shortly; first let's look at another transcript.

Session with Jeff: Hyperarousal

Jeff is a thirty-year-old male with PTSD, following a car accident in which he was the front passenger. His best friend, who was driving, was instantly killed. This exchange is early in the second session. Jeff is struggling with intense anxiety: pounding heart, sweaty hands, churning stomach, tightness in his chest, lots of thoughts about the accident and about whether he is going crazy. The therapist has already introduced the dropping anchor metaphor and explained the aims of the exercise:

Therapist:	So, just to be clear, this isn't a way to control your feelings—just like a real anchor doesn't control storms. It's a way to hold yourself steady, even as the storm rages inside you.
Client:	Okay, let's try it.
Therapist:	Okay, so there's a simple formula for doing this, which you can remember as A-C-E, "ace." The A of "ace" is for "acknowledge your thoughts and feelings." So the idea is to acknowledge what kind of thoughts and feelings are showing up for you. You want to kind of look inside yourself, as if you're a curious scientist trying to observe what's going on in there. So let's start with your mind; what kind of thoughts are going through your head right now?
Client:	Same as before—Dave's dead and it's my fault, and am I going crazy?
Therapist:	Okay, so acknowledge, and say to yourself, "I'm noticing scary thoughts."
Client:	Say it aloud?

Therapist:	Aloud or silently—whichever you prefer.
Client:	(*a bit unsure*) I'm noticing scary thoughts.
Therapist:	Okay. And you also acknowledge what's happening in your body. What's it like in your chest there?
Client:	It's really tight.
Therapist:	Okay. And your stomach?
Client:	Just like before—it's all churning.
Therapist:	Throat?
Client:	Yeah, there's um—there's a kind of lump.
Therapist:	And your hands?
Client:	They're um—yeah, they're sweaty.
Therapist:	Okay. So there are quite a few different feelings in there. So say to yourself—silently or aloud, doesn't matter—say, "I'm noticing feelings of anxiety."
Client:	I'm noticing feelings of anxiety.
Therapist:	Now the C of "ace" is for "connect with your body." So you've got all these anxious thoughts and feelings in here, and all of that is inside your physical body. So see if you can keep acknowledging the anxiety, and at the same time connect with your body. Just copy me. Try pushing your feet down into the floor. (*Therapist models this action, and client copies.*)... That's it. Feel the ground beneath you.
	Now try straightening your spine (*Therapist models this while talking. Client copies.*)... That's it. And notice how you naturally sit forward as your spine straightens. And notice your thighs resting on the chair beneath you; and keep those feet on the floor.
	Now slowly shrug your shoulders together, roll them around a bit, and loosen up your neck a bit. (*Therapist models these actions while talking. Client copies.*) That's it.
	Now how about stretching out your arms? (*Therapist stretches out and client copies.*) Yeah, that's it. Feel your arms moving, notice your upper back stretching.
	And take a moment to acknowledge there's a lot of anxiety here...and it's challenging and it's difficult... And again, say to yourself, out loud or silently, "Here's anxiety." (*Client silently nods his head, to indicate he is doing this.*) So notice—there are anxious thoughts and feelings here, and there's also a body around all that stuff—holding it, containing it all. And you can move and control it.
	So straighten your back again, and notice your whole body now...your hands, feet, arms, legs...that's it. (*Therapist models these actions. Client copies.*) Gently

Therapist: moving...and really noticing what those movements feel like... And having another stretch, a really big one... And noticing those muscles stretching...and how are you doing there?

Client: I'm okay.

Therapist: Excellent. So now the E of "ace" is for "engage in what you're doing." In other words, notice where you are, and focus on what you're doing. So take look around the room—up, down, and side to side... (*therapist looks around the room*) and notice five things that you can see... And also notice three or four things you can hear... sounds coming from me or you or the room around you... And also notice you and me here, working together, as a team.

So notice, there is anxiety here right now—scary thoughts in your head, and unpleasant feelings in your chest and throat, tummy—and around that anxiety there's a body, which you can move...and see if you can notice that body...and gently move it, have a stretch (*therapist moves, stretches, and client copies*)... That's it, take control of your arms and legs.

And also notice the room around you (*therapist looks around the room, client copies*)... So see if you can get a sense of it all—the feelings inside you, and your body around the feelings, and the room around your body... And also notice you and me here, working together as a team... (*playfully*) doing this *weird* exercise. (*long pause*) Okay, so those are the basic steps. Can we run through that again, and this time I'll talk less?

Client: Okay.

But I Want to Get Rid of the Storm!

Suppose the exchange above had gone a bit differently:

Therapist: And just to be clear, this isn't a way to control your feelings. It's a way to hold yourself steady—even as the storm rages inside you.

Client: But I don't want the storm to rage inside me.

Therapist: Of course you don't, it's really unpleasant. And I promise later we'll have a look at what we can do about that—but right now, what we're doing is dropping anchor, and that's not a way to control storms.

Client: So what's the point of it then?

Therapist: Well, basically there are three main aims... (*Therapist runs through the aims.*)

Such reactions are not uncommon, early in therapy: *That's not what I want. I want to get rid of these feelings. I want to stop feeling this way.* We can normalize and validate these wishes, and reassure clients we will soon address it: "Yes, absolutely. Naturally, you want to get rid of these feelings. They're very painful—and I promise you, we'll look at that shortly. I just want to be clear that, right now, with this particular skill, that's not the aim."

When the time is right, we compassionately explore the client's perfectly natural agenda of experiential avoidance—and gently undermine it through the oddly named process of "creative hopelessness" (chapter twelve). And when *is* the right time to do that? Well, as you know, there's no "fixed" or "right" order for TFACT—however, it's often useful to loosely follow this sequence:

1. Behavioral goals (extracting values if possible)

2. Dropping anchor

3. Defusion

4. Creative hopelessness

5. Acceptance

This sequence works well for two reasons: (1) to accept painful emotions is the hardest part of TFACT for most people, and it's usually much easier when dropping anchor and defusion skills are in place; and (2) when we establish goals first, they provide the motivation for acceptance: we make room for difficult feelings so we can do what matters.

Having said all that, we want to be flexible. So if a client remains opposed to dropping anchor and insists, "I just want these feelings to go away," we'd usually move into creative hopelessness.

Do We Have to Follow the A-C-E Sequence?

No, we don't. Some clients find it easier to first connect with their body before moving into the other stages. The ACE formula helps clients and practitioners learn and remember the three core components of dropping anchor; however, as therapy progresses, we want to encourage flexibility by playing around with the order. For example, we may go from E to C to A; or from C to A to E; or from A to C, then back to A, back to C, then to E, and so on. (You'll see an example of this in the next chapter.)

How Long Does Dropping Anchor Go For?

Exercises continue until the client has good control over their physical actions and is psychologically present: engaging in the session, attentive and responsive to the therapist. Presence might be indicated by nonverbal responses (e.g., facial expressions, body posture) or verbal responses (e.g., speaking readily, asking or answering questions, verbalizing thoughts and feelings).

Usually two to four minutes is enough—but in cases of intense fusion, overwhelming emotions, or dissociation, this may go for much longer; on rare occasions, even ten to fifteen minutes. At the other extreme, when clients only "drift off" slightly or "zone out" a little, a ten-second version might be enough.

Occasionally in supervision, a practitioner complains, "We dropped anchor, but the client was still really fused at the end." This represents a misunderstanding. Dropping anchor is not a script we follow for a set amount of time or a fixed number of repetitions; it's an interactive process that continues for as long as necessary. If the client is "still really fused," then we are not "at the end"; we keep going and work with that fusion:

> Therapist: (*Acknowledging*) So notice, your mind is still beating you up here, still telling you all the things that are wrong with you. And we're not trying to stop your mind from doing that; the aim is simply to acknowledge it. So say to yourself, "I'm having thoughts that XYZ (*XYZ = thoughts the client is fusing with*)." And at the same time, notice there's a body here you can control, even with all these thoughts present...

Similarly, sometimes a supervisee complains that the client was "triggered" by dropping anchor; they were feeling relatively calm and at ease before the exercise, but when they started it, difficult thoughts and feelings (usually anxiety) showed up. This doesn't happen often, but when it does, it's a good opportunity to practice flexible responding. We might say:

- So notice what's happening now. Your mind is fueling the emotional storm, making it bigger and stronger. Is it okay to keep working with this?

- Remember, we're not trying to make the storm go away; anchors don't control storms…

- So now, say aloud, "I'm noticing my mind worrying"…and "I'm noticing feelings of anxiety"… and "I'm noticing the storm getting stronger"…

- So noticing those thoughts and feelings are here right now, also stand up, just like I'm doing, and ever so slowly, let's stretch…and notice that even though the anxiety storm is raging, you have control over your arms and legs…

In this manner, we continue working with the anxiety until the client is anchored. (In chapter twenty we'll explore how this plays a central role in working with panic attacks.)

Scaling Client Responses

There are two useful scales for tracking client responses when dropping anchor—one for contact with the present moment, and the other for control over physical action.

For contact with the present moment, we say, "On a scale of zero to ten, where ten means you're fully present here with me, you know, you're engaged and focused and really tuned in to what we're doing, and zero means you've completely drifted off, you've sort of checked out of the room, gone off somewhere else in your head, lost track of what we're doing or what I'm saying—the very opposite of focused and engaged…then zero to ten, how present are you right now?"

For control over physical action: "On a scale of zero to ten, where ten means you've got full control over your physical actions—what you do with your arms and legs, hands and feet—and zero means you're completely frozen, locked up, can't move at all…then zero to ten, how much control do you have over your actions right now?"

Both of these are useful scales to establish early on in therapy. They help us track a client's responses and gauge the need to go for longer. If a client answers seven or eight, that's usually enough to end the exercise, and if they reach nine or ten, that's excellent. Below a seven, we probably need to keep going, and ramp up the physicality of the exercise, for example, stand up and stretch, walk around the room, or reach out and drink a glass of water.

These scales are particularly useful for telehealth, especially audio-only. They enable us to do regular check-ins: "Zero to ten, how present are you?" or "Zero to ten, how much control do you have over your actions?"

When Do We Introduce Dropping Anchor?

As mentioned earlier, if during intake a client is overwhelmed, having flashbacks, or experiencing extremes of arousal, it's wise to put all other tasks on hold and teach them to drop anchor. Similarly, if a client turns up (to any session) in a state of extreme hypo- or hyperarousal, although we obviously want to know what has happened, our *first* priority is to help them respond effectively to their physiological state; *later*, once they are centered and engaged, we can find out what triggered their reaction.

So basically, the sooner we introduce dropping anchor, the better. If we introduce it in session two (i.e., the session after intake), we might say, "There's a lot more I'd like to ask you about, but as I said earlier, a big part of our work here is learning new skills to handle all these difficult thoughts and feelings more effectively—take the power and impact out of them—and so if it's okay with you, I'd like for us to make a start on that. Would that be okay?"

Debriefing

In this section, we'll look at how to debrief dropping anchor exercises. After an exercise ends, useful questions to debrief it include:

- What happened? What did you notice? What changed?

- Is it any easier for you to engage with me, to be more present?

- Are you able to focus more on what I'm saying? Tune in to what we're doing?

- Do you have more control over your physical actions now—over what you can do with your arms and legs and mouth?

- Are you less hooked by these difficult thoughts and feelings? Are you less "swept away" or "jerked around" by them?

- Are you able to be present with me, even with that difficult stuff still here?

Note that we don't ask if anxiety has reduced, the memory has gone, or the client is "feeling better." That would send the wrong message. (Of course, emotional pain *does* usually reduce—but in ACT that's a bonus, not the main aim.) So if the client says something like "Wow; I feel a lot better. My anxiety has really dropped," we could reply, "That's not uncommon. So by all means, enjoy that when it happens. But please don't expect it; that's not the aim." If the client seems confused, surprised, or disappointed, we then clarify what the aim is. (We may also encounter the flipside: "It's not working" or "It didn't help." In other words, they expected to feel relaxed, calm, or happy. Once again, this requires patient clarification.)

When a client *can* talk freely—as in the earlier transcript with Jeff—we ask about their thoughts and feelings *before* launching into the exercise. But if a client can't or won't speak—as in the transcript with Lottie—we can "work blindly" to begin with. Then once the client is centered, engaged, and ready and able to speak, we can find out what happened:

- What was going on for you?

- What sort of difficult stuff showed up for you? What sort of thoughts, emotions, memories?

We also explore how this skill could be useful outside the therapy room:

- So what just happened there—do you ever have reactions like that outside this room? What do you usually do when that happens? Suppose you were to run through this exercise next time that happens—how do you think it might help?

- How might this skill be useful: At home? At work? At play? In your relationships? (When, where, with whom, doing what?)

Modifying

As with any intervention, first and foremost we need to take our clients' individual needs and circumstances into account. Below we'll go through some ways to modify dropping anchor exercises for different issues.

Modifications for Flashbacks and Intrusive Thoughts

We can think of a flashback as a state of extreme fusion. The client is so fused, they do not experience it as a "memory" (a "recording" or "impression" of a past event). It's as if this event is happening in reality—right here and now. There is no sense of "I"—the observer—noticing this experience; no sense of historical narrative attached.

Dropping anchor is a good first-line intervention for flashbacks. However, in the *Acknowledge* phase, we name the private experience as "a memory." For example: "Here is a memory," "I'm having a memory," or "My mind is replaying a memory." So by the end of the first ACE cycle, we may be saying: "Acknowledge, there's a painful *memory* here right now…and some painful feelings that go with it…and around all that is your body…so again, just move and stretch a little…and notice you can control your actions even with this *memory* present…and notice there's also a room around you…and see if you can get a sense of it all at once…the memory, and the feelings, and your body, and the room around you…and you and me working here together, as a team…"

Our next step is to link this memory to a historical narrative. (To understand the science behind this, and how you might explain it to clients, see Extra Bits.) As soon as the client can speak freely, we ask what the memory is, then add that information into the naming. For example: "Here is a memory of the car crash," "I'm having a memory of family violence," "My mind is replaying a memory of sexual assault."

Practical Tip

It's important to name memories nonjudgmentally. If a client uses a phrase like "Here is a memory of that bastard ruining my life," it's likely to increase fusion.

We use similar modifications for intrusive distressing thoughts, acknowledging them with phrases like "Here is a thought" or "Here's that thought again," or "I'm having a thought about XYZ."

Modifications for Distractibility

Many types of mindfulness practice develop your ability to focus. Initially, they have you focus your attention on some specific stimuli (e.g., the flow of your breath). And of course, after a while your attention wanders. The moment you realize this has happened, you acknowledge it and note what distracted you (e.g., thoughts, feelings, sights, sounds). And then, you refocus on the chosen stimuli. When we help clients develop task-focused attention in this manner, it's a useful antidote to distractibility and disengagement, and a good practice for disrupting worrying, rumination, or generally "getting lost in thought."

We can easily adapt dropping anchor to serve such purposes. After two or three rounds of ACE, as the client becomes more centered and engaged, we ask them to focus their attention on something—their breathing, or the sensations in their feet, or the sounds in the room—and keep it there. And then, as with any attention-training practice, we encourage them to notice when and by what they get distracted—and then refocus. You can do this for several minutes (or much longer) before ending the exercise. In Extra Bits you'll find a script for traditional attention training through mindfulness of the breath, and another that incorporates this practice into dropping anchor.

Modifications to Disrupt Problematic Behavior

We can use dropping anchor to disrupt almost any problematic overt or covert behavior. We modify the *Acknowledge* component as follows:

- For covert behavior such as worrying, ruminating, and obsessing: *Here's ruminating, I'm having obsessive thoughts, I'm noticing my mind criticizing me, Worrying again.*

- For urges to do self-defeating behavior: *I'm noticing the urge to cut myself, Here's an urge to drink, Wanting to scream.*

- When clients "catch themselves in the act" of doing something problematic and they want to cease, they first acknowledge, *Doing it again; time to stop.* They then go on to acknowledge their thoughts and feelings.

Aside from these modifications, the rest of the process is the same. Cycling through ACE will often help clients interrupt the problematic behavior or help prevent them from acting on an urge.

Modifications to Develop Core TFACT Skills

As therapy progresses, we may extend the *Acknowledge* component to develop acceptance skills—encouraging clients to notice, name, allow, and open up to their feelings. We may also do this for defusion—taking more time to notice, name, and allow—then actively observing the flow of cognitions. We may also extend the *Connect* component: spend much longer on tuning into the body to develop somatic awareness or practice interoceptive exposure (i.e., exposure to physical sensations). See Extra Bits for tips on how to modify exercises not only for all of the above, but also to develop values, committed action, and self-as-context.

Homework

After dropping anchor for the first time, it's good to set it as homework and encourage daily practice, clearly linking it to issues raised in session.

Assigning Homework

Depending upon the purpose of the homework, we may introduce it by saying things like:

- This is your "go to" whenever emotional storms blow up.

- Do this whenever you get hooked by your thoughts and feelings.

- You can use this with flashbacks, to help yourself unhook from the memory and get back into the here and now.

- When you're all caught up in worrying, you can use this to pull yourself out of it.

- This is "first-aid for emergency shutdown." If you're starting to zone out, or freeze up, or check out of the room—or if you sense that you're about to—this is what you need to do immediately.

We also clarify that after the exercise finishes, the idea is to focus on and engage in the activity you are doing, unless of course that activity is problematic—in which case, the aim is to stop it, and instead do something more life enhancing.

And we always emphasize the need for regular practice:

Therapist: The idea is to practice several times a day—especially at times when you're not too distressed. You know, when you're just a little bit anxious, or angry or upset about something. Like when you're stuck in a line or traffic jam, or you're running late for an appointment, or someone does something that irritates you. If you practice this a lot when you're just a little bit distressed, it builds up your psychological muscles, so then you'll be able to handle it when the really difficult stuff shows up. Would you be up for that?

Client: Yeah, I'll try.

Therapist: And also, see if you can do a ten-second version of this, any time you're "drifting off"—you know, when you're a bit lost in your head, not really focused on what you're doing. And I do mean literally ten seconds. You just acknowledge whatever thoughts and feelings are present, and come back into your body—straighten up or stretch or push your feet down—and then notice where you are, and refocus on what you're doing.

In Extra Bits, you'll find a client handout on dropping anchor, with hyperlinks to audio recordings, varying in length from one to eleven minutes. You can encourage clients to listen to one or two of them, daily.

Following Up on Homework

At the start of the next session, we aim to debrief the homework and troubleshoot any problems.

DEBRIEFING

When following up on homework, we ask when and where the client practiced it, what happened, and what difference it made. Did they modify the practice? Were they able to notice and name their thoughts and feelings? Allow themself to be present without a struggle? Did they take control of their physical actions? Refocus and engage in activities?

TROUBLESHOOTING

Two common problems with any mindfulness homework are (a) people misuse it to try to control their thoughts and feelings, or (b) they don't do it. We've already covered the first problem; we'll address the second in chapter eighteen.

Occasionally a client says, "It's fine dropping anchor when I'm alone, but I don't want to do it around other people because they might judge me." Their assumption is that dropping anchor needs to involve obvious physical movements, such as stretching. But this is erroneous. You can easily drop anchor in ways that others can't observe. For example, if you're socializing, you can take a moment to acknowledge your inner world, gently push your feet into the floor or straighten your spine, then refocus on the conversation—without anyone else knowing. Ideally, we'd ask the client to practice this in session, to ensure they get the hang of it.

Sometimes a client complains they were "too overwhelmed to drop anchor," or says, "By the time I realized what was happening, it was too late." There are three aspects to dealing with such issues: regular "mindful check-ins," planning ahead, and "building up."

Mindful check-ins. We can encourage clients to do "mindful check-ins" throughout the day: to pause for a few moments and notice their thoughts and feelings, and gauge how tense, stressed, or upset they are. This way, they learn to recognize when they are getting "wound up" or "things are building up"— and drop anchor "before it's too late."

Planning ahead. We can encourage clients to anticipate and prepare for high-stress situations. When and where are emotional storms or dissociative states most likely? Doing what and with whom? Ideally, as therapy progresses, clients will use more and more TFACT strategies to prepare in advance for such challenges. Even briefly dropping anchor before entering a high-stress situation can make a significant difference.

Building up. A useful metaphor is the idea of joining a gym to get fit. If you go straight for the heaviest weights on your first visit, you'll injure yourself. So you start lifting light weights, and over time, you build up your strength until you can safely lift the heavy ones. But even then, you still first do warm-ups with the light ones.

The same principle applies to dropping anchor (or any other new skill): clients first practice in less challenging situations; and they do so repeatedly, progressively building up their skills. Eventually they can apply these skills, even under high-stress conditions. Together, therapist and client brainstorm situations and events that are useful for "building psychological muscles"; anything that triggers mild-to-moderate levels of stress, tension, or difficult emotions provides a good opportunity for practice.

Where to Next?

The more distressed, shut down, or emotionally dysregulated the client, the more important it is to continue doing this "bottom-up" work in session. So we want to keep these exercises going in subsequent sessions, further developing the client's ability to drop anchor. But where to, after that? Do we continue the bottom-up emphasis, primarily working with emotions, sensations, and the body (as in chapters twelve, thirteen, fourteen, twenty-two, and twenty-three) or introduce some "top-down" work with cognitive defusion (as in chapters ten and eleven)? If emotions, sensations, and physiological reactions are the predominant issues, then the first option is probably better. Alternatively, if fusion predominates (e.g., hopelessness, reason-giving, rumination, worrying, self-judgment), then defusion is probably the best option. However, either option is fine; we tailor what we do to suit the needs and capabilities of each unique client. And at any point, if we get stuck working on one core process, we can freely shift to working on an another.

> **EXTRA BIT**
>
> In *Trauma-Focused ACT: The Extra Bits*, chapter eight, you'll find (a) a client handout on dropping anchor, with hyperlinks to free audio recordings; (b) a generic script for dropping anchor; (c) a script for training attention through mindfulness of the breath; (d) a script incorporating mindful breathing into dropping anchor; and (e) notes on incorporating memories into historical narratives.

Takeaway

"Dropping anchor" is a term for hundreds of different exercises based on the ACE formula: *Acknowledging* your inner world, *Connecting* with your body, and *Engaging* in what you are doing. We can introduce it at any point in any session, and it's especially useful as a first-line response to extremes of arousal, dissociation, flashbacks, extreme fusion, or emotion dysregulation. It's also a good foundation for defusion and acceptance. Simple to teach, easy to learn, nonmeditative, trauma sensitive, accepted across many different cultures, and useful with a huge range of problems: the sooner we introduce it, the better.

CHAPTER NINE

Flexible Sessions

Congratulations. You've just made it through the longest chapter in the book! In this much shorter one (breathe a sigh of relief), we'll explore how to structure our sessions. And like anything in TFACT, we want to be flexible. If you're going around in circles, sessions full of compassionate listening but no active practice of TFACT skills, then clearly you need more structure—but don't cling rigidly to the sequence I'm suggesting, which is:

1. Do a brief mindfulness practice.

2. Review homework.

3. Set an agenda.

4. Work through the agenda, item by item.

5. Assign homework.

Let's take a closer look at each of these items.

A Brief Mindfulness Practice

It's useful to start each session with a brief mindfulness exercise, lasting three to five minutes. This helps the client and therapist center themselves and primes both for an experiential session. (And it's especially useful with clients who don't practice between sessions.)

Practical Tip

After debriefing a client's first formal mindfulness exercise, we can ask, "Would it be okay to start each session doing something like this?" Most clients agree, making it easy to kickstart later sessions with some mindfulness.

Early on in therapy, we may use dropping anchor to start a session, but later, as the client's repertoire of TFACT skills grows, we may choose exercises that focus more on defusion, acceptance, self-compassion, or self-as-context. Ideally, we also include values in these exercises:

Therapist: Is it okay to kick off with a short centering exercise to help us both get into the space for a productive session?

Client: Sure.

Therapist: Okay, so building on what we did last session... (*Connecting with the body*)...taking a moment to adjust your position in the chair...straightening your spine, and letting your shoulders drop...and gently pushing your feet into the floor...getting a sense of the ground beneath you...

(*Engaging with the outside world*)...and fixing your eyes on a spot, or closing them if you prefer...and tapping into a sense of curiosity...as if you are a curious scientist, exploring the world around you...and noticing what sounds you can hear... coming from you...and from me...and from the room around you...and from outside the room...

And noticing how you can shift your focus between these different sounds... like you can focus in on my voice...or you can focus on the traffic noise outside...or you can focus on the sound of the air conditioner...

(*Acknowledging thoughts*)... And see if you can notice the difference between the sounds you hear and the thoughts that go with them...notice how as soon as you hear a new sound, your mind locates where it is and labels it with words or pictures... I'm going to make a sound now, and notice what your mind does... (*therapist taps fingers on a hard surface for several seconds, then stops*)...and now I'll make another sound, and again, notice how your mind locates it and labels it... (*therapist taps foot up and down on the floor for several seconds, then stops*)...

(*Connecting with the body*)... And now noticing your body in the chair...and straightening up...and having a stretch...and holding that stretch...and really noticing the sensations of the muscles stretching...and doing that again, but this time, doing it in slow motion, and really noticing all the tiny subtle sounds you make as you do so...

(*Acknowledging thoughts and feelings*) And noticing what thoughts and feelings are showing up for you right now...noticing whether they are pleasant or unpleasant or neutral...and using that phrase "I'm noticing" to silently acknowledge whatever is showing up...and taking a moment to tune into your values...to connect with why you came here today...to remind yourself what's important to you, deep in your heart...what and who you care about enough that you came here today...and take a moment to acknowledge that even though difficult thoughts and feelings showed up for you, you didn't let them prevent you from being here...

We typically finish this exercise by connecting with the body and engaging with the outside world through the five senses. We then debrief it, teasing out relevant points and tuning in to values and values-based goals. (And if you prefer a shorter exercise, you can do the mindfulness of sounds component as a standalone.)

Review of Homework

The next step is to follow up on the homework: What did the client do? What happened, and how was it helpful? And if the homework involved practicing a mindfulness skill, how often and for how long did they do it? We also inquire about difficulties or adverse outcomes, and we troubleshoot any problems the client encountered. And if clients haven't done their homework (yes, hard to believe, I know, but amazingly enough, on rare occasions this happens!), we address this as in chapter eighteen.

Setting an Agenda

It's a good idea to set an agenda for sessions. Some therapists initially resist this, complaining it's "too directive." However, once they accept their discomfort and try it out, they find sessions become far more productive. Furthermore, most clients respond very well; the agenda helps them collect their thoughts and prioritize what's important. Indeed, for clients prone to "problem hopping" (jumping from one problem to another, without creating an effective plan or strategy), learning to prioritize problems is an essential skill.

The choice point offers a simple way to do this: "What would you like to focus on today: working on unhooking skills or getting busy with towards moves?" Another simple tool is the "bull's eye," illustrated below.

The bull's eye is widely used for exploring values and setting goals, but it's also a good visual aid for setting an agenda:

Therapist: So you can see this little tool divides life up into four main areas—work, relationships, health, and leisure. If we could pick just one of those areas to focus on—to start making some positive changes there—which would you prefer?

Client: Um, I think, relationships.

Therapist: Okay. Is there one relationship we could focus on today?

YOUR VALUES: *What do you want to do with your time on this planet? What sort of person do you want to be? What personal strengths or qualities do you want to develop? Please write a few words under each heading below.*

Work/Education: includes workplace, career, education, and skills development.

Relationships: includes your partner, children, parents, relatives, friends, and co-workers.

Personal Growth/Health: may include religion, spirituality, creativity, life skills, meditation, yoga, nature; exercise, nutrition, and/or addressing health-risk factors.

Leisure: how you play, relax, or enjoy yourself; activities for rest, recreation, fun, and creativity.

THE BULL'S EYE: make an X in each area of the dart board to represent where you stand today.

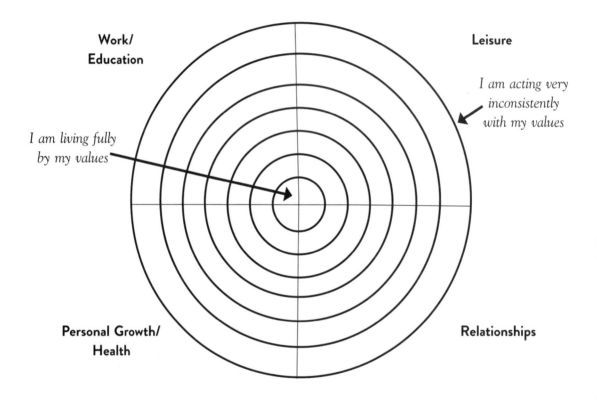

Adapted from *Living Beyond Your Pain* by J. Dahl and T. Lundgren by permission of New Harbinger Publications (Oakland, CA), www.newharbinger.com.

The Bull's Eye

So how do you prioritize? There is no "official" TFACT way to prioritize items on an agenda, but the following sequence works well:

1. Risk of self-harm. If there's significant risk that clients may harm themselves, this obviously takes priority over anything else. (See chapter twenty-six.)

2. Teamwork troubles. Many things can cause tension or discord in the therapeutic relationship: the client missing sessions, not paying bills, or being aggressive or dismissive; the therapist being coercive, invalidating, or lacking in empathy. We want to identify the problem and address it as soon as possible. (See chapter nineteen.)

3. Session stoppers. Next on the agenda are client behaviors that stall or disrupt the session: repeatedly coming up with reasons why therapy can't work or why they can't change, refusing to do exercises, problem hopping, continually changing topics, and so on. (See chapter nineteen.)

4. Homework horrors. If clients aren't doing their homework, we want to find out what the barriers are and help the client overcome them. (See chapter eighteen.)

5. Other issues. For the remaining problems, there are several ways to prioritize:

    a. Encourage the client to choose: "Out of all the issues you're dealing with currently, which one would you like to tackle first?"

    b. Use the bull's eye; ask the client to pick just one quadrant, and the most pressing problem within it.

    c. Focus on whichever seems to be the least difficult issue—the one most likely amenable to quick but significant change.

Working Through the Agenda

Once the agenda is agreed upon, we work through it, item by item. Occasionally an entire session may focus on just the first item, but often we can cover several.

No matter what issues the client chooses to focus on, in each session, we "dance around the triflex." We begin each session with "being present," which gives us a secure foundation for "opening up" (defusing from, accepting, and responding with self-compassion to difficult cognitions and emotions). And if clients become overwhelmed at any point, we drop anchor and bring them back to the present; then, when they're centered and willing, we venture forth once more into "opening up."

The same holds true for "doing what matters." Clarifying values, setting goals, and creating action plans can sometimes trigger overwhelming emotions or extreme fusion. If so—yes, you guessed it—we help clients drop anchor. Then, once they are present and centered, we gently return to values and committed action. Naturally, some sessions focus far more on one aspect of the triflex than the others, but usually all three are involved to some extent.

When clients are in challenging situations, with little hope of short-term resolution, a useful tool to cope is "the challenge formula" (Harris, 2015). This tool helps us to see that no matter how great the challenge we are facing, we are not powerless. We have choices, as summarized below.

The Challenge Formula

In any challenging situation, no matter what it may be, we always have two or three of the following options:

1. Leave.

2. Stay and live by your values: do whatever you can to improve the situation, make room for the inevitable pain, and treat yourself kindly.

3. Stay and do things that either make no difference or make it worse.

Of course, option one—leave—isn't always available. For example, if you're in prison, you can't just leave. If you've got a serious illness, or lost a loved one, you can't simply leave that situation; wherever you go, the problem goes with you. But, at times, leaving is an option—in which case, seriously consider it. For example, if you're in a toxic relationship, an awful job, a violent neighborhood, or a profession that exposes you repeatedly to traumatic events (e.g., emergency services or armed forces), consider: is your life likely to be richer, fuller, more meaningful if you leave than if you stay?

Now if you can't leave or won't leave, you only have options two and three. Unfortunately, for most of us, option three comes quite naturally: *Stay and do things that either make no difference or make it worse.* In challenging situations, we easily get hooked by difficult thoughts and feelings and pulled into self-defeating patterns of behavior that either keep us stuck or exacerbate our problems. For example, we may turn to excessively using drugs and alcohol, fighting with or withdrawing from loved ones, dropping out of important parts of life, or zillions of other self-defeating behaviors.

So the path to a better life lies in option two: *Stay and live by your values, and do whatever you can to improve the situation.* And of course, you can't expect to feel happy when you're in a really difficult situation; it's a given there will be painful thoughts and feelings. So the second part of option two— *make room for the inevitable pain, and treat yourself kindly*—is very relevant.

In the WHO's ACT protocol for refugee camps, the challenge formula comes early in session one. Obviously, option one is impossible if you're in a refugee camp—you can't just up and leave—but options two and three are both available. For example, there are people who share the tent with you, and you can treat them with kindness, warmth, and openness—or you can treat them with aggression, coldness, or hostility. And the choices you make each day will alter your experience within that tent. Likewise, when you step outside the tent, you can be kind and friendly to your neighbors, or distant and hostile. And you can join in with community activities, such as singing or prayer, or you can isolate yourself. So all day long, you have choices that will affect your quality of life within the camp.

It goes without saying that we need to be incredibly compassionate and validating of the client's difficulties when we present the challenge formula. Provided we do so, it's usually very empowering. It helps people realize they have choices, even in awful situations. And it's especially important for clients where those challenging situations are likely to persist, such as clients working in the armed forces and emergency services, those living in prisons and other hostile environments, and those continually exposed to racism, sexism, or other forms of prejudice and discrimination. As part of option two, we always emphasize the importance of reaching out to supportive others: friends, family, community, and so on. This may take many forms; for example, in the case of systemic prejudice and discrimination, this could involve forming or joining groups that are politically active and campaigning for change.

Practical Tip

We want to end each session safely, the client within their window of flexibility. So we need to keep an eye on the clock and make sure we allow enough time to help clients drop anchor (or use other methods to center themselves) before the session ends.

Homework

Ideally every session ends with a homework task. In early sessions, the therapist typically suggests these, but as therapy progresses, it becomes increasingly collaborative. (And if the homework task is a mindfulness practice, have the client practice it in session first so you can troubleshoot any problems.)

Before finalizing homework, we should assess: "On a scale of zero to ten, where ten means 'This is totally realistic, I'm definitely going to do this, no matter what,' and zero means 'This is completely unrealistic, there's no way I'm ever going to do this!'—how realistic is it that you will do this?"

If clients rate themselves lower than a seven, that bodes poorly for success, so we should change the task: make it smaller, simpler, and easier until the score reaches at least a seven.

EXTRA BIT

In *Trauma-Focused ACT: The Extra Bits*, chapter nine, you'll find a printable version of the bull's eye and a client handout on the challenge formula.

Takeaway

There's no official way to structure sessions in TFACT, but the principles in this chapter are often helpful. In every session, we dance around the triflex: being present, opening up, and doing what matters; and the challenge formula helps apply these processes to ongoing difficult situations.

In part two, we covered the important considerations for beginning therapy. Now let's delve into the first of the three interweaving strands of TFACT—living in the present.

PART THREE

Living in the Present

CHAPTER TEN

Slipping the Shackles of Fusion

I'm a lousy therapist. I don't know what I'm doing. I'm going to screw this up. Does your mind ever tell you things like this? Yeah, mine too. We have a lot in common with our clients! Most people think there is something wrong with them for "thinking negatively," so clients are greatly relieved when their therapist, in classic ACT style, discloses, "You know, your mind is a lot like mine. The things your mind says to you are so similar to the things my mind says to me."

Although we'll cover many different defusion methods over the next two chapters, I want to emphasize the importance of normalization. Many clients with trauma consider their minds to be "damaged" or "broken." So over and over again, in a myriad of different ways, we convey the message: *your mind is not defective; there is nothing wrong with you for thinking this way; the thoughts you are having are normal, natural, and valid; we all have minds that think like this.*

What Is Fusion?

Fusion means that cognitions dominate our awareness or our actions (or both). This can cause problems in the following ways:

A. Cognitions dominate our awareness. Examples include worrying, ruminating, obsessing, dwelling on the past, fantasizing, catastrophizing, "analysis paralysis," blaming, judging, and so on. This makes it hard to focus on the task at hand, engage in the activity we're doing, or be fully present with others. As a result, we do things poorly, miss out on important aspects of our experience, or cut ourselves off from others.

B. Cognitions dominate our actions. When we fuse with our thoughts, beliefs, attitudes, assumptions, schemas, judgments, rules, and reasons, they "dictate" our choices; we behave rigidly, in ways that are usually problematic; we do things that take us away from our values.

Technically, fusion means responding to cognitions with narrow, inflexible repertoires of behavior, and defusion means responding with broad, flexible repertoires. And these are not all-or-nothing states; we might be "very fused" or "a little fused," "completely defused" or "slightly defused." (With clients, we talk about "getting hooked" and "unhooking yourself," rather than fusion and defusion.)

In a state of fusion, cognitions seem like:

- commands, rules, or laws we have to obey

- important things that require our undivided attention

- good advice to follow

- threats we need to fight with or avoid

- statements of absolute truth

In a state of defusion, we see our cognitions for what they are: strings of words or pictures, changing from moment to moment, continually coming and going. They may or may not be true. And regardless of whether they are true or not, we don't have to obey them, follow their advice, treat them as threats, fight with them, avoid them, or give them our undivided attention.

The aim of defusion is *not* to reduce believability in thoughts, or make them go away, or reduce emotional pain—although all these outcomes are very common. The aim *is* to enable flexible responding to cognitions—so they don't dominate us, so we can act effectively and utilize them if helpful. (If that surprises or confuses you, please repeat the Hands as Thoughts exercise in chapter two, to clarify the costs of fusion and the aims of defusion.)

Form Versus Function

In TFACT, instead of looking at thoughts in terms of their "form" (i.e., whether their content is true/false, positive/negative, optimistic/pessimistic, rational/irrational, and so on), we look at them in terms of "function" (i.e., the effect they have on behavior).

A so-called "positive thought" (i.e., positive in terms of its content) may have negative functions (i.e., problematic effects on behavior). For example, a positive thought like *I'm fantastic at my job, and I know better than anyone else how to do it* may foster narcissistic behaviors that have a huge negative impact on workplace relationships.

Similarly, a so-called "negative thought" (i.e., negative content) may have positive functions (helpful effects on behavior). For example, the negative thought *I might fail this exam* may motivate a student to study sufficiently. If our thoughts have helpful functions (i.e., they help us to behave like the sort of person we want to be), then we let them guide us. If not, we allow them to come, stay, and go in their own good time—neither fighting nor avoiding them.

First Dance in the Dark, Then Lead to the Light

I've previously used this poetic term in other textbooks to emphasize the importance of a calm, patient, empathic approach to defusion. When our clients are lost and stumbling in the thick darkness of fusion, most of us have a strong urge to quickly flick on the bright flashlight of defusion to illuminate the way out. But we need to be cautious. If we rush into defusion too quickly, then despite our best intentions, it's likely to fail: to invalidate the client, trigger resistance, or backfire and create even more fusion. So we first empathize with the client, listening with openness and curiosity, looking at things from their point of view, understanding how they feel, acknowledging their difficulties, and validating their emotions.

"Dancing in the dark" means responding authentically and compassionately to the client while they are fused—helping them to feel heard, seen, understood, and validated. Typically, this doesn't take long. Sometimes therapists spend most or all of the session doing this work, and that can be counterproductive. For example, suppose the client is a "therapy veteran"; they've been in therapy for years, have told their narrative many times before, and yet they remain firmly stuck. They like attending therapy because of the empathy, understanding, and kindness they receive, but their self-defeating behavior does not change. In this case, doing yet another session comprised mostly of reflective listening, validating, and empathizing will not help the client to make meaningful life changes. If anything, it's likely to reinforce their fusion and sense of stuckness.

On the other hand, if the client has never been to therapy before and is disclosing sexual abuse for the first time, that's a very different scenario. We may spend much longer dancing in the dark with this client, to good therapeutic effect. However, if they should start dissociating or becoming overwhelmed while they are trying to talk about their trauma, we need to introduce practical skills straight away to help them handle that reaction. If we just sit and listen and ask questions and empathize while the client is dissociating or becoming overwhelmed, that's obviously harmful.

In other words, as with everything in TFACT, we need to tailor what we do to suit each unique client; what's useful or appropriate for one person may not be for another. Once we've danced in the dark long enough for the client to trust us as a dance partner, we can then start gently "leading them to the light." In other words, we introduce a core ACT process—not necessarily defusion; whichever process seems most likely to be helpful—and use it to compassionately guide them to a place of greater psychological flexibility.

Flexible Terminology

In TFACT, we often use the term "story" to encapsulate any type of cognitive content. However, occasionally a client finds this term invalidating. If so, we would immediately reply, "I'm so sorry. I wasn't trying to trivialize or discount what you're saying. All I mean by 'story' is a collection of words or pictures that convey information. I won't use that term again, if you prefer." This will usually salvage the situation, but to minimize the risk of invalidation, we may prefer not to use the term "story." Good alternatives include cognitions, beliefs, narratives, schemas, themes, statements, assumptions, ideas, accounts, histories, and judgments.

Even the term "thoughts" can sometimes elicit a negative reaction:

Therapist: Do you notice how these thoughts about being worthless keep popping up?

Client: They're not *thoughts*, they're facts!

Therapist: (*pauses for a few seconds*) Okay, how about we call them something else—like cognitions or self-judgments?

Client:	But they are *true*!
Therapist:	You sound as if you're expecting me to challenge you?
Client:	Well—yes. That's what the other therapist did.
Therapist:	In some models of therapy there's a big focus on whether your thoughts are true or false—but not in this one. In ACT, we don't get into that.
Client:	Oh. *(looks surprised)* Okay.
Therapist:	What we're interested in is what you do when these cognitions show up. If you give them all your attention, or do what they tell you to do, does that help you to build the sort of life you want? If it does, there's no problem. But if not, are you interested in learning how to unhook from them?

Clients are most likely to insist their thoughts are true when previous therapists have disputed them or made dismissive remarks like "It's just a thought." Clients are often surprised to find that this *isn't* going to happen in TFACT. (Indeed, one of the most impressive things about defusion is that it reduces the believability of false or inaccurate cognitions without needing to dispute them.)

Some clients have heard that "Thoughts are not facts," a phrase that can easily be invalidating. If so, we can explain that "facts" are indeed a type of thought:

Therapist:	The brain generates thousands upon thousands of thoughts all day long. Some of them are facts, some are opinions, some are judgments, some are lyrics from songs or lines from movies or popular sayings or jokes—or a zillion and one other things. Did you ever have some really weird thought pop up and wonder, *Where the hell did that come from?*
Client:	Man, you have no idea—the shit that goes through my head!
Therapist:	Yeah, mine too. So when I use the word "thought," I mean it as a catch-all phrase, to include all of these different things—from hard facts everyone would agree with to crazy weird shit that comes from who knows where. If you prefer, I can use the term "cognition."

Exploring Thoughts

We can usually identify fusion without directly asking about it. As the client tells us why they've come, what they've been through, and what their problems are, we're likely to observe plenty of fusion with all the categories mentioned in chapter two: past, future, self-concept, reasons, rules, and judgments. Sometimes, however, direct questions are useful, such as the ones below:

To elicit self-concept:

- If I could listen in to your mind when it's beating you up, what are the nastiest things I'd hear it saying about you? What kind of things does it judge you for?

To elicit past and future:

- Do you ever get caught up dwelling on the past? On what sort of things?

- Do you worry much? About what? What does the future look like to you?

To elicit reasons and rules:

- What stops you from doing X (*desired behavior*)?

- What keeps you doing Y (*problematic behavior*)?

To elicit judgments:

- What does your mind have to say about that?

To explore the origins of cognitions:

- Does this remind you of anything from your past? What's the earliest you can remember having such thoughts? Did anything happen back then that feeds into this?

To explore what triggers these thoughts:

- How often do these thoughts show up? When? Where? With whom? Doing what?

- Are these thoughts connected to something that really matters to you? Someone or something you deeply care about?

Identifying Themes

We're interested not only in thoughts, but also in the emotions, urges, sensations, memories, and impulses that accompany them. We may ask:

- How do you feel when your mind says these things?

- Do any emotions show up? Urges? Sensations? Impulses? Memories?

A useful strategy for defusion or acceptance is to identify themes that link all these private experiences. There are two ways to initiate this: as a teacher and as a detective.

TEACHER MODE

In teacher mode, we give the client a list of common patterns of fusion and ask which they relate to. In Extra Bits, you'll find three such worksheets: "Twelve Common Themes," which lists core beliefs, narratives, and schemas; "Big Six," which lists the six main categories of fusion; and "Relationship Roadblocks," which lists common cognitive patterns that fuel interpersonal problems. (You can also use lists from other models—for example, the eighteen schemas of schema therapy, or the twelve types of "dysfunctional" thinking in cognitive therapy—but remember that in TFACT we don't dispute cognitive content or evaluate thoughts as "distorted" or "dysfunctional.")

Teacher mode is most useful for groups, clients with limited self-awareness, or settings with limited time. In this mode, we might say, "Often our thoughts cluster around themes, and as a first step in unhooking, it's useful to identify what they are. This sheet lists some of the most common ones. Does your mind tend to favor any of these?"

DETECTIVE MODE

In detective mode, much like Sherlock Holmes, we "put the pieces together" and reach a conclusion that makes sense of it all. For example:

- Many of these thoughts and feelings seem to revolve around a common theme, and I'm not quite sure how to phrase it—I'm tempted to call it "unmet needs" because it seems to be about how your needs aren't getting met by other people; like they aren't taking into account what you really want. Does that seem about right?

- A lot of these thoughts and feelings seem to be about doing things "right" and "properly" and to a really high standard—and beating yourself up if you don't manage. I usually call this "perfectionism"; are you okay with that term?

- There are so many painful thoughts and feelings and memories here, going all the way back to your childhood, and they all seem linked to the same theme: "I'm a failure."

After suggesting a term, we check: "Is that a fair way to summarize it?" (and of course, we change it if the client doesn't approve). Better still, the client names the theme:

Therapist: So there's a whole stack of pain linked to this issue—thoughts and feelings and memories, going all the way back to age four, when your mom's boyfriend first started beating you. Now suppose we could somehow magically put all those thoughts and feelings and memories into a documentary that contains them all. And you might never show this documentary to anyone—or you might choose to share it with someone you really trust. But the idea is to come up with a short title that encapsulates the main theme. I know there are a few different ones, but we just want the main one, and a few words that sum it up. For example, the catch-all theme that fits everyone's documentary is "not good enough." So, you can use that if you like—the "not good enough" theme—but maybe you can come up with your own, like the "rejection" theme or the "useless" theme. Any ideas?

Client: Um, I think maybe, worthless, or um, unlovable?

Therapist: Okay. We can always change it later. For now, can we call this the "worthless, unlovable" theme?

Client: Sure.

Identifying themes helps clients to notice and name their cognitions—the first two steps in almost all defusion techniques—and it's good to make this explicit:

Therapist: One of our aims here is to spot that theme as it shows up in our sessions; we want to call it out, catch it in the act. Because as you get better at actively noticing this theme—and all those feelings and memories that go with it—you start to take some of its power away. It's the first step in learning to unhook.

We then ask for permission: "So is it okay to talk about it this way?" Once the client consents, we can use this as a term of reference throughout our sessions:

*   Is this feeling linked to "I'm a failure"?

*   And that triggered the "abandonment" theme?

*   Do you notice what your mind just did there? Another version of "Bad Mother"?

*   When you get hooked by "can't trust them," what do you do?

Strategies Galore

There are well over a hundred different strategies for defusion described in various texts (for an overview, see *ACT Made Simple*, 2nd ed., pages 140 to 155 [Harris, 2019]). In this chapter, we'll focus on just a few of them, beginning with the five simple strategies of *Notice*, *Name*, *Normalize*, *Purpose*, and *Workability*.

Notice

All defusion strategies begin with noticing the presence of cognitions. To help clients get better at this, we might ask, "What are you thinking right now?" or "If I could listen into your mind, what would I hear?" In formal mindfulness exercises, we might say, "Notice what your mind is doing right now; is it silent or active?" or "Notice your thoughts; are they pictures or words, or more like a voice in your head?"

Name

As we notice our cognitions, we usually also name, or "label," them. Initially we tend to use generic terms like "thoughts," "thinking," and "mind." Then we may get more specific or playful: "Here's the 'unlovable' theme again," "There goes 'radio doom and gloom.'" Often we help clients develop these skills through formal exercises such as "I'm Having the Thought That…," which we'll look at shortly.

Normalize

Most clients have the idea that there is something wrong with them for having so many "negative" or "weird" thoughts (especially if they've been told their thinking is "irrational," "distorted," or "dysfunctional"). So normalizing not only helps facilitate defusion but also fosters self-acceptance. We may say, "Thoughts like this are normal. Your mind sounds a lot like mine," or "These thoughts make perfect sense given what you've gone through; they're a completely normal reaction."

Purpose

We can reframe even the most "negative," "problematic," or "unhelpful" thoughts by considering them in terms of the mind's purpose. We convey, in many different ways, that these cognitions are the mind's attempts to protect us and meet our needs: to help us avoid what we don't want or get what we do want. Below are a few examples of how we might explain this—first in teacher mode, then in detective mode.

TEACHER MODE

Worrying, catastrophizing, predicting the worst. This is your mind trying to prepare you, to get you ready for action. It's saying, *Look out. Bad things are likely to happen. You might get hurt. You might suffer. Get ready. Prepare yourself. Protect yourself.*

Ruminating, dwelling on the past, self-blaming. This is your mind trying to help you learn from past events. It's saying, *Bad stuff happened. And if you don't learn from this, it might happen again.* So you need to figure out: Why did it happen? What could you have done differently? You need to learn from this so you're ready and prepared and know what to do if something similar should ever happen again.

Self-criticism for recurrent problematic behavior. This is your mind trying to help you change. It figures if it beats you up enough, you'll stop doing these things.

DETECTIVE MODE

In detective mode, rather than explaining, we invite the client to figure out the mind's purpose. We may say, "Usually when our minds are saying these things, there's an underlying purpose; they're trying to protect us or help us to get something. Any idea about what your mind might be trying to do?"

Useful questions include:

- What might it be trying to protect you from?

- What might it be trying to help you get? Or avoid?

- Is it pointing to something that really matters to you?

- Could it be trying to help you change your behavior?

We can usually quickly identify that pretty much any unhelpful thought or thinking process serves the purpose of protection, self-care, changing behavior, or getting our needs met. (Below you'll see examples for hopelessness and reason-giving, and in later chapters you'll see how to do this with suicidality, fear of trusting, and harsh self-judgment.) Not only does this facilitate defusion, but it enables us to readily segue into other processes, such as self-compassion and values, as we explore alternative, healthier methods of self-care, self-protection, changing behavior, or meeting needs.

After highlighting the purpose, we can introduce the Overly Helpful Friend metaphor (Harris, 2015).

The Overly Helpful Friend

So basically, your mind is like one of those overly helpful friends—you know, one of those people who's just constantly trying to be soooo helpful that they end up getting in the way, making things harder. Genuine intention to help—but actually doing the complete opposite. Well, that's what's going on here. Your mind's intention is not to (therapist names the adverse effects of fusion, specific to this client [e.g., "make you feel worthless"]). But unfortunately, that's the effect it's having.

For clients who believe in evolution, we can add impact to these explanations by talking about the evolutionary origins of such thinking processes (see "Caveman Mind Metaphors" in Extra Bits).

Workability

The principle of workability offers a simple way to defuse. Instead of examining thoughts in terms of their content, we look at how we respond to our thoughts, and how those responses affect us. Basically, we ask: When you let these thoughts guide you, where does that take you? Towards the life you want, or away from it?

A good first step is to identify the problematic behavior that results from fusion. This may be covert (e.g., worrying) or overt (e.g., social withdrawal). In detective mode, we ask questions like:

- When these thoughts show up, what do you usually do?

- What happens if you do what they tell you to do?

- If I were watching you on a video, how would I know that you had been hooked by these thoughts? What would I see you doing or hear you saying?

In teacher mode, we can pull out an Away Moves Checklist (see Extra Bits) that lists common patterns of fused behavior and ask which are relevant. Once we know what the fused behavior is, we can then ask a workability question:

- And in the long term, what direction does that take you?

- And would you call that a towards move or an away move?

- And is that more like the sort of person you want to be—or less?

- And what (or who) does that take you away from?

Of course, we ask these questions with genuine curiosity and compassion. (No point scoring, judging, or shaming the client.) Here's an example:

Therapist:	So when your mind starts laying into you—pulling out the "damaged goods" theme—what usually happens?
Client:	I get really down.
Therapist:	So if I were watching a video of this, what would I see or hear you doing on that video that would tell me, "Wow! Siobhan has really gotten hooked by this! She's really down"?
Client:	Different things. Like, if it was at home in the evening, you'd probably see me going into my bedroom and crying.
Therapist:	And who does that take you away from?
Client:	Mike. He hates it when I leave him.
Therapist:	So, it takes you away from the sort of relationship you'd like to have with Mike?
Client:	(*sighs, looks downcast*) Yeah.
Therapist:	That's hard. Can I ask what you're feeling right now?
Client:	I'm not sure. I'm just...really down.
Therapist:	Where are you feeling this in your body?
Client:	(*tearing up*) My eyes. (*wipes tears away, apologizes*) Sorry.
Therapist:	Please—tears are always welcome in this room. They show you're in touch with something very important.
Client:	(*looking down*) Thanks. I'd like to stop crying so much. I can't help it.
Therapist:	What you're going through is tough. Tears are only natural. Unfortunately, society teaches us that we need to hide them away—because, if I'm crying, what does that mean?

Client:	You're upset?
Therapist:	Well, usually, yes. Although I have been known to cry at weddings.
Client:	Me too.
Therapist:	But when I am upset, and I'm tearing up, society says, "That's not okay." I'm supposed to hold back my tears—because if someone sees me crying, what might they think about me?
Client:	You're weak.
Therapist:	Yup. I'm weak, I'm a softy. Need to toughen up a bit. (*playfully*) Swallow a concrete pill.
Client:	(*faint smile*) Tell me about it.
Therapist:	So, in this room, we don't play by those rules. Tears are always welcome; let 'em flow freely.
Client:	Thanks.
Therapist:	And what about the rest of your body? Are you feeling this anywhere else?
Client:	(*sighs heavily*) Yeah. It's like there's a plank on my chest.
Therapist:	A heavy one? (*client nods*) You also look like you're kind of...sinking into the chair?
Client:	Yeah, I am.
Therapist:	So, I'm guessing here, tell me if I'm off track, that what you're feeling here, is... sadness?
Client:	Yeah.

Note how the therapist normalizes and validates the client's reactions and helps develop her skills in noticing and naming emotions. The therapist now returns to workability and asks about what happens when the client gets hooked in other situations, such as work and social events. The therapist then summarizes:

Therapist:	So when you get hooked by the "damaged goods" theme, it pulls you away from some really important things: quality time with Mike, important meetings at work, joining in and engaging when you're socializing...
Client:	Yeah.

Therapist: So I'm wondering, would you like to learn a new way of responding to these thoughts, that's very different from what you normally do?

Bringing It All Together

When clients can notice and name their thoughts, acknowledge them as normal, recognize their purpose, and look at them in terms of workability—that's a whole lot of defusion! In the transcripts that follow, notice how these strategies are combined.

THERAPY SESSION: DEFUSION FROM DOUBT AND HOPELESSNESS

Therapist: You look doubtful. (*noticing and naming*) What's your mind saying to you?

Client: Honestly? It's saying this is a crock of shit.

Therapist: (*normalizing*) Well, I have to tell you—those kinds of thoughts are so common. Most of my clients have them at the start. (*self-disclosure*) And to be honest, I had the same ones myself, when I first had therapy.

Client: Really?

Therapist: For sure.

Client: Look, I've tried therapy before. I just don't think this is going to work. I'm sorry—I'm too fucked up. I don't think you can help me.

Therapist: (*normalizing, purpose*) Well, there's a reason why those kinds of thoughts are so common. Do you know why?

Client: (*joking*) Because therapy's a crock of shit?

Therapist: (*laughing*) Well, there are plenty of folks who'd agree with you about that, but the reason your mind says this stuff is that it's actually trying to protect you.

Client: What do you mean?

Therapist: (*purpose*) Well, therapy *is* a risk. You've tried before and it didn't work, and so now your mind is trying to save you from what might turn out to be yet another painful, disappointing experience.

Client: (*a bit surprised*) Yeah, well, it's got a point, hasn't it?

Therapist: (*purpose*) It sure has! A very valid point. Your mind is doing its single most important job here; trying to protect you from getting hurt.

Client: (*shrugs*) It's just stating the truth—I'm a hopeless case.

Therapist:	*(self-disclosure—to model noticing and naming)* I'm noticing I have an urge to debate this with you, try to convince you that's not true. *(workability)* But I don't think that would work, do you?
Client:	*(chuckles)* No. As I said, I'm a lost cause.
Therapist:	*(workability)* Cool, so let's not waste any time on debating that. *(naming)* So here's the situation: your mind says, "This won't work. I'm a hopeless case." *(workability)* So there's a choice to make right now about how you respond to these thoughts.
Client:	They're not thoughts! They're facts.
Therapist:	*(warmly)* I honestly don't mind what we call them—facts, cognitions, words—the point is your mind says, *(naming)* "This won't work. I'm a hopeless case."
Client:	Why do you keep saying "your mind"? It's not my mind.
Therapist:	Oh. Err, maybe I should call it something else. What do you call the part of you that generates thoughts?
Client:	It's my brain.
Therapist:	Okay. *(noticing and naming)* So right now, your brain is stating, "This won't work. I'm hopeless." And there are basically two options *(workability)* about how you respond to that statement. One option is, you end the session because your brain says it won't work. The other is, you let your brain keep saying that, and we continue the session and see what happens. So, there's a choice point here: what are you going to do?
Client:	Well, I'm here, aren't I?
Therapist:	Yep, you are. And there's a choice to make right now; your brain says this won't work, so do you get up and leave, or do you carry on?
Client:	Well, I guess... I'll carry on.
Therapist:	*(warm, genuine)* Thank you so much. I can see how hard this is for you. And I really appreciate that you're willing to stay here and give it a go, even though *(naming)* your brain says it's pointless. I really appreciate it.
Client:	*(surprised)* Okay.

Whatever reasons clients give as to why they can't, won't, or shouldn't change their behavior, we can use the same five steps to help them defuse: *notice, name, normalize, purpose, workability.* For example, suppose the client has a philosophy of nihilism:

Client:	Look, the fact is, life has no meaning. *Nothing* has any meaning. There's no point in doing anything—because it's all fucking meaningless.
Therapist:	(*notice, name*) Those are valid thoughts. (*normalize*) Many great philosophers throughout history have said similar things. And I'm wondering—have other people tried debating those ideas with you?
Client:	Yes.
Therapist:	And who won?
Client:	Me. 'Cause I'm right.
Therapist:	Well, I am *never* going to debate this with you. (*purpose*) The fact is, these thoughts, this philosophy—has a protective purpose. It keeps you safe.
Client:	What d'you mean?
Therapist:	Well, see, that philosophy helps you avoid taking risks, trying new things, leaving your comfort zone. Because every time you even think of doing those things, your mind says, "There's no point" and talks you out of it. So it saves you from all the anxiety that shows up when we do those things. And it also saves you from the possibility of getting hurt—because sometimes when you try new things, they go badly. So in the short term, this way of thinking keeps you safe and reduces your anxiety. (*workability*) At the same time, life involves choices. Meaningless or not, each day you choose whether to eat or starve; have a shower or not. Be polite to me or not. And while all those choices may be equally meaningless, they do have different consequences. (*speaking slowly, with great compassion*) So there's a choice for you to make right now. One choice is to stop therapy because your mind says it's meaningless—and if that's the choice you make, nothing changes; life goes on exactly as before. The other choice is, we carry on working together and find out what's possible—even though your mind says it's pointless.

As long as we are kind, warm, and compassionate when we present these options to a client, they are unlikely to say "Let's stop." After all, they've come to us for help; and they've often pushed through a lot of discomfort to reach us. However, if a client ever does say, "Let's stop," a pragmatic response is, "Well, you're already here—so how about we give it another ten minutes?" If they choose to continue, we express our genuine appreciation, while also acknowledging their commitment.

Having said all that, we don't want to be coercive. So if the strategy above doesn't help, or the client now seems to be "going along with it" grudgingly, or you get the sense they're just trying to please you, you'll want to press pause and explore those possibilities with openness and curiosity (as discussed in chapter nineteen).

Here's a shorter example:

Therapist:	*(debriefing a dropping anchor exercise)* So what did you get out of that?
Client:	Ah...I don't think it's for me.
Therapist:	Oh. Why not?
Client:	Err...it's just not me. I don't do this kind of stuff.
Therapist:	Oh—well, that's good.
Client:	*(surprised)* What do you mean?
Therapist:	Well, our aim here is to try new things; things you haven't done before—new approaches to dealing with your emotions. So *(noticing, naming, normalizing)* when you're having thoughts like "It's just not me" and "I don't do this," that indicates we're on the right track. Like, if you were thinking, "Oh yeah, this is me, I'm so comfortable doing this"—well, *that* would *not* be good; because it'd mean you're staying in the comfort zone, doing the same old thing—and we know that isn't working for you.
Client:	Oh. *(thinks)* Well, what I meant is, you know—doing this stuff—it feels weird.
Therapist:	Yes, absolutely. *(normalizing)* That's what it feels like when you step out of your comfort zone and try something new. *(purpose)* This is your mind looking out for you: the message is, "Be careful, you're entering new territory; this is risky." As we do this work together, these kinds of feelings will show up, and *(normalizing)* your mind will say things like that over and over again. And *(workability)* there's a choice for you to make: do we give up on this work because your mind says, "That's not me," or do we let your mind say that and carry on?

THERAPY SESSION: DEFUSION FROM SELF-JUDGMENT

Client:	I should have sorted this out a long time ago. I'm so pathetic.
Therapist:	*(noticing and naming)* Do you notice how you keep slapping these really harsh judgments on yourself?
Client:	And so I should! I'm fucking pathetic!
Therapist:	*(normalize)* Well, we all judge ourselves, and sometimes that helps *(purpose)*—sometimes it keeps us in line, stops us from getting too big for our boots—and other times it kicks our ass into gear. *(workability)* But I'm wondering...most of the time, when you use that tactic—beating yourself up, judging and criticizing—does it actually help you?

Client:	(*pauses, considers*) No, but it's true. I am pathetic.
Therapist:	I can notice my own mind arguing against that statement, but (*workability*) I don't think it would be helpful if I tried to debate about it. Do you?
Client:	No. Because it's true. There's no debate about it. I *am* pathetic.
Therapist:	(*compassionately*) I feel a twinge of pain every time I hear you talk about yourself that way. I'm wondering...what's it like for you to be on the receiving end of all that self-judgment?
Client:	(*looks sad*) Pretty shitty.
Therapist:	I'll bet. You look sad.
Client:	I am.
Therapist:	I'd feel the same way if I was getting hammered by all that criticism. Are you feeling that sadness in any particular part of your body?
Client:	Here (*touches central chest*).
Therapist:	Like a "heaviness in the heart"?
Client:	Yeah.
Therapist:	Yeah. Constant self-criticism takes a toll.
Client:	Yeah.

If something like this were to happen later in therapy, we would probably move into acceptance of emotions and self-compassion; however, at this point, such a move could easily fail or backfire. Therefore, the therapist continues with defusion.

Therapist:	So I'm wondering, (*workability*) when you get hooked by all these self-judgments, what typically happens?
Client:	What do you mean?
Therapist:	I mean, do you tend to do towards moves—things that make your life better? Or do you tend to do the opposite, away moves?
Client:	The opposite, of course. Shows how pathetic I am, doesn't it?

Therapist:	(*noticing and naming*) Do you notice how quick your mind is to judge you? It doesn't give you a break, does it? (*workability*) And it seems like when these judgments hook you, they pull you into away moves.
Client:	Yeah.
Therapist:	Like some of the things you mentioned earlier—drinking, staying in bed, isolating yourself?
Client:	Yeah, or just giving up on shit. Doing nothing.
Therapist:	(*workability*) So if we could do some work on learning how to unhook from all that self-judgment, to help you cut back on the drinking, get out of bed, socialize, and be more productive, would that be useful for you?

Actively Teaching Defusion Skills

So far we've been talking about "informal" or "indirect" defusion: the therapist's repeated use of comments and questions involving the five strategies: *notice, name, normalize, purpose, workability*. This helps clients become more conscious of their cognitions and see them from a new perspective. But this is only the start. The essential next step is to explicitly teach defusion skills—as a formal in-session exercise—and encourage the client to practice them for homework.

Defusion Metaphors

It's often useful at this point to introduce the Hands as Thoughts metaphor, as follows: "Before we start learning how to unhook, can I take you through a quick exercise to help you understand what we're trying to achieve?" This metaphor quickly clarifies the costs of fusion and the benefits of defusion, and it highlights two essential points: (a) defusion is not a way to get rid of thoughts (the hands are still present at the end), and (b) we don't dismiss or ignore thoughts; if we can use them constructively, let's do so.

There are many other metaphors for defusion. For example, we can talk about spam emails; pop-up advertisements on Instagram or Facebook; or annoying commercials on TV. If we use these services, this unwanted stuff will keep showing up. But when it does, we have a choice: we don't have to read a spam email from start to end; we don't have to click on a pop-up ad; and we don't have to keep watching TV during the commercials.

I'm sure you can think of many others; just be wary of what is playfully called "metaphor abuse": pumping out metaphor after metaphor in the hope that a concept will "get through." With metaphors, "less is more"; so stick to a few and reuse them often. (And if clients aren't learning to defuse or accept, don't introduce more metaphors; move into active skills training.)

Learning How to Notice Cognitions

If cognitive fusion is not a significant issue for a client, then we move on to other parts of the model: experiential avoidance, remoteness from values, and so on. But when it is a major issue, the first step in defusion is to consciously notice cognitions. Most people can easily do this, but sometimes a client says things like "I'm not having thoughts" or "I don't know what I'm thinking." If clients lack the ability to consciously notice their cognitions, we can:

1. Explain that "Everything you say or write is a thought. When we say thoughts aloud, we call that 'speech'; and when we write them down, we call that 'text'; but when we keep them 'inside our head,' we call them 'thoughts.'" From here, we can teach clients to notice the thoughts they are saying aloud. For example, if they say things like "I'm stupid," we might reply, "So the thought 'I'm stupid' just popped up. How often do you have thoughts like that?"

2. Invite clients to sit silently for one or two minutes and just "Notice what you want to say." Or alternatively, give them a piece of paper and pen, and ask them to "Write down anything you want to say." This includes things like "I don't want to say anything," "I've got nothing to write," "This is weird," and so on.

3. Take them through exercises designed to help them "hear" or "observe" their thoughts, as discussed in the next chapter.

4. Ask clients to *silently* sing a song, or *silently* repeat a well-known saying—and notice how they can "hear it" inside their head.

Practical Tip

When clients have difficulty identifying cognitions or emotions, focus on the ones that show up throughout the session. Don't get sidetracked into trying to get them to remember what they were thinking and feeling at various times outside of the session.

Defusion Exercises

We start by teaching relatively easy defusion skills and then progressively build up to more challenging ones (which we'll cover in the next chapter). Two simple exercises to begin with are "I'm Having the Thought That…" and Naming the Theme.

"I'm Having the Thought That..."

This is one of my favorite exercises (adapted from Hayes et al., 1999). The instructions that follow are the same as we'd give to a client. Please try it on yourself with a harsh self-judgment that tends to hook you.

First, pick a thought.

Now put that thought into a short sentence—in the form "I am X." For example, *I'm not smart enough* or *I'm too fat*.

Now for ten seconds, let that thought hook you. Buy into it. Believe it. Give it your full attention.

Now, silently replay that thought—but this time, insert a phrase at the start: *I'm having the thought that...* (For example, *I'm having the thought that I'm unlovable*.)

Now do that again, but this time insert another phrase: *I notice I'm having the thought that...* (For example, *I notice I'm having the thought that I'm worthless*.)

So did you get a sense of unhooking yourself; stepping back or separating from the thought? (If you didn't, please try again with another one.) With a client, we debrief this as follows:

Therapist: So what happened to the thought?

Client: It didn't bite as hard.

Therapist: Did you get a sense of stepping back from it? Like there's a bit of space between you and the thought?

Client: Yeah. It kind of shifted a bit.

Therapist: (*referring back to the Hands as Thoughts exercise*) So if this is totally hooked (*puts hands over face*) and this is completely unhooked (*lowers hands to lap*), can you show me with your hands what happened?

Client: Err, it was like... (*puts hands over face*)...this... (*lowers hands to chest height*)

Therapist: Cool. So you've just learned an unhooking skill.

We can then revisit this technique throughout our sessions. Here are two examples:

Client: Let's face it. I'm a lost cause.

Therapist: So you're having the thought that you're a lost cause?

Client: I can't believe how pathetic I am.

Therapist:	Could you say that again, but this time, put a phrase in front of it: "I'm noticing the belief that…"?
Client:	Say that aloud?
Therapist:	Well, you don't *have to*, but if you're willing to, it's better if you say it aloud.
Client:	Okay. "I'm noticing the belief that I'm pathetic."
Therapist:	Did that make any difference?
Client:	Yeah, I unhooked a bit.

Alternative phrases to "I'm noticing" include "I'm having a…" "Here is…" and "My mind's telling me…" (These are terms we've already been using when dropping anchor, and they apply equally to emotions, urges, memories, sensations, and so on: *I'm having a feeling of anger* or *I'm noticing the urge to smash something.*) Although we've focused on fusion with self-judgment, we can apply this method to any cognitive content: *I'm having thoughts about getting hurt, My mind's telling me she's going to leave me.*

Naming the Theme

This defusion strategy works best with a small sheet of paper or index card. On one side, the therapist writes down key thoughts linked to a common theme. (In telehealth settings, both parties have a piece of paper, and both write down the same thing.)

Therapist:	(*holding up a sheet of paper that lists ten of the client's recurrent difficult thoughts*) So this stuff (*points to the writing*) keeps showing up, and hooking you, right?
Client:	Yeah.
Therapist:	And still okay to call it the "worthless, unlovable" theme?
Client:	Yeah.
Therapist:	Okay. (*flips the sheet over*) So on the other side here, I'm writing a phrase that I hope will help you unhook. (*Therapist writes in large block capital letters and reads it aloud while doing so.*) "Aha! Here it is again! The worthless, unlovable theme. I know this one." (*If it's telehealth, the therapist asks the client to do the same on the back of their own paper; if "in person," the therapist passes the sheet to the client*). So this is an experiment. Obviously I hope it'll be useful, or I wouldn't ask you to try it, but I never actually know for sure. So part one is you read through all those thoughts—silently, inside your head—and you really let them hook you, reel you in. Then once you're really hooked, you flip it over and silently read to yourself what I've written on the other side there. And as soon as you've done that, you check in with me, tell me what happened.

Client:	Okay. (*reads the first side, looks distressed*)
Therapist:	Looks like you're hooked.
Client:	I am.
Therapist:	Okay, now flip it over, and read the other side.
Client:	Okay. (*reads the other side; face lifts a little; looks at the therapist, slightly surprised*)
Therapist:	What happened?
Client:	Yeah, it helped. It kind of contains it.
Therapist:	Helps you step back a bit? Unhook?
Client:	Yeah.
Therapist:	Okay, now just let that paper rest on your lap (*client does so*) and acknowledge—those thoughts are there, right now—and how many times has your mind told you this stuff?
Client:	Millions.
Therapist:	Yeah, so you don't really need to read that paper—you know all those thoughts by heart—so acknowledge they're here right now...and also any feelings that go with them...and at the same time, have a stretch, notice your body moving...and notice the room around you...so those thoughts are here right now, they're not going away...and there's your body around them, which you can move and control...and there's a room around your body...and you and me here, working together...and how are you doing there?
Client:	(*smiling*) Good.
Therapist:	Give me a number. This is zero (*puts hands over face*)—zero means completely hooked—thoughts are totally dominating you, controlling what you do. And this is ten (*lowers hands to lap*)—completely unhooked—thoughts are still there but they're not jerking you around, you don't have to obey them or give them all your attention, you can just let them be there while you get on with your life. What number are you?
Client:	About an eight.
Therapist:	Great.

The zero to ten fusion scale above helps to track the client's responses. Had the client given a low score at the end, the therapist would probably have moved into dropping anchor.

Thanking Your Mind

This popular defusion strategy (Hayes et al., 1999) involves not only noticing and naming but also appreciating the purpose of the thoughts in question.

> Therapist: So basically, next time your mind starts saying that, see if you can, with a sense of playfulness, say to yourself something like "Ah, thanks mind. I know you're trying to look out for me. But it's okay—I've got this." And if your mind replies, "Ah, you're such a loser!" then once again, you say, "Well, thanks for sharing." Basically, you don't debate, you don't defend, you don't let your mind pull you into an argument. With a sense of humor, you thank your mind for its comments, and carry on with what you're doing. And each time it tries to hook you, same thing: "Thanks, mind!"

Note: the "thanks, mind" part isn't essential. If you prefer, you can use a phrase like "Here's my mind trying to keep me safe again." You can also go a step further with this strategy and write a compassionate letter to your mind—see Extra Bits.

Clarification and Psychoeducation

The concept of defusion can be a tricky one, and we often need to clarify what it is and isn't.

ACKNOWLEDGING AND ALLOWING VERSUS DISMISSING OR IGNORING

A common misconception among both clients and newbie ACT therapists is that defusing from thoughts means dismissing or ignoring them. We may explain:

> Therapist: So I just want to be clear, we're not dismissing these thoughts. If they're telling us about something important that we need to deal with or face up to, reminding us about something that really matters, then we make use of that. We get into action, we address the issue, we do something constructive—we use that information to launch us into towards moves. On the other hand, if there's nothing useful in them, we let them sit there and do their thing, and we get on with our life.

Similarly, to distinguish defusing from ignoring, we might say, "This is not the same as *ignoring*. Have you ever been to a café or bar and there was music playing in the background that you really didn't like, or someone behind you with a loud, annoying voice? And did you ever try to ignore it? Yes? And what happened?"

Most clients will report that trying to ignore or "not hear" a loud noise—a barking dog, a lawnmower, a car alarm—makes it bother them more. We can then say, "Yeah, so the trick is to acknowledge the noise is there. Don't try to ignore it or block it out. And don't struggle with it, either. Allow it to play on in the background, acknowledging it's there—and focus your attention on what you're doing."

BUT I WANT TO GET RID OF THESE THOUGHTS!

Suppose a client says, "But can't I get rid of these thoughts?" We may reply, "I'm guessing you've tried that already. What are some of the methods you've used?" We then quickly elicit four or five of the strategies they've employed to try to get rid of these cognitions (e.g., drugs, alcohol, positive thinking, distraction). Then we say, "So all these methods work in the short term to make those thoughts go away—but they soon come back again, right?"

We could follow that with some brief psychoeducation about neuroplasticity, explaining that the brain can't delete old neural pathways; it can only lay down new ones on top of the old ones. (And if clients have previously tried disputing their thoughts, we can point out: "Even when you know, logically and rationally, that your thoughts aren't true, that doesn't stop them from coming back, right?") We may continue:

Therapist: Unfortunately, there's no delete button in the brain. There's no way to eliminate deeply entrenched thinking patterns. It's like, if you learn to speak Chinese, you won't eliminate English; you'll have English *and* Chinese. So we can't subtract old patterns of thinking—but we *can* add new ones. So for example, when "I'm a loser" pops up, we can go, "Aha. There's the 'loser theme' again."

Homework

For homework we may suggest:

Therapist: Like any new skill, this requires practice. So I'm going to suggest a few things that I think would be really helpful, if you could do them on a daily basis.

Client: Okay.

Therapist: So first thing is, throughout the day, there'll be lots of times you get hooked. That's a given. The moment you realize it, see if you can unhook yourself. So step one is to notice what's hooking you and then use the phrase... (*Therapist specifies the defusion phrase they have practiced in session* [e.g., *"I'm having the thought that..."* or *"Thanks, mind!"*]) Often noticing and naming it will unhook you, at least a bit. But if you're still quite hooked, the second step is to look at these thoughts in terms of towards and away moves. Ask yourself, "If I obey these thoughts, or give them all my attention—where will that take me? Towards or away from the stuff that really matters to me?" And if that's still not enough, if you're still hooked, the third step is to drop anchor. How does that sound to you?

EXTRA BIT

In *Trauma-Focused ACT: The Extra Bits* chapter ten, you'll find (a) three worksheets: "Twelve Key Themes," "Big Six," and "Relationship Roadblocks"; (b) Checklist for Common Away Moves; (c) Caveman Mind Metaphors; (d) a link to a humorous YouTube video on "Thanking Your Mind"; and (e) an exercise on writing a compassionate letter to your mind.

Takeaway

The five main strategies we've covered in this chapter—notice, name, normalize, purpose, and workability—are simple and practical. We can combine them in many different ways to start shaping defusion skills right from the first session.

Metaphors for defusion—such as Hands as Thoughts—are useful, but they don't build new skills. We need to follow them with active skills-building exercises, which we practice in session and encourage as homework.

CHAPTER ELEVEN

Heavy Lifting

In the last chapter we looked at quick, simple defusion techniques based on noticing, naming, normalizing, purpose, and workability. Now we'll look at some more challenging skills and special considerations for trauma. But first, let's discuss a very important topic: cognitive flexibility.

Cognitive Flexibility

If I had a dollar for every time I've heard someone say, "ACT doesn't change your thinking," then I'd probably spend it all on chocolate. (And believe me—it would be A LOT of chocolate!) The thing is, ACT *does* change our thinking—dramatically. It changes the way we think about our minds, our bodies, our thoughts, our emotions, how we want to live, who we want to be, why we do what we do, what matters to us, and so on.

However, ACT doesn't achieve this by challenging, disputing, disproving, or invalidating thoughts. Nor does it encourage people to avoid, suppress, distract from, or dismiss their thoughts. ACT helps people to change their thinking through (a) defusing from unhelpful cognitions and cognitive processes and (b) developing new, more effective ways of thinking, *in addition to* their other cognitive patterns. As mentioned earlier, there's no delete button in the brain. We can add new ways of thinking, but we can't subtract old ones.

So, above and beyond fostering cognitive defusion, ACT actively cultivates cognitive flexibility. ACT practitioners actively encourage, model, and teach effective cognitive processes such as flexible perspective taking, reframing, compassionate self-talk, values-based problem solving and strategizing, motivational self-instruction, examining behavior in terms of workability, nonjudgmental labeling of thoughts and feelings, and so on.

These new ways of thinking are not to help people control their feelings, but rather to develop psychological flexibility. So, for example, in some models, a therapist may ask, "Is there another way you can think about this?" And typically, the aim of such a strategy is to reduce emotional distress. In ACT we may ask something similar, but with a different aim: to foster values-based action: "Is there another way you can think about this that might help you to deal with it more effectively—more like the person you want to be?"

So, next time you hear someone claim that ACT "doesn't change your thinking," you know what to say: "Buy Russ Harris some chocolate!" Now, let's take a look at some other methods of defusion.

Going Further with Defusion

There are countless methods for fostering defusion, beyond the simpler techniques we've covered so far. I'll share some of my favorites below.

Observing the Flow of Thoughts

Many defusion practices train clients to observe the ongoing flow of their thoughts, without getting pulled into it. (These are also good practices to help develop self-as-context, or the noticing self, because they facilitate a sense of being "the observer" of your thoughts.) We might introduce them as follows:

Therapist: When we're ruminating, worrying, obsessing, or just dwelling and stewing on stuff, we miss out on a lot, right? We can't focus, we can't engage in what we're doing. It's like our thoughts are a raging river, and we get pulled into it and we can't get back out. Do you relate to that?

Client: Yeah. Happens all the time.

Therapist: So it's really useful to learn how to step back from that river and watch it flow on by, without getting pulled into it. This is basically the antidote to worrying and ruminating. We can't stop these thoughts from arising, but we can learn to let them float on by without getting swept away by them.

Leaves on a Stream (Hayes et al., 1999) is a popular ACT exercise for observing the flow of your thoughts. You visualize a gently flowing stream with leaves on the surface of the water, and imagine placing your cognitions onto the leaves and letting them float on by. (For a recording and script, see Extra Bits.) Common variants include clouds floating through the sky, waves rising and falling in the ocean, and trains pulling into and out of a station.

However, because exercises like this typically require sitting still and closing your eyes to visualize, we can modify them for two groups of clients: (a) those who find visualization hard or impossible (technically known as "aphantasia"), and (b) those who tend to "drift off," fall asleep, have flashbacks, or dissociate during eyes-closed exercises.

For both groups, a good alternative is Hearing Your Thoughts (Harris, 2018). In this exercise, with your eyes open and fixed on a spot, you "listen in" to your mind; you notice your thoughts as if listening to a voice speaking, paying curious attention to auditory qualities such as volume, pitch, tone, speed, and emotion. (For a recording and script, see Extra Bits.)

For homework, you might suggest, "Practice this for five minutes twice a day, or ten minutes once a day. And it's also a great exercise to do in bed, when you're finding it hard to sleep."

Getting Out of the River

When clients keep worrying, ruminating, or obsessing, it's useful to practice "getting out of the river" of repetitive negative thinking (an exercise inspired by Wells, 2009).

Therapist:	The idea here is to learn how to recognize when you've fallen into the river—and how to get yourself back out of it. So basically, the idea is that you start worrying now, as much as you can, and really get caught up in it. And then, every twenty seconds, I'm going to press pause and get you to stop for ten to twenty seconds. And then we'll go again. We'll do six rounds, about three to four minutes in total—is that okay?
Client:	Yeah. Okay.
Therapist:	Great. We'll ease into it. We'll start off with daydreaming and then we'll move on to worrying.

We now ask the client to daydream about something, like a book, movie, or exciting event; an issue they're passionate about; or a pleasurable memory. After twenty seconds of daydreaming, we say:

Therapist:	And pause. And what is your mind saying right now? (*Client shares their thoughts.*) Okay. So there's a choice now. One option is to jump back into the river—but if instead of that you want to stay present, how could you do that?
Client:	Look around the room?
Therapist:	Yup, so acknowledge whatever thoughts are present...and at the same time notice what you can see and hear...and have a stretch...and notice you and me, working together.
Client:	So this is pretty much dropping anchor?
Therapist:	Yeah, it's a variant on the theme.
Client:	Got it.
Therapist:	Okay. So let's go again, daydreaming for another twenty seconds. (*Therapist sits silently for twenty seconds.*) And pause. So what thoughts are showing up now? (*Client shares their thoughts.*) Okay, so again there's a choice—those thoughts are present right now, and you can either engage with me or go back into the river. Just try engaging for a few seconds. (*Client does so.*)

After six rounds of daydreaming—with a ten-second pause between each—we debrief the exercise. The key point is, whenever we catch ourselves daydreaming, we have a choice: jump back into the river, or focus on and engage in something else. Note how each time the client "gets out of the river," the therapist prompts them to acknowledge the thoughts that are present; if this step is omitted, the exercise is likely to function as distraction.

Next, we say, "So now, let's ramp up the difficulty." This time, we ask the client to worry or ruminate about a difficult issue, and we follow the same steps: twenty seconds in the river—ten to twenty seconds to engage (while acknowledging the thoughts that are present)—then repeat; again, for six rounds (three to four minutes in total). After this, we debrief, emphasizing that we all get repeatedly "pulled into the river," but we can, with practice, get better at realizing it and faster at getting back out.

For homework, we suggest, "Practice this for three to four minutes twice a day. Find a quiet place, sit down, and set a timer to go off at twenty seconds. Then start worrying (or ruminating). Each time the bell rings, pause: notice your thoughts; have a stretch; engage in the world. Then reset for another twenty seconds." We add, "Also, throughout the day, whenever you find yourself swimming in that river, press pause. Take at least ten seconds to stretch and look around, get a sense of where you are, what you're doing—and then make a choice: will you jump back into the river, or focus on something else?"

"Worry Time"

The popular concept of "worry time" fits very well with TFACT, provided we modify it. The idea is that if you worry a lot, you put aside five to fifteen minutes each day, at a specified time, during which you do nothing but sit down and allow yourself to worry. For the rest of the day, when worries pop up, you say to yourself, *Not going to worry about this now. I'll do it in my worry time.* To make this strategy ACT-congruent, there are two tweaks:

A. When worries pop up, say to yourself, *Thanks mind. I know you're trying to help. And I'll tackle this later in my worry time. For now, I have to focus on other things. So by all means, keep generating those worries—but just know, I can't give them my attention right now.*

B. When you get to the "worry time," don't passively sit there and allow yourself to worry; instead, respond to your worries effectively. Either practice observing the flow of your worries or getting in and out of the river; or tease out values from beneath the worries, and use them to create an action plan (see chapters fifteen and sixteen).

This strategy works well in conjunction with the defusion methods above—and we can also use it for ruminating and obsessing.

The Big Three: Write; Move; Expand Awareness

Three techniques are especially useful for tricky, sticky fusion: writing thoughts down, physical movement, and expansive awareness. (And again, we can adapt these methods for all private experiences: emotions, urges, memories, physical sensations, and so on.)

Writing Thoughts Down

Writing thoughts down is a powerful method for defusion; seeing them in black and white creates a sense of distance, separation, or "stepping back." Either party can do the writing, but it's often more engaging for clients if they do it themselves. (If working via telehealth, both client and therapist have a pen and paper, and we explain: "So you write this down at your end, and I'll write the same at my end.")

The gist of this intervention is: *So there are your thoughts; you can see them, in black and white. But they don't have to control what you do. So what are you going to do next?* In the transcript below, the client is fused with hopelessness.

Therapist:	Do you notice how often these thoughts keep showing up? Would it be okay if I jot some of them down, so we can have a look at them?
Client:	Sure.
Therapist:	Okay. (*Speaking the client's thoughts aloud while simultaneously writing them down on a large sheet of paper.*) "This is a waste of time." "There's nothing I can do." "It's pointless." "It's too late." "My life is fucked." (*Gives the paper to the client.*) So those thoughts keep cropping up, over and over, right?
Client:	Yeah.
Therapist:	So I'm curious about what you're going to do next.
Client:	What do you mean?
Therapist:	Well (*pointing to the paper*), those thoughts are here, right? You don't like them, you don't want them—but here they are. And the question is: what will you do next? With those thoughts present, you can do things that make your life better—or you can do things that make it worse. For example, suppose you wanted to make this therapy session go really badly, what could you do?
Client:	I suppose I could just not listen to you.
Therapist:	Yeah. That's one option. Anything else you could do—you know, if you really wanted to make this unpleasant?
Client:	I suppose I could insult you.
Therapist:	Yeah. Or grab some books from the bookcase and throw them at me. Or break the window. Or set fire to the carpet. Any other ideas?
Client:	Steal your wallet?

Therapist:	Yep, exactly. Or you could even just refuse to talk to me. On the other hand, if you wanted this to be a pleasant and productive session, what are some things you could do?
Client:	Err, I'm not sure.
Therapist:	Well, how about what you're doing right now? You're engaging, talking to me, listening, thinking about the questions I'm asking you, being polite and cooperative...
Client:	Oh, right—yeah, I see.
Therapist:	So you can choose to keep doing more of that—which will keep the session flowing—or do some of the other things, which will bring it to a crashing halt.
Client:	Right.
Therapist:	So which are you going to choose?
Client:	(*playfully*) Don't worry—I'm not going to steal your wallet.
Therapist:	(*chuckling*) So here's the thing: in each moment there's a choice point. We can choose to do something that makes life worse—or makes it better—even when difficult thoughts and feelings are present. And I don't expect your mind to agree with me. I expect your mind to go, "That's bullshit!" and say some of these things again (*points to the paper*). Is it doing that?
Client:	(*playfully*) How'd you know?
Therapist:	(*chuckling*) Because that's what minds do. And your mind is never going to agree with me on this—but the good thing is, it doesn't have to. So let's not waste time trying to convince your mind. What I predict is, throughout our work here, your mind's going to keep saying this stuff (*points to the paper*) over and over again—here in the room and outside it—and each time those thoughts show up, there's a choice point.

This intervention touches on ideas covered earlier, but the physicality of the paper adds some "oomph!" (It also works well via telehealth; after writing each thought down, we hold the paper up to the camera so the client can see it.) This strategy is useful with any cognitive content: reason-giving, rules, judgments, self-concept, core beliefs, schemas, and so on. When we write these cognitions down and help clients notice that they have choices—*even though* these difficult thoughts are present—it's a powerful experience.

And we can modify this strategy in many ways. For example, suppose a client keeps problem hopping or getting hooked by worries that pull them off topic:

Therapist:	(*noticing*) Have you noticed how your mind keeps jumping from one thing to another? It seems like your mind won't give you any peace at all. As soon as we focus on one issue, your mind pulls you to another.
Client:	Yeah, I know. I can't help it. It never stops. There's so much going on.
Therapist:	From where I'm sitting, it looks exhausting. What's it like for you, having your mind jerk you around like that?
Client:	Yeah, it is exhausting.
Therapist:	(*normalizing*) Everyone's mind does this at times. (*purpose*) It's like your mind wants to keep on top of all these issues; doesn't want you to forget anything. (*workability*) The problem is, if you keep letting your mind hook you this way, what happens?
Client:	I just keep worrying.
Therapist:	Yeah, for sure. And if we let that happen in our sessions, we're not going to achieve very much. So one of the most useful skills you can learn here, to help you with X (*mentions some of the client's therapy goals*), is to recognize when you're getting hooked, distracted, and pulled off task—and learn to unhook yourself from those worries and refocus on the task at hand.
Client:	Yeah, but look—these aren't just "worries." These are real problems!
Therapist:	You are right. They *are* real problems. Real, challenging, stressful problems—things that you need to deal with. And there's an essential skill you need, if you want to deal with them effectively. Do you know what it is?
Client:	Er, no.
Therapist:	It's called "task-focused attention," the ability to stay focused on a task. And the task we have here is to stick with one problem long enough to come up with a strategy that you can take home after the session and apply. So if we keep going off task, we won't get anywhere. So can we spend a bit of time working on this skill?

The term "strategy," as used above, could refer to any TFACT intervention: a defusion or acceptance skill, a value, a goal, a step-by-step action plan, and so on. Once clients understand the rationale for task-focused attention, they are usually willing to practice it in session. So we write down five to ten of the client's main worries (i.e., the thoughts that keep hooking them in session). Then we point to the paper and say, "Each time these show up, there's a choice point. We can stick to the problem we're working on and stay with it until we have a strategy, or we can let these other things pull us off track."

We then put the paper somewhere clearly visible (e.g., on the couch beside the client, on the floor in front of them). Later in session, when the client mentions other thoughts on the paper, we can say,

"Do you notice what your mind is doing right now? (*pointing to the paper*) That's right there, on the list. And now there's a choice point—do we let this pull us off track, or do we stay on course?"

PLACING THOUGHTS ON OBJECTS

If you're not keen on writing thoughts down, you can instead invite the client to imagine placing the thoughts on top of an object. For example: "Can I ask you to imagine something? Imagine collecting all those thoughts and placing them in a little pile on the couch, beside you. Just on top of the cushion." From there, the intervention is the same: "Okay, so all those thoughts are in a pile, right there on the cushion. And they're not about to suddenly disappear. So now there's a choice to make…"

Physical Movement

If a client starts to "freeze" in response to those thoughts on the paper, we can say:

Therapist: Okay, so you seem to be locking up a bit there. Let's see if you can reverse that. Notice, the thoughts are there, and at the same time, push your feet into the floor…and straighten your back…and stretch out your arms… (*Therapist continues giving such instructions until the client is freely mobile.*)… So notice (*pointing to the paper*), the thoughts are right there with you, but they don't control you; you can choose what actions you take with your arms and legs, hands and feet…

Physical movement is useful for defusion because it helps us to notice that difficult thoughts are present, but they do not have to control our actions. The basic intervention (always preceded by lots of normalizing and validating) is:

Therapist: Notice these thoughts (*points or refers to the paper or object, or speaks some of the client's thoughts aloud*) are present…and also notice, they do not control your arms and legs. Check it out for yourself; move them around. You are in control of your actions.

From this point on, there are many options. We could invite the client to stand and walk around, to stretch or shift position, to do a tai chi or yoga move, to mindfully drink a glass of water, and so on.

Expanding Awareness

Expanding awareness in the presence of difficult thoughts and feelings—without trying to distract from them—can facilitate defusion at any point in any session. Clients have already been doing this when dropping anchor, so we can readily play around with it and use it as an "add-on" or alternative to any of the interventions above:

Therapist: So notice those thoughts are here…and without trying to ignore them or distract yourself, see if you can expand your awareness…what else can you notice here, in addition to those thoughts? (*Therapist now prompts client to notice what they can see, hear, touch, and so on. After a minute or so, the therapist says...*) So there's a whole lot going on in this moment—so many things you can see and hear and touch—in addition to all those thoughts. So the question is, how much attention and energy do you want to invest in these thoughts? If they're telling you something useful and important that's going to improve your life, you want to make good use of them. But if they're not doing that, how about you let them sit there, and put your energy and attention into something more life enhancing?

Playful Defusion

ACT is well known for playful defusion techniques, such as singing thoughts, saying them in silly voices, or saying them extremely slowly (Hayes et al., 1999). Naturally, we want to be cautious about using these methods with trauma, because if we aren't careful, they may come across as dismissive or trivializing. So it's arguably safer to hold such methods back for later sessions, once clients are clear on the aims of defusion and have practiced other techniques such as those described earlier.

"Playing with your thoughts" involves putting them into a new context where you can readily recognize that they are constructs of words or pictures; this neutralizes their power, making it easier to unhook from them. Typically these methods highlight either the visual properties of thoughts (i.e., "seeing" them), their auditory properties (i.e., "hearing" them), or both. The best way to learn these methods (in my opinion) is to try them on yourself and notice what happens; you'll likely find that some work well, and others don't. If you find one or two that really help you to unhook, experiment with them over the next few days. However, if any technique makes you feel trivialized or mocked, then don't use it (and obviously, we'd say the same to our clients).

Playful Visual Techniques

On a piece of paper, jot down several of the thoughts that most frequently hook you and distress you. For each technique below, select which of these thoughts to work with, go step-by-step through the exercise, and be curious about and open to whatever happens.

Thoughts on Paper

Write two or three distressing thoughts on a large piece of paper.

Now hold the paper in front of your face and get absorbed in those thoughts, for about ten seconds.

Next, place the paper on your lap, look around you, and notice what you can see, hear, touch, taste, and smell.

Acknowledge the thoughts are still with you. Notice they haven't changed at all, and you know exactly what they are—but does their impact lessen when you rest them on your lap instead of holding them in front of your face?

Now on the paper, underneath those thoughts, draw a stick figure (or, if you're artistic, a cartoon character). Draw a "thought bubble" around those words, as if they are being thought by the stick figure. Now look at your "cartoon": when you see your thoughts like this, does it make any difference to the way you relate to them?

Try this a few times with different thoughts and stick figures. Put different faces on your stick figures—a smiley face, a sad face, or one with big teeth and spiky hair. Draw a cat, a dog, or a flower with those very same thought bubbles coming out of it. Does this change the impact of those thoughts? Does it help you to see them as words?

Computer Screen

You can do this exercise either in your imagination or on a computer. First write (or imagine) your thought in standard lowercase black text, on the computer screen. Then, play around with it. Change it into different colors, fonts, and sizes, and notice what effect each change makes. (Bold red uppercase letters may sometimes hook people; if so, change to a lowercase pale pastel color.)

Then change the text back to black lowercase.

And now, play around with the formatting:

- Space the words out, placing large gaps between them.

- Run the words together—no gaps between them—so they make one long word.

- Run them vertically down the screen.

Finally, put them back into normal formatting.

How do you relate to those thoughts now? Is it easier to see that they are words?

Karaoke Ball

Imagine your thoughts as words on a karaoke screen. Imagine a "bouncing ball" jumping from word to word across the screen. (If you like, imagine yourself on stage, singing along.)

Repeat this several times, with different thoughts.

Changing Settings

Imagine your thought in a variety of different settings. Take about five to ten seconds to imagine each one, then move on to the next. See your thought written:

- in playful colorful letters on the cover of a children's book

- as stylish graphics on a restaurant menu

- as icing on top of a birthday cake

- in chalk on a blackboard

- as a slogan on a T-shirt

WORKING WITH IMAGES

We can adapt most of the methods above for images. For example, you can imagine your images on TV, computer, and smartphone screens—and play around with colors, size, contrast, saturation, and brightness, or add text and subtitles. You can also visualize them in different settings: on a book, postcard, or painting; on a billboard as you're driving past; or on the side of a kite, flying through the sky.

Playful Auditory Techniques

Now play around with the auditory properties of your thoughts and notice what difference it makes. Does it help you to perceive them as sounds, noises, or speech?

Silly Voices

Say your thought in a silly voice—either silently or out loud. (Out loud is often more helpful, but obviously you need to pick an appropriate time and place.) You might choose the voice of a cartoon character, movie star, sports commentator, or someone with an outrageous accent. Try several different voices and notice what happens.

Slow and Fast

Say your thought—either silently or out loud—first very slowly, then at superfast speed (so you sound like a chipmunk).

Singing

Sing your thoughts—either silently or out loud—to the tune of "Happy Birthday." Then try it with a couple of different tunes.

Smartphone Apps

Speak your thought aloud into a smartphone app that plays it back, humorously altering your voice.

For example, the "Super Voice Changer" app will play your speech back in the voice of Darth Vader, Wall-E, Donald Duck, and many others. And the "AutoRap" app turns whatever you say into a rap song, with a drumbeat and music in the background.

Create Your Own Techniques

Now invent your own techniques. Put your thought in a new context where you can "see" it or "hear" it. You might visualize your thought painted on a wall, printed on a book, embroidered on the tutu of a ballet dancer, carved into a tree trunk, trailed on a banner behind an airplane, tattooed on a bicep, or inked in beautiful italics on a medieval manuscript. You could paint it, draw it, or sculpt it. You could imagine it jumping, hopping, or dancing; or visualize it moving down a TV screen, like the credits of a movie. Alternatively, you might imagine hearing your thought recited by a Shakespearean actor, playing on a podcast, emanating from a robot, or sung by a rock star. So be creative, invent your own, and encourage your clients to do likewise.

Homework

We may suggest clients practice playful defusion whenever they get the opportunity. It's often most useful when they're finding it hard to unhook. So, for example, if they've already used other defusion methods, and they're still hooked, they can pick one of the thoughts that's most difficult and start playing around with it. Then they can pick another, and so on.

Defusion Likes Company

All six core ACT processes are important; they all interconnect and reinforce each other. And sometimes therapists get stuck because they over-rely on one process while underutilizing others. Consider a client who has a core belief like "I'm worthless and I don't deserve to live," stemming back to horrific childhood trauma, and they are repeatedly fusing with it, triggering serious self-destructive behavior. In this case, defusion skills alone are unlikely to be enough. Defusion will be helpful, for sure—but we'll also need to bring in self-compassion, values, acceptance, dropping anchor, and so on.

I mention this because therapists sometimes complain, "I've tried lots of defusion, but we're not getting anywhere." This indicates the need to bring in other parts of the model. As an example, let's consider fusion with rules—a major factor in issues such as fawning (i.e., extreme "people pleasing") and perfectionism.

When clients are fused with rules such as "I have to do it perfectly; I mustn't make mistakes" (perfectionism) or "I have to keep everyone happy; my needs don't matter" (fawning), three strategies are especially important and useful:

1. Defuse from the rule (*notice, name, normalize, purpose, workability*).

2. Find the underlying values and explore flexible ways of living them.

3. Make room for the inevitable discomfort and be kind to yourself.

Let's unpack these strategies a bit.

Defuse from the rule (notice, name, normalize, purpose, workability). By now, you've read enough about noticing, naming, and normalizing, so let's skip straight to purpose and workability. Perfectionistic rules can serve many useful purposes: they can motivate you to work hard, be productive, and do good-quality work; protect you from making mistakes or underperforming; gain you praise, approval, or respect; help you achieve important goals; and boost your self-image as efficient, productive, reliable, a "performer"—while helping you escape a negative self-concept such as "I'm unworthy."

Similarly, people-pleasing rules can motivate you to look after and take care of others; protect you from rejection or hostility; gain you approval, affection, or gratitude; help you avoid conflict and increase positive interaction in relationships; and boost your self-image as caring, kind, helpful, a "giver"—while also helping you escape a negative self-concept such as "I'm unlovable."

So after uncovering, normalizing, and validating these benefits, we may summarize: "There are real payoffs to following these rules; this is your mind protecting you from stuff you don't want, and helping you to get things you do want."

From there we can turn to workability: We help clients to recognize that when they follow these rules rigidly, treat them as laws that must always be obeyed, the costs are usually significant: chronic stress, high anxiety levels, exhaustion, compulsive rituals, lack of motivation, or depression. In addition, in the long term, following these rules usually reinforces negative self-concepts. For example, following perfectionistic rules about achievement reinforces the belief "I'm only worth something when I'm getting good results; when I'm not successful, I'm worthless." Following rules about always pleasing others reinforces "I'm not important; my needs don't matter."

Once clients recognize these long-term costs, we can consider more workable options. We may say, "There are many benefits to following this rule, and obviously you don't want to lose those. So what if there's a way to keep most of those benefits while also starting to bend those rules a little?" This naturally leads into the next strategy...

Find the underlying values and explore flexible ways of living them. With some gentle, compassionate digging, we will always find values beneath these rigid rules. With perfectionism, we usually find values such as efficiency, reliability, competence, and responsibility. With people pleasing, we tend to find values such as self-protection, giving, caring, and helping. The aim is to then live by these values *flexibly*—acting on them in ways that enhance well-being and improve quality of life.

Make room for inevitable discomfort and be kind to yourself. When people start to bend or disobey rigid rules, all sorts of uncomfortable thoughts and feeling show up: fear, anxiety, reason-giving, and so on. This is inevitable; when we step out of our comfort zone, we get discomfort. So to handle all those difficult thoughts and feelings, acceptance and self-compassion skills are essential.

Obviously, there's more to these issues than the strategies briefly outlined above. For example, we usually need to bring in self-as-context and self-compassion to work with the client's self-concept. Also, rigid rule following is frequently accompanied by harsh self-criticism—and some clients (especially those with perfectionistic tendencies) will say this helps motivate them to do things that matter to them; we address this common sticking point in chapter fourteen.

The key point here is that while defusion is helpful in itself, it's far more potent when combined with other core processes, so be sure to bring them in if you're not making headway. (And if you're hungry for more on working with rigid rules, see the sections "I Don't Deserve Kindness" in chapter fourteen, "Clarifying Motivation"—which is all about "people pleasing"—in chapter fifteen, and "Defusion from the Rule 'Don't Trust'" in chapter twenty-eight.)

EXTRA BIT | In chapter eleven of *Trauma-Focused ACT: The Extra Bits* (downloadable from Free Resources on http://www.ImLearningACT.com), you'll find a script and audio recording of "Hearing Your Thoughts"; a client handout on "Playing With Thoughts"; and a link to an e-book called *Preempting Your Mind*, which goes further with some of the strategies mentioned above.

Takeaway

Exercises such as Hearing Your Thoughts, Leaves on a Stream, and Getting Out of the River are powerful antidotes to rumination, worry, or the myriad of other ways we get "lost in our thoughts." Playful defusion techniques can also be effective—although we need to be cautious when using them, particularly with clients dealing with trauma-related issues, to prevent invalidation. As for writing thoughts down, physical movement, and expanding awareness: keep these at the top of your toolkit because they can facilitate defusion from just about anything (especially when combined with dropping anchor).

CHAPTER TWELVE

Leaving the Battlefield

The ongoing war with unwanted thoughts and feelings takes its toll. Like combat in the real world, the battle with our inner experiences is exhausting—and comes with heavy casualties. And while we're all experientially avoidant to some extent (yes, it's normal, folks!), the more extreme this tendency, the more problems it creates.

Unfortunately, to the client, these unwanted inner experiences truly *are* the enemy, and their only two options are to fight them or run away. To open our clients to a third option—acceptance—we need to undermine their attachment to the other two. We do this through a process called…

Creative Hopelessness

Creative hopelessness means creating a sense of hopelessness in the agenda of emotional control: *I must control how I feel; I have to get rid of these bad thoughts and feelings and replace them with good ones.* As you know, this agenda fuels much unworkable action: self-harming, avoidance of intimacy, social withdrawal, and so on. Through gently and compassionately undermining this agenda, we hope to open clients to an alternative: the agenda of acceptance.

Creative hopelessness (CH) is rarely a once-off intervention; usually we need to revisit it several times. (But it gets quicker and easier each time around.) Like anything in TFACT, there are numerous ways of doing it, but all CH interventions basically boil down to three questions: *What have you tried? How has it worked? What has it cost?*

What Have You Tried?

The first CH question is *What have you tried so far to get rid of these difficult thoughts and feelings?* For example:

Client: I'm sick of feeling this way. I want to feel normal again.

Therapist: Of course you do. These feelings have been jerking you around for a long time.

Client: So how do I get rid of them?

financial costs?" Then we take several minutes to help the client connect with the true costs of over-relying on these strategies.

At this point, a quick reminder: mild experiential avoidance is rarely a problem and can even be life enhancing, but high levels come with significant costs. So we now uncover those costs in each category of DOTS. For example: "You've mentioned a few distraction strategies there; have there been any costs of using those? Any problems with relationships? Health issues? Work problems? Financial problems?"

For each category of DOTS, there are specific costs we want to highlight:

Distraction: "Has this ever resulted in a sense of wasted time or energy—as if you're not really spending your time on things that are truly important and meaningful to you? Or a sense of wasted money, or energy? Or missing out on life?"

Opting out: "Has this ever resulted in missed opportunities? Or a sense of missing out on people, places, situations, or activities that are important and meaningful? Or a sense that life is getting smaller?"

Thinking strategies: "Do you ever spend a lot of time caught up in your thoughts? Maybe missing out on life? Or finding it hard to focus? Ever been awake at three in the morning thinking this through?"

Substances: "Could these be damaging your health in any way? Are there any other costs—financial or work maybe? Any effects on your relationships?"

If we can identify ten to fifteen costs (in total), that's usually enough; typically that takes three to six minutes.

You've Worked Hard!

We now want to validate the client's steadfast effort:

Therapist: You've really worked hard at this. You have tried and tried for a long, long time to avoid and get rid of these painful thoughts and feelings. No one can call you lazy! You've put in a lot of effort. And no one can call you stupid; we all use these strategies. We all distract ourselves; we all opt out or back off from the difficult stuff; we all try to think our way out of pain; and we all use substances of some form or another, even if it's just aspirin or chocolate. And why? Because everyone around us recommends these strategies—friends, family, doctors, health and fitness magazines... This is the conventional wisdom, right? It's the same advice from everybody: "Make these thoughts and feelings go away!"

Client: Are you saying that's wrong?

Therapist: Not at all. I'm saying, you and me and everyone else I know, we've all grown up in a culture that's bombarded us with this message our whole lives. So it's completely natural that you're doing all this stuff. And what keeps it going is the short-term payoff; because *short term*, it gives you relief. But long term, it's costing you. Some of these strategies have drawbacks. They're taking a toll. I mean, *in the long term*, are they really giving you the sort of life you want?

Practical Tip

Sometimes a client may say, "So am I supposed to just suck it up and get on with it?" or "So what do I do; just give up?"

We could reply, "No, not at all. I'm guessing you've already tried that? (*Client says yes.*) And did it work to give you the sort of life you want? (*Client says no.*) Okay, so, that's yet another strategy we won't use."

How Are You Feeling?

By this point, most clients will have had an emotional reaction: commonly sadness, anger, or anxiety. But this is often mixed with relief, because we are powerfully validating the client's experience: we're acknowledging just how hard they have been working (often following well-meaning advice) and the painful fact that in the long term, it's not giving them what they want.

To gauge their reaction, we ask, "I'm wondering how you're feeling right now. Like, for a lot of people, this process brings up some sadness or anxiety or anger—anything like that for you?" And whatever emotions they report, we normalize: "That's a completely natural reaction. You've been stuck in a vicious cycle for a long time, through no fault of your own—and it's painful to face that. It hurts." (And of course, if the emotions are overwhelming, we drop anchor; or if the client fuses with harsh self-judgment—"I'm such a loser. This just confirms how stupid I am"—we segue into defusion. But these reactions are uncommon.)

Are You Open to Something Radically Different?

Now that we've identified the costs of war, it's time to suggest leaving the battlefield. We may say, "You've been trying hard for a long time to get rid of this stuff—and it's really taking a toll on you. So I'm wondering if you're up for something different. The skills I'd like to introduce you to are completely and radically different from everything else you've mentioned. A brand new way of responding to your feelings. Would you be up for that?"

Many clients will say yes; some will say they don't know; and a few will ask anxiously, "What does it involve?" Whatever they say, we reply, "Well, let me take you through a little exercise to help you understand what's involved." We then move on to…

Dropping the Struggle

Following creative hopelessness, we introduce a metaphor about dropping the struggle with difficult thoughts and feelings, and this signposts the route to acceptance. My favorite metaphor for this purpose is Pushing Away Paper (chapter two) because it quickly highlights the costs of experiential avoidance and the benefits of acceptance. At the end of the exercise, the paper is still present, emphasizing this is not a way to get rid of unwanted thoughts and feelings. Nor is it a way to dismiss or ignore them; the exercise highlights that painful emotions hold valuable information, but we can't utilize it if we're busy pushing them away.

If Pushing Away Paper is inappropriate (e.g., because the client or therapist has neck or shoulder problems), a good alternative is the Struggle Switch metaphor (Harris, 2007).

The Struggle Switch

Therapist: Imagine that at the back of our mind is a "struggle switch." When it's switched on, it means we're going to struggle against any physical or emotional pain that comes our way; whatever discomfort shows up, we'll try our best to get rid of it or avoid it.

Suppose what shows up is anxiety. (*We modify this to fit the client's issue; instead of anxiety it may be anger, sadness, painful memories, urges to drink, and so on.*) If my struggle switch is on, then I absolutely have to get rid of that feeling! It's like, *Oh no! Here's that horrible feeling again. Why does it keep coming back? How do I get rid of it?* So now I've got anxiety about my anxiety.

In other words, my anxiety just got worse. *Oh, no! It's getting worse! Why does it do that?* Now I'm even more anxious. Then I might get angry about my anxiety: *It's not fair. Why does this keep happening?* Or I might get depressed about my anxiety: *Not again. Why do I always feel like this?* And all of these secondary emotions are useless, unpleasant, unhelpful, and a drain on my energy and vitality. And then—guess what? I get anxious or depressed about that! Spot the vicious cycle!

But now suppose my struggle switch is off. In that case, whatever feeling shows up, no matter how unpleasant, I don't struggle with it. So anxiety shows up, but this time I don't struggle. It's like, *Okay, here's a knot in my stomach. Here's tightness in my chest. Here's sweaty palms and shaking legs. Here's my mind telling me a bunch of scary stories.* And it's not that I like it or want it. It's still unpleasant. But I'm not going to waste my time and energy struggling with it. Instead I'm going to take control of my arms and legs and put my energy into doing something that's meaningful and life enhancing.

So with the struggle switch off, our anxiety level is free to rise and fall as the situation dictates. Sometimes it'll be high, sometimes low; sometimes it will pass by very quickly, and sometimes it will hang around. But the great thing is, we're not wasting our time and energy struggling with it. So we can put our energy into doing other things that make our lives meaningful.

But switch it on, and it's like an emotional amplifier—we can have anger about our anger, anxiety about our anxiety, depression about our depression, or guilt about our guilt. (*At this point, we check in with the client:* "*Can you relate to this?*")

Without struggle, we get a natural level of discomfort—natural, given who we are and what we're doing. But once we start struggling, our discomfort levels increase rapidly. Our emotions get bigger, and stickier, and messier; hang around longer; and have much more impact on our behavior. So if we can learn how to turn off that struggle switch, it makes a big difference. And what I'd like to do next, if you're willing, is show you how to do that.

Other popular metaphors for dropping the struggle include "Tug of War with a Monster" and "Struggling in Quicksand" (Hayes et al., 1999; both described in Harris, 2019, *ACT Made Simple, 2nd edition*, pages 106–108). All these metaphors convey the concept of acceptance: what's involved, how it works, and the rationale behind it. But that's just the start. The next step is to actively teach acceptance skills, which we'll cover in the next chapter.

 EXTRA BIT In *Trauma-Focused ACT: The Extra Bits*, chapter twelve, you'll find (a) the "Join the DOTS" worksheet, (b) what to do when clients mention prescription medications, and (c) a link to a YouTube animation of the Struggle Switch metaphor.

Takeaway

Creative hopelessness undermines the agenda of emotional control by looking at it in terms of workability. This paves the way for acceptance. As long as we are kind and understanding, clients find this process validates their experience: they've tried hard to control the way they feel, but it's not working over the long term and life is getting worse.

We first explore three basic questions: What have you tried? How has it worked? What has it cost? We then acknowledge how hard they have worked, compassionately validate the client's emotional reaction, and ask whether they are open to trying something different. If the answer is yes, we follow up with a metaphor about dropping the struggle, which sets the stage for actively learning acceptance skills.

(e.g., cognitions, emotions, sensations, memories). The aim in models that embrace this concept of exposure is to (a) get clients in contact with stimuli they fear, and (b) maintain that contact until distress or anxiety significantly lowers.

The problem is, this popular concept of exposure is based on scientific research that is now quite old, and somewhat questionable. In contrast, *inhibitory learning theory* offers a contemporary account of exposure, which differs significantly from older models (Arch & Craske, 2011; Craske et al., 2014). Inhibitory learning theory (IHL) suggests that habituation is *not* the main mechanism for positive behavioral change following exposure.

IHL proposes that when clients contact fear-evoking stimuli during exposure, they learn new, more effective ways of responding—and these new learnings then inhibit (but do not eliminate) older responses. The research referenced in the previous paragraph shows there is no correlation between the drop in distress/anxiety during exposure and the positive behavioral changes that result.

Said differently, even when clients have no change at all in distress/anxiety levels during exposure, significant positive behavioral change can happen. And on the flipside, clients may have large drops in distress/anxiety during exposure without any positive behavioral change at all. (If you're surprised by this, please do read the papers referenced above; times are changing, and IHL increasingly influences many models of therapy.)

In summary then, according to IHL, when effective behavior change occurs through exposure, it is not because of a drop in anxiety or distress, but from learning new, more flexible responses that inhibit the old, ineffective ones.

Now ACT's model of exposure is not *identical* to that of IHL, but the two are extremely similar and complementary. In ACT, we define exposure as "organized contact with *repertoire-narrowing stimuli* to facilitate *response flexibility*." Again, let's unpack that.

By "repertoire-narrowing," we mean that when we contact these stimuli, our behavior narrows down to a small range of rigid, ineffective responses. "Repertoire-narrowing stimuli" is a much bigger category than "fear-evoking stimuli." Repertoire-narrowing stimuli may evoke fear, sadness, guilt, shame, anger, or any other emotion. Our primary concern is not what emotions these stimuli evoke, but the narrow behavioral repertoires they cue.

To understand ACT-style exposure, see the choice point diagram below. Repertoire-narrowing stimuli—emotions, cognitions, situations—are at the bottom. ("Situations" include any context where you can see, hear, touch, taste, or smell repertoire-narrowing stimuli in the external world, such as people, places, objects, events, and activities.) Away moves are the narrow repertoires that result from repertoire-narrowing stimuli.

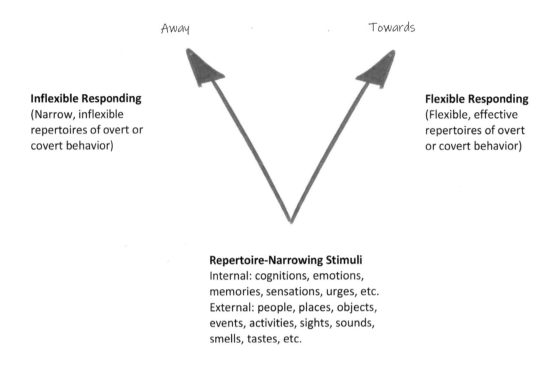

Away   Towards

Inflexible Responding
(Narrow, inflexible
repertoires of overt or
covert behavior)

Flexible Responding
(Flexible, effective
repertoires of overt
or covert behavior)

Repertoire-Narrowing Stimuli
Internal: cognitions, emotions,
memories, sensations, urges, etc.
External: people, places, objects,
events, activities, sights, sounds,
smells, tastes, etc.

In ACT, the aim of exposure is not to reduce distress or anxiety (although this commonly occurs). Rather, it is to respond more flexibly to repertoire-narrowing stimuli so you can be more effective in doing things that create a meaningful life. "Response flexibility" includes emotional flexibility, cognitive flexibility, and behavioral flexibility. And on the choice point, these flexible responses are called towards moves. (John Forsyth and Georg Eifert clearly laid out the procedures for ACT-style exposure in their 2005 textbook, *ACT for Anxiety Disorders* [Eifert & Forsyth, 2005]; TFACT builds upon that excellent foundation.)

So what has all this got to do with acceptance? Well, when we turn with openness and curiosity toward difficult, painful, or threatening private experiences that we usually try to avoid—and we willingly allow them to be present without letting them control our behavior—that *is* exposure! It's organized contact with repertoire-narrowing stimuli, to facilitate response flexibility.

Of course, there are many private experiences we find easy to accept: pleasant emotions, happy memories, comforting thoughts, and so on; accepting those experiences is *not* exposure. But when we accept *difficult, unwanted* emotions and cognitions that usually trigger problematic behavior—*that* is exposure.

Graded Exposure

"Graded exposure" means gradually exposing yourself to repertoire-narrowing stimuli in a way that enables you to remain psychologically flexible at each step. Earlier, I mentioned the gym metaphor: you don't go straight for the heaviest weights; you start with light ones and build up over time. The same principle applies with graded exposure; we encourage clients to develop their acceptance skills over time: begin with less challenging private experiences, work up to more difficult ones.

For example, when clients are highly avoidant of anxiety, we may initially focus on accepting just one physical sensation—like a racing heart or a knot in the stomach. We could then choose another one, and so on. From there, we can move on to other components of anxiety, such as thoughts and urges, until the client can accept all aspects of the experience. Here's a playful way to communicate this:

Therapist:	Do you know that old joke, "How do you eat an elephant?"
Client:	(*smiling*) One mouthful at a time.
Therapist:	Corny as it is, there's a lot of wisdom in that joke. Rather than trying to deal with some massive overwhelming emotion, we want to focus on one small bit at a time.

THE THREE COMPONENTS OF AN EMOTION

There are three experiential components to any emotion: sensations, urges, and cognitions. We can work with any of these elements during exposure and acceptance.

Sensations

For many people (but not everyone), physical sensations in the body are the predominant experiential aspect of an emotion. For example, with anxiety, clients may notice muscle tension, shaking, sweating, numbness, knots in the stomach, a lump in the throat, tightness in the chest, a racing heart, and so on.

Urges

All emotions come with urges and impulses. With anxiety, there may be urges to worry, seek reassurance, take drugs, drink alcohol, smoke a cigarette, distract oneself, leave a situation, and so on.

Cognitions

Cognitions are an intrinsic element of all emotions and urges. For example, when experiencing anxiety, clients may have thoughts like *I've screwed it up, Something bad is going to happen, I can't stand this,* and so on. Note that "cognitions" is a broader term than "thoughts." Cognitions may include the labels we give to the experience (e.g., anxious, nervous, jittery, shaken), the meaning we make of it (e.g., "I feel scared so that means I'm in danger"), and the images or memories that go with it.

As you'd expect, we use defusion to work with the cognitive component of emotions, so since we've already covered that, we'll now focus on the other elements: sensations and urges. (You'll notice, though, that I often talk about "emotions, urges, or sensations" for ease of discussion.)

Values-Guided Exposure

In ACT, the primary aim of exposure is to help people live by their values so they can build more meaningful lives. This is a big difference from other models, where the primary aim is to reduce anxiety or distress, and we need to make it explicit before formal exposure begins:

Therapist: (immediately following the Pushing Away Paper exercise) So I just want to be clear about the main benefit of learning how to do this. It's so that when these difficult thoughts and feelings show up, instead of doing away moves, like (mentions problematic behaviors the client commonly does in response to the emotion), you can do towards moves, things that help you build the sort of life you want. So is it okay if we take a moment just to clarify what those towards moves are?

We now help the client to reconnect with their towards moves, recapping the values or goals previously established. (And if we don't yet have this information, we need to gather it now, as outlined in chapter five.) We can repeatedly use this information to facilitate acceptance:

Therapist: So let's just take a moment to really get in touch with what this is all about. We're doing this work so that you can be more like the sort of dad you really want to be—patient with the kids, playing with them more. And it's also about the husband you want to be—more loving, more giving, more open.

In the worst-case scenario, if the client can't identify any towards moves at all, we have two options, both equally valid:

A. We put acceptance on hold and move into values clarification, as described in chapter fifteen; then return to it later, once values-based goals are established.

B. We carry on with acceptance but use vague, generic terms, such as "self-caring" or "caring for others" as values, and "building a better life" as a goal. We would say, "So for now, how about we say your main motivations are 'self-caring' and 'building a better life'?"

Actively Building Acceptance Skills Through Exposure

Everything we've covered in the previous chapter and this one paves the way for actively learning acceptance skills. So now we need to use exposure techniques to bring an emotion or urge into the room:

Therapist: If you were learning to play guitar, we'd need to have a guitar here for you to practice on. And it's the same with these new skills for handling emotions—we need to bring the emotion into the room, so we can work with it. I'm wondering, are you feeling it at all, right now?

If a difficult emotion, urge, or sensation is already present, then we start working with it. But if not, we need to evoke it, as described below. Anxiety is the main emotion that clients with trauma-related disorders try to avoid. But it's rarely if ever the only one; anger, shame, sadness, guilt, and loneliness are also commonly avoided. The good news is, acceptance skills are transferrable: we can use the same tools and techniques with any emotion, sensation, or urge, including feelings of numbness, emptiness, and physical pain. So we can help clients develop acceptance skills with any unwanted feeling that arises.

For example, suppose the client really struggles with sadness, but they can't tap into it during the session. If so, they are likely to feel frustration, disappointment, or anxiety—in which case, we work with *those* emotions instead. Fortunately, the strategies below work well to help most clients access difficult emotions.

RELIVE A MEMORY

We can help the client to relive a memory of a time where they were intensely feeling this sensation or urge. (At this point in therapy, we don't want clients to deliberately recall traumatic memories; there are many precautions we need to take for such work, as discussed in chapter thirty. So we help the client pick a memory of something moderately stressful, but not traumatic. And if we can't safely do that, it's better not to use this particular method.) Useful questions to ask include:

- Can you recall the last time you were feeling this urge/sensation?

- Can you describe it to me as if it's happening right now? Where are you? What can you see and hear? Who are you with? What's going on? What are you feeling?

Once the client contacts their emotion in the memory, we can ask:

- And as you're sitting here with me, right now, is that feeling starting to show up? Can you feel it in your body at all?

IMAGINE A FUTURE SCENARIO

We can help the client vividly imagine a forthcoming difficult situation, and ask the same questions as above:

- Can you describe it to me as if it's happening right now? Where are you? What can you see and hear? Who are you with? What's going on? What are you feeling?

And again, once the client contacts the emotion in the imaginary scenario, we can ask:

- And as you're sitting here with me, right now, is that feeling showing up at all?

DO AVOIDED TASKS

If clients are avoiding difficult tasks, such as making a phone call, sending an email, starting a study assignment, making an appointment, writing a resume, researching a job, joining a group, putting in an application, and so on, we can encourage them to do these things during the session.

LET YOUR GUARD DOWN

Some clients "keep their guard up" in session (i.e., do things that give them a sense of safety and protection, such as covering their legs with a coat, adopting an arms-folded posture, or keeping their cell phone switched on and by their side). We could encourage them to experiment with changing that: put aside the coat, unfold their arms and adopt a more open posture, or put the phone away.

SET CHALLENGING GOALS

Almost always, when we start actively setting goals in session that are going to pull the client out of their comfort zone, difficult sensations and urges will show up: feelings of anxiety or urges to change the topic, end the session, or stop the exercise.

URGE-EVOKING EXERCISES

In session, we may be able to organize contact with stimuli that usually trigger urges for the client. For example, if smoking or binge eating is the issue, you might ask the client to bring in a pack of cigarettes or a sample of the food they binge on, and ask the client to look, touch, taste, or smell these items and notice the urges that arise.

For the urge surfing exercise described later in this chapter, I like to work with urges to swallow. The client places a grape, or a piece of chewy candy such as Mentos, on top of their tongue and lets it sit there, without chewing or swallowing. Saliva rapidly builds up—and with it, the urge to swallow. We then coach the client to acknowledge and allow the urges to swallow or chew, without acting on them. (See Extra Bits for a script.)

FEAR-EVOKING EXERCISES

To evoke fear and anxiety, there are many well-established techniques we can draw upon that are used in many other models, such as asking clients to hyperventilate. We cover these in chapter twenty: "Compassionate, Flexible Exposure."

ANTICIPATORY ANXIETY

Often, just anticipating the forthcoming exercise is enough to trigger anxiety—in which case, we can work with that:

Therapist: I'm wondering, now that you're about to take the plunge and practice this new skill, what kind of feelings are showing up?

Client:	I'm a bit nervous.
Therapist:	Okay. So how about we work with your nervousness? Where are you feeling this in your body?

In addition, the urge to avoid the exercise almost always arises:

Therapist:	Are you noticing any urge to try to get out of the exercise?
Client:	Err, yeah.
Therapist:	How about we work with that urge? Where are you feeling this in your body? Are you tensing up anywhere? Noticing any impulses in your arms, legs, hands, feet?

Safety and Defusion Before Intense Experiential Work

As we do this work, all the safety factors discussed earlier come into play. This includes checking that the client is genuinely willing (not coerced); continually tracking their responses, to ensure they're within their window of flexibility (i.e., able to focus, engage, and control their physical actions); and dropping anchor as needed, to keep them within that window. It's also wise to preempt fusion: "As we do this, your mind is probably going to say some unhelpful things, so see if you can let it chatter away in the background, like music playing in a supermarket."

If fusion does arise during the exercise (e.g., "This is silly," "I can't do it"), we notice and name ("So notice what your mind is doing here") or normalize and acknowledge the purpose. ("It's natural to have thoughts like that. It's a challenging exercise, and your mind wants to save you from the discomfort.") Alternatively, we can link to values: "Let's take a moment to connect with why you're doing this in the first place… (*Therapist recaps the client's values and goals.*) So can we keep going, even though your mind says 'It's bullshit'?" And if all that is still not enough, we can bring in the "big three" from chapter eleven: write, move, expand awareness.

NAME the Emotion

Once a difficult emotion or urge is present, we can start cultivating acceptance. (And there's a huge range of exercises we can draw upon; the few we cover here are the tip of the iceberg.) One popular practice is to NAME the emotion or urge (Harris, 2009b). The acronym, NAME, stands for:

N—Notice the sensations

A—Acknowledge by name

M—Make room

E—Expand awareness

Using these components, we go through an exercise with our client to help them develop acceptance.

NOTICE THE SENSATIONS

The NAME process begins with noticing the physical sensations of an emotion or urge:

Therapist: So where are you noticing this in your body?

Client: My chest.

Therapist: What's it like in there?

Client: It's tight. Feels kind of hard to breathe.

Therapist: Anything else you notice in there?

Client: My heart!

Therapist: What's it doing?

Client: Pounding away.

Therapist: Okay—so tight chest, pounding heart. Anywhere else you're feeling this?

Client: Errr—my throat.

Therapist: Yeah? What's the feeling in there?

Client: It's kind of—like a lump there. Like I can't swallow.

We continue this for a minute or so, identifying what the sensations are like and where they are in the body. Often, we ask leading questions: "Are you feeling anything in your face? Noticing anything in your jaws? How about in your throat? Neck? Shoulders? Chest? Abdomen?"

If we're working with an urge, we'd ask, "Are you noticing the urge or impulse to do something? Is there anywhere in your body you particularly feel that? Is any part of your body tensing up, getting fidgety or jittery? Are you noticing any tension in your arms, legs, back, shoulders, neck?"

ACKNOWLEDGE BY NAME

Therapist: So what would you call this emotion?

Client: It's anxiety!!!

Therapist:	Okay. Could you just take a moment to acknowledge this feeling by name? Say "I'm noticing anxiety."
Client:	I'm noticing anxiety.
Therapist:	Does it make any difference when you say that?
Client:	Not really.
Therapist:	Okay, so can we try that again, but this time, a bit differently—and as well as saying the words, see if you can *really notice* what you're feeling. The idea is to help you sort of step back and watch the anxiety, instead of being in the thick of it. Have you ever been outside when it suddenly starts pouring rain—and then you take shelter in a doorway or something—and you can watch it pouring down without getting drenched by it?
Client:	Yeah.
Therapist:	So noticing and naming what you're feeling usually helps you do the same thing; it doesn't stop the anxiety, just helps you step back a little, so you can watch it.
Client:	Okay.
Therapist:	Cool. So this time, say, "I'm having a feeling of anxiety, and I'm noticing it in my chest, throat, and tummy."
Client:	"I'm having a feeling of anxiety, and I'm noticing it in my chest and throat and tummy."
Therapist:	Any difference that time? Any sense of stepping back, watching it?
Client:	Yeah, it did kind of help me to do that, a little.

Noticing sensations and acknowledging them by name can sometimes have dramatic effects—and occasionally, no effect at all. Most clients will be somewhere in between these extremes. If there's little or no obvious benefit, we take that in stride: "Okay," "Cool," "No worries," or some similar response, delivered with warmth and openness.

If a client is finding it hard to name an emotion, we can make suggestions: "Is it sadness, maybe?" And if they are using more colloquial language (e.g., "nerves," "jittery," "shaky"), we might say, "Sounds like that might be anxiety?" Naming urges is much simpler: "I'm noticing the urge to shout," "Here is the urge to smoke," and so on.

Practical Tip

There's rarely only one painful emotion showing up, so it's often helpful to ask about others (e.g., "Is it all anxiety—or are there other feelings too? Any sadness or anger or shame?")

We can also usefully speak metaphorically about "layers" of emotion: "Often underneath our anger, there's another emotion—like fear or guilt or sadness. See if you can peel off the top layer; is there maybe something else underneath?" If other emotions are present, we work with whichever the client finds most difficult.

MAKE ROOM FOR IT

We have a huge range of techniques for helping clients to open up and make room for these difficult sensations, and usually we combine several. Popular methods include:

- **Noting Properties:** noticing and describing the physical properties of a feeling—size, shape, temperature, movement, borders, and so on

- **Physicalizing:** imagining the feeling as if it's a physical object

- **Breathing into it:** imagining, sensing, or visualizing your breath flowing into and around the feeling

- **Expansion:** using the metaphor of expanding around the feeling

Throughout this process we encourage the client to observe the feeling with genuine openness and curiosity. For example:

Therapist:	So out of all those different areas, where is it bothering you most?
Client:	In my gut.
Therapist:	Okay. So see if you can observe this feeling as if you're a curious scientist who's never seen anything quite like this.
Client:	Okay.
Therapist:	And you're focusing in on just this one feeling, in your tummy...
Client:	Right.
Therapist:	And just like a scientist, you're aiming to discover something new here—maybe something you've never noticed before.
Client:	I normally try not to notice it!

Therapist:	That's right. This is the very opposite of what you usually do. Are we okay to keep going?
Client:	Okay.
Therapist:	(*noting properties*) So can you give me a sense of the shape and size of this feeling? Like, with your finger, could you trace the outline for me?
Client:	(*tracing a circular shape, mid-abdomen*) It's mostly here.
Therapist:	And flat like a pancake, or more like a 3D object?
Client:	It's like a ball.
Therapist:	A ball? Right. And where is it sitting? Like is it at the surface or deep inside or…
Client:	Err, it's quite deep—sort of right in the middle.
Therapist:	And what's the temperature in there? Are there any hot spots or cold spots?
Client:	Errmm—it's, it's—I never thought about it before—It's kind of hot.

In addition to the above questions, we could ask:

- Is it moving or still?

- Light or heavy?

- Are the edges well defined or vague and blurry?

- Can you notice any vibration or pulsation or movement within it?

- Is there any pressure in there?

- Any burning, tingling, throbbing, cutting?

After this, we may move into "physicalizing" (Hayes et al., 1999):

Therapist:	(*physicalizing*) Now, I'm wondering if you could imagine this feeling as if it's a physical object inside you.
Client:	Okay.
Therapist:	So is it liquid, solid, or gaseous?
Client:	Solid.
Therapist:	And light, heavy, or weightless?

Client:	Oh, heavy.
Therapist:	And if it had a color, what would that be?
Client:	Black.
Therapist:	So it's like a hot, heavy, solid, black ball—in the middle of your tummy.

In addition to the above questions, we could ask:

- Is it transparent or opaque?

- All one color, or several?

- If you could reach in and touch the surface, what would it be like: rough, smooth, wet, dry?

Keep in mind, a small number of people find visualization extremely difficult (I'm one of them); so if clients struggle with these visual elements—skip 'em! And note: there's no attempt to change the feeling (e.g., make the ball smaller or dissolve it). Often that kind of change spontaneously happens, but it's not something we're aiming for; the purpose of the exercise is to accept the feeling *as it is*. So if it does reduce in size and intensity: nice bonus, not the main aim.

The next step is to breathe into the feeling, which most people find quite soothing. (But if it triggers unpleasant reactions, skip it.)

Therapist:	(*breathing into it*) Now see if you can gently breathe into this—no big dramatic breaths—just gently, breathing in, and imagining your breath flowing into and around this feeling... (*Therapist pauses for a few seconds, as client does this.*)...that's it, slowly and gently... (*pause*)...breathing into it... (*pause*)...breathing around it... (*pause*)...not trying to get rid of it, just letting it be there, and breathing into it... (*pause*)...are we okay to keep going?
Client:	Yeah, we can.
Therapist:	(*expanding around it*) Great...so as you're breathing into it, keep observing this feeling...look at it from all angles...from the front and the back, the top and the bottom...and see if you can kind of open up around it...kind of like you're expanding around it, making lots of space for it...and just taking a moment to connect with why you're doing this—so you can be more playful with the kids, more loving with your wife, more like the dad and husband you want to be...and in the service of those values, opening up and making room for this feeling...and are we still okay to keep going here?
Client:	Yeah, yeah.

Therapist:	So I'm wondering, is it getting any easier to let this feeling be there? To just kind of have it there, without fighting it?
Client:	Well, I don't really like it...
Therapist:	Of course not. Who would? I'm not expecting you to like it at all, I'm just wondering if you're getting that sense of just letting it be, without struggling?
Client:	Yeah, yeah. I'm getting that.
Therapist:	So on a scale of zero to ten, where ten means no struggle at all, "I'm absolutely willing to make room for this feeling (*extends her arms outward and sideways in a posture of openness, to accentuate the point*) and let it be here, even though it's awful"; and zero means "I absolutely have to get rid of this feeling right now (*crosses her arms tightly across her chest, in a posture of closing off*), I can't bear it a moment longer, I need it gone"; and five is the halfway point we call tolerating it or putting up with it...where are you now on that scale?
Client:	Ten is no struggle?
Therapist:	Right—you're absolutely willing to have it, without fighting it, no matter how bad it is.
Client:	I'm probably a seven.
Therapist:	That's great. Can we keep going with this, a bit longer?
Client:	Okay.
Therapist:	Great. So, keep observing this feeling. And notice...this feeling is not you; it's something passing through you, just like clouds pass through the sky.

Note how the therapist introduced a willingness scale, where ten = complete willingness (i.e., zero avoidance, complete acceptance), and zero = no willingness (i.e., zero acceptance, maximal avoidance). This is a useful subjective measure of experiential acceptance. In some sessions, clients may reach a ten, but often they don't—and that's not a problem. (I'm sure you can relate to this; at times, we're pretty good at accepting painful feelings; at other times, we suck at it.) Over time, with practice, we expect clients to improve their acceptance skills; if they can reach a seven, that's a good start.

Kind Hands

Often at this point, we bring in the Kind Hands exercise to foster self-compassion:

Therapist:	I invite you to take one of your hands and turn it palm upward (*client does so*) and see if you can fill that hand with a sense of real kindness...you've used this hand in a lot of kind ways in your life, right? Did you cuddle your babies, when they were upset?
Client:	For sure.
Therapist:	Hold your kids' hands when they were scared?
Client:	Uh-huh.
Therapist:	Used it to help other people lift things, move things, do things?
Client:	Yep.
Therapist:	So see if you can get a sense of that kindness and support that you've given to others, and in some way, put it into this hand right now—as if your hand is filling up with kindness.
Client:	Okay.
Therapist:	Now I'm going to give you a choice here—either rest this hand gently on top of your tummy, or, if you prefer not to actually touch, just hover it slightly over the surface. (*The therapist takes their own hand and rests it on their own tummy, to demonstrate. The client follows suit.*) Great. And see if you can send that kindness inward—you might feel it, or imagine it, or sense it—a sense of warmth and kindness and support, flowing into you.

Some clients, for reasons discussed in chapter eight, do not want to touch their body, so always give them the option of letting their hand hover, rather than directly touching. Another option is to cup their hands together, rest them in their lap, and then imagine, feel, or sense the kindness "filling up the cup"; and from there, flowing up the arms, into the body, and into the pain (or numbness).

Therapist:	And see if you can send that warmth and kindness into and around this feeling... breathing into it...expanding around it...see if you can soften up around it, hold it gently...hold it like it's a crying baby, that needs comforting...and what's happening?
Client:	(*eyes slightly teary, voice softer*) It's err—yeah—I'm, err—it's good (*breathes a sigh of relief*).
Therapist:	Okay to keep going?
Client:	Yeah.

Therapist: Ten is complete willingness to have this feeling, zero is totally unwilling, five is tolerating it. What are you at now?

Client: I'm at a nine.

EXPAND AWARENESS

We end with E: *Expand awareness* (similar to *Engage*, in dropping anchor). Returning to our Kind Hands exercise…

Kind Hands: Conclusion

Therapist: So in finishing up, notice there's anxiety here…and also notice that sense of opening up, making room for it, letting it be…and notice that around this feeling you have a body…and perhaps, having a stretch?… (*therapist stretches, client copies*)…and also noticing the room around you…what you can see and hear…and breathing in the air, noticing what that's like…and noticing you and me here, working together, (*playfully*) doing these weird exercises (*client smiles*)… So how was that?

What Do I Do Next?

As a part of debriefing the exercise, we say: "So, the question is, after you've done this, what next? Well, if what you're doing is important, meaningful, life enhancing—then you keep doing it, and give it your full attention; really focus on it, and get absorbed in it. But if it's not really important or taking you toward the life you want, then the idea is to stop, and do something else that is."

Usually, by this point in therapy, we've already explored questions like "If this urge/emotion wasn't controlling you, what would you do differently?" But if not, now is a good time to do so. Of course, some clients have no idea what to do differently, in which case we can make suggestions, such as scheduling pleasant activities (chapter sixteen) or doing self-soothing practices (chapter twenty-three).

When Clients Can't Label Their Emotions

Some people have little or no ability to name their emotions. Technically this is known as "alexithymia"—which, in Greek, means "no words for feelings." In such cases, we work on emotional literacy: teaching clients to distinguish and label different emotions, much as we would a young child. When we see evidence that the client is feeling something (e.g., they look or sound angry, sad, anxious, guilty), we ask them to tune into their body, notice where they are feeling it, what it's like, and what they feel like doing. We can then help them label the emotion: "You feel like crying and curling up into a ball? Tears in your eyes? Heavy chest? That is sadness"; "You feel like yelling, hitting, smashing things? Fists clenched? Jaws tight? Heart pounding? That's anger." And so on. We may start with the "big four"—sad, mad, glad, scared (sadness, anger, joy, fear)—and then gradually expand the repertoire. (With a quick google search, you'll find many free "emotion charts," useful for this work.)

Duration of Exercises

Most acceptance exercises last from two to twenty minutes. The duration varies hugely, though, depending on the client's issues, their level of experiential avoidance, and the ACT skills they already have. For example, with a client extremely high in experiential avoidance, phobic of their own emotions, we might start with a sixty-second exercise. Next time, we may increase it to ninety seconds, and after that, to two minutes, and so on.

Practical Tip

The longer the duration, the more important it is to regularly connect with values throughout the exercise. We might say, for example, "And just take a moment to connect with why we're doing this" or "And remind me, what's this in the service of?"

Surfing Urges and Emotions

The term "urge surfing" was originally coined by psychologists Alan Marlatt and Judith Gordon as part of their mindfulness-based approach to working with drug addiction (Marlatt & Gordon, 1985). It's an acceptance technique utilizing the metaphor that urges are like waves: they rise, peak, and then fall. (The same metaphor also applies to emotions.) And the idea is to "surf" the wave, rather than resist it. This means you observe the inner experience mindfully—and allow it to rise and peak and fall again, without acting on it. We can bring in surfing exercises either as an addition to or as an alternative to NAME exercises.

INTRODUCING THE WAVE METAPHOR

Therapist:	You know how a wave in the ocean starts off small, then it gathers speed, and it grows bigger and bigger, until it reaches a peak—and then it gradually subsides?
Client:	Yeah?
Therapist:	Well, the same thing happens with emotions and urges. They're like waves. As long as we don't resist them, they rise, they peak, and they fall—usually quite quickly. But if you resist a wave, what happens?
Client:	You get slammed.
Therapist:	Yep, the wave smashes you around. So the aim in this exercise is to make room for those waves—to surf them, instead of resisting them.

BUT MY WAVES LAST FOREVER!

Sometimes clients will protest that their waves go on and on and on for ages. We would compassionately validate, "Yes, that's right. At the moment, they do. And there's a good reason for it. It's because you're doing the same thing that we *all* naturally, instinctively do: you're resisting them."

Following that, we would recap what the client usually does in response to urges/emotions. We might say, "And what I mean by that is you tend to…*here, we recap a few of the client's main inflexible responses: fight with them, ruminate about them, worry about them, try to distract yourself, try to push them away*)…and whenever we respond to them that way, it makes them go on for ages. No one ever taught you how to surf them, so you've never experienced what I'm talking about; but what you'll find when you try it is that the waves usually rise and fall pretty quickly."

HOW TO SURF

Urge surfing and emotion surfing exercises utilize the basic steps of NAME. To surf an urge or emotion—rather than be "slammed," "dunked," or "wiped out" by it—you first *Notice* the sensations and *Acknowledge* the experience by name. Then, in the *Make room* phase, you use the metaphor of a wave: observing the experience as it rises, peaks, and falls. We can ask clients to rate the wave, on a scale of zero to ten: ten is the strongest this urge or emotion has ever been (the highest peak ever), and zero means it has completely disappeared.

Therapist:	How strong is it now?
Client:	It's about a seven.
Therapist:	Can we keep going?
Client:	Okay.
Therapist:	Remember, no matter how big that wave gets, it can't get bigger than you. And if you give it enough space, then sooner or later it will peak, and then subside. So breathe into it, open up around it, make lots of space…
Client:	I hate it.
Therapist:	So notice your mind, trying to hook you… Can you let your mind have its say, and carry on?
Client:	Okay.
Therapist:	And what's the wave up to now?
Client:	It's a nine, I think.
Therapist:	Okay. So keep observing. Notice where you're feeling it. Let it be there.

Client:	Okay.
Therapist:	And remind me—what values is this in the service of?
Client:	Caring.
Therapist:	For who?
Client:	For myself, my family.
Therapist:	Cool. So let's go back to that willingness scale again—zero to ten, in the service of caring for yourself and your family, how willing are you to make room for this wave?
Client:	About an eight.
Therapist:	Great. So keep observing the wave. And notice...the wave is not you; it's something passing through you. Zero to ten, what's the wave at now?
Client:	It's going down. I think it's about seven.
Therapist:	Interesting.

Waves usually rise and fall within three to ten minutes—urges typically faster than emotions. The exercise finishes with the E of NAME: *Expand awareness*. (This is the same as in the Kind Hands exercise, so I won't repeat it here.)

When discussing the exercise afterward, we clarify:

- While the waves typically rise and fall quite quickly, they often don't go all the way to zero.

- This isn't a way to control waves or make them go away; we are simply making room for them, allowing them to rise and fall in their own good time. In challenging situations, the waves will continue to rise and fall—and then rise and fall again—and so on.

- If we make room for the wave to flow through us, we won't get slammed or swept away by it, and it often falls more quickly than we expect. This frees us up to do important, meaningful, life-enhancing things.

Debriefing and Homework

When debriefing any exercise, we ask how the client found it, what they got out of it, and how it could be helpful outside of session. We also link it back to values: "This is very different from what you've been doing, and being a new skill, it's naturally tricky and challenging. So take a moment to acknowledge that you're doing this in the service of something important..."

For homework, we encourage regular practice, supported by audio recordings and handouts (see Extra Bits). Naturally, we want to encourage as much practice as possible—while at the same time tailoring this for each unique client, given they vary enormously in how much they're willing to do. This is a good time to revisit the weight-lifting metaphor:

> *Therapist:* You know all those little moments throughout the day when you're *a bit* anxious or sad or irritable—not having a full-blown emotional storm, but just *a bit* worked up, *mildly* stressed—well, think of those as "the "light weights." Practice on those to build up your "psychological muscles," and then work up to the "heavy weights," those really intense emotions. The ideal plan would be to practice at least one long exercise—using the audio recording, if you like—at least once a day daily, but also fit in as many short versions as you can, at times when you're a *bit* stressed or wound up.

Catching Experiential Avoidance "In the Act"

Experiential avoidance typically shows up in many different ways throughout a session, especially "gating" and "skating." By "gating," I mean behaviors intended to lock up or hold back emotions. Clients may do this through biting their lips, clenching their teeth, sighing, looking away, going silent, shifting their position in the chair, changing their body posture (e.g., folding arms, covering eyes), leaving the room, reaching for tissues, shrugging, fidgeting, digging their nails into their palms, laughing in a forced or inappropriate way, and so on.

By "skating," I mean skating over the surface of particular topics and issues, to avoid the painful emotions that go with them: *Nothing much happened, can't recall, it was okay, that's old news, don't go there, all good, went well, nothing to report, no worries, next, moving on, oh you know what it's like, why dwell on it, it's over and done, who cares anyway, doesn't matter, same old shit, I'm over it.* This may include racing through a narrative, omitting important details, or rapidly changing the topic.

Obviously we don't tackle every bit of experiential avoidance; that would definitely alienate our clients. But it's often useful to shine a mindful spotlight on these behaviors and turn them into opportunities to practice acceptance. For example, in the transcript below, one of Ravi's therapy goals is to improve communication, connection, and intimacy with his partner. However, whenever the therapist asks about his feelings, Ravi pauses, strokes his chin, frowns, and then after a few seconds says, "That's an interesting question," or "I've never thought about it."

> *Therapist:* I notice that when I ask you about your feelings, you reply, "Interesting question" or "I've never thought about it." And I'm not sure if you're saying that because you don't want to talk about it, or because you find it difficult to know what your feelings are.
>
> *Client:* Yeah, that's an interesting question.
>
> *Therapist:* Ah, see, there it is again. Now I'm willing to be wrong about this, but my guess is, when you reply that way, it kind of helps you skate over some unpleasant feelings that you'd rather not contact. (*The therapist resists the urge to ask, "What do you think about that?" knowing it would only invite the client to get caught up in his*

thoughts.) The thing is, you really want to improve things with your partner, and one of the skills you need for that is the ability to tune into your feelings: to notice what they are and name them. Would you be willing to do this right now? Can I take you through an exercise to help you? (*The therapist now takes Ravi through a quick body scan and helps him to notice and name his feelings.*)

Going Further with Acceptance

The exercises above focus mainly on the first three As of acceptance (*acknowledge, allow, accommodate*). Let's look at ways to go further: the fourth A (*appreciate*), self-as-context, and flexible thinking.

APPRECIATE

Once clients are sitting with an emotion, making room for it, we may then segue into appreciation: "Our emotions are basically messengers, loaded with important information. So now that you've made some room for it, let's see if you can extract the wisdom from this emotion—tune into it, and see what it's offering."

We may then ask questions like:

- What is this emotion telling you to address or face up to?

- What is this emotion telling you to do differently?

- What is this emotion telling you really matters to you?

- (If we've done work on values) What values does this link to?

- (If we've worked on self-compassion) Can you use this feeling as a reminder to be kind to yourself?

- (If working on compassion, empathy, or connection with others) How can this emotion help you to understand others? Who in your life may be feeling something similar? What might help them at those times?

Questions like this quickly tap into values, needs, desires, or important issues that need to be addressed; so if there's still time in session, we can start translating this into values and committed action, as in chapters fifteen and sixteen.

Of course, a client might occasionally interpret an emotion in a way that is unhelpful. For example, when we step out of our comfort zone, emotions such as fear and anxiety are inevitable, but a client might interpret them as "telling me not to do it." If this happens, we can return to workability:

Therapist: So your sense is that these feelings are "telling you not to do it?"

Client:	Yeah, I think so.
Therapist:	Well, that's possible—but...if you follow that advice, where does it take you? Toward or away from the life you want?
Client:	Err, away. (*confused*) So, are you saying I should ignore it?
Therapist:	No. Not at all. I'm just wondering if there's another way to interpret this feeling, that might help you keep moving forward.
Client:	Errrmm—this is risky?
Therapist:	Yeah. "This is risky. It's new territory. Be cautious. Take care of yourself."
Client:	Right, yeah. It does feel risky.
Therapist:	Of course it does. You don't know what's going to happen. Anxiety tells you to be careful; prepare; look after yourself.

SELF-AS-CONTEXT

Throughout therapy, we repeat numerous variations of the above exercises, and as we do so, we can plant seeds for self-as-context (the noticing self). For example, it's often useful to end acceptance exercises with the ancient Sky and the Weather metaphor—which is thousands of years old, found in Hinduism, Buddhism, and Taoism.

The Sky and the Weather

Therapist:	Your thoughts and feelings are like the weather, always changing from moment to moment; sometimes pleasant and enjoyable; sometimes extremely unpleasant. But there's a part of you that can step back and notice those thoughts and feelings—just like you've been doing in this exercise. And that part of you is a lot like the sky. The sky always has room for the weather—no matter how bad it gets. The mightiest thunderstorm, the most turbulent hurricane, the most severe winter blizzard—these things cannot hurt the sky; and sooner or later the weather always changes. And sometimes we can't see the sky—it's obscured by clouds. But it's still there. And even when they are thick, dark thunderclouds, if we rise high enough above them, sooner or later we'll reach clear sky. So more and more, when the emotional weather is bad, you can learn to take the perspective of the sky: to safely observe your thoughts and feelings; to open up and make room for them.

In later sessions, we can repeatedly refer back to this: "You are not your emotions. See if you can open up and make room for this, like the sky makes room for the weather."

Similarly, when clients are surfing emotions or urges, we may say things like "A wave is not the ocean. Waves rise out of the ocean and go back into it. In the same way, you are not your emotions or urges—these things continually rise, and peak, and fall away."

THINKING FLEXIBLY ABOUT EMOTIONS

When an unwanted emotion is present, our mind often reacts to it in a harsh, judgmental way (e.g., *It's bad, horrible, awful, unbearable, getting in the way of my life; I have to get rid of it; it means something is wrong with me*). So as well as encouraging defusion from those judgments, we encourage new ways of thinking *about* them, to facilitate acceptance. For example, we may encourage clients to say to themselves:

- This emotion is normal; it's a normal reaction to a difficult situation.

- Emotions are like the weather, and I am like the sky.

- Emotions are like waves: they rise, and peak, and fall. This emotion is intense now, but soon it will pass.

- I have room for this feeling; no matter how big it gets, it can't get bigger than me.

- I'm willing to make room for this feeling, even though I don't like it.

- It can't harm me; I don't need to fight it or run from it.

- I don't have to let this control me; I can have this feeling and choose to act on my values.

- Like all feelings, this one will come and stay and go in its own good time. I don't need to fight it.

- Drop anchor, weather the storm.

- Make room for it.

- This is an opportunity to practice my new skills.

(You may notice the similarity between these responses and the popular CBT strategy "cognitive reappraisal"; the big difference is that cognitive reappraisal usually aims to reduce the emotion, whereas these cognitive reframes aim to accept it.)

EXTRA BIT   Chapter thirteen of *Trauma-Focused ACT: The Extra Bits* includes (a) a handout on practicing acceptance skills, (b) a script for urge surfing with a grape or Mentos, and (c) a link to an e-book on working with anger.

Takeaway

There are so many takeaways in this chapter. Here are the main ones:

- The four As of acceptance are *acknowledge, allow, accommodate, appreciate.*

- From an ACT perspective, emotion dysregulation means inflexible responding to emotions: fusion, avoidance, and unworkable action. The antidote is learning to respond flexibly.

- Identifying the positive functions of "negative" emotions—how they motivate, illuminate, and communicate—fosters acceptance.

- Exposure in ACT is defined as "organized contact with repertoire-narrowing stimuli, to facilitate response flexibility." When we practice acceptance of unwanted private experiences that trigger problematic behavior, that *is* exposure.

- Acceptance is always in the service of values and values-based goals.

CHAPTER FOURTEEN

Self-Compassion

There are numerous definitions of self-compassion. My own is very simple—just six words: "Acknowledge your pain, respond with kindness." In other words, self-compassion involves consciously acknowledging your pain, hurt, and suffering, and in response, treating yourself with kindness, caring, and support.

Self-compassion has always been an intrinsic part of ACT, but in the 80s and 90s it very much hovered in the background. John Forsyth and Georg Eifert brought it to center stage in the early 2000s (Eifert & Forsyth, 2005), and since then, it's stayed firmly in the spotlight. Self-compassion is important for everyone—especially when working with trauma. Many of our clients have not only experienced horrific events in the past but continue to face ongoing difficulties. They may be struggling with physical, emotional, psychological, or spiritual pain, often of the most extreme nature. So we aim to help them respond to their suffering with genuine kindness and caring. Unfortunately, this is easier said than done.

Words Matter!

For most people (practitioners included), self-compassion doesn't come naturally; we usually only learn it when we go down the path of therapy, self-help, or spiritual development. Far more commonly, we respond to our pain by:

- fighting with it

- trying to escape or avoid it

- fusing with it

- denying, trivializing, or dismissing it

- blaming, judging, and criticizing ourselves

- tolerating or "putting up" with it

- worrying, ruminating, or obsessing about it

Self-compassion is radically different from all of the above—so it's hardly surprising we encounter many misconceptions about it. Many people find it incredibly difficult; for those with entrenched self-hatred, it can trigger much anxiety. So it pays to go slowly, to introduce self-compassion gently and flexibly, one small step at a time. We can instigate it formally—that is, explain the concept, then do an exercise—or informally, which means we bring it fluidly into our experiential work without announcing "This is self-compassion." You saw an example of the informal approach in the last chapter, where the therapist introduced the Kind Hand exercise.

With the formal approach, the language we use is important because some clients react negatively to the term "self-compassion"; they equate it with being weak, selfish, or self-pitying or as something religious. So a simple way to introduce it—without using the word "self-compassion"—is with the Two Friends metaphor.

The Two Friends Metaphor

Therapist: Suppose you're traveling with a friend. And it's really tough. It's a dangerous journey and all sorts of terrible things keep happening. It's knocking you around, and you're really struggling to keep going. Now as you carry on with the journey, what kind of friend do you want by your side? A friend who says, "Ah, shut up! Stop your whining. I don't want to hear about it. Stop being such a wimp. Suck it up and get on with it!" or a friend who says, "This is really shit. But hey, we're in this together. I've got your back, and I'm with you every step of the way"?

Client: Yeah, I'd go for the second one.

Therapist: Yeah, me too. So what kind of friend are you being to yourself? More like the first or the second?

Client: The first.

Therapist: Yup, we all do it. We beat ourselves up, come down hard on ourselves. Most of us are pretty bad at being like the second friend. Would you be interested in learning how to do that?

Other useful metaphors to draw out the qualities of self-compassion include the friendly teacher or coach, who is warm, supportive, and encouraging (as opposed to harsh, critical, uncaring), or the loving parent who comforts and soothes the distressed child (as opposed to ignoring, criticizing, or yelling at them).

Self-Compassion and Secure Attachment

John Bowlby was a British psychiatrist who is best known as the originator of attachment theory (Bowlby, 1969). With trauma-related interpersonal issues, it's often useful to explain a bit about this theory because it makes sense of self-defeating behavior in relationships (see chapter twenty-eight).

Attachment Theory in a Nutshell

A newborn infant is totally helpless, entirely dependent on its caregivers for protection and nurture (without which, it dies). So thanks to millions of years of evolution, infants are born with strong instincts to seek out and stay close to caregivers who will protect and nurture them. To use Bowlby's terminology, infants make "bids" to their caregivers for closeness, companionship, comfort, protection, caretaking, reassurance, and sustenance. At birth, the basic bids are crying, whimpering, or scream-ing—but as a child grows, they develop many other ways of seeking protection and nurture.

If a caregiver responds positively to these bids—that is, if they reliably give the child nurture, comfort, and sustenance (and do so far more often than ignoring a bid or responding with hostility)—the child develops a "secure attachment style" within that relationship. In other words, the child learns that their caregiver (or "attachment figure") is safe, reliable, and responsive in meeting their needs, and therefore feels secure in that relationship. Not surprisingly, there is a strong correlation between secure attachment styles in childhood and the ability to form secure intimate relationships later in life.

Insecure attachment styles (of which there are several types) develop when a caregiver is *not* reli-able and responsive, when they ignore the child's bids or respond with hostility. This correlates with difficulties forming secure intimate relationships in later life—an almost universal problem following chronic childhood abuse or neglect.

Spot the Similarities

It's easy to see the similarities between self-compassion and secure attachment. When we are in pain, hurting, and suffering, we need comfort, reassurance, and nurture. Our painful thoughts and feelings are "cries of distress"—and, when we show self-compassion, we respond to these with kind-ness, caring, and support. And the more reliably and sensitively we do so, the greater the benefit. Over time, with the regular practice of self-compassion, we develop a "secure attachment style" with our-selves: a sense of trust in our own ability to support, nurture, and look after ourselves.

A similar process goes on in therapy: the client seeks solace, support, and security, and the thera-pist reliably responds with kindness and caring. (Indeed, for some clients, this may be the first such relationship they've ever had.)

Through values and committed action, we help clients build healthy loving relationships with others who will be there for them in kind and supportive ways. At the same time, we help them develop useful skills for actively supporting themselves, especially when lonely or isolated; self-compas-sion is foremost among them.

Building Blocks of Self-Compassion

Kristin Neff, the world's top researcher on self-compassion, describes self-compassion in terms of three processes: (a) mindfulness, (b) kindness, and (c) common humanity (Neff, 2003).

Mindfulness and kindness need no elaboration. "Common humanity" is Neff's term for that sense of commonality we feel when we recognize that others suffer as we do: that recognition that we're all in the same boat, struggling with "the human condition." When we transpose Neff's three elements onto the hexaflex, "mindfulness" maps onto defusion (unhooking from self-judgment), acceptance (opening up), and contacting the present moment (acknowledging your pain); and "kindness" maps onto values and committed action (kind words and actions). And if we take self-as-context to mean "flexible perspective taking," this is where common humanity goes. Diagramatically, it looks like this:

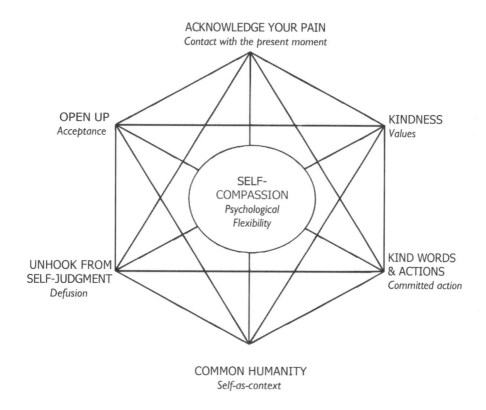

Self-Compassion and the Hexaflex

I think of this diagram as representing the six "building blocks" of self-compassion. We can work on any one (or several) of these building blocks at a time; and as therapy progresses, clients can "stack them up" into stronger, broader repertoires of self-compassion. Let's take a quick look at each one.

Acknowledging Pain

The first building block is usually the kind, caring, nonjudgmental noticing and naming of whatever is painful or difficult. We often need to distinguish this from self-pity:

Therapist: Acknowledging our pain means being honest with ourselves about how much this really hurts—without dwelling on it, wallowing in it, or turning it into self-pity. So, for example, we wouldn't say, "This is awful. I can't bear it any longer. I've never felt so bad. Why me? It's not fair." That's self-pity, which only makes things worse. We want to acknowledge our pain in a simple, kind, and honest way—just as you'd acknowledge the pain of a friend who was suffering.

If clients can't pinpoint the exact feeling(s), we can use terms like "suffering," "grief," "hurt," "loss," "pain," or "heartbreak," or phrases like "Here is suffering," "I'm noticing heartbreak," or "I'm having a feeling of emptiness." And it's often useful to include terms such as "here and now" or "in this moment." When we say, "Here and now, I'm noticing anxiety" or "In this moment, loneliness is present," this helps us to remember that thoughts and feelings are transient—continually changing, like the weather. Even amid times of the greatest suffering, our emotions keep changing; sometimes we feel better, other times, worse. "Here and now" we may be noticing anxiety; later we'll be noticing a different emotion.

Other phrases we could use include "This is an instant of," "This is a moment of" or "This is an experience of" (e.g., "This is a moment of great sorrow" or "This is an instant of frustration"). We can encourage clients to experiment with such words and find a phrase that resonates. Neff recommends "This is a moment of suffering"—a poetic phrase that appeals to many. However, some folks prefer more down-to-earth language, such as "This really hurts."

Opening Up

When we make room for painful thoughts and feelings, that's an act of kindness in itself; it relieves suffering in a way that's much healthier than many things we do to avoid it. So any acceptance practice fits nicely here.

Unhooking from Self-Judgment

Defusing from self-judgment (and its close relatives: self-criticism, self-loathing, and self-hatred) is a huge part of self-compassion. So any defusion practice fits nicely here.

Common Humanity

Common humanity involves the deep recognition that suffering is something we have in common with all other humans. We acknowledge and empathize with the pain of others; we consciously recognize that they too are suffering with their own life difficulties. If we're fused with self-pity and the idea that no one else suffers as we do, that not only fuels disconnection from others, but also ramps up experiential avoidance. When we recognize the suffering of others, and see our commonality, this facilitates a sense of belonging and connection, while also fostering acceptance.

Our repeated normalizing of our clients' thoughts and feelings, including our own self-disclosure, lays the ground for common humanity. However, we need to be careful that it's not misinterpreted as trivializing or minimizing the client's pain:

Therapist: Often when we're hurting the most, our mind tells us that we're alone in our pain—no one else is going through this—everyone else is happier or better off than we are! I know that's often what my mind says to me; does your mind ever tell you something like that? (*Client agrees.*)

The thing is, when we get hooked by that, it usually just makes us suffer even more. So it's often useful to remind ourselves that everybody hurts, everybody suffers in their own way. Obviously in different ways, to different extents—but no one gets a free pass; we'll all be touched by loss and hurt and hardship—many, many times in our lives. But it's very important that you don't use this as a way to discount or trivialize your pain; the fact is, you're hurting, and you want to acknowledge that, not minimize it! The idea is to acknowledge your pain, and at the same time, see it as part of being human—something you have in common with everyone else.

Client: So how do I do that?

Therapist: Well, one way is to create a phrase to remind yourself, like "Everyone suffers. This is part of being human" or "Everybody hurts. It's the human condition."

We then encourage the client to add this phrase to other self-compassion practices.

THE SKY PERSPECTIVE

Earlier, we aligned common humanity with self-as-context, when defined as "flexible perspective taking." But you'll recall that self-as-context also means "the noticing self"—and this also plays a role in self-compassion. When you access the psychological space of the noticing self, you are like the sky and your cognitions and emotions are like the weather. So when that weather involves intensely painful emotions, horrific memories, and harsh self-judgmental narratives, it's an act of self-kindness to observe it all from the safe perspective of the sky; to recognize there's so much more to you than those terrible events from the past or those hateful self-judgments; and to let it all flow through you, instead of consuming you.

Kindness

At the core of self-compassion is the value of kindness. And although it's often buried under layers of fusion and avoidance, the Two Friends metaphor usually quickly uncovers it. Any variant on this question is usually helpful: "If someone you deeply care about were suffering like you are right now, what would you say to them, and what would you do for them?"

If this stumps the client, we can prompt them: "If you wanted to send them the message 'I see you're hurting, I care about you, I'm here for you,' what kind of things would you say and do?" (And of course, we can modify these questions. For example, if the client loves dogs, we could ask how they'd respond if they saw a dog suffering.) Questions like this not only tap into kindness, but naturally segue into committed action.

Kind Words and Actions

Committed action involves translating the value of kindness into both covert behavior (e.g., kind self-talk, kind imagery, Loving-Kindness Meditation) and overt behavior (kind, caring, supportive deeds and actions).

KIND SELF-TALK

Kind self-talk involves speaking to ourselves in ways that are kind, encouraging, and supportive. This may include anything from validating our pain (*Wow! This is really hard to bear*) to compassionate self-encouragement (*I can handle this; I can do this; I'll get through this*). Any type of question about what you'd say to a friend or loved one if they were suffering will usually generate ideas. We then suggest:

Therapist: Throughout the day, whenever these difficult thoughts and feelings show up, the idea is to acknowledge what you're feeling, and acknowledge that it's painful, and remind yourself to respond with kindness and caring. And it's good to have a catch-phrase you can say to yourself. For example, what I say to myself is, *This really hurts. Be kind.* So if that appeals to you, you could use that; but if you want to come up with your own phrase, that's even better. Any ideas?

Clients learn to first defuse from harsh self-talk, then say something kind and supportive. For example, suppose after making a mistake, a client fuses with "I'm a loser." Kind self-talk may go like this: *Aha. Here's the loser theme again. Okay, I know I screwed up. But hey, I'm human. Everyone makes mistakes.*

Perfectionistic clients may remind themselves, *I'm having the thought I need to do this perfectly. And hey, I really don't have to. "Good enough" is okay.*

Clients struggling to develop a new skill or pattern of behavior may say to themselves, *Here's the "give up" story—but I'm not buying it. What I'm trying to do here is really difficult—and today was a bad day. I'll have another crack at it tomorrow. Over time, I'll get better.*

Clients who compare themselves harshly to others may say, *Aha! Here's my mind comparing me again—trying to beat me into shape. And I don't have to go along with that. What matters is working on myself, doing what I care about.*

Earlier we talked about cognitive flexibility: defusing from unhelpful cognitive repertoires and adding in new, more flexible ways of thinking. We don't try to ignore, avoid, or distract ourselves from self-judgmental thoughts; nor do we attempt to dispute or eliminate them; we accept that they are present (and will continue to recur), unhook from them…*and* talk kindly to ourselves.

Practical Tip

Always check the tone of the inner voice. If clients are saying kind words, but the tone of their inner voice is harsh, sarcastic, or uncaring, it will not have the desired effect.

KIND IMAGERY AND MEDITATION

There are many imagery and meditation practices that foster self-compassion. Particularly powerful are "inner child" or "younger you" exercises, where you imagine yourself traveling back in time to comfort and care for yourself as a child or adolescent (chapter twenty-nine). Loving-Kindness Meditation is also very powerful (chapter thirty-one).

KIND SELF-TOUCH

There are many variants of kind self-touch, such as the Kind Hands exercise in the previous chapter. We encourage clients to experiment and find what's best for them. Options include:

- One hand on the chest, the other on the abdomen
- Both hands on the chest
- Both hands on the abdomen
- Hugging yourself gently
- Hugging yourself while also gently stroking your arms
- Gently massaging an area of tension or tightness
- Gently holding your face in your hands—plus or minus massaging your temples

KIND DEEDS AND ACTIONS

The sky's the limit when it comes to actions of kindness, caring, and support for oneself: practicing TFACT skills, spending quality time with others; doing basic self-care such as healthy eating and regular exercise; making time for rest and relaxation; doing hobbies or sports or other pleasurable, restorative activities; attending therapy; self-soothing; and so on.

But note: any activity that's primarily motivated by fusion or experiential avoidance is unlikely to function as self-compassion. So it's essential that behavior is primarily motivated by kindness and is done in a flexible, mindful way.

We also explain: "You don't have to do anything dramatic. Even the tiniest little act of self-kindness counts." And if clients are stuck for ideas, we suggest some. For example, we may use self-disclosure: "To give you an idea, here are some little acts of self-kindness I did today. I did some stretching of my back and neck…had a long, hot shower…played around with the dog, had a laugh with my son watching some silly YouTube videos…ate some healthy stuff for breakfast. And just before you got here, I sat outside for a couple of minutes, and closed my eyes—just to hear the birds and feel the sun on my face."

Appreciate

Previously we looked at the four As of acceptance: *acknowledge, allow, accommodate, appreciate*. Appreciation plays a huge role in self-compassion. When clients appreciate the purpose of their difficult cognitions, emotions, and physiological reactions, this makes a kind response easier.

> Therapist: So this is the crazy thing; when your mind and body generate all these painful thoughts and feelings, they're actually trying to help you. All those difficult thoughts, painful emotions, fight or flight, freeze or flop—they all stem from one overarching purpose: your mind and body trying hard to protect you, keep you safe.
>
> Client: Yeah well, that may be, but I still don't like it.
>
> Therapist: Of course you don't! Who likes pain and discomfort? No one wants it, no one chooses it. Life has hit you hard—and your mind and body responded the best way they know. You didn't ask for all this suffering; life dumped it on you. And it hurts. And when life hurts this badly…we need some kindness.
>
> Client: (*nods thoughtfully*) True.

Barriers to Self-Compassion

Let's now take a quick look at some of the most common barriers to self-compassion—and how we can overcome them.

Fusion and Getting Overwhelmed

Even going gently, one building block at a time, self-compassion may trigger a slew of difficult thoughts and feelings. Clients may become fused with self-judgment (*It was my fault. I deserve what I get*) or overwhelmed by difficult emotions and memories. If this happens, you know the drill: drop anchor and defuse.

It's Selfish, Self-Indulgent, or Weak

If clients complain that self-compassion is selfish, self-indulgent, or weak, we can approach it this way:

Therapist: This kind of work is new and different, so naturally it's uncomfortable. And your mind is trying to help you avoid that discomfort by coming up with reasons not to do it—it's selfish or weak. So how about we let your mind do that...and at the same time, consider this: if your best friend was struggling, going through a really tough patch, would you support them?

Client: Of course.

Therapist: And if they accepted your help and kindness, would you judge them as selfish or weak?

Client: No...

Therapist: So notice the double standard. If your friend deserves kindness and caring in their time of need, so do you.

Client: But that's different.

Therapist: Of course your mind is never going to agree with me; it will keep saying *this is selfish, this is weak*. So there's a choice point here. If you let these thoughts push you around, where does that take you?

Client: Back into my hole.

Therapist: Have you ever flown on a plane?

Client: A few times.

Therapist: You know what they say about oxygen masks? Put your own on first, before you try to help anyone else? You can think of this the same way: take better care of yourself so you can take better care of others.

Motivation

Clients may say, "I have to be tough on myself. That's what stops me from screwing up," or "This is how I motivate myself. If I go easy on myself, I won't get anything done." We want to validate that in the short term, this can indeed be motivating; but in the long term, it usually has the opposite effect. The well-known Carrot and Stick metaphor is useful here:

The Carrot and Stick Metaphor

Therapist: (*playfully*) You have a pet donkey, right? Carries your goods to the marketplace?

Client: (*playing along*) Err, yeah, of course.

Therapist: And there are two ways to motivate that donkey, right? Beat it with a stick—and it carries the load to escape the beating. Or coax it with carrots—and it carries the load to get more carrots. The more you use carrots, the healthier and happier your donkey. But the more you rely on the stick, the more battered, bruised, and miserable your donkey becomes. So being hard on yourself—is that carrot or stick?

Client: Yeah, it's the stick. But then how am I supposed to motivate myself?

Therapist: Well, luckily, we have something much better than carrots—we have something called "values."

From here therapy segues into learning self-motivation through values, values-based goals, and compassionate self-encouragement. The Two Coaches metaphor (similar to the Two Friends metaphor) is often useful for perfectionistic clients and others who cling to self-criticism for motivation.

The Two Coaches Metaphor

Therapist: So what's your favorite sport? (*Client answers.*) Okay, so let's imagine there are two teams of equally talented players, and they each have a coach. The first coach motivates the players through being harsh, judgmental, and critical and focusing on everything the players do wrong: "That was pathetic!" "You're useless!" "You're not even trying!" "I can't believe you did that!" "How many times do I have to tell you?" "You screwed up this, you messed up that, and you completely loused up the other."

The second coach motivates the players through kind, supportive feedback and encouragement, acknowledging what they do right as well as what they do wrong: "You did A, B, and C really well today. And I can see you're improving at D and E. And I was stoked you remembered to do H and I when J happened. I notice you seem to be struggling a bit with F and G; let's have a look at what's going on there, and see how you can improve on that. Yeah, I know you messed up with X and Y, but hey—we're all human; we all make mistakes. Don't beat yourself up about it; let's go over it and see what you can do differently next time something like that happens."

There are lots of published studies on this topic—and what we know is that harsh, critical, judgmental coaching in the long term leads to demotivated players and poor performance. Kind, supportive coaching is far more effective; players are more motivated and performance is better. Have you ever had a coach/teacher/ manager/parent who used the harsh, critical method with you? What was that like for you? Which method are you using on yourself?

Religious Connotations

Some people see self-compassion as a religious practice, which can be problematic, either because they are nonreligious or because they see it as something from a religion at variance with their own. The easiest way to avoid this is to introduce it in a nonreligious way (e.g., the Two Friends metaphor). If, despite this, religious concerns arise, we have an honest, open discussion about it. We talk about how self-compassion is an important part of most, if not all, religions; however, these days it is a widespread secular practice, studied intensively by scientists because of its benefits for health and well-being.

Little or No Experience of Receiving Compassion

Some people have had such hard lives, they've rarely experienced genuine compassion from others; and without this, it's hard to be compassionate to themselves. We can encourage and support such clients to:

- Put effort into finding and building relationships with people who are likely to be compassionate: caring friends, a loving partner, friendly neighbors.

- Join groups or communities or programs—religious, spiritual, self-development, or self-help—where compassionate support is likely.

- Look for and reflect on examples of compassionate behavior in the outside world, including movies, books, TV shows, friends, and family.

- Practice being compassionate to others, then see if they can do the same for themselves. Again, Loving-Kindness Meditation is good for this purpose.

"I Don't Deserve Kindness"

At times clients may say things like "I don't deserve kindness. Other people do, but not me." (This is obviously linked to larger narratives around unworthiness.) Rather than challenge or dispute this idea, we help clients to notice, name, and defuse from it. We may then ask, "If you follow the rule 'Never seek kindness, and never expect it,' what does that help you avoid?" If the client doesn't know, we explain that if you never *seek* kindness, you avoid all that anxiety about whether or not you'll receive it. And if you never *expect* kindness, you avoid being hurt or disappointed if others don't treat you well. We can usually link this to childhood: "In your house, seeking or hoping for kindness from your caregiver(s) was a recipe for pain and suffering. It was much safer to give up on it. So this way of thinking is basically your mind looking out for you."

From there, a good strategy would be to write the thoughts down:

Therapist: So your mind has issued a decree here: "I do not deserve kindness." Is it okay if I write that down? (*Client agrees. Therapist writes it on a sheet of paper in large block* capitals.) And your mind backs this up with a bunch of other statements, like "I'm worthless," "It's my fault," "I'm bad." (*Therapist writes these under the first statement, then holds the paper up.*) That about right?

Client: Yeah.

Therapist: And I don't agree with any of these things—but I think it would be a waste of time trying to debate that with you, right?

Client: My last therapist tried that—but we didn't get very far.

Therapist: I'll bet. Your mind's been saying this for such a long time. Nothing is likely to stop it now. So... (*Therapist places the paper on a spare chair, the writing clearly visible to the client.*)...that's what your mind has to say. Basically, the rule is: no   kindness allowed! And you feel you have to go along with that, right?

Client: I don't really think of it as a rule. It's just what I do.

Therapist: Yeah, that's the thing. (*pointing again*) You've been doing it for so long, you don't even see it as a rule.

Client: It's who I am. Life's simpler that way.

Therapist: Gotcha. There are real benefits to living your life that way. And it's the same for all of us—when we've been doing things a certain way for a long time, it's uncomfortable to even think about the possibility of doing something different. And so I want to let you know, I greatly appreciate the effort you are making.

Client: What do you mean?

Therapist: I mean I'm genuinely impressed that you keep coming to see me—even though your mind keeps saying that (*points again to the paper*). Each time you come here, you're looking after yourself, doing something to support and take care of yourself. Every moment we work together here, you're breaking that rule (*points again to the paper*). And that's a hard thing to do.

Client: I hadn't really seen it that way.

Therapist: From where I'm sitting, it's kind of cool. Is it okay if we carry on working here, even though your mind keeps saying that stuff?

Client: Okay.

Therapist: I really appreciate that. What's it like for you to be disobeying that rule?

Client: I feel anxious.

Therapist:	Yup, that's a normal feeling to have when you disobey deeply held rules. It's almost like breaking the law.
Client:	Yeah, it is.
Therapist:	So see if you can open up, let that feeling be there. (*Therapist runs through a quick version of the NAME exercise. Once the client has accepted the feeling, the therapist points again to the paper.*) So notice, the rule is still there—but it's not controlling you. And if this is the feeling you need to make room for, to take your life in a better direction, are you willing to do that?
Client:	Yeah.

Opening Old Wounds

Sometimes as clients start being more self-compassionate, lots of old "psychological wounds" start to open. This is very painful and can be overwhelming. Here's one way to explain what's happening:

The Orphanage Metaphor

Therapist:	Imagine that you've taken a job at an orphanage—one of those old-fashioned ones like you've seen in the movies. And it's your first night shift. And you're walking down the corridor, and you hear a child crying, in the dormitory. So you go in...and there are about twenty kids in there, all fast asleep in their beds—except for this one child, who's quietly sobbing into her pillow. So you very quietly go over to this child and you sit beside her on the bed, and in a whisper (so you don't wake up the other kids) you ask her what the matter is. And she tells you she's really sad and scared, and you say some kind words to comfort her...but, you just aren't quiet enough...and two kids on either side wake up...and they see you there, and they want your attention too...so they start crying, and you try to comfort them too... but now the kids around them are waking up...and they also want your attention, so they start crying...and before you know it the whole dormitory is full of kids crying, telling you how scared and sad they are, asking you to comfort them.
	So if you wanted to help those kids calm down, feel secure, you'd first need to respond with kindness and reassurance. If you yell at them or threaten them, they may get quiet—but they won't be calm or secure. And if you run off and leave them—well, *you'll* get some relief, but the kids will just be hurting even more.
	So you might say, kindly and calmly, "It's okay, kids. I'm here, and I'm not leaving you. I'm staying." And then you might go around the room, say a few words of comfort to each child—and promise to talk later when you have more time.

Most clients get this metaphor without need for further explanation. We can then refer back to it in later sessions: "This pain you're feeling right now—it's like one of those distressed kids in the orphanage, crying out for comfort. How are you going to respond?"

Homework

For homework we can encourage clients to practice regularly with any combination of self-compassion "building blocks." For one client, we may focus on kind self-talk. For another, we might encourage daily practice of the Kind Hands exercise. For yet another, we might emphasize small daily actions of self-kindness.

We can also encourage clients to create their own mini self-compassion rituals; for example, do a two-minute version of Kind Hands before getting out of bed in the morning and before going to sleep at night; or add it in to dropping anchor.

> **EXTRA BIT** In *Trauma-Focused ACT: The Extra Bits* (downloadable from "Free Resources" on http://ImLearningACT.com), chapter fourteen contains scripts for a number of self-compassion exercises, including Loving-Kindness Meditation.

Takeaway

Self-compassion—acknowledging your pain and responding with kindness—is an intrinsic part of TFACT. Because it can be challenging, it's useful to chunk self-compassion into building blocks and introduce them one or two at a time. Sometimes clients quickly develop this ability; at other times, it's painstakingly slow. However, as we say to our clients, every step counts, no matter how small it may be.

CHAPTER FIFTEEN

Knowing What Matters

Although the word "optimism" is rarely mentioned in ACT texts, the model is inherently optimistic and hopeful. ACT assumes we can all reduce our suffering and build meaningful lives—no matter where we have come from, what we have been through, and what we are facing now. Of course, we don't teach people to challenge pessimistic thoughts and replace them with optimistic ones—or to hope all their problems will magically disappear—but through values and committed action, we actively instigate a hopeful, optimistic stance toward life.

No matter what's going on in our life, no matter how hard it may be, no matter how horrific our past—we can learn how to practice self-compassion, live by our values, and appreciate what life has to offer. This doesn't magically eliminate our pain, solve our problems, and make us happy—but it does reduce psychological suffering and enable us to enjoy life more and live meaningfully in the face of our challenges. In this chapter, we'll look at the pivotal role of values in helping us achieve this.

Bringing Values to Center Stage

Values are desired qualities of behavior: the qualities you want to bring to your actions right now, and on an ongoing basis. One way to describe them to clients is "your heart's deepest desires for how you want to behave as a human being; how you want to treat yourself, others, and the world around you." In contrast to *goals*, which describe outcomes we are aiming for: what we want to have, get, or achieve in the future, *values* describe how we want to behave in this moment and on an ongoing basis. For example, if you want to "have a great job," that's a goal; if you want to "be responsible and reliable," those are values. To "get married": goal; to "be loving": value. To "buy a house" for your family to live in: goal; to "be supportive and caring" toward your family: values. To "go traveling": goal; to "be curious, open, appreciative, and adventurous" while you are traveling: values. To "have a child": goal; to "be loving and nurturing": values. To "make new friends" or "be popular": goal; to "be warm, open, and understanding": values.

If you want power, fame, money, solitude, happiness, popularity, beauty, respect, a big house, a great body, a flashy car, people to treat you well or find you attractive—those are all goals, not values; they all describe outcomes you are seeking, as opposed to desired qualities of your own behavior.

This distinction matters because even when goals are a long way off, or seemingly impossible, it's empowering to live by our values, here and now. For example, a value such as "being kind" can under-pin the smallest of actions (such as holding a door open for someone) to the largest long-term goals (such as becoming a therapist). It may take you years to achieve that long-term goal, but you can live the value of kindness every day, in a thousand ways, through things you say and do.

We can use values as a compass to guide us through life: to inspire the goals we set and the actions we take, and to motivate us to do the hard work of pursuing our goals, even when doing so gives rise to painful thoughts and feelings. Our values can also guide how we behave *as we pursue* our goals, for example, how we treat ourselves and others as we attempt to get our needs met in relationships. Values hover in the background of every session—and as therapy progresses, we increasingly bring them to the foreground.

Gradually Getting to Values

Let's quickly retrace our early steps toward values. Often, we first touch on them in the intake session, teasing them out (without calling them "values") from the goals we establish for therapy. Thereafter, we repeatedly connect with them through the concepts of workability, towards moves, and choice points. For example, when clients report life-enhancing behaviors they've done outside of session, we may ask, "So did that feel more like a towards move or an away move?" or "The way you did that—how would you describe those qualities?" or "What were you standing for in that moment?" "Did you like who you were as you handled that?" "Anything you're proud of in the way you went about that?"

And when clients talk about their away moves, we ask, "When you do that, what or who does it take you away from? And what do you miss out on, or lose?" or "What does that get in the way of?" or "What would you prefer to do, instead?"

We also tap into values when we explore emotions, with questions like "What do these feelings tell you that you care about, or need to do differently? What do they suggest you want to stand for—or against?"

Then, as therapy progresses, we may start explicitly using the word "values" in our questions: "Which values is this in the service of?" or "As you practice that skill/pursue that goal/take that action, what values will you be living?"

Through such interventions, we gather much useful information about values, values-congruent goals, wishes, needs, desires, important domains of life, important relationships, behaviors the client wants to stop or reduce, and behaviors the client wants to start or increase. This is all golden material for both values and committed action.

Beginning Sessions with Values

When starting sessions with a quick mindfulness exercise, it's often useful to flavor it with values. For example:

Therapist: So taking a moment to center yourself...pushing your feet into the floor...straightening your back...letting your shoulders drop...fixing your eyes on a spot...and opening your ears, noticing what you can hear...with openness and curiosity... sounds coming from me...and from you...and the room around us...and outside the room...and now, consciously tuning in to what you care about, deep in your heart... reminding yourself of what matters enough that you made the effort to come here today...

Therapist: (*specifically mentioning values, values-congruent goals, and important relationships or domains of life the client has previously mentioned*) And perhaps reflecting on some of the things you've mentioned...like caring for yourself and your kids...being loving and attentive...being real and open...being courageous in facing your fears...getting back into the workforce...and looking after your health...and taking a moment to acknowledge, this matters to you...and this is what our work is all about.

Into the Spotlight

When we wish to bring values into the spotlight, we might say:

Therapist: Can we take a few minutes to talk about something important? You've been working hard, stepping out of your comfort zone, learning new skills so that you can unhook from those difficult thoughts and feelings—and that's been pretty challenging, right?

Client: That's an understatement.

Therapist: Yeah, it is. And so, I wondered if we could look at the big picture: where's all this leading? As I said on the first session, our ultimate aim is to help you build a meaningful and fulfilling life. And so far we've been working mainly on one aspect of that—learning how to deal with difficult thoughts and feelings. But there's another really big piece to this, which is taking action: doing what's needed to actively build a better life. So I'm wondering, could we shift the focus to that?

Client: Okay.

Therapist: Great. So the first step is getting to know what your values are. And by "values," I mean your heart's deepest desires for how you want to behave; how you want to treat yourself, others, the world around you. You've already mentioned some of your values, like... (*mentions a few values*)...so I'm wondering, could we explore this in a bit more depth?

At this point, reactions may vary from openness, curiosity, or enthusiasm to hopelessness, anger, or cynicism. Negative reactions indicate fusion or avoidance, and we respond with dropping anchor, defusion, acceptance, and self-compassion, as we'll cover in chapter nineteen. But many clients are receptive. If a client asks, "What's the point?" or "How's that going to help?" it's important we answer that question—but we want to keep it short, not give a lecture. We also want to ensure that the client is genuinely willing to explore values, not just "going along with it" to please the therapist. Here's how we might address both these issues:

Client: I don't see how that will help.

Therapist: Well, it can help in quite a lot of ways. One, when we know our values, it helps us make better choices—do things that work better for us. Two, they're like a sort of inner compass that can guide us through life, help us to find our way, give us a sense of purpose. Three, they provide motivation—give us the strength and courage to do what really matters. Four, when life is dull and gray, they add some color to it. And five, when you act on them, they give you a sense of fulfilment—a sense of being true to yourself, living life *your* way, behaving like the sort of person you really want to be, deep in your heart.

Client: I don't have time that for crap. I have real problems to deal with.

Therapist: Yes, you do. And that's where we're headed next: taking action to solve your problems, to make your life better. Knowing your values helps you do that, because they help you choose what you're going to stand for, and how you're going to treat yourself and others as you tackle these issues.

Client: Yeah, but, look—I can't just snap my fingers and rebuild my life. I've got a lot of shit to deal with.

Therapist: Yes, absolutely; you have so much shit to deal with. And you're so right—rebuilding your life is not quick and easy. It's a slow and challenging process. And it happens through making small changes, over time—and that's difficult. And values give you the motivation to do that hard work. So, look, I don't want to push you into this if you're not ready. We can certainly spend more time learning how to handle your thoughts and feelings, if that's what you prefer. I mean, I think you're ready for this—but I'll be guided by you.

Client: (sighs) Well, alright then. If you say so, let's do it.

Therapist: Can I be honest? It sounds like you're just saying that to please me. Doesn't sound like you're really interested.

Client: Well, yeah. I'm skeptical.

Therapist:	Skepticism is cool with me. Please don't believe anything just because I say it; your experience is what matters.
Client:	Okay. Well, alright then, let's get on with it.
Therapist:	Errm, you know what? I'm a bit hesitant. Because…it still feels like you're just going along with it to please me. And you really won't get anything out of it if you do it that way.
Client:	So how am I supposed to do it?
Therapist:	Well, this is about you. It's about who you want to be. Deep inside. What sort of person you want to be; what sort of relationships you want to build; what you want to put out into the world in this one precious life that's ticking away. Does that interest you?
Client:	(*pauses; then answers quietly*) Yes.
Therapist:	What's showing up for you now?
Client:	(*tearing up*) I feel kind of sad.
Therapist:	That's a good sign that we're on the right track.

As clients first start explicitly connecting with values, it's not uncommon for their eyes to tear up and emotions such as sadness to arise. Once we're sure the client is genuinely willing, we ask them to pick one area of life they wish to improve (e.g., work, health, leisure, or an important relationship) and go on to explore values within that domain.

Two Surefire Ways to Values

My apologies. The above heading is false. It was a deliberate attempt to deceive you. The truth is, nothing in TFACT is ever "surefire" (unfortunately). However, either of the exercises below will help *most* people connect with values.

Connect and Reflect

The Connect and Reflect exercise involves thinking about someone you care about and reflecting on what you like to do together. (It was inspired by Kelly Wilson's "sweet spot" exercise, Wilson & DuFrene, 2009.) What follows are bare bones instructions for you to flesh out with your own words. Go slowly with this exercise, allowing plenty of time for the client to process each instruction. (They may speak or stay silent throughout; either is fine.)

There are two parts to the exercise:

Connect and Reflect—Part A

- Think of someone you care about who is active in your life today—someone who treats you well, whom you like to spend time with. And remember a time, recent or distant, when you were together, doing an activity you like.

- Make this memory as vivid as possible.

- Relive it. Feel it emotionally.

- Look out from behind your own eyes onto the scene: Notice where you are... Time of day?... Indoors or outdoors?... Weather? Scenery? Temperature?... What's the air like? What can you see?... What can you hear?... What can you touch...taste...smell?

- Notice the other person—what do they look like? What are they saying or doing? What's their tone of voice, the expression on their face, their body posture, the way they are moving?

- In this memory, what are you thinking?... And feeling? And doing? What are you doing with your arms...legs...mouth? Are you moving or still? Get into your body (in this memory); what does it feel like?

- Savor the moment. Make the most of it. What's it like? Really appreciate it.

Allow the client at least a minute or two to savor the memory. Then move on to part B, either as a conversation or silently, allowing the client time to process each question.

Connect and Reflect—Part B

- Now step back and look at the memory as if you're watching it on a TV screen. Focus on yourself. What are you saying and doing? How are you interacting with the other person? How are you treating them? How are you responding to them?

- What qualities are you showing in this memory? For example, are you being open, loving, kind, fun-loving, playful, connected, engaged, interested, appreciative, honest, real, courageous, intimate?

- What does this remind you about the sort of person you want to be; the way you want to treat yourself and others; the sort of relationships you want to build; how you want to spend your time?

Connect and Reflect—Debrief

After the exercise, discuss the client's responses to the questions in the last two bullet points in part B to highlight the values elicited in the exercise.

Connect and Reflect—Modifications

We can easily modify this exercise, asking the client to remember any activity they enjoy (or used to enjoy) with others or alone—at home, at work, or at play—and connect with it as above. We then ask similar questions to those in part B:

- What qualities were you showing in this memory?

- What does this remind you about the sort of person you want to be? About how you want to spend your time?

- How do you want to treat XYZ? (*XYZ = objects, people, places involved in the activity*)

Whom Do You Look Up To?

Another option is to ask, "Whom do you look up to/respect/admire?" This could be a historical figure, a fictional character in a book or movie, someone the client knows personally, or someone they know about from the media.

Once the client picks someone, we ask questions like "What is it about them you admire/respect?" "What do you like about their personal qualities, their personality?" "What are they like as a person?" "How do they treat other people?" "What do they stand for?" "If you had to choose two or three words to describe their best attributes, what words would you use?"

After we have those answers, we can ask, "So are those qualities you'd like to bring into play in your own life?" If the answer is yes, we've identified values. (This method was used in the WHO's ACT protocol. Participants were asked to pick someone in the refugee camp they respected, then describe this person's qualities—especially how they treated other refugees.)

Practical Tip

You can usually tell when people are truly connecting with values because they tend to be very present, open, and willingly vulnerable, with a sense of vitality and freedom. This is often accompanied by a softening of their face and voice, and openness in their body posture. So if discussing values seems a bit stale, dry, or "heady," this usually means the client is not truly connecting with them; they're merely "paying lip service" or intellectualizing them. To encourage connection, ask them to imagine living these values: What would it look and sound like? And how does it feel as they imagine it?

Choosing Values

One of the great things about values is that the moment we choose them, they are ours. Here's how we may explain this:

Client: I'll be honest with you. I want to say "loving" and "kind," but when I look at what I've been doing, it's pretty obvious those aren't my values.

Therapist: Well, I'm glad you raised that. You see, society says that what we do reflects our values. But what research shows us is that a lot of the time, what we do does *not* actually reflect our values—because we get hooked by our thoughts and feelings and pulled *away* from our values. You see, values are "desired qualities of behavior." They're how we want to behave, if we could choose. So if there's any value you'd like to have—then by definition, it's already your value; it's a quality of behavior you desire. If you'd like to be loving, then being loving is one of your values. If you'd like to be kind, then kindness is one of your values.

Client: But I'm not doing anything kind or loving.

Therapist: So you've hit on something important: the difference between values and actions. For any given value, you can either act on it, or not. If you want to act on the values of kindness or being loving, then even if you've never done so in your life, you can start today.

Three Additional Paths to Values

If for some reason the exercises and methods above don't suit you or your client, there are many other approaches. Just for good measure, here are three more:

CONVERSING ABOUT MEANINGFUL ACTIVITIES

Conversations about activities the client finds meaningful (or used to) often unearth values. We might ask:

* What do you do for fun/leisure/relaxation/entertainment/creativity?

* What makes you feel proud/accomplished/fulfilled?

- When do you experience a sense of belonging/being fully alive/doing something important/ connecting deeply with someone or something?

- When are you at your best in your marriage/with your family/as a friend/at work? What are you like to be around at those times? How do you treat others? How do you treat yourself?

Especially powerful are conversations about "meaningful pain," where a client has done (or is doing) something deeply meaningful even though it was (or is) incredibly painful—such as supporting a loved one through a serious illness, or standing up for their beliefs and ideals even though it comes with significant personal costs.

MONITORING DAILY ACTIVITIES

Monitoring activity is especially useful for clients presenting with extreme apathy, disengagement, low motivation, or hopelessness. Clients use worksheets like those in Extra Bits to monitor what they do from hour to hour, rating each activity for meaningfulness, vitality, and workability. The completed records raise clients' awareness of how they are spending their time and how that affects them, which leads to fruitful discussions about what enhances life and what drains it.

This is usually our best starting point for deeply depressed or apathetic clients. It helps them recognize things they are doing that keep them stuck—paving the way to try something different. They also discover activities that make life better, so we can explore how to build on these and tease out the values from beneath them.

VALUES CARDS AND CHECKLISTS

Checklists—such as the one below—are a good way to work with values in "teacher mode." First clients select an area of life they want to improve (e.g., work, education, health, play, parenting, friendship, intimate relationship). Then they look through or fill in a values checklist.

FORTY COMMON VALUES

Values are your heart's deepest desires for how you want to behave as a human being. They describe how you want to treat yourself, others, and the world around you. (This is not a list of "the right" values; there are no "right" or "wrong" ones. It's like your taste in ice cream. If you prefer chocolate but someone else prefers vanilla, that doesn't mean their taste is right and yours is wrong—or vice-versa. It just means you have different tastes. So these aren't the right or best values; they're just to give you some ideas. And if your values aren't listed, there's room at the bottom to add them.)

Pick an area of life you want to enhance, improve, or explore (e.g., work, education, health, leisure, parenting, friendship, spirituality, intimate relationship). Then consider which values in the list below best complete this sentence: *In this area of my life, I want to be…*

Read through the list, and if a value seems very important in this area of life, put a V by it. If it's somewhat important, put an S. And if it's not that important, put an N.

In this area of my life, I want to be…
1. Accepting: open to, allowing of, or at peace with myself, others, life, my feelings, etc.
2. Adventurous: willing to create or pursue novel, risky, or exciting experiences
3. Assertive: respectfully standing up for my rights and requesting what I want
4. Authentic: being genuine, real, and true to myself
5. Caring/self-caring: actively taking care of myself, others, the environment, etc.
6. Compassionate/self-compassionate: responding kindly to myself or others in pain
7. Cooperative: willing to assist and work with others
8. Courageous: being brave or bold; persisting in the face of fear, threat, or risk
9. Creative: being imaginative, inventive, or innovative
10. Curious: being open-minded and interested; willing to explore and discover
11. Encouraging: supporting, inspiring, and rewarding behavior I approve of
12. Expressive: conveying my thoughts and feelings through what I say and do
13. Focused: focused on and engaged in what I am doing
14. Fair/just: acting with fairness and justice—toward myself and others
15. Flexible: willing and able to adjust and adapt to changing circumstances
16. Friendly: warm, open, caring, and agreeable toward others
17. Forgiving: letting go of resentments and grudges toward myself or others
18. Grateful: being appreciative for what I have received
19. Helpful: giving, helping, contributing, assisting, or sharing
20. Honest: being honest, truthful, and sincere—with myself and others
21. Independent: choosing for myself how I live and what I do
22. Industrious: being diligent, hardworking, dedicated
23. Kind: being considerate, helpful, or caring—to myself or others
24. Loving: showing love, affection, or great care—to myself or others
25. Mindful/present: fully present and engaging in whatever I'm doing
26. Open: revealing myself, letting people know my thoughts and feelings
27. Orderly: being neat and organized
28. Persistent/committed: willing to continue, despite problems or difficulties
29. Playful: being humorous, fun-loving, light-hearted
30. Protective: looking after the safety and security of myself or others
31. Respectful/self-respectful: treating myself or others with care and consideration
32. Responsible: being trustworthy, reliable, and accountable for my actions
33. Skillful: doing things well, utilizing my knowledge, experience, and training
34. Supportive: being helpful, encouraging, and available—to myself or others
35. Trustworthy: being loyal, honest, faithful, sincere, responsible, and reliable
36. Trusting: willing to believe in the honesty, sincerity, reliability, or competence of another
37. Other:
38. Other:
39. Other:
40. Other:

Forty Common Values Checklist

Clients can obviously redo the checklist above for other areas of life, and often they'll find that many values recur across different domains. Values cards serve the same purpose; usually a pack contains forty to fifty cards with a different value printed on each. The client picks a life domain, then sorts the cards into three piles: very important, somewhat important, and not important. With either method, the client then chooses two or three "very important" values to "play around with" (i.e., experiment with various ways of acting on those values throughout the day) in the week ahead.

Practical Tip

Many therapists like cards and checklists because they're easy to use compared to other methods. However they can become somewhat superficial or intellectual exercises, where the client chooses words but doesn't really connect with them. Therefore, these methods work best as a second-line intervention, to flesh out values work *after* you've first done more experiential work, as above.

Barriers to Values

As with anything in TFACT, at times things will not go smoothly. So let's take a look at some common barriers to values.

"I Don't Know!"

Have you ever had a client who answers, "I don't know" to every question about values? If not, you're lucky! When this happens, rather than keep asking questions, we might say, "It's clear that right now, you really don't know. So would you be willing to do an exercise to find out?" We then can then work through a values checklist or do a Connect and Reflect exercise.

Similarly, when clients say, "I don't have any values," we may reply, "Yes, I can see that's how it appears. And there are two possible explanations. One is that you don't yet have any values; the other is that you do already have them, but you don't realize it. And either way, we can work with that. If you're willing to do an exercise with me, it will help you find the values you already have—or create them from scratch.

Confusion with Outcome Goals

Clients often use the word "value" as a synonym for "like" or "want." For example, consider these statements: I value financial security, I value being slim, I value having friends, I value power and influence, I value inner peace, I value good health. These are not values, as ACT uses the word; they don't describe desired qualities of behavior. They are describing outcome goals—things we want to have, get, achieve, or complete—whereas values (as mentioned earlier) describe how we want to behave, here and now, and on an ongoing basis, whether we achieve our goals or not.

This distinction is important, because we can't control whether or not we achieve a desired outcome, but we can control whether or not we live by and act on our values. Of course, if a desired outcome is important to us, we can change our behavior to increase our chances of achieving it—but there is never a guarantee we will succeed. So when clients identify outcome goals, we want to first validate them, then tease out the underlying values, and then translate them into action plans.

The following metaphor usually helps clients distinguish between values and outcome goals:

Where You're Going and How You're Traveling

Therapist: A goal is like a destination—a place you're traveling toward, such as Paris or New York. Values are how you want to behave while you're traveling—how you want to treat yourself, and other people, and the things you encounter along the way. For example, do you want to be kind and helpful to other travelers, or mean, or pushy or distant? Do you want be open to and curious about your experiences while traveling, or closed off and uninterested? Do you want to treat your body caringly, or neglectfully? So the goal is the endpoint, the final destination, whereas values are how you want to behave along the journey—and how you want to behave when you get to the end.

The transcript below illustrates how to shift from focusing on an outcome goal to identifying a value. The client is a thirty-year-old male with chronic pain syndrome and PTSD following a physical assault a year earlier. During the attack, he sustained a back injury, after which he had spinal surgery, which has only exacerbated the pain:

Client: Look, the one thing I value most is my health. And I can't have it! I used to run marathons for fuck's sake—now I can hardly fucking walk!

Therapist: I can only begin to imagine how difficult that is. You look really upset.

Client: Of course I'm fucking upset. Wouldn't you be?

Therapist: Yes, I would for sure. Anyone would.

(The therapist now asks the client to notice what he's feeling, and the client reports sadness and anger. They then do a quick version of NAME the emotion, incorporating the Kind Hands exercise. The client has done this before, so no explanation is needed; it takes about four minutes. The therapist then returns to the topic of values.)

Therapist: So here's the thing. Of course you want to have good health—and at this point, you don't, and that's really painful. And one of our aims here is to get you doing everything possible to improve your health as much as you can. With that in mind, can you tell me a bit about how you want to treat your body?

Client: I want to fix it. I want to get it working again.

Therapist:	For sure. And here's the thing: nobody knows for sure how long that will take, or how much improvement there will ultimately be, right?
Client:	No.
Therapist:	But what we do know is, the better you look after your body today, the better your chances are for the future.
Client:	Right.
Therapist:	So if you were to really take care of your body—as it is today—as well as you possibly could, what would you do?

The therapist has helped to shift the client from the goal of "get my health back" to the value of self-care (i.e., "taking care of your body"). The next step will be to translate this value into committed action—exploring things the client can do on a daily basis to take care of his body.

Confusion with Emotional Goals

Sometimes as we work on values, clients fall back on emotional goals. In the transcript that follows, the client has been focusing on their relationship with their children and has stated, "I value calm and peace." Again, the word "value" is a synonym for "I want"—and the client has described an emotional goal—how they want *to feel*—not a value.

Therapist:	(*making the emotional goal obvious*) So you want to feel more calm, more peaceful?
Client:	Yes.
Therapist:	Yeah, me too! And you know, what you're describing there is what we technically call an *emotional goal*—in other words, how you want to *feel*. So you want to *feel* peaceful, *feel* calm. And I am so with you on that! I think we all want to feel calm and peaceful. But of course, it's impossible to feel that way all the time—life is stressful and full of difficulties, and at times we're all going to experience anxiety and sadness and anger, and so on. Remember we talked about how emotions are like the weather, always changing—sometimes wonderful, sometimes dire?
Client:	Yeah. I prefer the good weather.
Therapist:	Yeah, don't we all. But the thing is, values are very different from emotions. Values are not how we want to feel; they are how we want to *behave*—how deep in our hearts we want to treat ourselves and others and the world around us, no matter how we are feeling, whether we feel peaceful and calm or anxious and sad. So suppose I have a magic wand here—a real one, that actually does magic. And when I wave this magic wand, all those stressful thoughts, and memories, and

emotions—are like water off a duck's back—no longer hold you back in any way... then, how would you treat your children differently?

Client: Err, well—I wouldn't yell at them all the time.

Therapist: So how would you talk to them when they're acting out?

Client: Well, calmly.

Therapist: Okay, so you'd talk more calmly. How else would you treat them?

Client: Well, I wouldn't be so hard on them. Wouldn't be so strict.

Therapist: So instead of strict and hard, you'd be more what?

Client: Relaxed!

Therapist: Meaning that you'd relax some of your expectations for your kids' behavior? You'd give them more leeway, more freedom, less demands?

Client: Err, yeah.

Therapist: So you'd be more easygoing, more flexible?

Client: Yeah, definitely.

Therapist: Anything else? Any other ways you'd treat them differently?

Client: I guess I'd listen to them more. And laugh more.

Therapist: So you'd be more attentive? More playful?

Client: Err, yeah. We'd have more fun.

Therapist: So you'd be more fun-loving?

Client: Yeah.

Therapist: So you'd behave quite differently toward the kids—you'd be acting more calmly, more easygoing, flexible, playful, fun-loving, attentive. So if our work here could help you to treat your kids that way, both at times when you feel calm and peaceful, *and also* at times when you feel anxious or sad or angry—would that be useful for you?

We can use the same approach when clients express other emotional/psychological states they want to have (e.g., confidence, high self-esteem, relaxation, contentment, fulfilment, satisfaction, joy—or the classic "I just want to be happy").

In all these cases, the client's (usually unconscious) rule is "I have to first achieve this psychological/emotional state before I can behave like the person I want to be." In ACT, we overturn that rule and introduce a different way of living: *I can behave like the sort of person I want to be—even when I don't feel the way I want to.* (However, if a client remains fixated on emotional goals, we put values on hold and return to creative hopelessness.)

Fusion with Rules

If clients seem rigid, heavy, burdened, or trapped—as opposed to having a sense of vitality, openness, and freedom to choose—they are probably fusing with rules rather than flexibly contacting values. The examples below illustrate the difference:

Being loving = value

I MUST always be loving, no matter what! = rule

Being kind = value

I SHOULD be kind at all times, even when people are abusive = rule

Being efficient = value

I HAVE TO ALWAYS be efficient, and I MUST NEVER make any mistakes = rule

Basically, rules are strict instructions you have to obey—usually readily identified by words like have to, must, ought, should, right, wrong, always, never, do this, don't do that, can't until, won't unless, can't because, and so on. There are countless ways to act upon our values, in even the most difficult situations. Rules, in contrast, tend to limit our options and narrow our behavior, and the more tightly we adhere to them, the less choice we have. Thus, fusion with rules often prevents us from acting effectively.

In addition, fusion with rules tends to "suck all the life" out of values. Instead of meaning and vitality, clients fused with rules are likely to experience pressure, obligation, guilt, shame, or anxiety. Often this manifests as worrying: "Am I doing it right?" "Am I doing it enough?" "Am I doing it too much?" So we help clients notice, name, and unhook from the rules, and return to the underlying values.

Fusion with Reasons

Fusion with reason-giving often shows up as we do this work. One form this takes is "I don't deserve a life." We could respond to this just as to "I don't deserve kindness" in chapter fourteen. Another version is "I don't care about anything," which we respond to as with nihilism, as in chapter ten.

Sometimes clients use the recurrence of certain thoughts as evidence that they are a bad person, or that they don't truly have the values they profess to (e.g., "I know I say that I want to be about love and kindness—but that can't be right because I have all these hateful thoughts").

Take the case of Maria, a fifty-four-year-old woman whose twenty-six-year-old son, Nick, was addicted to heroin. Maria's trauma stemmed from multiple distressing incidents involving

Nick—including several life-threatening overdoses, hospital admissions, medical complications, legal issues, and many aggressive confrontations where he would yell abusive remarks, threaten violence, or even threaten to kill himself if Maria did not give him money. At times Maria would have thoughts like *I wish he would just die* or *We'd be better off if he'd never been born.* These thoughts would then trigger a cascade of self-judgment: *What kind of mother would think that way? I'm horrible, I made him the way he is.*

What we're dealing with here are intrusive thoughts, and we can help clients respond to them with the methods in chapters ten and eleven. It's also helpful to equate these thoughts to ineffective problem solving:

> Therapist: This is basically your mind in problem-solving mode. The problem here is a relationship that's causing lots of pain. And the solution your mind comes up with is "look for ways to end it"—which includes the other person dying, or an alternative reality where they never existed. But the thing is, that's your mind on autopilot, generating those solutions. You don't consciously choose those thoughts. They just pop up. And the fact that they distress you tells you something, doesn't it? Like, if you *really* didn't want him alive, those thoughts wouldn't bother you, would they? The fact they bother you so much suggests the very opposite.

> Client: I never thought about it like that.

> Therapist: Yeah, well—it doesn't stop there. See, first your mind creates these thoughts and then it starts to see *them* as a problem. It's like, "Hey. These thoughts are bad!" So now it starts judging you, telling you how bad you are; it figures, if it can just beat you up enough, then maybe you'll stop thinking that way. But what does your experience show you; does beating yourself up actually help?

> Client: No, it doesn't.

> Therapist: So how about we revisit that self-compassion stuff?

Experiential Avoidance

Living by our values is a way to make life richer, more fulfilling, more meaningful. At times this gives rise to pleasurable and enjoyable feelings—especially when we do so in nonchallenging situations. At other times, though, acting on our values will trigger painful thoughts and feelings—especially when we leave our comfort zone to tackle life's challenges.

Fear of failure, fear of responsibility, fear of rejection, fear of making mistakes, fear of the unknown, are all commonplace—as are many other fears and anxieties. And of course, fear and anxiety are never barriers in and of themselves, but experiential avoidance often is. If clients are unwilling to make room for all those difficult cognitions and emotions, they will resist connecting with or acting on their values. In such cases, we segue into defusion, acceptance, and self-compassion as required—and then we return to values.

Clarifying Motivation

When we do things motivated primarily by fusion or experiential avoidance, they are rarely satisfying—and when we reflect on this consciously, we are likely to see them as away moves. But If we do those same things mindfully, motivated primarily by values, they are much more fulfilling, and we're likely to consider them towards moves.

For example, if you "want solitude," that's a goal, not a value; it just means you want to spend time alone. Now if this goal is primarily motivated by fusion with "no one likes me" or avoidance of social anxiety, then it's not based on values, and it will likely be an unsatisfying experience. But if this same goal is primarily motivated by values such as self-caring, being creative, being mindful, it will be a different—and much more fulfilling—experience. We help clients to discriminate these differences not by giving them a didactic lecture, but by guiding them experientially. In the transcript that follows, the client is a thirty-eight-year-old woman who spends a lot of her time and energy people pleasing, and finds it exhausting. But she finds it hard to distinguish this behavior from acting on her value of helpfulness.

Client:	I'm a bit confused, because I think my values pull me into away moves.
Therapist:	Can you give me an example?
Client:	Yeah, like one of my main values is being helpful. So at parties and social events and family get-togethers, you know, I'll always be running around looking after everyone, helping whoever's running it—organizing, putting out food, topping up drinks, helping out in the kitchen—and really, I'm doing it because it reduces my anxiety. I get really anxious if I'm trapped in a conversation, or if people ask me personal things—so it helps me to keep moving, and it saves me from all that awkwardness and anxiety.
Therapist:	You've really highlighted something important there. Motivation matters. When we do something motivated by avoidance—trying to avoid difficult situations, thoughts, and feelings—it's not satisfying. And that's what you're describing. When we do something motivated by values, it's different. Have you ever done something helpful not to avoid anxiety or awkwardness, but just because you really wanted to, deep in your heart?
Client:	Oh yeah. Like, my Gran—she's in a hospice—and I go visit her every couple of weeks and take her out in her wheelchair.
Therapist:	And what's that like?
Client:	It's nice. You know, she was always really kind to me, when I was little. But it's hard—it's sad to see her like she is now.
Therapist:	And so even though you know you're going to feel sad, you visit her?

Client:	Yeah, well—she's my Gran!
Therapist:	And when you're doing that—does it seem like you're being the person you want to be?
Client:	Oh yes.
Therapist:	And what about when you're running around at a party, avoiding getting trapped in conversations; does that seem like you're being the person you want to be?
Client:	No.
Therapist:	Right. So helping out your Gran—that's living your values. Helping out at the party—well, the value's still there, but it's kind of in the background, isn't it? I mean, what's driving you most?
Client:	Yeah, trying to avoid anxiety.
Therapist:	Yeah. Big difference.

In trauma literature, we often read about "survival strategies," "co-dependent behavior," "people pleasing," "fawning," "submissiveness," and so on. But when we look at these behaviors through a TFACT lens, we see they are all primarily motivated by fusion and experiential avoidance. My favorite interventions to distinguish these motivations from values are all variants on the magic wand question:

- If I could wave a magic wand so that everyone on the planet automatically loves you, treats you well, and approves of everything you do—no matter what you do—would you still go ahead and do this? Or would you do something different?

- If I could wave a magic wand so that there's no chance of failure, no chance of things going wrong—all those things you're most afraid of, they can't possibly happen—would you still do this?

- If I could wave a magic wand so that you had no fear—would you still do this?

- If I could wave a magic wand so that all those rules about what you should or shouldn't do, or the "right" thing to do, or what you're supposed to do, or what others expect you to do—they lose all their power over you, they no longer dictate what you do—would you still do this?

Let's continue the transcript from above, to see how we can use such questions in session:

Therapist:	So if I could wave a magic wand so that next time you're at a party you behave like the sort of person you really want to be, deep inside, and nothing stops you from that—no thoughts, no feelings; nothing can stop you, because this is magic, right?—how would you behave differently?

Client:	Well, I'd still help out, because…I like helping out.
Therapist:	Would you help out as much as before?
Client:	No, probably not.
Therapist:	So what would you do instead, if you weren't so busy helping out?
Client:	I'd talk to people more. You know, get to know them.
Therapist:	And let them know you?
Client:	Ooh, that's scary.
Therapist:	But this is magic, right? If magic happened, so fear lost all its power over you…
Client:	Yeah, I'd let them get to know me a bit better.
Therapist:	And what values would that be living—if you talk to people, get to know them and let them know you?
Client:	Err, I'm not sure…
Therapist:	Would it be any of the values on that list?
Client:	(*scanning the list*) Ummm…genuine…open…trusting…
Therapist:	Courageous?
Client:	Yes!
Therapist:	So if our work here could help you to do that, that would be useful?
Client:	I don't think I could.
Therapist:	You look worried.
Client:	I am.
Therapist:	What's showing up for you?
Client:	I'm scared.
	(*The therapist takes the client through a brief NAME exercise to make room for anxiety, then continues.*)
Therapist:	So even thinking about acting on those values brings up anxiety, right? And your mind doesn't like that. So what does it tell you to do?
Client:	Don't do it!

Therapist:	Yep, follow the rules. And your mind has laid down some very clear rules about what you can and can't do. Let's go through them. Number one is, obviously, "Be helpful!" What are some others?
Client:	Well, don't talk to anyone for too long. Keep moving.
Therapist:	Yeah. And what are you allowed to talk about?
Client:	Oh, just jokes or small talk.
Therapist:	And you're not allowed to talk about…?
Client:	Personal stuff. Nothing deep or meaningful.
Therapist:	And what does your mind threaten you with, to stop you from breaking those rules? What does it warn you will happen?
Client:	Oh you know, they'll find out what I'm really like.
Therapist:	And then?
Client:	And then they won't like me.
Therapist:	And then?
Client:	Well, they won't want to know me.
Therapist:	And then?
Client:	I'll be alone.
Therapist:	And that's a pretty big threat, isn't it?
Client:	Yeah.

The therapist has now identified the fusion and experiential avoidance that motivates the client's behavior and identified the values they've "lost." There are many ways to go from here: exploring ways to act on those values (openness, honesty, trusting, and courage) in social situations; defusion from rules; making room for the anxiety that will inevitably accompany these new behaviors. If time allows, the therapist can also explore the client's comment "They'll find out what I'm really like": tease out fusion with self-judgment, and move into self-compassion. (If there's insufficient time, the therapist would follow this up in the next session.)

Homework

For homework, we could ask clients to reflect on their values, write about them, talk about them with a loved one. We could also ask them to track when and where they act on their values, and what happens when they do so. (See the various homework worksheets in Extra Bits.)

If, however, the client is already clear on at least some of their values, we can ask them to nominate an area of life (e.g., work, relationships, health, or leisure) and specify two or three values to "play around with" in that domain. Alternatively, we can invite them to experiment with "flavoring and savoring" (Harris, 2015).

Flavoring and Savoring

Therapist: Each morning, choose one or two values that you want to bring into play through-out the day. So, for example, you might pick "playfulness" and "openness." You can choose different ones each day, or always keep them the same—up to you. Then, as you go through your day, look out for opportunities to "sprinkle" those values into your activities—so whatever you're saying or doing, see if you can give it the flavor of those values. And as you flavor it, savor it! You notice what you're doing and you actively savor the experience—just like savoring your favorite food or music—you tune in, notice what's happening, appreciate it.

Most clients respond well to this suggestion, but a few have great difficulty with "savoring," which indicates the need to work on mindful appreciation skills, as in chapter twenty-seven.

 EXTRA BIT   In *Trauma-Focused ACT: The Extra Bits*, chapter fifteen, you'll find values checklists, information about values cards, activity-monitoring worksheets, various homework worksheets, the "Bull's Eye," and the "Life Compass."

Takeaway

Values are the foundation of the whole ACT model. Like a compass, they give us direction, keep us on track, and help us find our way when we get lost. Clients often find it hard to connect with their values because they are buried under layers of fusion and avoidance. This is especially so with clients who are disconnected from their feelings or have an impoverished sense of self. But over time, with gentle, patient persistence—and huge amounts of understanding and compassion—we can usually get there. We may discover values hiding in many places, especially in narratives about what's lacking or missing, in experiences that give a sense of vitality and meaning, and in the important messages carried by painful emotions. Once values are unearthed, they become a powerful source of motivation and inspiration for the difficult work of building a meaningful life.

CHAPTER SIXTEEN

Doing What Works

The dual aims of TFACT are to reduce psychological suffering and build a meaningful life. To achieve these outcomes requires committed action: living by and acting on our values, in ways both great and small. Committed action is a truly huge umbrella; it encompasses not only goal setting, action planning, problem solving, and formal exposure, but also any type of empirically supported behavioral intervention, from behavioral activation for depression to social skills training for interpersonal problems.

The brunt of work in this stage involves helping our clients to reclaim, open, or expand important areas of life they've been avoiding, and most sessions have a dual focus on (a) translating values into actions, and (b) overcoming barriers. In the first part of this chapter, we'll review the main elements of this work; in the second part, we'll look at a transcript that illustrates them; and in the third part, we'll cover strategies to facilitate committed action despite the many challenges of trauma.

From Values to Actions

In a typical session, we invite clients to select a domain of life or a problem to work on and choose the values they want to put into play. We then help them set goals, create action plans, and implement them. In some cases, this may involve abandoning areas of life that are toxic (e.g., ending an abusive relationship, leaving an unsafe workplace, or staying away from people and places that facilitate problematic drug use). As you'd expect, such work usually triggers painful thoughts and feelings, so we often have to segue into defusion, acceptance, or self-compassion, and then return to the task at hand.

Useful Questions for Goals

After asking the client to pick a life domain they wish to improve, or a specific problem they'd like to address, we can ask questions such as:

- What values do you want to bring into play here?

- What do you want to stand for?

- What do you want to be about in the face of this?

- Who do you want to be as you address this?

- What do you want to model for others?

The client identifies one to three values they want to bring into play, which we then use to set SMART goals. There are various versions of the SMART acronym; I prefer the following:

S—Specific

M—Motivated by values

A—Adaptive

R—Realistic

T—Time-framed

(If you're not familiar with these terms or are unsure how to set SMART goals, see Extra Bits.)

Goals into Action Plans

Next, we break those goals down into action plans:

- When and where will you do this?

- What's the first step? And then what? And then?

- What equipment, resources, and skills will you need?

- What unhooking skills will you need?

- On a video, what will that look like and sound like?

Often, we can "cut out the middleman": move directly from values to actions without the intermediate step of goal setting. (We did this in the WHO protocol because we thought goal setting would add an unnecessary level of complexity. This is also a good option for clients who dread, resent, or feel overwhelmed by setting goals.) If we follow this path, then after choosing values, we ask, "So what are some small, simple actions you can take straight away, to start living these values? Little things you could say and do, not too demanding?" And we emphasize "thinking small":

Therapist: You know the saying "The journey of a thousand miles begins with one step"? So let's think small here. What's the smallest, easiest step you could take?

LONG-TERM GOALS

Initially TFACT focuses on short-term goals and action plans: what do you want to achieve in the next few hours, days, or weeks? But later, we look at longer-term goals, such as finding a partner or changing career. (Of course, it doesn't have to be that way around; we can look at long-, medium-, or short-term goals at any point in therapy.) When breaking these goals down, we have the client consider: What do I need to start doing *right now* to have the best chances of achieving this in the future? What short-term and medium-term goals will take me closer toward it?

So, for example, if a client has a long-term goal of finding a partner, short-term goals may include researching and joining dating platforms, starting new activities where they are likely to meet suitable people, or maybe even working on social skills. Medium-term goals may be going on dates or sharing activities with potential candidates. Similarly, if the long-term goal is to find a new job or change career, short-term goals may be researching different work options, seeing a career counselor, or writing a resume. Medium-term goals may be learning new skills, getting work experience, or going for interviews.

VALUES-BASED PROBLEM SOLVING

Problem solving in TFACT differs from other models because it is explicitly values based. Thus, after defining a problem, we explore: "What do you want to stand for in the face of this?" or "What values do you want to bring into play?"

From there, we follow all the traditional steps of formal problem solving. We brainstorm possible courses of action, consider the pros and cons of each, and combine the best ideas into an action plan. We then implement it, track the results, and modify it as needed—depending on what worked and what didn't. (The challenge formula comes in very handy here.)

ANTICIPATING OBSTACLES

Once clients have established an action plan, we ask, "Can you think of anything that might get in the way of this?" We then help them figure out how to deal with those obstacles, should they arise.

It's wise to explore a "fallback option" or "contingency plan"; if a particular course of action can't be pursued for one reason or another, there are always many other ways to act on the underlying values. But without planning ahead, clients may not realize this. So we may ask, "You know that saying, 'The best laid plans of mice and men often go awry'? If this all goes pear-shaped, what's your plan B?"

Willingness

Willingness is essential. We check repeatedly that clients are *willing* to take action—even if it's scary, painful, and difficult. We remind them that they don't *have to* do it; it's a personal choice. And we ensure it's in the service of their own values and goals, as opposed to pleasing or complying with the therapist.

Earlier we looked at "willingness" as a synonym for acceptance: the willingness to make room for your thoughts and feelings, in the service of living your values (as opposed to reluctantly or half-heartedly making room for them, which we call "tolerance"). Here "willingness" refers to a quality of behavior: doing things willingly as opposed to resentfully or begrudgingly. And we need to clearly distinguish "willing" from "wanting":

Client:	I don't really want to do it.
Therapist:	Of course you don't. It's bringing up a lot of uncomfortable thoughts and feelings. And you don't have to do it. The question is, is it important to you? Are you willing to do it, even though you don't want to?
Client:	I don't see the difference.
Therapist:	Well, suppose I had cancer. Now I do not *want* to have chemotherapy or radio-therapy or surgery—but I'd be *willing* to have them in order to cure my cancer. So if something is important, we can be willing to do it even though we don't want to do it. Have you ever done something resentfully or half-heartedly?
Client:	Yeah.
Therapist:	So that's the opposite of willingness. And did you notice how dissatisfying it was?
Client:	Yeah. I get it. But I don't feel willing to do it.
Therapist:	Yeah, for sure. Because willingness isn't a feeling. It's more like an attitude: "This matters to me, I care about this—so I'm prepared to do it even though I have lots of uncomfortable feelings, and lots of thoughts about not doing it."

MOTIVATION

Given that new behavior is challenging, motivation is an important aspect of willingness. This is where values come into their own. Like the mythical philosopher's stone that transforms base metals into gold, values can turn any activity into something meaningful and intrinsically rewarding. With this aim in mind, we can ask:

So when you do this, will it be…

- a towards move/taking you closer to the bull's eye/moving toward the life you want to build?

- doing something new/trying something different—rather than doing the same old thing/ staying in the rut?

- getting closer to/more in line with the sort of person you want to be, deep in your heart?

- likely to have any benefits for you or the people you love?

Monitoring and Scheduling

In the previous chapter we discussed encouraging clients to monitor their daily activities and gauge them in terms of vitality and workability. This provides a lot of valuable information about what the client does that *is* workable—and what they do that *isn't*. It's often a great springboard for committed action: the idea is to do more of the behaviors that *are* workable, and explore alternatives to the ones that are not.

Hand-in-hand with monitoring goes scheduling. We encourage clients to fill in worksheets (see Extra Bits) to schedule life-enhancing activities for the week ahead. This advanced planning instigates and maintains positive behavior change and is especially important for clients who are apathetic, demotivated, or depressed. If they don't plan ahead, they often find themselves spending time in unfulfilling ways. Scheduling can be done anywhere from a day to a week in advance—and the more planning and organizing an activity requires, the earlier this should start.

If clients have no idea of meaningful things to do with their time, this itself plays a big role in maintaining or exacerbating their suffering. In such cases, we can present them with a list of pleasant activities. (You'll find one in Extra Bits, but a google search for "list of pleasant activities" will give you lots of alternatives.) As therapy progresses, we can help clients engage mindfully in these activities while defusing from and accepting the difficult thoughts and feelings almost certain to arise.

Exploring and Experimenting

"If you always do what you've always done, you always get what you've always gotten."

This quote by Jesse Potter (often erroneously attributed to Henry Ford) speaks to the problem of behavioral rigidity. When facing difficult situations, behavioral variability is (usually) adaptive—but our default setting is to fall back into long-established patterns. And on occasion, that may be effective. But very often, by the time clients come to therapy, they are stuck in narrow, rigid repertoires of behavior that are not working to give them the results they want; and often, they aren't even aware of this.

So we encourage them to explore other options, experiment with new and different ways of doing things. And inevitably, this is risky. When we step out of our comfort zone and try new things, there's always a risk of failure. There are no guarantees. Things may go wrong; things may backfire; things may even get worse. So anxiety—and all the reason-giving that goes with it—is virtually guaranteed, and we repeatedly normalize and validate it. And we ask, "Are you willing to make room for these difficult thoughts and feelings, in order to do what matters?"

And what if the client is *not* willing? Glad you asked.

THE HARD BARRIERS

Again and again, as we do this work, we will push up against the HARD barriers:

H—Hooked

A—Avoiding discomfort

R—Remoteness from values

D—Doubtful goals

H = Hooked

Clients will repeatedly get hooked by reason-giving: their minds will come up with many different reasons for why they can't, shouldn't, or shouldn't even have to take action: "I don't deserve a life," "I'll only fail if I try," "Something bad will happen," "I'll get hurt," and so on.

The antidote is defusion—especially notice, name, normalize, purpose, workability. The mind's main "purpose" for virtually all forms of reason-giving is protection: saving you from pain, keeping you from taking risks. And the workability question is always some version of "If you let those thoughts dictate your choices, where does that take you?" We may add, "You can't stop your mind from saying these things, but you can unhook from them."

A = Avoiding Discomfort

Personal growth and meaningful change means stepping out of your comfort zone. This inevitably brings up discomfort in the form of difficult thoughts, sensations, emotions, memories, and urges. If clients aren't able to open up and make room for these experiences, they won't do the things that really matter. To overcome this barrier, we do more work on developing or applying acceptance and self-compassion skills.

R = Remoteness from Values

Why would clients bother to do this challenging stuff if it's not important or meaningful? If clients are ignoring, neglecting, or forgetting their values; or being pulled away from their values by fusion (e.g., with rules); or merely paying lip service to certain values to please the therapist, then they will not have the desired effect. The antidote is to help clients truly identify and connect with their values, and recognize they will be living these values with every step they take.

D = Doubtful Goals

As mentioned in chapter nine, after agreeing on an action plan, it's useful to gauge how realistic it seems, on a scale of zero to ten. If a client scores less than seven, it's doubtful they will follow through. So we explore: Are their goals excessive? Are they trying to do too much, or do it too quickly? Or perhaps even trying to do it perfectly? Are they trying to do things for which they lack the resources (such as time, money, energy, health, social support, or necessary skills)?

If so, we change the goals: make them smaller, simpler, easier, and matched to the client's resources—until the client's realism score goes up to at least seven.

The idea is to run through these common barriers with the client, see which ones are relevant, and come up with plans to deal with them. (In Extra Bits, you'll find a HARD barriers worksheet.)

Transcript: Therapy Session with Mark

This is an extract from session six with Mark, a thirty-four-year-old former army officer. Mark developed PTSD after a tour of duty in which his friend was shot through the head and killed. He has since left the army. He lives by himself, has become socially withdrawn, and feels intensely lonely. In line with his values of "courage, self-care, and friendship," he wants to reestablish social contact with friends and family. He would like to start by reaching out to his oldest friend, Jake.

Therapist:	Any hesitation about doing this? Does anything show up for you when you talk about that as a possibility?
Client:	I guess there is a little bit of um, a resistance, because you know, I don't want to have to talk about stuff too much and I also feel, like, embarrassed that I haven't kept in contact.
Therapist:	So those are valid concerns. Do you notice anything happening in your body right now? Uncomfortable feelings?
Client:	Yeah. Got like a, like a pain in my gut here.
Therapist:	What's it like in there?
Client:	Like tight or something.
Therapist:	Tight? And what kind of shape and size?
Client:	Like a ball. (*uses his finger to draw a circle around his abdomen*)
Therapist:	And what would you call this feeling?
Client:	Maybe, like fear or something?
Therapist:	Fear? Well, that's to be expected. As we start to talk about making changes in your life to build a new future, there will probably be a lot difficult thoughts and feelings showing up.
	(*The therapist takes the client through a ninety-second NAME exercise to help him accept the fear. Following this, they explore reason-giving...*)
Therapist:	So as we've discussed before, your mind is like a reason-giving machine, and it's going to crank out a whole lot of reasons not to do this. Can I get you to jot some of these down?
Client:	Okay.
	(*The therapist prompts the client to identify reason-giving, with questions such as "How's your mind trying to talk you out of this?" "What's it warning you might go*

wrong?" The client writes down each reason on a sheet of paper. This continues for three minutes. The thoughts include: *Don't want to talk about what happened, He's moved on, He's got no time for me, We're too different, He won't want to talk to me, I'm too fucked up, I've got nothing to say, He's got a life and I haven't, I got nothing, I am nothing. I'm going nowhere.)*

Therapist: There we go. So your mind's really doing a hatchet job, isn't it? "I got nothing. I am nothing. I'm going nowhere." And my guess is this isn't unique to Jake; your mind would say this if you think about reaching out to just about anyone.

Client: Yeah, it would.

Therapist: I mean, there might be a few little tweaks on the theme, but it'd basically be "I'm nothing, got nothing, they don't want me, I don't like talking..."

Client: Probably, yeah, yeah.

Therapist: *(pointing to the paper)* So how are you going to unhook from that?

Client: Um...I can call it the "Don't Do It!" story?

Therapist: Sounds good to me. Can I get you to write that on the back?

(On the back of the paper, the therapist asks Mark to write, in large, bold letters: *Aha! Here it is again! The "Don't Do It!" story. Thanks, mind. I know you're trying to save me from pain—but it's okay—I've got this handled.* [Mark has already used these techniques in previous sessions.] The therapist asks Mark to silently read to himself all the negative thoughts written on the paper—and emphasizes, "And see if you can really let them hook you." The therapist then asks Mark to flip the paper over and silently read the statement on the back. Mark finds this very helpful: his score on the fusion scale [chapter ten] drops from an eight to a three.)

Therapist: So all of this stuff—these thoughts and feelings: fear, embarrassment, pain in the stomach, self-judgment—I predict they're going to keep showing up as barriers, to stop you from doing the stuff that makes your life better.

Client: I think you're right.

Therapist: Any idea what your mind might be trying to save you from?

Client: Um yeah, embarrassment? Fear? Failure?

Therapist: Yup. Fear, embarrassment, getting hurt. So your mind's a lot like my mind; this is what they do to protect us. And there's a choice here. Do you give up on doing the stuff that's important, because of all these difficult thoughts and feelings, or do you make room for them, and do what really matters?

Client:	I'm not giving up.
Therapist:	What are you going to do?
Client:	I'm going to call him.
Therapist:	You know, my mind's telling me you'll think this sounds corny, but the truth is, I feel privileged to hear you say that. I mean, I can see that this is painful for you and I know you've been through an incredibly rough journey and I can see your mind generating all of these reasons to give up—and yet you're willing to keep going. That's inspiring.
Client:	Thanks.
Therapist:	So what's the very first step?
Client:	Um, well, just pick up the phone, I guess.
Therapist:	Okay. So I'm going to put you on the spot here. I'm going to ask you a question, and before you answer I want you to just use that noticing part and just notice what your mind says and notice what feelings show up in your body. Okay? So the question: When are you going to call him? Give me a day, date, time. Take a few seconds. Just notice what your mind says. Notice what feelings show up in your body.
Client:	Okay.
Therapist:	What are you noticing in your body?
Client:	Uh, my stomach went a bit tight. There are bits that are like jumpy.
Therapist:	What did your mind say?
Client:	It's just like scanning for I don't know... Is he going to be available? Will he pick up? What will we do?
Therapist:	Can I get you to jot those things down too, please? Will he be available? Will he pick up? What will we do? (*Mark writes them down.*) And how would you describe this feeling?
Client:	Um, worried.
Therapist:	Worried? So if that's showing up right now just talking about it, we can pretty much guarantee it's going to show up in the real situation.
Client:	Yeah, you're right.
Therapist:	Are you willing to make room for this stuff?

Client:	Yes. Yeah for sure.
Therapist:	Cool. So let's plan it. When are you going to make the call? Day, date, time?
Client:	Okay, say Wednesday, after work—about sixish.
Therapist:	So, let's role-play it. I'll be Jake. You pick up the phone. Just kind of...let's just kind of play with this. You've kind of, you've got the phone there and I'm Jake. (*Client and therapist both pretend they are talking into cell phones.*) Uh, hello?
Client:	Hey, Jake, how are ya?
Therapist:	Uh, who's this?
Client:	It's Mark.
Therapist:	Mark...Mark! Okay!
Client:	Hey, buddy, what's going on? Long time!
Therapist:	Wow. It is a long time. What the fuck happened to you?
Client:	(*awkwardly*) Err...yeah...well, err...
Therapist:	Okay let's pause. What's showing up?
Client:	Uh, a bit embarrassed, a bit of fear, a bit of I don't know what to say.
Therapist:	Okay. What was your mind actually saying while you were talking to Jake?
Client:	Uh, you know, this is stupid. Hang up.
Therapist:	Well, that's what your mind's going to say on the day. So I'm wondering, is it worth maybe rehearsing a bit—preparing what you're going to say?
Client:	Yeah I could um, I could just you know practice maybe what I'm going to say—like where I've been, why I didn't keep in touch.
Therapist:	Great. So let's say you chat with him for a few mins, and then...what are you going to ask him? Like, are you going to suggest catching up, doing something together?
Client:	Uh, yeah—maybe see if he wants to go for a beer or play some basketball, shoot some hoops.
	(*They now role-play this part of the conversation, and again the therapist asks Mark to check in, see what's showing up. Once again, Mark reports embarrassment and anxiety and thoughts about backing out.*)

Therapist: So in the service of those values of courage, self-care, and friendship, are you willing to make room for all of that?

Client: Yes I am.

Therapist: On a zero to ten scale, how realistic is it that you will do these two things: (a) go home and rehearse and plan this conversation, and (b) actually make that phone call on Wednesday at 6 p.m.?

Client: Uh...I'd like to say ten but uh, I would say, realistically, about eight.

The transcript above illustrates the two key themes of this chapter: translating values into goals and actions, and overcoming HARD barriers. Note the use of role-play to bring the action plan to life, and the repeated segues into defusion and acceptance.

Additional Strategies for Committed Action

With trauma-related disorders, there are often many barriers to committed action, so we typically need multiple strategies to help clients do what truly matters to them. In this section, we'll explore several options; the idea is to add these on to the methods we've already covered.

Savoring and Appreciating

In the last chapter, we discussed "flavoring and savoring." We can extend this practice to all committed action, on an ongoing basis, by repeatedly tuning in to underlying values and mindfully appreciating what happens as a result. This plays a big role in ongoing motivation. For example, many clients with trauma-related disorders suffer from high social anxiety—especially with regard to fear of negative evaluation. Social withdrawal is understandably common. But even when clients do attend social events, they often "white-knuckle" it: "tough it out" and "get through it" with little or no satisfaction or enjoyment. Afterward, they typically judge the event—and their own social "performance"—extremely negatively: "It was horrible," "a waste of time," "hated every minute of it," "I was useless," "I couldn't talk to anyone," "I hid in the corner," and so on. Naturally, this bodes poorly for future socializing.

So when such clients attend social events, we can encourage them to notice and appreciate all those little moments where they manage to make eye contact (even fleetingly), or share something personal, or establish a sense of connection. That way, even if the overall experience is stressful and dissatisfying, there are moments within it they can appreciate. And over time, as their skills improve, they are likely to have more of those meaningful moments. (Of course, mindful appreciation is a skill that usually requires formal practice: see chapter twenty-seven.)

Cognitive Flexibility and Committed Action

As discussed earlier, ACT helps people not only to defuse from unhelpful cognitions but also to develop new, more effective ways of thinking. Let's quickly look at three types of flexible thinking that TFACT encourages to facilitate committed action: reframing, reinterpreting, and motivational self-talk.

REFRAMING

"Reframing" means looking at something from a different perspective, which then changes the way you respond to it. TFACT is full of reframing—especially about what's in our control and what isn't. For example, at times clients fuse with thoughts like *I'll fail* or *It won't work*. After normalizing those thoughts, we often present this reframe: "The truth is, we have no control over whether we will achieve a goal or not, but we do have a lot of control over the actions we take to try and achieve it. So even though there are no guarantees, we can give it our best shot. And if we fail, at least we know we tried. But if we give up because our mind says, 'It won't work,' then that's obviously not taking us toward the life we want."

Sometimes, clients get hooked by the narrative "I can never have the life I want," and often they can back this up with incontrovertible evidence based on their past trauma history. If so, we validate that the life they have is not the one they wanted, and we help them make room for the painful feelings that are inevitable and practice self-compassion. After much validation, and with great compassion, we may help them reframe this situation: "It's truly awful what you've been through. No one should have to experience that. The question is, what next? Where to from here? You probably know that old saying: 'We don't get to choose the deck of cards life deals us—but we do get to choose how we play them.'" In other words, the challenge now for the client is how to make the most of the life they have—even though it's not the one they want.

At other times clients may protest, "It's too late." In this case, a useful reframe is that old Chinese proverb: "The best time to plant a tree was twenty years ago; the second best time is now." In other words, we agree, it would have been better to start earlier—but that's not in the client's control; what is in their control is to take action now. (We could add, "Your mind will keep saying it's too late—and every time it says that, there's a choice for you to make.")

REINTERPRETING

The more difficult, challenging, or threatening a situation, the more likely it is to trigger fusion with judgments, themes, rules, reasons, schemas, or core beliefs. And in turn, that fusion shapes the way we interpret the situation. All too often, our initial automatic interpretation is unhelpful—in the sense that it doesn't help us to act effectively, guided by our values; rather, it triggers self-defeating patterns of behavior. So when clients face these situations, we encourage them to drop anchor and unhook from that first interpretation, and consider alternative perspectives that can help them to handle it better. In other words: "How can I think about this differently, in a way that's going to help me act effectively?"

For example, a client prone to aggressive verbal behavior is very anxious and furious because her partner is three hours late in returning home from work. While dropping anchor, she might say to herself something like *My mind's in judgment mode*, or *My mind's telling me she did this on purpose to hurt me*, or *Here's the "She doesn't care" theme!* She makes room for her anger and anxiety and reminds herself of the values she's been working on: being kind, patient, and understanding.

She thinks to herself, *If I let myself get hooked by "She doesn't care," I know what's going to happen. I'll start shouting, yelling, blaming as she comes through the door, and we'll have a huge fight. I don't want that. My values are kindness, patience, and understanding. How would a kind, patient, understanding partner interpret this situation?*

She may then consider, *It's not really her fault; other people screwed up the project and made it run late. And she's usually good at getting home on time. And she's called me twice to apologize and explain. Blaming and yelling just pulls me away from the partner I want to be. So I'm going to use this as an opportunity to practice my new skills. I'm going to drop anchor and practice the Kind Hands exercise.*

There are similarities here to the CBT strategy of cognitive reappraisal; the big differences are that there's (a) no disputation of cognitions and (b) no attempt to escape, avoid, or control emotions. We defuse from unhelpful cognitions, accept the emotions, and take a new perspective on the situation to enable effective values-guided action. (And that's why I've called this "reinterpreting" rather than "reappraising"—to reduce confusion. In ACT terminology, this comes under the umbrella of "flexible perspective taking.")

The basic steps of this strategy are:

1.   Drop anchor, unhook from your thoughts, make room for your feelings.

2.   Consider: What values do I want to bring into play? What outcomes do I want to aim for?

3.   Consider: How can I look at this in a different way that helps me to act effectively?

(Keep in mind, we don't necessarily need to follow this order; steps 2 and 3 are interchangeable. And if clients are not struggling with cognitions and emotions, they can skip step 1.)

MOTIVATIONAL SELF-TALK

It's often useful to have clients prepare in advance some motivational prompts: short catchphrases they can use to nudge themselves into action, keep them going, or foster their willingness. Here are some examples:

•   This is hard, but it's important.

•   Every step counts.

•   Rome wasn't built in a day.

•   Just make a start; once you're over the speed bump, it gets easier.

- I don't have to do it perfectly. It's okay to make mistakes.

- Little by little does the trick.

- I can do this—even though it's uncomfortable.

- I don't want to do this, but I'm willing to.

- I don't *have to* do this; I *choose* to.

- Here's an opportunity to live my values.

- Thinking about it won't get it done.

I'm sure you can think of many others. Indeed, there are many famous quotes and sayings we can recruit for this purpose. For example, when I'm finding it hard to keep writing because my mind says it's rubbish, I remind myself of Ernest Hemingway's quote: "The first draft of anything is shit!" At other times, when my mind beats me up for not writing fast enough, I remind myself of Aesop's saying: "Slow and steady wins the race." Usually this self-talk keeps me going. The key ways to keep motivational self-talk ACT-congruent are to (a) make it realistic, (b) not try using it to avoid or get rid of unwanted thoughts and feelings, and (c) ensure it's aligned with values.

"I Just Don't Know How to Do It!"

Sometimes clients will identify a value but then fuse with *I don't know how to do this*! For example, clients who tend to self-sacrifice, people-please, or be overly responsible for others may want to take better care of themselves but have little or no idea of what this looks like behaviorally. To help them with this, we may:

- suggest they watch movies and TV shows, or read books, and (a) look for actions of self-care the characters take, and then (b) consider how to translate that to their own life;

- teach them assertiveness skills, including basic psychoeducation about their rights and the rights of others, how to say no, and how to set boundaries;

- suggest they google "self-care activities" to find a huge number of suggestions;

- ask them to complete activity-monitoring worksheets, rating each activity on a self-care scale of zero to ten (ten = very caring for self, zero = not at all caring for self); and

- ask them to imagine a role reversal: "If you were caring for someone else, what would that look like/sound like? Now how can you do something similar for yourself?"

In addition, such clients will need good acceptance skills, because self-care will trigger much anxiety, and defusion skills, to unhook from rules like "I must put others first" and "I am unworthy."

Although the example above is for self-care, these basic strategies can be modified and adapted for any value a client does not know how to operationalize.

Is Attention Training Needed?

You may recall that in chapter eight we touched on the importance of attention training as an antidote to distractibility and disengagement. If clients find it hard to focus on or engage in a new values-based activity, they probably won't find it very satisfying; and if it's a complex task, they probably won't do it well. In such cases, we can introduce (or revisit) attention-training practices (e.g., traditional mindfulness of the breath) and encourage clients to practice them regularly. The idea is to develop their focusing skills and apply them to these new activities.

Setbacks Happen

Committed action is a bumpy road. As our clients expand their lives through acting on their values, they will have successes and failures, breakthroughs and setbacks. At times things will go better than they ever expected; at other times they will go horribly wrong.

When setbacks happen, the first step is to acknowledge how painful that is, make room for the feelings, and practice self-compassion. This includes both defusion from harsh judgments (*That was a total waste of time, This shows how useless I am*) and compassionate self-talk (*At least I tried, Everybody has setbacks, Tomorrow is another day*).

The second step is reflection: *Even though overall it did not go well, were there any moments—no matter how brief—where things did go well, or I had a sense of being more like the person I want to be? Is there anything I can learn from this? What worked? What didn't work? What could I do more of, less of, or differently next time around?*

This reflective practice not only reframes setbacks as learning opportunities, but also acts as an antidote to the harsh judgments mentioned above. It also often suggests new homework activities.

EXTRA BIT   In *Trauma-Focused ACT: The Extra Bits*, chapter sixteen, you'll find worksheets for setting SMART goals, values-based problem solving, overcoming HARD barriers, monitoring, and scheduling activities.

Takeaway

When translating values into actions, we help our clients set goals, create action plans, solve problems, and learn skills; we facilitate flexible contact with important aspects of life the client has been avoiding (technically, this is exposure); and we encourage experimentation with new behaviors. We continually check that clients are genuinely willing and their goals are realistic. We can expect the HARD barriers—*Hooked, Avoiding discomfort, Remoteness from values, and Doubtful goals*—to arise repeatedly; and to help clients get past these, we use defusion, acceptance, connection with values, and SMART goal setting.

CHAPTER SEVENTEEN

Undermining Problematic Behavior

How do we do TFACT with substance abuse, suicidality, social withdrawal, self-harming, aggression, gambling, reckless risk taking, self-neglect, self-harm, hygiene, lying, stealing, compulsive checking or cleaning, fawning, excessive bed rest, procrastination…or just about any other problematic behavior you can think of? I'm so glad you asked! In this chapter, we'll explore a four-step approach to undermining any type of problematic, destructive, or self-defeating behavior. Once you have a handle on this, you can figure out how to use TFACT with almost anything.

Function Matters!

Before we get into the four steps, I want to introduce (or renew your acquaintance with) the concept that underpins them: "functional analysis." This means figuring out the "functions" of a behavior: the effects it has, or what it achieves, in a particular situation. When we focus on any problematic behavior, functional analysis is the best place to start because it opens many possibilities for specific, carefully targeted interventions.

To figure out the functions of a behavior, we need to know (a) what triggers it—the "antecedents," and (b) what the immediate outcomes are—the "consequences." Antecedents can include situations, cognitions, emotions, urges, sensations, memories; anything you can see, hear, touch, taste, and smell; and physiological states, such as thirst, hunger, illness, or fatigue. (On a choice point diagram, antecedents always go on the bottom.) So basically, antecedents are anything present—in your inner or outer world—that directly triggers (or, to use the technical term, "cues") the behavior in question.

If the immediate outcomes are such that the behavior continues or increases, they are known as "reinforcing consequences," or "reinforcers"; they reinforce the behavior. Conversely, if the immediate outcomes are such that the behavior discontinues or reduces, they are known as "punishing consequences," or "punishers"; they punish the behavior.

Once we know the antecedents and consequences for any given behavior, we know its functions: the effects it has, or what it achieves, in this situation. For example, suppose that a client, alone in their apartment at night, has intense feelings of anxiety (antecedents) that trigger the overt behavior of smoking marijuana. They smoke a joint, and the immediate outcomes are (a) their anxiety disappears, and (b) they feel calm and relaxed. These outcomes keep the habit going—so they are reinforcing consequences. We now know at least two functions of smoking marijuana in this particular situation: to avoid anxiety and to feel relaxed. The diagram below shows how we could plot this out on a choice point; in this case, the client sees smoking marijuana as a "bad habit" that they want to kick, so it goes on the away arrow. (If desired, you can write the reinforcing consequences in a "payoffs" box, as illustrated.)

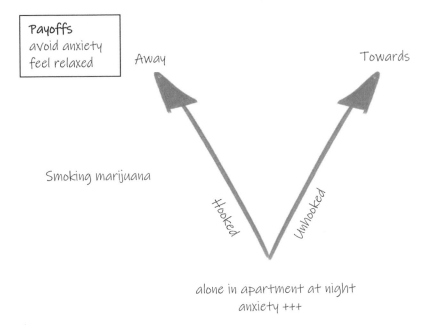

Now let's consider the functions of smoking marijuana for a different person in a different situation. This client is a sixteen-year-old at a party. As he sees his friends taking turns smoking a joint, he experiences feelings of excitement, a pleasurable sense of risk taking and adventure, and the desire to join in. These thoughts and feelings are the antecedents for what he does next: smokes the joint. The immediate outcomes are an enjoyable feeling of doing something cool and adventurous and a sense of camaraderie and belonging to the group. These outcomes make it more likely that he will do the same

2

thing in similar situations in the future—so they are reinforcing consequences. Therefore, the main functions of this behavior are fitting in with his social group and the excitement of risk taking.

In the choice point diagram below, the client sees this behavior as something he wants to keep doing, in line with his values of social connection, having fun, and being adventurous—so it goes on the towards arrow.

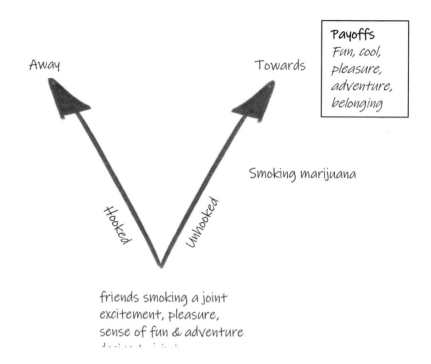

Away

Towards

Payoffs
Fun, cool, pleasure, adventure, belonging

Smoking marijuana

Hooked

Unhooked

friends smoking a joint
excitement, pleasure,
sense of fun & adventure

Both examples above analyze what is *reinforcing* behavior. At other times, if a desired behavior is reducing in frequency, we may analyze what is *punishing* it. The figure below illustrates the choice point in terms of antecedents, behaviors, and consequences.

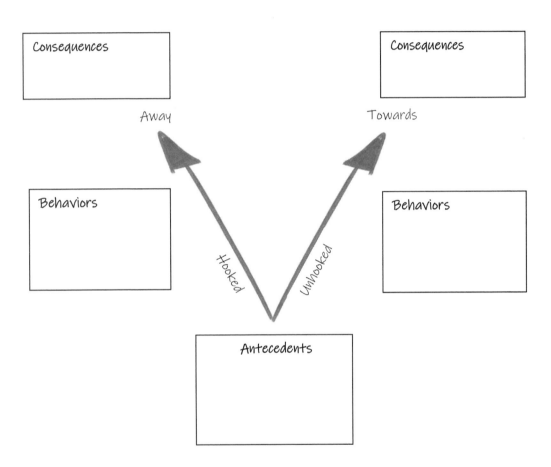

Four Steps to Undermine Any Problematic Behavior

When a client wants to reduce or stop a problematic behavior, we typically go through a four-step process, answering the following questions:

1. What triggers the behavior?

2. What are the costs and benefits?

3. What's a good alternative?

4. What skills are needed?

Before we explore these four steps, a practical note: When we wish to undermine any problematic behavior, we first need to specify what it *involves*: what is the person actually saying and doing? Specifically, what would we see them doing and hear them saying if we watched it on a video recording? (Covert behaviors, such as worrying and ruminating, can't be seen or heard on a video, so instead we specify them as "worrying about XYZ" or "ruminating about ABC.")

So, for a behavior described as "taking drugs," we want to know what substances are taken, how, in what quantities, and with what frequency? And for a behavior described as "social withdrawal": does that mean canceling social events at the last minute, staying home when friends are out partying, refusing to answer phone calls, or staying in one's bedroom to avoid other people in the house?

Usually, some gentle questioning is necessary. For example, when clients say they want to "stop procrastinating," we ask, "What are you putting off doing?" (e.g., are they avoiding completing a tax return, or going to the gym, or having a difficult conversation?). Then we ask, "What do you do instead? What would I see and hear if I watched a video of you procrastinating?" (e.g., do they stare at a wall, go for a walk, surf the net, play video games, read books, hang out with family, stay in bed?). Once we have this information, instead of a vague, nonspecific term like "procrastinating," we can work with a specific description of the behavior, such as "watching TV instead of going to the gym."

Question One: What Triggers the Behavior?

Having specified the behavior, we want to know: what are the antecedents? What situations, thoughts, and feelings typically trigger it? Are there particular people, places, events, activities, cognitions, memories, emotions, sensations, or physiological states that cue this behavior? (If a behavior is triggered by many different situations, thoughts, and feelings, we focus on the most common ones. And if the triggers are predominantly private experiences, we may focus primarily on the cognitions and emotions, rather than situations.)

If clients aren't sure what triggers their behavior, one good option is to suggest they keep a diary: write down when and where they do it, and what they were feeling and thinking immediately beforehand. (There's a worksheet for this in Extra Bits.) Another option is to help the client recall, as vividly as possible, the last time they did the behavior, then "rewind" the memory to the moment immediately before they started doing it and see if they can remember the thoughts and feelings present at that moment.

Experiment on Yourself

A great way to learn the strategies in this chapter is to apply them to yourself. If you're willing to do this, pick an *overt* behavior you'd like to reduce. (It's easier to work with overt behaviors when you're new to this). You can use the "Functional Analysis Worksheet" in Extra Bits, or a blank sheet of paper, and begin by writing down a specific description of the behavior. Then, write down the antecedents.

Question Two: What Are the Costs and Benefits?

Any type of behavior has both benefits and costs. It's not *essential* to identify the benefits, but it's often helpful, because (a) it gives clients insight into why they keep doing this, and (b) it helps to validate the behavior, which facilitates self-compassion. Basically, the benefits of any behavior boil down to either or both of the following:

- You get to escape or avoid an "aversive stimulus" (i.e., something you don't want)

- You get to approach or access an "appetitive stimulus" (i.e., something you *do* want)

Remember, when the benefits are such that the behavior continues or increases, we call them reinforcing consequences. Below are some common reinforcers for problematic behaviors.

The behavior helps us to:

- escape or avoid challenging people, places, situations, or activities

- escape or avoid unwanted cognitions, emotions, memories, or sensations

- get our needs met

- gain attention

- gain approval

- get others to do what we want

- "look good" to others

- "fit in" with others

- feel better (e.g., relaxed, calm, happy, safe)

- feel righteous (we are "in the right," and others are "wrong")

- feel like we are successfully following important rules

- feel like we are working hard on ourselves or our problems

- feel like we are making sense (e.g., of life, the world, ourselves, others)

- feel comfortable by doing something familiar

There's a truly vast number of possible reinforcers—but most of them will fit under one or more of the broad categories above (usually several). Useful questions to identify them include:

Any idea what's keeping this behavior going?

Does it have any benefits you can identify?

Does it help you get something you want?

Does it help to save or protect you from something you don't want?

If clients can't answer these questions, we have three options. One option is to explore a bit more: "What usually happens—the moment you start doing this? Is there a moment when you first start doing it when there's a sense of getting something you want or getting away from something you don't want?"

A second option is to show clients the list of common reinforcers above (using the worksheet in Extra Bits).

And a third option is psychoeducation. For example: "There are three big benefits to worrying: (a) it helps us prepare for bad things that might happen; (b) it pulls us into our thoughts, which helps us to escape from feelings in our body; and (c) it feels like we're working hard on our problems."

Occasionally, despite our best efforts, we just can't figure out what's reinforcing the behavior—and that's okay. It's useful, not essential; we don't *have to* know the benefits in order to change behavior. It's much more important to get clear on the costs of the behavior.

When clients are contemplating changing their behavior, they are already aware of some of the costs—otherwise, why change? And often, they have already told us some of them. However, we now prompt them to reflect more deeply (just as in creative hopelessness). For example:

Have you noticed any costs or drawbacks to this behavior? Any unintended negative consequences?

Is there anything important that you lose or miss out on when you do this?

Does it lead to anything in your life that you don't really want?

Does it hold you back from anyone or anything important?

Does it take you away from any important values or goals?

And if we see some area of the client's life that their behavior is impacting negatively—but the client doesn't yet see it—we prompt them. We might say, for example, "I can't help wondering: what effect does this have on your relationship with your partner?"

After identifying costs, we give a compassionate and nonjudgmental summary, looking at the behavior in terms of workability. The basic script is as follows: "So it seems that DEF (*antecedents*) tend to trigger G (*specific behavior*), which has some real benefits, such as HIJ (*reinforcing consequences*), but also some significant costs, such as KLM (*adverse outcomes*). For example:

> Therapist: I'm going to have a go at summarizing this, and please tell me if I don't get it right. It seems like often in the evenings, lots of anxious thoughts and feelings show up for you, as well as these bad memories. And when you get hooked by that stuff, you drink beer and wine. And there's a real short-term benefit: it reduces your pain, helps you unwind, helps you forget. But in the long term, it's affecting your health and well-being. You don't sleep well, and you're often hungover, which affects your work performance. Your anxiety's getting worse, not better. Your wife is upset. Your kids are upset. You're missing out on the family life you want. And you're not being the sort of husband or father you want to be.

Experiment on Yourself

Okay, back to you again. What are the costs and benefits of your own behavior that you selected in the previous exercise? Please think about it carefully and identify as many as possible. Write them down, then summarize the information gathered so far, as exemplified above.

Question Three: What's a Good Alternative?

The third step is to consider what new, effective behavior the client will do (instead of the old, problematic one). For example:

- If you don't yell at your kids when they bug you, what will you do instead?

- If you don't stub cigarettes on your arms when these memories resurface, what will you do instead?

- If you don't get drunk after you quarrel with your partner, what will you do instead?

This brings us full circle to the previous two chapters: new, effective behaviors, guided by values. For example, regarding the bullet points above, the client may choose these new behaviors: (a) instead of yelling, they may patiently make an assertive statement, or accept it's happened and make a joke out of it, or talk calmly and honestly about their feelings; (b) instead of self-harming with cigarettes, they may firmly massage their arms and forearms, or do some stretching, or commence a self-soothing practice; or (c) instead of getting drunk, they may just have one or two drinks, or do a self-compassion practice, or go for a run around the block.

Experiment on Yourself

Now back to you again. So if you don't do what you normally do when all that difficult stuff shows up, what will you do instead? Write down a new, values-guided behavior, and consider:

- What values does this serve?

- What difficult thoughts and feelings go with it? Are you willing to make room for them?

- Is this at least a seven out of ten, in terms of how realistic it is? If not, make it simpler and easier, until you can score at least seven.

Question Four: What Skills Are Needed?

We now need to identify what skills the client needs to respond flexibly to (a) the antecedents to their old behavior, and (b) the HARD barriers to their new behavior. For example, do they need skills in defusion? Acceptance? Self-compassion? Urge surfing? Dropping anchor? Connecting with values? If the client already has these skills, we explore how to apply them. But if these skills are lacking, we help clients develop them.

Experiment on Yourself

So, one last time, back to you: What skills do you need to handle the antecedents to your problematic behavior and to overcome the HARD barriers to your new, effective behavior? How will you apply them?

EXTRA BIT

In *Trauma-Focused ACT: The Extra Bits* (downloadable from "Free Resources" on http://www.ImLearningACT.com) in chapter seventeen, you'll find (a) a generic functional analysis worksheet, (b) a choice-point-based functional analysis worksheet, and (c) an undermining problematic behavior worksheet.

Takeaway

We covered four steps in this chapter for undermining problematic behavior, involving the following four questions:

1. What triggers the behavior?

2. What are the costs and benefits?

3. What's a good alternative?

4. What skills are needed?

These steps are guidelines, not commandments. We don't always have to cover all of them, and we can readily change the order as desired. What I'm hoping and trusting is that you can now, using these guidelines, figure out how to use TFACT with just about any problematic behavior you encounter.

CHAPTER EIGHTEEN

Overcoming Barriers, Maintaining Change

Are you currently putting off any important tasks? Are there things you could be doing that you know full well will improve your life—but you're not doing them? Of course there are! Because you're human. And this is something we have in common with our clients. So when a client reports that they haven't done their homework, one good response is, "You are so like me!" We then explain to the shocked client, "We all do it. We all say, 'Yes, I'm going to do X and Y and Z'—and then we don't do it. It's normal." We then check to see if the client is fusing with self-judgment or struggling with shame or anxiety—and if so, we segue into dropping anchor, defusion, acceptance, or self-compassion, as needed.

After this, we put this issue onto the agenda for the session. If the client is reluctant to do this, we could say, "I know you want your life to be better…you've mentioned things like (*recaps some of the client's therapy goals*)…and the only way to make that happen is to follow through on this stuff, outside of our sessions. And the problem is, whatever stopped you from following through last time is likely to stop you again, this time and next time—unless we figure out how you can overcome it. So can we just spend a few minutes to figure out what the obstacle is, and come up with a strategy to overcome it?"

The Main Barriers to Committed Action

If clients aren't following through on committed action between sessions, we need to take a good look at…ourselves! Much of the time, clients don't follow through because therapists skip important steps, such as specifying the behavior, linking it to values, checking for willingness, anticipating obstacles, preparing a contingency plan, or ensuring a realism score of at least seven.

We also need to consider: is the therapeutic alliance strong? If not, we work on improving it.

Finally, we consider whether there are any HARD barriers. Is the client *Hooked*, *Avoiding discomfort*, *Remote from values*, or pursuing *Doubtful goals*? If so, we bring in the antidotes: unhooking; accepting discomfort; connecting with values; and SMART goals.

Maintaining Change: The Seven Rs

It's one thing to start some new type of life-enhancing behavior; it's another thing to keep it going. So how can we help our clients sustain their new patterns of behavior? There are hundreds of tools out there to help us with this challenge, but we can pretty much bundle them all into "the seven Rs": reminders, records, rewards, routines, relationships, reflecting, and restructuring the environment.

Reminders

Clients can use all sorts of simple tools to help remind them of their new behavior, for example, a pop-up or screensaver on their computer or smartphone with a key word, phrase, or symbol. Or there's the old favorite of writing a message on a card and sticking it on the fridge or bathroom mirror. This might be just one word, like "Breathe" or "Pause" or "Patience," or a phrase like "Letting go" or "Caring and compassionate." Alternatively, they could put a brightly colored sticker on the strap of their wrist-watch or their computer keyboard—so each time they use these devices the sticker reminds them to do the new behavior. And on top of all that, there are smartphone apps; for example, the "ACT Companion" app will send you brief messages about different aspects of ACT throughout the day. (These strategies are also good for clients who keep "forgetting" to do their homework.)

Records

Clients can keep a record of their new behavior throughout the day, writing down when and where they do it and what the benefits are. Any diary or notebook—on paper or on a computer screen—can serve this purpose. (Worksheets are handy, too.)

Rewards

Acting on one's values is (usually) intrinsically rewarding—and becomes even more so when we encourage clients to practice mindfully appreciating the experience. However, additional rewards are helpful to reinforce the new behavior. One form of reward is kind, encouraging self-talk, such as saying to oneself, *Well done. You did it!* Another form of reward is sharing success and progress with a loved one who is likely to respond positively. Some clients might prefer more material rewards. For example, if they sustain this new behavior for a whole week, they get to buy or do something that they really like, such as get a massage or buy a book.

Routines

We can explain to clients, "If you get up every morning at the same time to exercise or do yoga, over time that regular routine will start to come naturally. You won't have to think so hard about doing it; it will require less 'willpower'; it will become a part of your regular routine." We can then encourage them to experiment: see if they can find some way to build a regular routine or ritual around their new behavior so it starts to become part of their everyday way of life. For example, if they drive home from work, then every night, just before they get out of the car, they might do two minutes of dropping anchor, and then consider what values they want to bring into play when they go through the front door into their home.

Relationships

It's easier to study if you have a "study buddy"; easier to exercise if you have an "exercise buddy." So we can encourage clients to find a kind, caring, encouraging person who can help support them with their new behavior. (Sometimes the therapist is the only person who can play this role.) Ideally clients check in with this person on a regular basis and share their progress (as mentioned in "Rewards") in person or via text or email. Or they can use the other person as a "reminder." For example, a client might say to their partner, "When I raise my voice, can you please remind me to drop anchor?"

Reflecting

We can encourage clients to regularly reflect on how they are behaving and what effect it is having. They can do this via writing it down (i.e., through records) or in discussion with another person (i.e., through relationships). Or they can do this as a mental exercise throughout the day or just before bed. We might ask them to take a few moments to reflect: *How am I doing? What am I doing that's working? What am I doing that's not working? What can I do more of, or less of, or differently?*

Restructuring the Environment

Clients can often restructure their environment to make their new behavior easier. For example, if the new behavior involves healthy eating, they can restructure the kitchen: get rid of or hide away the junk food and stock the fridge and pantry with healthy stuff. If the new behavior is drinking water and tea in the evenings, instead of beer or wine—they can remove the alcohol. If they want to go to the gym in the morning, they could pack up their sports gear in their gym bag and place it beside the bed or somewhere else obvious and convenient, so it's all ready to go as soon as they get up. (And of course, when they see the gym kit, it acts as a reminder.)

So, those are the seven Rs: reminders, records, rewards, routines, relationships, reflecting, and restructuring the environment. The idea is to be creative; help your clients mix and match these methods to create their own strategies for lasting change.

| **EXTRA BIT** | In chapter eighteen of *Trauma-Focused ACT: The Extra Bits*, you'll find a client handout on the seven Rs. |

Takeaway

If clients aren't following through on homework or sustaining their new behaviors, we want to make that a top priority for the session. We can usually quickly identify the barriers and introduce useful tools to get past them—especially the seven Rs.

CHAPTER NINETEEN

When Things Go Wrong

In 1887, British engineer Albert Holt, pioneer of the long-distance steamship, reportedly wrote, "It is found that anything that can go wrong at sea, generally does go wrong, sooner or later." For some unknown reason, this later became known as Murphy's law: "Whatever can go wrong, will go wrong." (So there you go; don't say you didn't learn anything in this book!)

Murphy's law is just as relevant to therapy as to steamships; if you can imagine something going awry in TFACT, the chances are, sooner or later, it will. So this chapter is to help us prepare in advance. I've chunked it into five sections: (1) backfired experiments—when interventions fail or trigger adverse reactions; (2) session stoppers—when clients behave in ways that disrupt or stall the session; (3) teamwork troubles—interpersonal tensions between client and therapist; (4) working on ourselves—overcoming our own fusion and avoidance in session; and (5) preparing ourselves for a challenging session.

Backfired Experiments

Everything we do in therapy is an experiment; we never know for sure what will happen. Even a simple question or innocuous comment can sometimes trigger an extreme adverse reaction. So inevitably our experiential work will sometimes fall flat, fail miserably, or have unintended negative consequences.

Three common reasons for backfiring experiments are:

- The therapist does not establish ACT-congruent goals for therapy.

- The therapist does not clearly link experiential work—especially mindfulness and acceptance practices—to the client's ACT-congruent therapy goals.

- The therapist encourages the client to talk about traumatic events but relies on reflective listing and supportive counseling instead of helping the client develop new skills for flexible responding.

Watch out for these mistakes (they're easy to make when you're new to TFACT) and remedy them as soon as you realize they've happened.

When things go awry in session, we want to model, instigate, and reinforce TFACT processes as a response. This usually involves some or all of the following:

- drop anchor

- explore and validate

- thank the client

- apologize

- clarify

- create a learning opportunity

Let's quickly go through these.

Drop Anchor

We are in the same boat as our clients; when something goes wrong, we experience all sorts of uncomfortable thoughts and feelings—especially anxiety. So we drop anchor ourselves, and help our clients do likewise. If the client is having a strong adverse reaction (e.g., fusion, extremes of arousal, dissociation), we run through the ACE process, to keep them within their window of flexibility. And as therapy progresses and the client learns more skills—defusion, acceptance, self-compassion, and so on—we bring those in too.

Explore and Validate

When things go askew, we ask about the client's thoughts and feelings, and we validate whatever is showing up. Then, with openness and curiosity, we explore: "Clearly that didn't go as intended. What happened?" We want to discover: Did the client misunderstand the aim? Did we go too fast or was the exercise too hard? Were they not truly willing to do it? Did the exercise trigger painful inner experiences, such as traumatic memories, intense emotions, or harsh self-judgments? Did we say or do something dismissive, uncaring, or invalidating?

Or did the exercise simply have a different effect from what was intended? For example, every defusion technique occasionally results in fusion; every self-compassion technique occasionally triggers self-judgment.

Thank the Client

When clients give us feedback that something went wrong, we thank them for it—even if it's harsh or abrasive (like "This is stupid!" or "It's not fucking working!"). We might say (and obviously we need to be completely authentic and genuine), "Thank you for being honest with me. I appreciate the feedback, because if something's not working for you, we need to sort that out, pronto."

Apologize

If the experiment backfired due to some error or misjudgment on our part, an apology is warranted. We might say, "I'm sorry. I can see now, I didn't clearly explain the purpose to you," or, "I'm so sorry. I wasn't expecting that to happen," or "I'm really sorry. I think I pushed you into that before you were ready for it." When we do this genuinely, it models authenticity, openness, and taking responsibility—while also repairing the breach.

Clarify

Is the issue one of misunderstanding? Maybe you didn't clearly explain the purpose of the exercise, or perhaps the client misunderstood it (e.g., expecting it to get rid of unwanted feelings)—or both. If so, you should calmly and openly explain what you had meant or intended. This may involve revisiting metaphors such as Hand as Thoughts, Pushing Away Paper, or, in the case of dropping anchor, a reminder that anchors don't control storms. In other cases, this may mean clarifying the use of particular terms: "I'm sorry. When I used the term 'story,' I didn't mean it's not true or you were making it up. It's just a more user-friendly way of talking, instead of using technical terms like 'cognition.' I certainly won't use that term again."

Create a Learning Opportunity

Can the client learn something useful from this unexpected, unwanted experience? The answer is usually yes—provided we foster openness and curiosity. We may say, "Obviously neither of us wanted this to happen, but given that it did, I'm wondering if there's something useful to learn from it." Possible lessons may include how to use defusion, acceptance, or self-compassion skills; how to respond flexibly to difficult emotions; and how to accept it when things go wrong and carry on doing what's important.

We may not need to go through all the above responses—one or two may be enough. What matters most is to stay present and respond with openness, curiosity, and compassion. As part of these conversations (and this also applies for session stoppers and teamwork troubles), we always inquire about the client's thoughts and feelings. We might say, "These kinds of discussions are quite confronting for most people—so I'm wondering, what's showing up for you?" Often all that's required is to validate their reaction, but sometimes it's necessary to bring in defusion, acceptance, or dropping anchor.

Session Stoppers

From time to time, we all have clients who behave "problematically" during the session. They may continually vent about their problems without letting us get a word in; or blame all the people in their life without ever looking at their own role in ongoing issues; or repeat the same narratives week after week without any obvious purpose. They may get bogged down in intellectualizing and "analysis paralysis." They may repeatedly talk over or interrupt us. They may keep "problem hopping"—moving rapidly from one issue to another, never sticking with one long enough to generate an action plan.

And let's be honest: haven't we all at times simply gritted our teeth and tried to put up with this behavior, and "get through the session"—rather than openly addressing it with the client? Usually, we do this because we get hooked by our own anxiety and reason-giving: *It would be rude of me to interrupt, They'll get upset if I mention it, It's good for them to vent, Maybe they just need to do this.*

"Press pause" (chapter four) is often a good intervention here: "Can I press pause for a moment? I'm noticing something happening here, and I'd really like to bring it to your attention. My mind's telling me you're going to be upset or offended by what I say, and I'm noticing a lot of anxiety in my body, and a strong urge just to sit here and not say anything about it. However, I'm committed to helping you create the best life you can possibly have. So, if I sit here and say nothing about this, then I don't think I'm doing my job properly; I don't think I'm being true to you, as a therapist. So, I'm going to do what matters here, even though my heart is racing—I'm going to tell you what I'm noticing."

Notice how, in doing this, we model five of the six core processes: contact with the present moment, defusion, acceptance, values, and committed action. And by now, we'll have our client's full attention!

Here's a shorter version: "Can I press pause for a moment? I'm wanting to talk about something that I think is going on, and my mind's telling me that I'm going to come across as rude or insensitive... however, I don't want to let my mind talk me out of it because I think it's really important...so, is it okay with you if I share what I think may be happening here?"

Then, with an attitude of openness and curiosity (unhooking ourselves from any judgments), we can compassionately and respectfully bring in the *notice, name, normalize, purpose, workability* strategies. When noticing and naming behavior, it's essential that our description is *nonjudgmental*. For example, we would *not* say, "You're being aggressive"—because that's a judgment about the behavior, and the client may take offense or argue that they're "not being aggressive." In contrast, here's a nonjudgmental description: "I notice that your voice is getting louder, and you've clenched your fists, and you're frowning."

Following this, we can normalize the behavior, consider its purpose, and look at it in terms of workability. Here's an example, for a client who keeps problem hopping:

Therapist:	(*noticing and naming*) What I've noticed is this pattern—we start talking about a problem or topic, but before we get a chance to come up with an effective strategy, you move on to another issue. Have you noticed this yourself?
Client:	Yes. That's because I've got so many problems to deal with!
Therapist:	(*normalizing*) Absolutely. And it's completely normal. My mind does it too. When we've got a lot of problems, our minds naturally jump from one to another. (*exploring the purpose*) This is your mind looking out for you; it's saying, "Look—you have to deal with *all* of this stuff. You can't neglect any of it. You have to cover all bases."
Client:	Yeah. It's always doing that.

Therapist:	(*workability*) The thing is, if we let your mind keep doing that in our sessions, you're not going to get much out of therapy. If we want to make these sessions effective, so that you can... (*mentions several of the client's goals*)...then we need to stay on task, focus on one problem long enough to come up with a plan or a strategy or something practical to do.

It's often nerve-racking to have these conversations with clients, but it fosters authentic, courageous therapeutic interactions. (And if at any point, the client reacts negatively—aggression, shutting down, crying, and so forth—we respond as we would for "backfired experiments.")

The next step is for client and therapist to collaborate on catching and interrupting the problematic behavior when it recurs. For example, we may make an agreement that either party can "call out" the behavior when it happens—and both parties will then pause for a few seconds. Continuing with the example of problem hopping:

Therapist:	So how about we try this: we agree to focus on one issue at a time, and stay with it for as long as necessary to come up with a strategy—something practical, that we can write down, so you can take it home and do it. And then, if there's time, we can move on to another issue. Would that be okay? And if at any point your mind tries to pull us off-task, switch over to some other issue, then either one of us can call it out. Can you think of a phrase we could use to name it when we see it?
Client:	Errmm, not really.
Therapist:	How about we just say "switching"—to indicate your mind's trying to switch problems?
Client:	You're going to say it? Or I am?
Therapist:	Either. I expect, to begin with, it'll be mostly me, but after a while, you'll start to catch your mind in the act, and call it out yourself. So basically, as soon as one of us notices what's happening, we say "switching." Then we pause for a few seconds—maybe take a slow breath or have a stretch—and then we refocus on the original problem.

This strategy provides an ongoing means of raising awareness of a problematic behavior, while also developing the client's ability to (a) interrupt it and (b) refocus attention on the task at hand. And of course, we don't need to stick to the agreed-upon phrase; we can use more playful comments, such as "There it goes again" or "Did you spot it?"

As therapy progresses, we phase out this strategy and instead simply ask, "And what do you notice going on right now?" or "What do you notice happening here?" We may then explore: "Where is this leading?" or "If we continue down this path, will that be a good use of our time?" or "Is this helping us work together as a team?"

Here's another example:

Therapist:	(*noticing and naming*) What I've noticed is, sometimes I'm talking and you interrupt and talk over me. Have you noticed this yourself?
Client:	(*surprised*) No, I haven't. I talk the same way to you I talk to everyone else.
Therapist:	(*normalizing*) Well, of course, we all interrupt and talk over each other at times. (*exploring the purpose*) And I'm guessing you do this because there's a lot you want to talk about, and you want to make sure we don't miss anything.
Client:	That's right. So, what the problem? Isn't that what therapy is about? Talking about shit? No one's ever had a problem with this before.
Therapist:	(*workability*) Well, the thing is, in order for us to be an effective team, we need to treat each other with care and respect, and that means—
Client:	Are you saying I don't respect you?
Therapist:	Do you notice how you just talked over me again? Each time you do that, for me, it feels a bit like a slap in the face. The message you send me when you do that is that what I have to say isn't important, isn't worth listening to. And that's quite hurtful; it gets in the way of us building a strong team.
Client:	Oh. (*goes quiet, looks thoughtful*)
Therapist:	And I really appreciate what you're doing right now. Instead of talking over me— you're listening. And that feels so different to me; so much more caring and respectful.
Client:	(*uncertainly*) Okay.
Therapist:	And again, I really appreciate you letting me talk—this is a really uncomfortable conversation—and it means a lot to me that you aren't talking over me. I already feel we're a stronger team because of it. So could we make that one of our tasks here? To spot patterns of behavior that get in the way of good, effective team-work—and press pause when they happen, and try something different?

Many clients have problematic patterns of interpersonal behavior, which show up in their relationship with the practitioner. After raising awareness of such behavior, as above, we can explicitly draw out its relevance to therapy goals such as building better relationships. We openly discuss the effect it has on the therapeutic alliance, then explore if it shows up in other relationships—and if so, what impact it has. We then get an agreement to catch it happening in session, press pause, then try something more workable. For example, we might invite the client above to experiment with active listening: paying curious attention to the speaker's face, mouth, and voice, and noticing the urge to interrupt without acting on it.

Teamwork Troubles

Sigmund Freud talked about "transference" and "counter-transference." I prefer the simpler term, "teamwork troubles": patterns of behavior that undermine the therapeutic alliance. (Not sure Siggy would approve of that term, but hey—each to their own.) When teamwork troubles arise, we first take a good, honest look at ourselves: *What am I saying or doing that might be causing or exacerbating this tension?* For example, have we been arrogant, dismissive, uncaring, pushy, argumentative, patronizing—or even overly zealous about ACT? (I've been guilty of all of these things at times!)

On the client's side, contributing behaviors may include trying hard to please you and agreeing with everything you say; debating, challenging, or contradicting everything you say; calling you names or disparaging your profession; using racist, sexist, or homophobic language; turning up late to sessions or repeatedly canceling at the last minute; excessively delaying payment; and so on.

Raising and Discussing Teamwork Troubles

We raise and discuss teamwork troubles just as for session stoppers (and if there are negative reactions, respond as for backfired experiments). We may say, "Not sure if you remember, back on our first session, I said the aim here is for you and me to work together as a team. The thing is—and I'm curious to know if it's the same for you—I don't feel like we're a strong team, and I wonder if we can talk about what's getting in the way of that, and how we can make it better?"

We then have an open and honest discussion, taking the greatest care to be respectful and understanding, while also being assertive. Judicious use of self-disclosure is helpful:

- When you use terms like "bitches" to refer to women, I feel really uncomfortable.

- When you say things like "You don't really care about me," I feel a bit hurt—because even if you don't believe it, I really do care, and I want our work here to be useful, to help you build a better life, and I'll be sad if that doesn't happen.

- When you keep saying, "This is all bullshit," I feel anxious; my mind says I'm not doing my job properly.

- When you don't pay your bills, I feel a bit resentful, and also a bit embarrassed, because I don't really want to hassle you about it.

We listen to the client's perspective, validating their feelings—then, as for session stoppers, agree to collaborate on catching and interrupting the problematic behavior if it recurs.

How Are We Contributing to Teamwork Troubles?

As mentioned above, we always want to look at our own role in teamwork troubles—and be willing to apologize. We can ask, "I've been thinking about my part in this—and I'm wondering, is there anything I've been saying or doing that is not landing well with you?"

If clients are not forthcoming, we may prompt: "I've been wondering if maybe I've been too XYZ—or perhaps too ABC?" If the client confirms our suspicion, we might say, "I sincerely apologize for that. I can imagine how unpleasant that was for you. And I'll take a different tack from now on. And if I ever slip back into that, please let me know straight away."

What Can We Learn from Teamwork Troubles?

When a client's behavior strains the therapeutic relationship, there's a great opportunity to learn from it—because usually it's creating problems in other relationships, too. We can often fruitfully explore:

A.   What is the client *hoping* will happen when they say or do these things?

B.   Is it having the effects the client hoped for? What effect is it having on the therapeutic relationship?

C.   What's the past history of the behavior? How old is it? Did it originate as a response to trauma or adversity? Did it serve some useful purpose in past relationships—to help protect the client or get their needs met?

D.   Does it happen in other relationships today? What effect does it have there?

The information we gather from these explorations is often extremely helpful for working with relationship issues (chapter twenty-eight).

Working on Ourselves

The therapeutic relationship is of central importance in TFACT. We aim to see each client as a rainbow: a unique work of nature unfolding in front of us; a privileged encounter we can savor and appreciate. We don't look at a rainbow and say, "Oh, how disappointing—if only that shade of indigo were a bit deeper." We admire the rainbow; and no matter how faint it may be, we feel privileged to witness it. And we aim to bring this same attitude to therapy: living our values; unhooking from judgments; paying attention with openness, curiosity, and compassion. (This metaphor is my homage to Carl Rogers, who famously said: "People are just as wonderful as sunsets if you let them be. When I look at a sunset, I don't find myself saying, 'Soften the orange a bit on the righthand corner.' I don't try to control a sunset. I watch with awe as it unfolds.")

When the alliance is strong, the client is motivated, and the session is going smoothly, it's easy to see a client as a rainbow. But it's not so easy when the client is deeply stuck: fused, avoidant, and responding negatively to our interventions. Usually when this happens, that "judgment factory" in our head goes into overdrive.

I've asked thousands of therapists to share judgmental thoughts they have about their clients during difficult sessions. Here are some common ones: *She doesn't really want to get better, I don't like him, She's a hopeless case, This guy's an asshole, She's not really trying, What on earth am I going to do with him? She's clearly borderline, He must be a narcissist, I wish she'd shut up, Oh no—here we go again, This is infuriating, I can't wait for this session to be over, How do I get him out of here? I should refer her on to someone else, This is a waste of time, Why do you keep coming back when we aren't getting anywhere? Will you shut up and let me get a word in? Can't you see it's your own fault? Why do you keep doing this?*

We've all had thoughts like this at times. We don't consciously choose them; they just "show up"—especially when the going gets tough. And having such thoughts is not a problem; it's normal, natural, and expected. But if we fuse with those thoughts: *big* problem! The client's not a rainbow, but a road-block! We see them as an obstacle—getting in our way, holding us back; a problem we need to solve. Naturally, this does not bode well for the session.

I've also asked thousands of therapists to share what away moves they make when hooked by their thoughts and feelings in a difficult session. Here are some common answers: *I just nod my head and listen and wait for the session to end, I become directive and pushy and tell the client what they need to do, I open up my toolkit and start frantically searching for tools and techniques, I end the session early, I suggest they see another therapist, I talk louder and faster, I become pushy and controlling, I disconnect and zone out, I give up on therapy and we just chat, I get defensive, I start trotting out metaphors, I become snappy or impatient.*

In other words, where there's a stuck client, we tend to find a stuck therapist. And thus the need to apply ACT to ourselves: to unhook from unhelpful cognitions, make room for our emotions, connect with our values, and be fully present with our clients. The good news is, the more we use ACT on ourselves, the better we'll be able to do it with our clients—so let's make a start on this, right now.

A Self-Development Exercise

Your mission, should you choose to accept it, is to identify your own away moves in therapy sessions, and map out a plan for working on them. I encourage you to write this out in the "Practitioner's Barriers Worksheet" (see Extra Bits). But if you are unwilling to write, then at least think very carefully about it. (It's so much more powerful if you write it, though; just saying.) You can do this either as a broad-focus exercise (i.e., covering a wide range of thoughts, feelings, and behaviors that occur with many different clients) or as a narrow-focus exercise, specific to just one client.

What Hooks You?

Write down client behaviors you find most difficult. And underneath that, write down all the difficult thoughts and feelings that show up for you in response. This may include difficult emotions (frustration, anxiety, guilt, boredom, hopelessness); judgmental thoughts about the client (such as those above); judgmental thoughts about yourself (*I'm a lousy therapist, I can't do this*) or the model (*TFACT doesn't work!*). Perhaps you also get hooked by perfectionism or other rigid rules: *I have to do this right, I mustn't get this wrong, I'm not experienced enough to do this, I can't admit that I don't know the answer*, or by reason-giving: *I can't do this experiential work because it will upset the client, I'm too anxious to do this exercise.*

What Are Your Away Moves?

Now write down what kind of values-incongruent, ineffective behaviors you do when fusing with or avoiding those thoughts and feelings.

What Are Your Towards Moves?

Write down several of your most important values as a practitioner (e.g., compassion, respect, authenticity). To help you with this, consider the following two questions:

1. Suppose I interview one of your clients and ask them, "What are your therapist's greatest qualities?" What would you like your client to reply?

2. Next, I ask them, "When you were at your rock-bottom worst, really struggling—how did your therapist treat you?" What would you like your client to reply?

Next write down towards moves that you already do in response to all those difficult thoughts and feelings that show up when you're challenged by your client's behavior.

And finally, write down towards moves that you'd like to start doing. This includes any unhooking skills you want to apply: tools, techniques, practices, or exercises; any combination of defusion, acceptance, contact with the present moment, self-compassion, and self-as-context.

After completing it, please keep the "Practitioner's Barriers Worksheet" handy. The idea is for you to revisit this regularly and use it as a guide for ongoing work on yourself.

Preparing Ourselves for a Challenging Session

The following exercise takes only two minutes. It's especially useful immediately before a session with a client whose behavior you find difficult. So if you see a name in your appointment book, and you have a sinking feeling, or anxiety, or a thought like *I hope they cancel*—please do this *before* that session begins.

Compassion for Your Client

Take a moment to think of your client.

Consider: *What does this client say or do in session that you find challenging? What difficult thoughts and feelings show up, in response?*

Acknowledge: *It's hard for you to work with this client. It's painful. It's difficult. It's stressful. So acknowledge it's hard, and be kind to yourself.*

Consider: *This client's "difficult" behavior results from fusion or avoidance. They are not intending to make your life hard. They are very deeply stuck. What might it be like for them to live that way? To be so stuck? To be jerked around by their thoughts and feelings, as if they are a puppet on a string? To be pulled into problematic patterns of behavior, over and over again, hurting and suffering as a result?*

Consider: *You only see this client for a short period of time, with days or weeks in between sessions. Yet even in that brief time, it's challenging for you. So what's likely to be happening in your client's other relationships—with friends, family, or coworkers? How much tension, conflict, or disconnection is likely? How painful must that be?*

Can you put this client's behavior to one side, and see the stuck, struggling human being behind it? This person, just like you, wants to love and be loved; to care and be cared for; to know and be known. And right now, it's hard for them to do that. But **you** can help. **You** can make this relationship different from many others. **You** can make it a secure and healing relationship, where your client's difficult behavior meets caring, understanding, and compassion. Don't underestimate the value of this; it is a great gift.

So take a moment to again think of your client—and truly acknowledge their struggles and their suffering. And at the same time, connect with your heart, and tap into your deepest reserves of warmth and kindness and caring. Then, holding on to your compassion, with your heart warm and open, go out and meet your client.

EXTRA BIT

Download *Trauma-Focused ACT: The Extra Bits* from "Free Resources" on http://www.ImLearningACT.com. In chapter nineteen, you'll find the "Practitioner's Barriers Worksheet" and an MP3 audio file of the Compassion for Your Client exercise.

Takeaway

We can't stop judgments from arising when clients behave in ways we find difficult, but we can defuse from our judgments, come back to our values, tune into our compassion, and engage with our clients mindfully. And when things go wrong, we can take a courageous, open, authentic stance—and speak about it honestly. Often, we avoid such conversations because we feel anxious or awkward—so we need to apply ACT to ourselves: are we willing to make room for our own discomfort, in order to live our values as practitioners?

CHAPTER TWENTY

Compassionate, Flexible Exposure

A quick reminder: ACT defines exposure as "organized contact with repertoire-narrowing stimuli, to facilitate response flexibility." (Or, in layman's terms: "getting in touch with difficult stuff, to learn more effective ways of responding to it.") And no matter what exposure involves—whether it's increasing physical intimacy, connecting with the body, or working with traumatic memories—one thing's for sure: it's uncomfortable. It gives rise to all manner of difficult cognitions, emotions, and sensations. So why on earth would anyone want to do it?

Values-Based Exposure

As discussed in chapter thirteen, exposure in TFACT is always in the service of values and values-based goals—and the motivation needs to be clear *to both client and practitioner*. What values and values-congruent goals is this serving? What will this enable the client to do differently?

The choice point diagram below illustrates the aims of TFACT-style exposure:

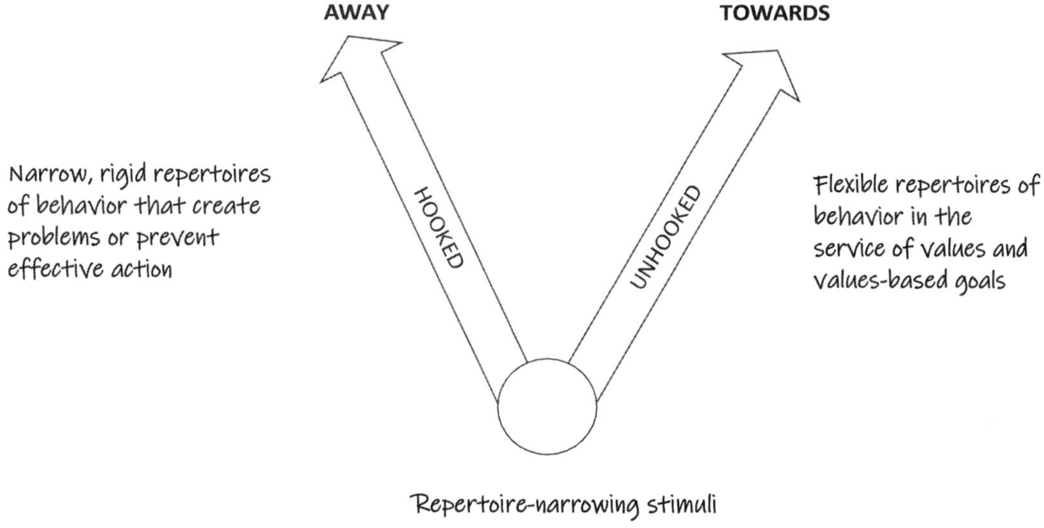

AWAY   TOWARDS

Narrow, rigid repertoires of behavior that create problems or prevent effective action

HOOKED   UNHOOKED

Flexible repertoires of behavior in the service of values and values-based goals

Repertoire-narrowing stimuli

We can explain the aims of exposure to clients as follows: "The idea of doing this exercise/learning this skill is so that next time you encounter this stuff (*mention repertoire-narrowing stimuli*) you can unhook from it/handle it better/respond more effectively—so that instead of doing (*mention away moves triggered by the stimuli*), you can do (*mention values and values-congruent goals*)."

Before, during, and after exposure, we repeatedly return to this motivation. We say things like "Let's take a moment to reconnect with what this is all about…" Then we mention the client's values-congruent goals, such as being a loving mother, getting back to work, regaining your independence, being there for your partner, gaining that promotion, being more courageous, and so on. (With some clients, we may initially do exposure in the service of vague values-oriented goals like "self-care" or "building a better life," but as therapy progresses, we want to get much more specific.)

What Do We Measure?

Because the primary aim of exposure in TFACT is not to reduce distress or anxiety but to increase emotional, cognitive, and behavioral flexibility, there's no need to measure the client's distress using the SUDS (Subjective Units of Distress Scale). Instead, we can use the three scales we introduced earlier—presence, control over physical actions (CPA), and willingness. A quick refresher:

PRESENCE SCALE

On a scale of zero to ten, where ten means you're fully present here with me—engaged and focused and really tuned in to what we're doing—and zero means you've completely drifted off, gone off somewhere in your head, lost all track of what we're doing, then zero to ten, how present are you right now?

CONTROL OF PHYSICAL ACTIONS (CPA) SCALE

On a scale of zero to ten, where ten means you've got full control over your physical actions—what you do with your arms and legs, hands and feet—and zero means you're completely frozen, locked up, can't move at all, then zero to ten, how much control do you have over your actions right now?

WILLINGNESS SCALE

On a scale of zero to ten, where ten means you're completely willing to have these difficult thoughts and feelings—to let them be here without trying to fight them or escape them—and zero means you're completely unwilling, you'll do anything possible to make them go away, then zero to ten, how willing are you to have them right now?

How Long Do Exercises Last?

Exposure activities may last for as long as the client is willing to continue. But if at any point the client can no longer sustain a high level of willingness, we immediately stop. (If we continue, this will just turn into yet another occasion of fusion or experiential avoidance.)

Most of the exposure exercises in this book vary from ten to thirty minutes, and I've provided approximate timings for quite a few of them. However, they may be much shorter. Often we decide with the client beforehand how long the practice will last. For example, if a client is very hesitant, we may agree initially to just one minute. After that minute is up and we've debriefed the exercise, if the client is willing, we may encourage them to try again for perhaps two or three minutes. And if they're still willing after that, the third time we may go for four or five minutes.

However, if we're doing a longer exposure exercise, we may not need to continue for the full agreed-upon time; if we reach a point where the client is scoring high on all three scales, the task has been accomplished, and we can stop.

Exposure and Response Flexibility

In TFACT we emphasize "exposure and response flexibility." We want clients to recognize that they have choices; that there are many ways of responding to these stimuli. So we don't tell clients what they *can't do*; rather we encourage them to choose more flexible responses in preference to their older, more inflexible ones.

This especially applies to "safety behaviors": overt or covert behaviors that clients do during exposure to escape or avoid anxiety or distress. For example, clients may try to distract themselves during exposure by counting or thinking about something else; or they may deliberately slow and deepen their breathing in order to relax. We watch carefully for safety behaviors—and if they occur, make the client aware of them. We gently point out it's interfering with their learning, and encourage them to refocus on the target stimuli.

Please keep in mind the following strategies to help clients build response flexibility during exposure.

Keeping It Safe

All the safety strategies discussed in chapter four are important, especially (a) a nonverbal gesture the client can use to ask for "time out," and (b) regular check-ins from the therapist to ensure the client is genuinely willing (as opposed to "toughing it out" or trying to please the therapist). And of course, we always aim to keep the client within their window of flexibility, so if at any point they seem overwhelmed or dissociative, drop anchor.

Move with the TIMES

TIMES is an acronym for Thoughts, Images, Memories, Emotions, and Sensations. During exposure, all sorts of difficult private experiences show up, and we can flexibly shift focus from one to another, as required: we "move with the TIMES."

For example, suppose we are working with a traumatic memory and the client gets hooked by self-judgment. We then shift focus to defuse from those self-judgmental cognitions. (If desired, we can track this with the zero to ten defusion scale discussed in chapter ten.)

Once the client has defused from these thoughts, we refocus on the memory. Now suppose a minute later, the client starts to dissociate; in that case, we help them drop anchor—and we track their level of presence and CPA. After the client is centered, we return to the memory.

And suppose shortly afterward, a huge wave of sadness shows up. We then segue into acceptance and self-compassion, and track the level of willingness. And once the client is accepting the sadness, we return to the memory.

The diagram below illustrates this process. At any point, we can help the client respond to any experience inside the triangle, using any process on the outside—and we can freely shift from one private experience to another: "moving with the TIMES." (In Extra Bits, you can find a copy of this diagram and an exposure record sheet.)

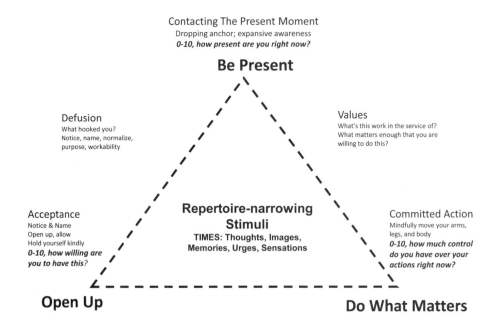

Move with the TIMES

"Difficult TIMES"

We can help clients get in touch with "difficult TIMES" through any of the methods explored in chapter thirteen: vividly remembering something painful, imagining a difficult future event, setting challenging goals, evoking urges, doing an avoided task, or working with anticipatory anxiety. Here are three additional methods:

CREATE UNPLEASANT SENSATIONS

Often clients' anxiety is triggered by unpleasant physical sensations—such as dizziness, shortness of breath, or choking. With a bit of creativity, we can help clients to recreate these sensations in session. For example, we can ask a client to hyperventilate: to breathe extremely fast, taking about two seconds for each full breath in and out. This usually gives rise to sensations such as dizziness or light-headedness, a tight chest, and pins and needles in the fingers.

Another method involves breathing through a narrow straw with one's nostrils pinched shut, for thirty to sixty seconds; this usually creates a feeling of shortness of breath or suffocation. A third involves swallowing repeatedly for one minute while really noticing the sensations, which usually creates choking sensations.

These inductions usually continue for about one minute after the first unpleasant sensations arise. (Exposure to physical sensations is technically called "interoceptive exposure.")

IMAGINE YOUR GREATEST FEARS

We can ask clients to vividly imagine what they fear (technically called "imaginal exposure"). In PTSD, this is likely to be the reoccurrence of something resembling the original trauma. However, as we discussed earlier, traumatic events may give rise to the full range of anxiety disorders, each of which have their own characteristic fears. For example, in panic disorder there are typically fears of going crazy, losing control, or having a heart attack; in social anxiety disorder, fears of being ridiculed, embarrassed, or rejected; in OCD, fears of doing something aggressive, lewd, or sacrilegious. So we can encourage clients to vividly imagine the events they fear most.

IN VIVO EXPOSURE

In vivo (Latin for "in life") exposure involves contacting a feared situation, activity, or object in real life. With the advent of telehealth, in vivo exposure has become much easier than before. For example, one of my clients was mugged while withdrawing cash from an ATM (automated teller machine) outside a bank—and had since avoided all banks and ATMs, as they triggered high anxiety. In one of our sessions, I was in the office, and he was in another location on his cell phone, and during the session I coached him through first approaching and then entering the bank, all the while defusing from and accepting his anxiety. Interacting via cell phones, tablets, laptops, or computers, we can help clients to approach all sorts of feared and avoided situations, activities, and objects during a session.

Exposure and Panic Attacks

The TFACT approach to panic attacks is summarized in the choice point diagram below. The away moves listed are behaviors that many people tend to do during a panic attack, primarily to try to avoid or get rid of unwanted thoughts and feelings. Clients learn to drop anchor, defuse from thoughts such as *I'm going to die/pass out/go mad/have a heart attack*, accept the physical sensations and urges of anxiety, act on their values, and focus on their values-guided activity. When they are responding this way, they may still have feelings of anxiety, but they are no longer having a "panic attack."

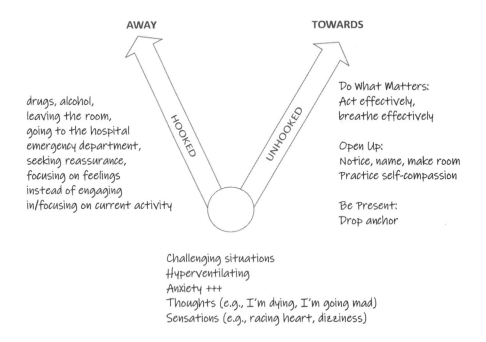

I'm going to illustrate the TFACT approach to exposure for panic attacks using the case example of Sergio.

Sergio was a thirty-four-year-old single male—a senior executive in a large manufacturing company. He presented with common symptoms of PTSD and panic disorder. His issues stemmed from a hiking accident nine months earlier in which Sergio's best friend slipped off a narrow mountain pathway and fell to his death. We're going to look at extracts from session six. By this point, Sergio was quite skillful in dropping anchor and had developed basic abilities in defusion and acceptance (although he was still resistant to self-compassion).

The figure below illustrates Sergio's thoughts, feelings, sensations, and urges (at the bottom of the choice point); his problematic responses (i.e., away moves); and the new, more effective responses (i.e., towards moves) he worked on developing through exposure.

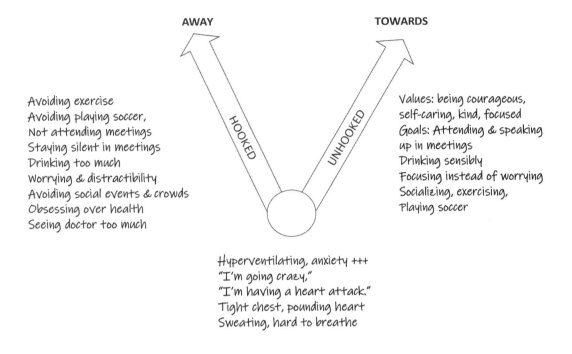

AWAY

HOOKED

Avoiding exercise
Avoiding playing soccer,
Not attending meetings
Staying silent in meetings
Drinking too much
Worrying & distractibility
Avoiding social events & crowds
Obsessing over health
Seeing doctor too much

TOWARDS

UNHOOKED

Values: being courageous,
self-caring, kind, focused
Goals: Attending & speaking
up in meetings
Drinking sensibly
Focusing instead of worrying
Socializing, exercising,
Playing soccer

Hyperventilating, anxiety +++
"I'm going crazy,"
"I'm having a heart attack."
Tight chest, pounding heart
Sweating, hard to breathe

Motivation

Sergio's values-based motivation for exposure was documented alongside the towards arrow of the choice point. Throughout exposure, his therapist would frequently return to these values and goals to remind Sergio of the purpose for this challenging work.

Psychoeducation for Panic Attacks

Psychoeducation about the cause and nature of panic attacks always precedes exposure. There are three main aspects to this (all of which the therapist covered with Sergio):

1. HOW STRUGGLING WITH ANXIETY AMPLIFIES IT

First, we introduce the struggle switch (chapter twelve) to illustrate how struggling with anxiety amplifies it. Then:

Therapist: So now even the slightest trace of anxiety—and even physical sensations that have nothing to do with anxiety, like when your heart is racing after exercise—will trip your struggle switch. Which instantly amplifies whatever anxiety is present. And hey, presto, the vicious cycle starts: anxiety about anxiety about anxiety, ending with a full-blown panic attack.

2. WHY IT FEELS DIFFICULT TO BREATHE

Most clients feel unable to breathe properly during panic attacks. So we explain:

Therapist: What happens is, you're breathing in and out so fast—hyperventilating—that your lungs don't have time to empty. It takes quite a few seconds to empty all the air from the lungs, and you're not giving it that long. So basically your lungs are still half full of air when you start taking your next breath—which means it's very hard to breathe in, because there's all that air already inside your lungs, taking up space. So what you need to do if you feel like you can't breathe properly is the complete opposite of what your mind is telling you: you need to actually *breathe out very slowly and very gently*, and ever so slowly, empty your lungs. *Then*, you'll be able to breathe in.

3. THE SENSATIONS OF HYPERVENTILATION ARE UNPLEASANT BUT HARMLESS

Therapist: Another thing that happens when you hyperventilate is that you breathe out lots and lots of carbon dioxide—so the level of carbon dioxide in your bloodstream drops to way below normal. And that then triggers a complex biochemical chain reaction that ends up altering the blood flow in different areas of your body—more blood to your face, so you flush; less to your fingers and brain, so you get pins and needles, or dizziness. The thing is, although that feels very unpleasant, it's actually harmless. But your mind *thinks* it's dangerous—so whoosh, up goes your anxiety.

Defusion

With Sergio, psychoeducation was followed by some defusion practice. Sergio noticed and named his most troublesome thoughts as "I'm going crazy" and "I'm having a heart attack." The therapist normalized these (*we all have thoughts about bad things happening*) and looked at their purpose (*your mind trying to protect you, keep you safe*).

Next the therapist emphasized, "These thoughts will keep coming back. Your doctor gave you a full check-up, your blood tests were fine, your ECG is healthy, your heart is great—and each time you've been to the emergency department, the doctors have told you you're fine—but none of that has stopped your mind from telling you you're going to have a heart attack. Same with going crazy; it's never happened, but even though you know that, and even though all these doctors have assured you it won't happen, those thoughts keep showing up. And there's a reason for that; you can never actually disprove those thoughts. No doctor or therapist can ever 100% guarantee that you won't have a heart attack or go crazy; you know logically and rationally that it's extremely unlikely, but no one can ever guarantee it—so that gives your mind wiggle room to say, *It still might happen*."

Sergio, following the advice of a popular self-help book, had vigorously disputed these thoughts many times—telling himself, *It's not true, It won't happen, I've never gone crazy, The doctors have examined my heart and it's fine*. And yet—the thoughts continued to occur. The therapist asked, "So given that these thoughts keep occurring, and your usual ways of responding to them are taking you away from the life you want, what might be helpful from the work we've already done?"

Sergio decided to use his favorite defusion technique: *Aha! Here's the panic theme, again. Hey, mind, I know you're looking out for me—but it's okay, I've got this covered*. The therapist got him to practice this technique with two of the "stickiest" thoughts—first fusing with them, then defusing, and Sergio agreed to use this method, if required, during exposure.

Beginning Exposure

Sergio had good dropping anchor skills, and the exposure session began with a one-minute version of ACE. Then the therapist encouraged Sergio to hyperventilate. Within a minute, Sergio was feeling dizzy, hot, anxious, and tight in his chest.

While encouraging Sergio to continue hyperventilating (for a minute more), the therapist obtained scores for presence, CPA, and willingness.

Therapist: Zero to ten, how present are you, right now?

Client: About eight.

Therapist: And zero to ten, how much control do you have over your physical actions, right now? Have a stretch, move your arms and legs, check it out.

Client: (stretching and moving) About a nine.

Therapist: Cool. And zero to ten, how willing are you to have these feelings, right now?

Client: Not very. About a three.

Exposure and Acceptance

The therapist then worked on acceptance. Key comments from the therapist (not including Sergio's responses) are recorded below. Three dots indicates a pause of around five seconds.

Therapist: So which of these feelings bothers you most?... Okay, so see if you can just open up and make some room for it... And notice it with curiosity... Look at it from all angles, above and below... Notice the shape and size...

Do you really have to fight with this feeling, or run from it? Can you make peace with it, even though you don't like it?... See if you can let it be there... Drop the struggle, open up, let it be...

And no need to keep hyperventilating, you can breathe normally now...

And is your mind saying anything unhelpful? Yes? Okay—so notice and name those thoughts, and come back to the feeling... And observe it as if you're a curious scientist who has never encountered something like this before...

> And let's update the numbers again, zero to ten for each one please—how present? Eight, okay. Control of your actions? Eight, okay. Willingness to have this feeling? Five, up from three. Cool. Are you okay to stay with this a bit longer? Great...
>
> So again, noticing with curiosity...and allowing it to be there...and remembering why you're doing this—courage, self-caring, freedom, expanding your life to the fullest...and are you willing to make room for this feeling, so you can do the things you want to do?... So opening up, making room, letting it be there, even though you don't like it... And if your mind is interfering, notice and name those thoughts, and come back to the feeling... Opening up... Letting it be...
>
> And the numbers again—present? Nine. Actions? Nine. And willingness? Seven, cool!... That's great work. So—no pressure at all—would you be willing to do that again?

Whichever scales we use, we want the scores to be at least a seven before moving on to the next round of exposure. If the client is willing to continue, we repeat the exercise but focus on a different sensation. For Sergio, there were four rounds of exposure, lasting twenty minutes in total. Each round focused on a different sensation: dizziness, pounding heart, chest tightness, a lump in the throat. And the final round ended with a minute of dropping anchor.

Can Physical Movement Be a Distraction?

If at any point during exposure a client's ability to control their actions drops below a seven, we get them to stretch, move, change position, reach out and pick up an object, and so on, until it's back to seven or higher. Of course, there is a risk that this movement could distract the client, so we rapidly refocus on the target stimulus:

Therapist: Okay, so five is a bit low; let's see if you can really connect with your body here. Have a really good stretch... And shift your position in the chair... And move your arms around, wiggle your fingers... And tap your feet up and down... That's it... Now what's the number? Seven? Great. So really notice this... Notice the feeling again, it's right there, *and* notice that even with this feeling present, you have control of your actions, so you can do things that are important... Now focus in on the feeling again...

What About Breathing Exercises?

When anxiety shows up, we want clients to drop anchor, make room for sensations and urges, unhook from thoughts, act in line with their values, and engage in what they're doing. (This is precisely what Sergio's therapist taught him to do.) If a client is doing all this, they *will* be experiencing anxiety—but they will *not* be having a panic attack.

If clients use a breathing technique for acceptance (e.g., breathing into and around a feeling to help open up, make room for it, allow it to be there), that's okay. But if they breathe in a particular manner to reduce anxiety, this is risky. Why? Because it easily pulls them back into the experiential avoidance/emotional control agenda, which is what fosters panic attacks in the first place. Therefore, breathing to relax should be discouraged.

Of course, hyperventilation does have unpleasant side effects, such as dizziness, pins and needles, and facial flushing—and we can teach clients to reverse these side effects through slow and gentle exhalation, rebreathing into a paper bag, or biofeedback using a capnometer. However, if we go down this path, we need to make it crystal clear that (a) although the sensations are unpleasant, hyperventilation is harmless; and (b) the breathing techniques are not intended to reduce anxiety; their purpose is to reverse the harmless but unpleasant physiological effects of hyperventilation.

If we omit this essential information, confusion is likely, and the client will likely use these techniques to try to avoid anxiety.

Learning Outcomes and "Expectancy Violation"

Inhibitory learning theory informs us that one way to increase the effectiveness of exposure is to maximize "expectancy violation": the difference between what you *expect* to happen and what actually *does* happen. The greater this difference, the greater the new learning. So before an exposure activity begins, the therapist asks the client, "What do you think might happen as we do this? What's your greatest fear?"

Sergio's reply to this question was, "I think it's going to be really difficult. I think I might lose it. It's going to be very hard. I don't know if I'll be able to do it. I might flip out."

The therapist does not (as in other models) try to reassure the client, or challenge their worrying thoughts, or help them make their predictions more realistic—because this would reduce the degree of expectancy violation. Instead, the therapist encourages openness and curiosity: "Okay, so let's note that that's what your mind is expecting—and let's see what happens."

After the exercise, the therapist explores the new learning, with questions like:

- So your mind predicted that X, Y, Z was going to happen. How accurate was that?

- What was different than what you expected?

- Was it as intense/difficult/challenging/hard to make room for as you expected?

- What did you learn from this? How might that new learning be helpful for you?

Sergio's replies to these questions included:

- "Well, it was really hard—but no, I didn't lose it. I didn't flip out."

- "Yes, it got a bit easier with each round—still hard, but—just, you know, got a bit easier—and I could flick off the struggle switch quicker."

- "Well, I didn't like the feeling…but I found I could have it there without fighting it."

- "I learned I can control my actions when anxiety is there."

Note that we don't focus on the erroneous content of thoughts, nor advocate disputing them. We focus on what happened during exposure, and what it was like to make contact with and open up to the target stimuli. We note the discrepancy between what "the mind" predicted beforehand and what actually happened—and we use this as an opportunity to reinforce earlier metaphors such as the Caveman Mind or the Overly Helpful Friend. We acknowledge: "Your mind will keep doing things like this—warning you of things that will hurt you. And sometimes it is spot on with its predictions, but a lot of the time, it's way off. And that's normal. That's a normal human mind just doing its number one job: trying to keep you safe."

Often at this point, it's useful to quickly recap the core concept of workability: that although the mind naturally predicts danger everywhere, we do have a choice about how we respond. We can notice these thoughts and consider—if we let them guide our actions, will that take us toward or away from the life we want? And if the answer is the latter, the client can use the unhooking skills they've learned in earlier sessions.

Ongoing Exposure

After in-session exposure, we encourage the client to practice doing similar exercises at home. Daily practice for fifteen to twenty minutes (in one sitting) is ideal, but we need to be flexible; any practice is better than nothing. So we could start with once a day for ten minutes, or twice a day for five minutes, or three times a week for three minutes—and build on it over time. (Light weights first; heavier weights later.) The "Home Practice" worksheet in Extra Bits and the motivational tools of chapters sixteen and eighteen (especially the "seven Rs") come in handy.

Some clients rapidly develop their ability to respond flexibly to difficult TIMES. For others, progress is slow, and patience is necessary. Sergio was in the first category. He practiced diligently for ten to fifteen minutes every day, and within two weeks, his emotional flexibility significantly improved. He became much better at accepting anxious feelings and defusing from anxious thoughts, while staying present and in control of his physical actions. He still experienced anxiety, but he no longer had panic attacks.

The next step for clients is to resume activities they've been avoiding—and as they do so, respond flexibly to the difficult TIMES that arise. For Sergio, this included playing soccer, attending and speaking up in meetings, and going to crowded social events.

Creating an Exposure Hierarchy

An exposure hierarchy sets out a number of steps, ranging from not at all difficult to extremely difficult, for the client to follow. We don't *have to* create an exposure hierarchy, but it's often useful to do so, as it maps out a clear pathway ahead.

For example, if a client is avoiding work because of a traumatic incident that happened there, their exposure hierarchy may begin with driving past the workplace, then going home. (If even this is too challenging, they may just drive half the distance to work, then go home.) After a day or two of this, the next step may be driving to work, parking in the parking lot, staying there for a few minutes, and then going home. After doing this a few times, the next step may be going into the building, having a cup of coffee in the staff lounge with a trusted colleague, and then going home. From there, the next step may be going back to their office, sitting at the desk, answering a few emails, then going home after five minutes. And so on and so on, until eventually they are back at work, on full duty.

The diagram below shows the top of an exposure hierarchy worksheet (see Extra Bits). In the top row, we write the values and values-based goals that motivate the exposure. The first column highlights willingness, the second specifies actions to take, and the third rates the expected difficulty of doing it.

MOTIVATION: I am doing this challenging work in the service of:		
1st column: In order to do what matters, are you willing to make room for difficult thoughts, images, memories, emotions, sensations, urges? Write Y for yes, N for no. **2nd column:** What you will actually do? For how long? How often? **3rd column:** Predicted degree of difficulty: 0 = none at all, 10 = extremely difficult		
Willing? Y or N	Actions I Will Take (i.e., what I will say and do): When; where; for how long; how often	Difficulty? 0–10

Top Part of an Exposure Hierarchy Worksheet

Let's walk through the steps of completing this worksheet.

Step One: Brainstorm and Rate

Before completing the worksheet, the therapist and client collaboratively brainstorm a range of actions (usually about ten to fifteen) that the client could take to reclaim this aspect of life, and the client rates each one zero to ten in terms of expected difficulty. It's best to do this initial brainstorming on a blank sheet of paper because it usually gets messy: clients often change their minds about the scores, so we end up crossing out one number and writing in another, which then alters the position in the hierarchy. Once brainstorming is complete, we then write the activities on the worksheet, arranged in sequence according to difficulty. And to save time, we can ask clients to do this after the session. (It's fine if several activities have the same rating, or if there isn't one assigned for every number.)

Let's look at an example for a client whose target problem is avoidance of intimacy.

Sophie is a forty-three-year-old female nurse in a same-sex relationship. Her past trauma history includes childhood sexual abuse by her brother, episodes of physical and verbal abuse in two brief heterosexual relationships in her twenties, and a sexual assault in a night club by a man who drugged her drink. Her current relationship has been going on for nine months and is the longest she has ever had. However, there is very little physical intimacy because it triggers extreme anxiety (which Sophie wants to avoid). She has basic skills in defusion, acceptance, dropping anchor, and self-compassion. Before brainstorming activities, the therapist explained:

> *Therapist:*   Remember we talked about working with light weights before moving to the heavy ones? For most of my clients with these issues, sex is the heaviest weight in the gym—whereas holding hands is a light weight. So can we brainstorm a range of activities—some easy, some hard, some in the middle? And the thing is, sometimes even just talking about the possibility of doing this stuff can trigger strong emotions or painful memories—so if that happens, you know the drill?

> *Client:*   Drop anchor?

> *Therapist:*   Yep!

They then brainstormed fifteen different activities varying in degree of physical intimacy, and Sophie rated each degree of difficulty. The table below shows only ten of them.

Willing? Y or N	Actions I Will Take (i.e., what I will say and do): When; where; for how long; how often	Difficulty? 0–10
	Lying on the bed, kissing, stroking, few or no clothes	10
	Lying on the bed, kissing, stroking, top clothes off	9.5
	Lying on the bed, kissing, stroking, clothes on	9
	Lying on couch, kissing, stroking, top clothes off	8
	Lying on couch, kissing, stroking, clothes on	7
	Sitting on couch, hugging, kissing, stroking, clothes on	6.5
	Sitting on couch, hugging and kissing, clothes on	5
	Sitting on couch, thigh-to-thigh, arms around each other, clothes on	4
	Sitting together on couch, thigh-to-thigh, holding hands, clothes on	3
	Sitting close to each other on couch, holding hands, clothes on	2

Extract from an Exposure Hierarchy for Physical Intimacy

For an experienced therapist, it usually takes about fifteen minutes to create a ten-to-fifteen item hierarchy. However, it can sometimes take much longer. If so, we don't have to complete it all in session; clients can finish it for homework. The example above took about thirty minutes because, as anticipated, talking about these activities triggered high anxiety, and several times they had to put the task on hold so the client could drop anchor, defuse, and make room for her feelings.

Upon completion, the therapist said, "So we don't want to start with the really heavy weights—like seven or above—but we don't have to start with the very lightest ones, either. Looking at this list, which would you be willing to start with?" The client chose "Sitting on couch, thigh-to-thigh, arms around each other, clothes on"—which she'd rated a four in terms of expected difficulty.

Step Two: Specify Duration and Frequency

The next step is to specify how often the client will do this activity and for how long. This information also goes on the worksheet. Sophie wrote:

> Sitting on couch, thigh-to-thigh, arms around each other, clothes on   4
> (10 minutes, 3 x a week)

Step Three: Check for Willingness

The final step is to check for willingness. A good way to do this is to ask the client to vividly imagine doing the exposure activity outside of session. For example, here's a portion of Sophie's therapy session:

Therapist: So take a moment to imagine yourself going ahead with this, as vividly as you can… notice what you can see, and hear, and touch, and taste…as if it's happening right now…and what's showing up as you do that?

Client: I'm scared.

Therapist: And where are you feeling that?

Client: My chest—it's really tight.

Therapist: Anywhere else?

Client: My throat.

Therapist: And what's your mind saying?

(The therapist spends a few minutes helping the client accept these feelings, through more exposure, ending with the Kind Hands exercise. Then continues…)

Therapist:	So if these feelings are showing up now, just from imagining it, you can pretty much guarantee that in the real situation, they'll be there even stronger. Are you willing to make room for these feelings, in order to do this?
Client:	Yes. I am. This is really important to me.
Therapist:	How will your mind try to talk you out of it?
Client:	Oh, the usual. *It's too scary. Don't do it. You'll get hurt.*
Therapist:	Are you willing to make room for those thoughts?
Client:	Yes.
Therapist:	Okay, let's write that in then. (*Therapist writes Y—for "yes"—in the willingness column.*)

If a client is ever unwilling to do something, we compassionately and respectfully acknowledge that: "Okay. Thank you so much for being honest with me. I'd hate for you to ever go ahead and force yourself to do this stuff if you're not truly willing." We then encourage them to move down the ladder and pick an easier task.

The ability to focus attention fully on the activity at hand—and refocus, whenever it wanders—is an important factor for success as the client undertakes these challenges, so we want to emphasize their use of this skill (and teach it, if it's lacking). For example, Sophie found as she worked through the hierarchy above, she often got distracted by anxiety or painful memories, which pulled her out of the intimate connection she wanted; so each time that happened, she noticed and named the experience, then refocused on her partner. (And naturally, HARD barriers will surface—which we address as in chapter sixteen.)

But what if a client avoids a desired meaningful activity because it triggers traumatic memories? For example, suppose a client wants to be sexually active with their partner but avoids it because they know painful memories of sexual abuse are likely to recur during it. If so, we first work with those memories directly, doing exposure as in chapters twenty-nine and thirty. After that, we use intimate activity for further exposure, as described above.

A Note on Sexual Problems

The exposure hierarchy above focused on increasing physical intimacy but did not extend into sexual intercourse because, at this point in therapy, the client considered that "off the table." Many clients with trauma-related issues suffer from sexual problems such as vaginismus, anorgasmia, dyspareunia, erectile dysfunction, premature ejaculation, delayed ejaculation, and low libido. Often clients don't mention these issues out of shame or embarrassment—even though they cause deep, ongoing distress. But these issues are common barriers to physical intimacy: the client avoids it because of the fear it would lead to sexual activity, which would then expose the aforementioned problems (and all the difficult emotions, cognitions, and memories that go with them).

The good news is, because fusion, experiential avoidance, and hyper- or hypoarousal usually play major roles in sexual dysfunction, many clients find that as therapy progresses and their psychological flexibility increases, their sexual functioning improves. But if sexual problems persist, behavioral sex therapy is warranted. For example, a "sensate focus" program is often extremely helpful. First developed by Masters and Johnson (1966), sensate focus programs involve a structured series of intimate mindfulness exercises that couples do together to deepen connection, tune into their bodies, and increase responsiveness to their own and each other's physical, emotional, and sexual needs. If your clients do TFACT first, the mindfulness skills they develop will complement and accentuate behavioral sex therapy, if it is later needed.

Variable Exposure

We'll finish off this chapter with the liberating concept of "variable exposure." Older models teach that you need to strictly "move up the ladder" of the exposure hierarchy, and an activity needs to be repeated until there's a 40 to 50% drop in the SUDS score *before* progressing to the next level. However, inhibitory learning theory suggests that new learning is more likely when we *don't* follow a strict progression, but instead practice "variable exposure": that is, freely moving up and down the hierarchy, without regard to level of difficulty. So, for example, one day you may do a task rated five; the next day, an eight; and the day after that, a three. (However, it's wise to begin with low-difficulty items to build confidence and prevent dropout or treatment refusal.)

From a TFACT perspective, if the client is *freely choosing* to act in line with their values and *willing* to make room for all the difficult thoughts and feelings that arise—we can encourage them to go ahead with it. In other words, it's fine for a client to jump straight from an item rated two to an item rated nine without the need to go through items rated three through eight—as long as they are willing.

EXTRA BIT — In *Trauma-Focused ACT: The Extra Bits*, chapter twenty, you'll find a "Move with the TIMES" diagram, an exposure record sheet, a "Home Practice" worksheet, and an "Exposure Hierarchy" worksheet.

Takeaway

TFACT's exposure principles are the same for all repertoire-narrowing stimuli—both internal (e.g., cognitions, emotions, urges, sensations) and external (e.g., people, places, objects, situations, activities). Compassionate, flexible exposure involves contacting these stimuli and learning to respond flexibly, in the service of values-based goals.

CHAPTER TWENTY-ONE

The Flexible Self

We all have a "self-concept," or "conceptualized self": a collection of narratives, opinions, judgments, and beliefs about who we are, what we are like, how we got this way, our strengths and weaknesses, our "good points" and "bad points," what we can and can't do, and so on. A self-concept is useful—but, like any cognitive content, when we *fuse* with it, problems ensue. Most commonly, clients fuse with a negative self-concept: *I'm broken, damaged, defective, worthless, incapable, incompetent, unlovable,* and so on. But at times, they may fuse with a positive self-concept, leading to problems with narcissism, arrogance, egotism, overconfidence, grandiosity, or entitlement.

Fusion with self-concept can present as "event centrality": an individual's perception that a traumatic event is central to their identity. The more someone's identity is based upon their trauma history, the more severe their symptoms and the worse the prognosis (Boals et al., 2010). So we want to help clients defuse from this trauma-centric narrative to experience that "there is much more to me and my life than these traumatic events in my past." One way to achieve this is to work explicitly with self-as-context (Boals & Murrell, 2016). When clients remain entangled in their self-concept to such a degree that it holds them back in life (e.g., "I'm too depressed to do that"; "I don't deserve a better life"; "Now that I've left the army, I'm a nobody"), and defusion interventions have not been as effective as desired, self-as-context can make all the difference.

In chapter thirteen, we explored how self-as-context (the noticing self) can foster acceptance, through metaphors like The Sky and the Weather. Now we'll explore how it can facilitate defusion from the conceptualized self.

Two Types of Intervention for Self-as-Context

Broadly speaking, when working with self-as-context (in the sense of "the noticing self"), there are two types of intervention we use: (a) metaphors that facilitate defusion from self-referential narratives, through conveying the message "you are not your thoughts"; and (b) mindfulness practices that develop the ability to take "the observer perspective," enabling you to "step back" and observe cognitions without getting caught up in them.

Metaphors for Self-as-Context

Popular metaphors for self-as-context include the Chessboard and Pieces (Hayes et al., 1999) and the Stage Show of Life (Harris, 2009a), both of which you'll find in Extra Bits. Here, I'll share my favorite: the Documentary of You (Harris, 2007).

The Documentary of You

This metaphor begins by discussing documentaries about the country in which the client lives.

Therapist:	So, I'm guessing you've seen quite a few documentaries about the United States on streaming services or news channels?
Client:	Yeah. Of course.
Therapist:	So, what kinds of things have you seen in those documentaries?
Client:	Well, recently, the presidential elections. Donald Trump, Joe Biden.
Therapist:	Right. What else?
Client:	Err, well, I guess things like "Me Too" and "Black Lives Matter."
Therapist:	Sure. What about famous events from the past?
Client:	Oh, wars. Like Vietnam...the Gulf War...Pearl Harbor.
Therapist:	Yeah. What about even further back in time?
Client:	The Civil War. Abraham Lincoln.
Therapist:	Right, and back to the present. Other famous people, apart from Trump and Biden?
Client:	Oh, lots of stuff on movie stars, athletes...Prince Harry and Meghan Markle.
Therapist:	What about nature or travel documentaries?
Client:	Oh yeah, Grand Canyon...Monument Valley...Mount Rushmore...Empire State Building...
Therapist:	And animals?
Client:	Yeah, grizzly bear...bald eagle.
Therapist:	Right. So you've seen some pretty positive documentaries about the US—and you've also seen some pretty negative ones. So, which type of documentary shows the *real* United States; the positive or the negative?

Client:	Well, both.

Therapist: I can see why you'd say that. But do you know how biased those documentaries are? Like, the camera crews film hours and hours of footage, and then they cut that down to just a few minutes of the most dramatic shots, and then they edit it together to tell an extremely biased story that represents the viewpoint and prejudice of the director.

Client: Yeah, good point.

Therapist: I mean, suppose I gave you one thousand hours of the world's greatest ever documentaries about the US. Would that be the same thing as the US itself?

Client: Err, no.

Therapist: What about a hundred thousand hours of documentaries? Would that be the same thing as the US?

Client: No.

Therapist: Right. I mean you'd see images that represent aspects of the US, and you could hear people's opinions about certain things going on in the US, but it couldn't even come close to the *reality*—to actually hiking the Grand Canyon or feeling the spray on your face from Niagara Falls, or sinking your teeth into a Coney Island hot dog.

Client: (*grimaces*) Not keen on hot dogs!

Therapist: Well, there you go, looking at a hot dog in a documentary, and eating one in real life—those are two very different experiences, right?

Client: Right.

Therapist: Now the human mind is like the world's greatest documentary maker. It's always filming: twenty-four hours a day…one hundred and sixty-eight hours a week… almost nine thousand hours a year. So by the time you get to age thirty, your mind's been filming for over a quarter of a million hours.

Client: Wow!

Therapist: And what percentage of that film gets stored in your long-term memory?

Client: One percent?

Therapist: Not even close. It's like a zillionth of one percent. I mean how much do you remember of yesterday? Or last week? Or last month?

Client:	(*nodding*) Good point.
Therapist:	So your mind makes this incredibly biased documentary about who you are—cutting out over ninety-nine-point-nine-nine percent of everything that you've done in your life—and then it says, "This is you. This is who you are." And the subtitle of that documentary is "You're not good enough."
Client:	Hmmm.
Therapist:	Right. So if a documentary about the US is not the US, then a documentary about you...is not you. And no matter what shows up in that documentary, whether it's false or true, positive or negative, ancient or recent, facts or opinions...the documentary will never be you.
Client:	I never thought of it like that.
Therapist:	And you know how you can tell that the documentary is not you?
Client:	How?
Therapist:	You step back and watch it. If you can *watch* a documentary, you can't *be* the documentary.

The Documentary of You metaphor builds on earlier defusion techniques involving noticing and naming cognitions, and exercises that involve observing them, such as Leaves on a Stream. And for homework, we can encourage clients to play with the metaphor: "Thanks, mind. You're playing my documentary again"; "Aha! Here's the 'broken me' documentary."

However, as discussed in earlier chapters regarding acceptance and defusion, metaphors by themselves are not enough for clients to develop new skills.

Mindfulness Practices for Self-as-Context

To fully develop self-as-context skills, we need to follow self-as-context metaphors with active mindfulness practices that foster the experience of the "noticing self." (In Extra Bits, you'll find a set of instructions that you can add to literally *any* mindfulness practice to serve this purpose.) So, for example, following an exchange like the one above, we could say, "So I'm wondering, would you be willing to do an exercise, now? It's about learning how to step back and watch that documentary, without getting caught up in it." We could then segue into a mindfulness practice such as the one below.

The Transcendent Self

The Transcendent Self exercise—also known as "the Observer Self" or "Continuous You" exercise (Hayes et al., 1999)—is often empowering and liberating for trauma survivors. Because it's quite long, we often leave it until later in therapy, when the client has developed good mindfulness skills. Space doesn't allow for the complete script, so I've put that into Extra Bits; here I've summarized what's involved and provided extracts to give you the general idea.

The aim is to help people access a sense of transcendence. In other words, to experience that no matter what trauma they've been through, and no matter what physical, emotional, or psychological damage they sustained, a very important part of them, the "noticing self," has transcended these events and come through unharmed.

For example, suppose my physical body has been horribly scarred or deformed; the part of me that notices those scars or deformations has not been harmed. And suppose I have horrific memories and painful emotions; the part of me that notices those memories and emotions has not been harmed. And suppose I have painful cognitions: *I'm broken, damaged, worthless; I can never have the life I wanted to live.* The part of me that notices those cognitions has not been harmed. Thus, a part of me has transcended the trauma.

Now if we try to convince the client of this, or explain it logically, or lecture them about it, it's likely to backfire; the client could easily disagree, argue about it, overanalyze it, or even feel invalidated. So instead, we help the client access this insight through their own direct experience, via mindfulness practices such as the Transcendent Self exercise.

This exercise typically comprises several different segments, each based on five repeating instructions:

1. Notice X.

2. There is X—and there you are, noticing X.

3. If you can notice X, you cannot be X.

4. X is one small part of you. It does not define who you are. There is so much more to you than X.

5. X changes. The part of you noticing X does not change.

With each segment of the exercise, X varies—typically starting with your breath, then moving on to your thoughts, emotions, memories, physical body, and the roles you play. Here's an example:

Therapist: Take a step back and notice, where are your thoughts?... Where do they seem to be located?... Are they moving or still?... Are they pictures or words? (*Pause five seconds.*)

And as you notice your thoughts, be aware you're noticing...there go your thoughts...and there you are noticing them. (*Pause five seconds.*)

>   If you can notice your thoughts, you cannot be your thoughts. (*Pause five seconds.*)
>
>   These thoughts are a part of you; but they do not define who you are; and there's so much more to you than these thoughts. (*Pause five seconds.*)
>
>   Your thoughts change continually...sometimes true, sometimes false...sometimes positive, sometimes negative...sometimes happy, sometimes sad...but the part of you that notices your thoughts does not change. (*Pause five seconds.*)
>
>   And when you were a child, your thoughts were so very different than they are today...but the you who noticed your thoughts as a child is the same you who notices them now as an adult. (*Pause five seconds.*)

We then run through the same steps with the client's emotions, memories, body, and the roles they play. We conclude:

Therapist: Your noticing self has been there all this time...and it's there right now, noticing my words, noticing your responses to them...noticing how you feel about what I say, and whether or not you agree...and more and more, you can look at your thoughts and feelings from this space, and see that there's so much more to you than these beliefs and judgments and stories about who you are...and there's also so much more to you than your memories, emotions, and urges...and ever so much more to you than your physical body and the various roles you play...so more and more, you can bring this larger sense of self to your life...to make that life fuller and more meaningful.

I recommend you read the full script *and* listen to the audio recording of this exercise (both in Extra Bits) to experience it for yourself.

As with every core ACT process, there are many different tools, techniques, metaphors, and exercises we can use for self-as-context (the noticing self), so if further work is needed, we have plenty of options. One of my favorites is the Good Self/Bad Self exercise (Harris, 2019). In this exercise, clients first fuse with and then defuse from *both* negative elements of self-concept ("Bad Self") and positive elements of self-concept ("Good self"), so they learn to "hold lightly" all aspects of the conceptualized self. (For a script, see Extra Bits.)

And a quick tip: if you google "The Guest House," you'll discover an amazing poem written in the thirteenth century by the Persian poet Rumi. It beautifully and profoundly encapsulates self-as-context through the metaphor of a guest house, in which thoughts and feelings are the guests, coming and going. (After working with self-as-context, you may want to give your clients a copy.)

The Impoverished Self

Some clients, usually those with complex trauma, have such an impoverished sense of self—such a limited concept of "who I am," "what I want," and "what I care about"—that we actually need to help them develop a self-concept. There are several strands of work involved in this process.

For a start, they need to access their feelings, which often requires mindful bodywork (chapter twenty-two) and the ability to observe, describe, and allow their feelings (chapter thirteen). They also need the ability to consciously notice their cognitions (chapter ten). Once they can access and observe their thoughts and feelings, a whole new world of self-knowledge opens up for them: they can start to consciously recognize what they like and don't like, what they want and don't want, and how they really think and feel about things.

Activity monitoring worksheets (chapter fifteen) and mindful appreciation skills (chapter twenty-seven) are also important: the former help clients learn more about what they like and want, and the latter help them to appreciate aspects of life that are meaningful and pleasurable. And if clients have no sense at all of what they like or want, scheduling pleasant activities (chapter sixteen) and self-soothing practices (chapter twenty-three) are usually helpful.

On top of this, it's usually necessary to learn assertiveness skills—especially how to say no, make requests, and set boundaries (chapter twenty-eight). After all, it's hard to know what you want or need for yourself if you have no concept of your own rights or you're constantly busy meeting the needs of others.

After doing all the above, we can usually get to values in a lot more depth. Then as clients develop a sense of what they want to stand for in life, what really matters to them, and how they want to treat themselves and others, they are more able to flesh out their self-concept.

> **EXTRA BIT**
>
> Download *Trauma-Focused ACT: The Extra Bits* from the "Free Resources" page on http://www.ImLearningACT.com. In chapter twenty-one you'll find (a) a script and audio recording for the Transcendent Self exercise, (b) instructions for fostering self-as-context in any mindfulness practice, (c) a script and animation for the Chessboard metaphor, and (d) a script for the Good Self/Bad Self exercise.

Takeaway

Experiential work with self-as-context (the noticing self) facilitates defusion from self-concept. This enables a more flexible sense of self, no longer defined or limited by self-referential judgments and narratives. It also facilitates transcendence: a sense of rising above one's trauma history. And on top of all that, it paves the way for formal exposure to traumatic memories. Clients are more willing to do such challenging work when they can see their thoughts, feelings, and memories as "a documentary" and know they can't be harmed through observing them.

CHAPTER TWENTY-TWO

Working with the Body

When humans disconnect from their bodies, they usually experience an unpleasant sense of lifelessness. They describe this as feeling numb, empty, hollow, dead inside; like an empty husk, a shell, a zombie, and so on: a state that's the very opposite of vitality.

The word "vitality" comes from the Latin word *vita*, meaning "life"; it refers to life force, energy, drive, and passion; feeling fully alive and participating fully in the world. Our bodies keep us alive, and our feelings remind us we're alive; so naturally when we disconnect from them, our sense of vitality is lost. One of our main aims in TFACT is helping clients get that vitality back, and connecting with the body (which includes somatic awareness and interoceptive exposure) is essential for this purpose.

Why Connect with the Body?

Here's a problem I often encounter when supervising clinicians. Practitioners have typically read a lot about trauma, and being knowledgeable about the benefits, they naturally encourage clients to connect mindfully with the body. The problem is, most clients *don't* have this knowledge—so they find these practices pointless, odd, or "more therapy bullshit." They also fear that connecting with their body will bring them into contact with unpleasant sensations, emotions, or memories—experiences they have tried hard to avoid. Either way, they are often reluctant to do the work involved.

So we need to clearly communicate how connecting with their body will help the client achieve their therapy goals. If we skip this or do it poorly, we can expect confusion or resistance. We may begin by explaining, "Our emotions are generated by nerve signals, which mostly come from muscles and organs inside our body and travel upward to the brain. That's why when we really *feel* an emotion intensely—like anger or fear or love—we feel it in our body. So the more you cut off from your body, the less aware you'll be of your emotions and feelings." We flesh this out with a relevant example (e.g., the racing heart, tight chest, and knotted stomach of anxiety) and then go on to highlight whichever of the nine points below are *clearly relevant* to the client's therapy goals.

1. Vitality

Clients may complain of feeling dead, lifeless, numb, empty, shut down—and may even turn to self-harming behaviors, such as cutting themselves or taking stimulants to "feel something." We may then say, "One of the big benefits of learning to reconnect with your body is that over time, it will give you a sense of vitality, coming back to life, feeling fully human."

2. Joy and Pleasure

We may explain, "Cutting off from your body helps avoid painful feelings—but also cuts you off from pleasurable emotions and feelings, like joy and happiness. So learning to reconnect with your body will give you access to the full range of emotions and feelings—both painful and pleasant. It will enable you to experience pleasure, love, and joy, as well as sadness, anger, and anxiety."

3. Control over Your Actions

We may explain, "The less aware you are of your emotions, the less control you have over your actions—over what you say and do, and how you react. If we're not aware of our feelings, they jerk us around like a puppet on a string." To clarify this, we can bring in the Kids in the Classroom metaphor (Harris, 2015).

Kids in the Classroom

Therapist: Remember when you were a kid and your teacher left the classroom? What happened? All hell broke loose, right? Well, it's the same thing with our emotions. Our awareness is like the teacher, and our emotions are like the kids. If we're not aware of our feelings, they act up, create havoc, run wild. The less aware we are of our feelings, the more they control our actions; they jerk us around like a puppet on a string and easily pull us in to problematic patterns of behavior. When the teacher returns to the classroom, the kids immediately settle down. Same deal when we bring awareness to our feelings; they lose their impact and their ability to jerk us around. They're still there, but they don't control us.

4. Wise Choices, Good Decisions

We may explain, "For effective decision making, and for generally making wise choices in life, we need access to our feelings and emotions. But the more we cut off from our body, the less access we have, so the more likely we are to make unwise choices or decisions."

5. Intuition, Trust, Safety

We may explore with clients how intuition is strongly dependent on access to our feelings. We may say, "Think of those 'gut feelings'—about whether you can trust someone or not. We can't access our gut feelings if we're not tuned in to our body. And more importantly, feelings in your body often alert you to threats and dangers that your conscious mind is not picking up. So without access to this information, you may unwittingly put yourself at risk." We would link this explicitly to relevant client issues, such as repeatedly falling into dangerous situations or having relationships with untrustworthy people.

6. Safety in Your Own Body

We may explain, "If you ever want to feel safe in your own body, you have to start exploring it and discovering better ways to handle the difficult feelings that are 'in there.' As long as you avoid doing this, you will never feel safe in your own body: it will be like a dark cave full of monsters that you want to avoid at all costs."

7. Success in Life

We may explain, "There is a direct correlation between success in life and what psychologists call 'emotional intelligence,' which basically means being aware of your emotions, noticing how they affect your behavior, and learning how to handle them more effectively. Research shows that if you want to be more successful in almost any area of life—as a parent, partner, in work or at play—the higher your emotional intelligence, the greater your likely success. And probably the fastest way to improve your emotional intelligence is learning to tune into your body and access your emotions."

8. Relationships

We may explain, "If we want to build strong, healthy relationships with other people—whether that's a partner, friends, children, family, and so on—we will be at a huge disadvantage if we don't have full access to our full range of emotions. Because building good relationships requires emotional intelligence, not just in terms of our own feelings, but also being able to tune into and handle the feelings of others."

We can flesh this point out with the following metaphor: "Have you ever watched part of a movie on TV without any sound? It's not very satisfying. The images may be great, but without music, or dialogue, or sound effects, you lose a lot of the experience. And if you watch carefully, you can still keep track of what's happening to some extent, but it's easy to misread what's going on. And that's what it's like when we interact with others while we're cut off from our feelings. We can easily misread what they want or don't want—their intentions, their feelings—and we easily lose track of how *our* behavior is affecting them." We then link this metaphor to relevant examples of the client's interpersonal problems.

9. Love and Intimacy

This final point will be relevant for many clients with relationship problems. We may say, "If you're in a loving, caring relationship, when you have those moments of genuine loving connection and intimacy, it usually gives rise to pleasurable feelings. But if you're cut off from your body, you won't get to enjoy them. Instead, you'll feel numb or empty, which makes intimacy and connection unpleasant—and feeds into that sense of disconnection and loneliness. And then because it's uncomfortable, you often end up actively avoiding intimacy. So by cutting off from pain, you also cut off from love."

The rationale we give for connecting with the body will vary from client to client, depending upon their unique situation—but at least some of the points above will be relevant to most clients. The key thing is to always link it clearly and directly to the client's therapy goals.

Tuning In to the Body

In TFACT, we help clients develop somatic awareness (the ability to mindfully tune into the body) right from the word go. This begins with dropping anchor—both the Acknowledge and Connect phases—and develops further through acceptance, self-compassion, and interoceptive exposure. However, we often need to go further, especially with clients who experience numbness.

There are four main ways to help clients tune into and connect with their bodies:

- Mindful movement and stretching

- Mindful body scans

- Mindfulness of posture

- Mindful self-touch

Before we discuss these methods, a reminder about graded exposure: begin by helping clients tune into "safe zones" of the body, and "safe sensations" within those areas. Then, if the client is willing, help them move up the exposure hierarchy to more challenging areas and sensations. And as difficult cognitions, emotions, and sensations arise, help clients stay within their window of flexibility by using their skills in dropping anchor, defusion, acceptance, and self-compassion.

Mindful Movement and Stretching

In session, we can encourage clients to do brief mindfulness exercises, focused on moving and stretching. The Connect phase of dropping anchor already includes this a little—but we can extend it much further:

Therapist: Now hold that stretch...and notice what that's like...tune into it...notice the sensations of stretching as if you're a curious child who has never encountered something like this before... Where are the feelings strongest?... Are they changing in any way?... Can you notice any tingling, pulsing, vibrating?... Can you notice any increase in temperature?... And can you notice what's happening in the adjacent areas of your body?... And, being careful not to injure yourself, are you willing to go a bit further into that stretch?... That's it... And noticing that sense of opening up... Noticing the muscles lengthening... Noticing the sensations changing...

In addition, we can encourage clients to experiment with Eastern mindfulness-based practices that center on movement and posture, such as yoga and tai chi, and to mindfully tune into their bodies when doing sporting activities—especially when these include stretching. And when clients notice tension or knots or stiffening in various muscles, we may also encourage them to mindfully stretch (or massage) those areas in session.

Practical Tip

In chapter thirteen, I mentioned a facet of acceptance called "harnessing": actively utilizing the energy of an emotion, channeling it into purposeful activity. When clients are very anxious, they may start shaking or trembling or become restless and fidgety. We can explain these reactions as byproducts of the fight or flight response: "This is your nervous system, priming your body for action." And then we can invite them to channel this energy into physical movement.

For a fit, healthy person (without chronic pain, physical injury, or other factors that limit activity), we may encourage them to run on the spot or do squats. And for the upper body: swinging arms around, or raising arms and clapping hands above the head, or even (in fit, strong people) doing push-ups. We encourage clients to do this mindfully until they get the sense of "expending all that pent-up energy." Usually, this takes a few minutes, and it promotes both acceptance of the anxiety and a rapid reduction of shaking and trembling. Once the exercise stops, the client is typically calmer, and their shaking or trembling significantly lessens or stops.

Mindful Body Scans

Mindful body scans are pretty much self-explanatory. They involve scanning parts of the body (or the whole of it), mindfully tuning into the physical sensations, acknowledging and allowing them to be there. Like any mindfulness practice, body scans may vary enormously in duration, taking anywhere from thirty seconds to thirty minutes. Generally, it's best to start with shorter exercises of three to four minutes, and build up the duration over time. We can then encourage clients to practice these exercises at home with scripts or audio recordings. (We may then opt to start sessions with a brief body scan, rather than dropping anchor.)

A quick caution: remembering earlier discussions about trauma-sensitive mindfulness, consider how each unique client may respond to lying still, eyes closed, for a prolonged period. Many clients will be okay with this, but not all. So to play it safe, you may wish to begin with scans that are eyes-open, involving plenty of movement—such as progressive muscle mindfulness (PMM). This has many similarities to progressive muscle relaxation (PMR), but there's one massive difference. The primary aim of PMR is to relax. However, in PMM there is *no emphasis* on relaxation; not one single mention of the word "relax." In PMM, the emphasis is entirely on noticing the sensations in your body and *allowing them to be as they are.*

For example, in PMR, a typical instruction is:

Therapist: Bring awareness to your feet. Tense the muscles by curling the toes and the arch of the foot. Keep the tension there and notice what it feels like. (*Pause five seconds*) And now *relax*. Letting go of the tension...noticing the new feeling of *relaxation*.

Conversely, in PMM, the instruction is:

Therapist: Bring awareness to your feet. Tense the muscles by curling the toes and the arches of the feet. Keep the tension there and notice the sensations this creates...on the top of your feet, and underneath them...and in your toes. (*Pause five seconds*) And now, see if you can, ever so slowly, ease off that tension...and notice what happens to the sensations in your feet as you do that...allowing them to be as they are, without any attempt to change them...and if they do change, simply noticing the new ones that appear.

In other words, PMM means mindfully scanning your body from head to toe while tensing and contracting muscles—but with *no attempt to relax* (even though this often happens as a side-effect). You can find a script in Extra Bits, which you're welcome to share with clients.

Practical Tip

For clients who tend to dissociate easily, especially those who "freeze up," encourage them to do PMM standing up, rather than sitting or lying down.

Mindfulness of Posture

There are many ways of working mindfully with body posture. For example, we may encourage clients to notice how they are holding themselves and explore how that feels; or we may give them feedback about the signals their posture sends. We may also invite clients to experiment with different stances, postures, and positions and explore what effects this has (on them and on us). We don't have space to cover this important topic here, but I've included an entire section on this topic in Extra Bits.

Mindful Self-Touch

Mindful self-touch is a powerful way of reconnecting with the body. Initially, clients may touch, tap, stroke, or massage "safe" parts of the body, through the clothes. (By "safe," I mean unlikely to trigger emotions, cognitions, memories, or sensations that the client is not yet ready or willing to have.)

For example, for clients with a history of sexual trauma, sexual areas of the body are unlikely to be "safe." Naturally, this will vary from person to person, so we always need to individualize what we do; however, often the arms, forearms, shoulders, or neck are good places to start.

Some clients may prefer to begin with a firm deep-tissue massage, their fingers really digging into the muscles and pushing hard. Others may prefer more gentle self-massage. Yet others may prefer to tap on or gently stroke those areas. Again, this varies from person to person, so we always want to ask the client what they prefer and invite them to experiment with various options, rather than assume we know what's best.

The client will initially do "through-the-clothes" self-touch of "safe" areas in session, for about five minutes, while we encourage them to tune into the sensations.

Thereafter, clients can create an exposure hierarchy to continue this work at home. This may involve experimenting with some or all of the following, listed below in order of (probably, for most people) increasing difficulty:

- Self-touch, through clothes, "safe" parts of the body

- Self-touch, bare skin, "safe" parts of the body

- Self-touch, through clothes, gradually extending into areas usually avoided

- Self-touch, bare skin, gradually extending into areas usually avoided

If the client is in a relationship with a supportive partner—and wanting to increase physical intimacy—then we would encourage them to experiment with different ways of both touching and being touched by their partner, especially through structured sensate focus exercises, as discussed in chapter twenty.

Homework

We can encourage clients to do any or all of these practices for homework. For clients who have been emotionally numb and deeply disconnected from their body for a long time, patience is essential. Although some clients rapidly learn to tune into and reconnect with their body and their feelings, for others, progress is slow—so much self-compassion is warranted.

EXTRA BIT   Download *Trauma-Focused ACT: The Extra Bits* from the "Free Resources" page on http://www.ImLearningACT.com. In chapter twenty-two, you'll find (a) a script for a traditional body scan, (b) a link to an e-book on working with posture, and (c) a script for progressive muscle mindfulness.

Takeaway

Working mindfully with the body is an important and central aspect of TFACT, intrinsic to acceptance, self-compassion, dropping anchor, and interoceptive exposure. We often go further with body work, using mindful movement and stretching, mindful body scans, mindfulness of posture, and mindful self-touch. However, we always need to clearly link somatic mindfulness—and its benefits—to the client's therapy goals; if not, we can expect confusion or resistance.

CHAPTER TWENTY-THREE

Sleep, Self-Soothing, and Relaxation

Many clients lack the necessary skills to establish healthy sleep routines, soothe themselves when distressed, and relax themselves when tense. Developing these essential life skills, the focus of this chapter, is an important part of committed action.

Sleep

Insomnia is an extremely common problem in trauma. Disrupted sleep can lead to increased irritability, anxiety, depression, daytime sleepiness, impaired performance at work, low energy, and so on. Clients may be reluctant to go to bed for fear of nightmares or to avoid a restless night of tossing and turning. Many resort to drugs, alcohol, or prescription medication to try to get better quality sleep—but often this just exacerbates the issue in the long term.

So if we can help our clients improve their quality of sleep, this will have positive effects on other clinical issues. In Extra Bits you'll find a client handout on "Sleep Hygiene," which covers the main components:

- restricting stimulants

- maintaining regular sleeping hours

- implementing wind-down rituals before bed

- blocking out light and noise in the bedroom

- exercising during the day

- minimizing pre-bedtime exposure to blue light (e.g., from phones, computers, TVs)

- limiting activity in bed to four things: sex, sleep, mindfulness, and relaxation

Naturally, when adjusting sleep routines, all the HARD barriers tend to show up, which we address as in chapter sixteen. We also need to be crystal clear about the purpose of practicing mindfulness exercises (e.g., Leaves on a Stream, mindful breathing, Kind Hands, body scans) in bed:

Therapist: Have you ever tried to make yourself sleep? And what happened? The more you tried to force sleep, the less effective, right? So it's very important not to fall into that trap here. If you're in bed, and you're not sleeping, trying to make yourself sleep is a recipe for failure. So instead, the idea is to use that time effectively. Instead of tossing and turning and worrying, you practice these skills we've been working on. That way, you're learning really useful skills that will help you with many other problems. And the good news is, these practices are very restful and restorative; not as much as sleep, of course, but a whole lot more than tossing, turning, stressing, worrying, and so on. And on top of all that, there's often a bonus—when you do these practices in bed, a lot of the time, after a while, you fall asleep. So you can enjoy that when it happens—and when it doesn't happen, at least you'll get the other benefits.

Nightmares are a common problem for clients with a history of trauma. Imagery rehearsal therapy (IRT) is a cognitive behavioral therapy for reducing the frequency and intensity of nightmares. The practitioner first gathers details about the content, frequency, and emotional intensity of the nightmares, then helps the client to "rewrite" the nightmares—changing the details so they become less threatening. The client then mentally rehearses the rewritten nightmares—first in session, and then at home, daily. Over several weeks, nightmares usually drop in frequency and intensity or become distress-free dreams. IRT fits beautifully with TFACT; see Extra Bits for more information.

Self-Soothing

To soothe means to calm, comfort, or provide relief from pain. Self-soothing involves learning to do this for yourself rather than relying on others—and, as you'd expect, overlaps considerably with self-compassion.

In many models, self-soothing strategies are avoidance-based: they emphasize reducing or removing pain or distracting yourself from it. The word "relief" comes from the Latin term *relevare*, meaning "to raise or lighten." Pain is a burden, and naturally we strive for relief from it; we want to "lighten the load." Many people assume that relief from pain means removing it, avoiding it, or distracting from it. But mindfulness-based approaches offer a radically different form of pain relief; this comes from dropping the struggle with pain, making room for it, and treating yourself compassionately.

Thus, TFACT-style self-soothing does not aim to avoid or get rid of pain. It involves calming and comforting yourself through (a) *first* accepting your pain and treating yourself in a kind and caring manner, and (b) *then* engaging in calming, comforting values-guided activities.

Is Avoidance-Based Self-Soothing Bad?

There is nothing "wrong" or "bad" about avoidance-based self-soothing (i.e., doing activities with the primary aim of reducing, avoiding, or distracting from pain). Undoubtedly, such activities can be helpful. Remember, TFACT only targets experiential avoidance when it is so excessive, rigid, or inappropriate that it becomes problematic—in other words, gets in the way of a rich and full life.

However, if the *primary aim* of self-soothing is to reduce, avoid, or get rid of pain, there are times this simply will not work. So in this sense, acceptance-based self-soothing is superior because we can practice it whether or not pain reduces. (Of course, pain commonly *does* reduce significantly as a by-product of acceptance and self-compassion. That's not the aim, but it's a nice bonus, to be appreciated when it happens.)

When Is Avoidance-Based Self-Soothing Problematic?

Many self-destructive experientially avoidant behaviors—including the inappropriate or excessive use of drugs and alcohol, overeating, gambling, and even (in specific contexts) self-harming—can be viewed as avoidance-based attempts to self-soothe. So naturally, we validate the adaptive functions of these behaviors: "These things have helped you in the past. They were good strategies, in the sense that they helped you get through all the bad stuff that was happening and cope with those painful feelings." Then we compassionately highlight the costs of continuing to use them, and once the client sees these behaviors as unworkable, we explore alternatives.

Self-Soothing Activities

"Soothe" is derived from the old-English word "sooth," which means "truth" or "reality." The first step in self-soothing is simply to acknowledge the truth or reality that in this moment, life is painful, and you are hurting. The next step is acceptance, using any technique you prefer. And the third step, after accepting the emotional pain, is to initiate a self-soothing activity.

Any mindfulness-based activity can serve this purpose—especially those that center on the five senses. Basically, we ask clients what they find comforting or calming to look at; listen to; smell; taste, eat, or drink; touch or be touched by; and do physically. The idea is to focus on, engage in, and actively savor these aspects of present-moment experience:

Sight: In terms of sight, we may ask clients, "What do you find comforting, calming, or soothing to look at?" We may prompt them to consider movies, paintings, sculptures, architecture, fashion, the sky and the weather, animals, plants, the "great outdoors," theater, dance, and so on. And then we can ask, "What self-soothing activities could you do that draw on sight? For example, could you watch movies, go to an art gallery, go for a walk in nature?"

Sound: Regarding sound, we may ask, "What do you find comforting, calming, or soothing to listen to?" We can inquire about types of music, favorite songs, sounds of nature, voices of particular people, prayer or chanting, religious hymns, and so on. And then we can ask, "How can you create self-soothing activities that draw on sound? For example, could you consider listening to your favorite music, joining a choir, singing favorite songs, praying, or chanting?"

Smell: For smell, we may ask clients about food, drink, scent, aroma, incense sticks, perfumes, freshly baked bread, roast coffee, the smell of their children's freshly washed hair, forest flowers, freshly cut grass, and so on. Self-soothing activities that draw on smell might include lighting incense sticks, massaging with a pleasant-smelling hand cream, putting smelling salts in the bath, baking bread, going for a walk in nature, "smelling the roses," and so on.

Taste: For taste, we may explore types of food and drink (that are life-enhancing rather than self-destructive when consumed). Self-soothing activities may involve eating or drinking a favorite food or drink slowly and mindfully and truly savoring the experience (instead of doing it rapidly and mindlessly).

Touch: We may prompt clients to consider both self-touching and being touched by others. This could include brushing hair, massage, stroking a dog or cat, cuddling or hugging or snuggling up against loved ones, having their back rubbed or their head stroked, running their fingers through grass, walking barefoot on the beach, taking warm showers or hot baths, getting a massage, and so on.

Physical activities: Last but not least, we can ask clients about physical activities, such as yoga, meditation, prayer, dancing, singing, hot baths, playing sports, arts and crafts, woodwork, fixing up the house, tinkering with the car, writing, reading, acting, getting out into nature, physical exercise, cooking, visiting museums or galleries, or gardening.

Experiment, Engage, Appreciate. If the questions above reveal that clients have little or no prior experience of self-soothing to draw on, we can ask them to experiment with a range of activities and actively notice what happens as they engage in them. And we want to clearly emphasize that the key to making any these activities truly self-soothing is to engage in them fully—to give the experience their full attention and actively appreciate it—while allowing their feelings to be as they are.

When Avoidance Creeps In

Despite our best intentions, many clients *will* do self-soothing activities with an avoidance agenda—primarily to avoid/escape/distract from pain. This becomes problematic when (a) the client complains "It's not working," or (b) the client is trying so hard to avoid pain, they don't engage in the activity.

In the case of the first issue, always ask what the client means by "not working." Usually they will report that the pain is not reducing or going away—indicating they are misusing it for avoidance. We then explain, "While self-soothing often reduces pain, it won't always. It's a way to support yourself, comfort yourself, be kind to yourself, in the midst of your pain. If the pain reduces, as it often does—by all means, appreciate it; but please don't make that your main aim, or you'll soon be disappointed."

For the second issue, we revisit creative hopelessness and dropping the struggle.

Relaxation Skills

If clients don't know how to relax in healthy, life-enhancing ways, that's a significant skill deficit. So we help them develop healthy relaxation skills, in the service of values such as self-care, self-support, and self-nurture. You can introduce any relaxation skill you like, from progressive muscle relaxation or guided imagery to slow breathing or biofeedback.

However, when we introduce relaxation techniques after several sessions of TFACT, there's potential for confusion and mixed messages, so we need to be crystal clear in our communication. We explain that (a) this has a totally different aim than all the mindfulness and acceptance skills, and (b) it's only likely to work in nonchallenging, nonthreatening situations. The metaphor of a Swiss Army Knife is useful.

The Swiss Army Knife Metaphor

Therapist: So this skill has a different aim than all the others. If you think of a Swiss Army Knife, the other skills are like the cutting blades, whereas this one is like the corkscrew. It serves a purpose—but it's a different one.

Client: How do you mean?

Therapist: Well, with all the other skills, the aim is to let your thoughts and feelings be as they are; acknowledge they are there, open up and make room for them, let them come and go in their own good time; we don't try to control them. But with relaxation skills, we're doing the opposite; we're actively setting out to cultivate feelings of calm and relaxation. So it's important to know this is only likely to work in nonchallenging, nonthreatening, low-stress situations. It's not likely to work in really challenging, threatening, high-stress situations.

We then give examples of each type of situation—emphasizing again that in challenging, threatening, high-demand situations, relaxation techniques are almost certain to fail—so instead, they should rely on dropping anchor, defusion, acceptance, and self-compassion.

What About Distraction?

"Distraction," like many psychological terms, can be understood in a variety of ways, but usually it refers to a class of behaviors that function as experiential avoidance: deliberately drawing attention away from unwanted cognitions and emotions to reduce emotional distress.

Flexibly "shifting attention" is different from "distraction." Contact with the present moment involves flexibly narrowing, broadening, sustaining, or shifting attention, as desired. Only when one shifts attention with the *primary aim of experiential avoidance* would we call it "distraction."

When used moderately, flexibly, and appropriately, distraction can be helpful. (We all do it!) However, like any form of experiential avoidance, when distraction is used excessively, inflexibly, and inappropriately, it becomes a *big* problem. (Consider: how much of your own valuable time have you wasted trying to distract yourself from your feelings? What have been the costs when you used distraction excessively or inappropriately?)

When we *first* accept our feelings, and *then* do some meaningful values-based activity, and then engage in it fully, that's an example of flexibly shifting attention. And this will usually be far more satisfying than doing that very same activity *without* acceptance, to distract ourselves from unwanted feelings. This is because of the paradoxical effects of experiential avoidance. For example, if you're trying to distract yourself from unwanted thoughts and feelings, and they don't reduce enough (or they temporarily go away but then rebound), you're likely to feel frustration and disappointment. ("I'm still not feeling any better!") Or you find it hard to engage in your new activity because you keep checking in on your feelings to see if distraction is working. Of course, these things don't always happen, but the more intense the emotional pain the client is trying to escape, the more likely they are to eventuate.

Now having said all that, if you want to teach clients distraction skills, then you can. If you teach them in the service of values (such as self-care), they would come under the banner of "committed action." But before you go down this path, there are three things to consider:

- Clients already have many ways of distracting themselves—and as we explored in creative hopelessness, these methods aren't giving them the long-term results they want. So there's a real danger of providing "more of the same."

- If we're using dropping anchor skillfully and flexibly, along with acceptance-based self-soothing, distraction isn't needed to cope with emotional distress. (I've been practicing ACT for almost two decades, and so far, I've never once needed to teach a client distraction.)

- As with relaxation, there's a danger of confusion and mixed messages. So you'd need to be crystal clear about how distraction differs from other skills, such as defusion, acceptance, and dropping anchor. Again, the Swiss Army Knife metaphor is useful.

EXTRA BIT   Download *Trauma-Focused ACT: The Extra Bits* from the "Free Resources" page on http://www.ImLearningACT.com. In chapter twenty-three you'll find client handouts on self-soothing and sleep hygiene, and information on imagery rehearsal for nightmares.

Takeaway

Many clients benefit from developing skills in sleep hygiene, self-soothing, and relaxation. Distraction is not "forbidden" in TFACT but is rarely if ever needed. When we introduce relaxation or distraction, we need to be crystal clear about how these techniques differ from mindfulness and acceptance skills, to prevent mixed messages and confusion.

CHAPTER TWENTY-FOUR

Working with Shame

Many of us have been taught that shame is demotivating—that it makes people shut down and avoid dealing effectively with their issues—whereas guilt is motivating because it helps people recognize they've done wrong and drives them to atone or amend.

The TFACT stance on this is somewhat different. From a TFACT perspective, no emotion is inherently "good" or "bad," "positive" or "negative." Problems don't happen because of the emotions themselves, but because of responding to them inflexibly. So if clients respond *inflexibly* to guilt (i.e., with fusion and avoidance), then it's likely to *demotivate* them, hold them back from values-based living. On the flipside, shame can be a powerful and effective motivator for life-enhancing change, once clients learn how to respond to it *flexibly*, which is the main topic of this chapter.

First Steps

The fivefold strategy of *notice, name, normalize, purpose, workability* is a useful place to start with any difficult emotion. Noticing, naming, and normalizing need no further elaboration, so let's consider purpose and workability.

Purpose

If we respond to it flexibly, shame can motivate us to repair social damage and cease behaviors that alienate others, illuminate the importance of treating others well and belonging to the group, and communicate "I have failed" or "I am defeated." So rather than treating shame as the enemy, we can explore how it has aided the client in the past. It will often have had at least some of the following benefits:

Reducing hostility: If we look ashamed to others, this often lessens the degree of their hostility, aggression, criticism, punishment, or judgment.

Eliciting support or kindness: If others know we feel ashamed, this may elicit their sympathy, kindness, support, or forgiveness.

Avoiding pain: Often, in the grip of shame, we avoid people, places, situations, events, and activities that trigger difficult thoughts, feelings, and memories—especially fears of negative evaluation, rejection, or punishment. In the short term, then, shame helps us escape or avoid pain.

Workability

As with any emotion, we want to explore:

A. What does the client typically do when shame arises?

B. How does that work in terms of building the life they want?

When shame shows up, most clients respond with fusion in some situations, avoidance in others. Fusing with the cognitive aspects of shame—*I'm bad, I'm worthless, I deserve to be punished*—commonly leads to social disengagement or withdrawal, self-punitive actions, or judgmental rumination about one's flaws and failures.

Experiential avoidance, on the other hand, may involve any of the usual suspects—from drugs and alcohol to distraction and self-harm. (Interestingly, some clients use anger and aggression to avoid shame. This is not a conscious strategy, but it's highly reinforcing because it makes people feel strong and powerful—a quick escape from the sense of weakness and inadequacy fostered by shame.)

Usually clients readily see that these are not workable ways of responding to shame. So we then identify more workable behaviors, using any of the methods we've covered in earlier chapters.

Skill Building

Typically, the first active skill we teach is dropping anchor—which immediately helps to "break the grip" of shame. From there we move to other core ACT skills: defusion from harsh self-judgments; acceptance of sensations and urges; and, most importantly, the "ultimate antidote" to shame: self-compassion.

In addition to building skills, psychoeducation and values work are both very important.

Psychoeducation

We can help encourage defusion, self-acceptance, and self-compassion by looking at the client's history. For example, did the client's caregivers or abusers or assailants say things that fueled shame (e.g., "You deserve this," "You're a slut," "You brought this on yourself," "You should be ashamed of yourself")? In cases of childhood abuse by a caregiver, the following psychoeducation is essential:

Therapist: The thing is, a child has to maintain a positive view of her caregivers—no matter what they do wrong—because they are the child's life support system. And it's not like the child consciously thinks this through. It's an automatic, unconscious self-protective mechanism. Because if the child consciously acknowledges that their life support system is a source of threat and danger, well, that's just terrifying. So when caregivers are abusive or neglectful, the child's mind *automatically* and *unconsciously* blames the child for it: *It's my fault.* That's how a child's mind protects them from a terrifying and painful reality.

Another essential piece of psychoeducation, specifically for sexual abuse, revolves around pleasure. Some clients feel deeply ashamed because they experienced pleasure or became sexually aroused during the abuse; the false narrative goes along the lines of "I enjoyed it" or "I must have wanted it" and therefore "It's my fault" or "I'm a freak." Some people can even experience orgasm during sexual assault—even though they were in pain, terrified, and hating it. We explain that these are involuntary physiological responses of the body; they have nothing to do with desire or enjoyment or "wanting it."

Therapist: Our sexual organs are built to get aroused or give pleasure when they're stimulated in certain ways. And we don't control that. Feeling pleasure or getting aroused doesn't mean you enjoyed it or wanted it. It's your body responding the way it's been designed to. It's like, some people are extremely ticklish, and absolutely hate being tickled—but when you tickle them, they laugh; and they'll keep on laughing—even while hating it and begging you to stop. Or sweating: it's not up to you how much your body sweats; it's a physiological response, outside of your control. So in no way do those automatic physiological reactions mean that you enjoyed it, wanted it, or made it happen.

Yet another common issue involves clients who "froze" during their trauma—and are now ashamed that they didn't fight or run. Brief psychoeducation about the freeze/flop response is invaluable, and after this we say: "Knowing this won't get rid of 'It's my fault' or 'I'm bad' or similar themes. They will keep popping up. But at least now you know the facts." From this point on, we can refer to narratives like "I'm bad" or "It's my fault" as "old programming" to facilitate defusion: "There's some more old programming showing up."

Values Work

Shame may relate to things the client has had done to them—or to things they have done to others. Either way, important values are usually sitting just beneath the surface, and gentle questioning can quickly tease them out. We may ask:

What does this feeling tell you…

- that you deeply care about?

- that you want to take a stand against?

- that you want to stand up for?

- that you want to do differently, going forward?

- about the way you ideally want to treat yourself or others?

- about what you need to address, face up to, take action on?

Any such questions can start a rich discussion that unearths values, which then become a springboard for new, effective actions. Through this process, shame can become a powerful motivator for values-guided behavior. This is very empowering; we can't change the past, but we can learn from it—and the wisdom thereby gained is a useful resource.

Scrunching Emotions

We'll finish this chapter with one of my favorite exercises: Scrunching Emotions (Harris, 2015). Although it focuses on shame, we can adapt this for any painful emotion, to foster acceptance and self-compassion and connection with values. (Like Pushing Away Paper, it isn't suitable for people with neck, shoulder, or arm issues.) In the script, three dots indicate a pause of about three to five seconds.

Step 1: Write

The client identifies a shame-triggering memory to work with. On a sheet of letter (or A4) paper, they write a few words (maximum of one sentence) to summarize it.

Step 2: Scrunch

Therapist: Now scrunch that up—the memory, and all the thoughts and feelings that go with it—and make it as small as you possibly can. Scrunch it really hard, no half measures... That's it... Now put it between your palms, and use both arms and hands to try to squash it even smaller... Push as hard as you can...and keep pushing.

Step 3: Squeeze

Therapist: Keep the pressure on, squeezing hard... Hard as you can... Making it as small as possible... And notice what this is like... How tiring is it?... How distracting is it?... How hard to do the things that matter, or engage in what you're doing?... How much time and energy have you spent trying to do this in your life?... And isn't it exhausting?... Given there is no "delete button" in the brain, no way to simply make this disappear, would you be open to trying something different?... You would? Great!

Step 4: Hold It Gently

Therapist: Now hold it as if it's a crying baby, or a whimpering puppy, or the hand of a loved one who is in deep distress... And notice the difference that makes... Is there some relief for you in this?... Is it less distracting, less tiring?... Notice how much more energy you have now to put into doing things that are meaningful...

Step 5: Consider What It Tells You

Therapist: Keep holding it this way, and consider: What does this tell you that you care about?... What values does this remind you of?... And also consider... You can't change the past, but you can influence the future... So going forward, what do you want to do in the world to make it a better place?... To help prevent things like this from happening again?

Step 6: Appreciate It

Therapist: Notice that when you hold it this way, this emotion can be your ally...reminding you of your values...motivating you to behave like the person you want to be... And even though it hurts like hell, it's giving you valuable information... This emotion comes about through your mind, brain, and body working together, to look out for you... So even though it hurts, see if just for a moment, you can appreciate it.

Step 7: Squeeze, Then Ease

Therapist: Now just for a few moments, go back to trying to squash it... Again, crush it hard; both hands, both arms, crushing it as hard as you can... And keep the pressure on, full strength, and notice how tiring this gets... And now, once again, hold it gently... like a crying baby, or a whimpering puppy, or the hand of a loved one in distress... And notice the difference... And cup it gently in both hands...and imagine the space around it filling up with warmth and caring and kindness...

Step 8: Self-Compassion

Therapist: And see if you can send this same warmth, caring, and kindness to yourself... Imagine it as a kind of energy...that flows from the cup of your hands...and flows up your arms and into your heart...and from there, flowing up and down your body... and wherever there is pain, tension, or numbness, this warm, kind energy flows into those areas...softening up and loosening up around them.

(The therapist now helps the client zoom in on specific areas of pain, tension, or numbness, and work with them as in other acceptance and self-compassion exercises: acknowledging pain and responding with kindness.)

Step 9: Drop Anchor and Debrief

The exercise finishes with a minute of dropping anchor. We then debrief it, exploring the impact of acceptance and self-compassion and teasing out values.

Takeaway

We can use TFACT with any difficult emotion, to transform it from an enemy to an ally. Although we have focused here on shame, the same strategies apply for anger, sadness, fear, anxiety, guilt, jealousy, and so on.

CHAPTER TWENTY-FIVE

Moral Injury

When for one reason or another, someone experiences repeated or major violations of their own morality (e.g., when a soldier is ordered to shoot civilians, or a worker helplessly witnesses systemic bullying and discrimination in the workplace, or a young man fails to stop his friends from violently beating up an innocent person), it can have profound psychological effects.

"Moral injury" refers to psychological damage sustained when one perpetrates, witnesses, or fails to prevent an act that transgresses their moral principles. It was first described in the US military, when service members returned from the Vietnam War with trauma-related symptoms that didn't fit a diagnosis of PTSD; they presented primarily with strong emotional reactions of shame and guilt, rather than fear and anxiety. Since then, moral injury has been reported in doctors, nurses, teachers, and in many other professions. (However, it can also result from traumatic events that have nothing to do with work—for example, failing to report knowledge of a sexual assault.) In this chapter, we'll explore how TFACT can lessen the impact of moral injury.

Pain Versus Injury

In many texts on moral injury, the terms used are somewhat vaguely defined. For the sake of clarity, here are some ACT-congruent definitions:

Values: desired qualities of behavior (without any judgment of "right" or "wrong")

Morals: principles or standards of "right" and "wrong" or "good" and "bad" behavior

Moral values: values that are judged by one's society or community to be right and good, also known as "virtues." For example, many societies and communities would judge values such as honesty, fairness, respect, kindness, and integrity to be "right," "good," or "virtuous."

Moral pain: painful cognitions and emotions (especially shame and guilt) that arise when one's moral principles are violated.

Moral injury: psychological, spiritual, or social damage that results from responding inflexibly to moral pain.

A Normal Reaction

Moral pain is a normal, natural reaction when one's morals are violated. In our own lives, we've all experienced the stress and anxiety of moral dilemmas: "What's the right thing to do?" And we all know the angst that results when we don't "do the right thing": the guilt, shame, or regret that arises when we compromise our own moral standards.

In addition, as practitioners, we've all experienced moral pain when we know our clients are victims of injustice, being abused by "the system," or being mistreated by others, yet, for one reason or another, we are unable to intervene.

Depending on the events and the moral principles violated, we can expect to feel any number of painful emotions, including anger, sadness, guilt, shame, sorrow, regret, fear, anxiety—and even disgust or contempt. Likewise, we can expect distressing cognitions to arise—typically involving themes of injustice, betrayal, unfairness, blame, criticism of self or others, questions of right or wrong, and so on. These painful emotions and cognitions are normal, valid reactions, requiring acceptance, defusion, and self-compassion. And if we respond to them flexibly, there is no moral injury. Only when we respond *inflexibly* to this pain—with fusion, experiential avoidance, and unworkable action—does moral injury occur.

Presentations of Moral Injury

Moral injury, like any other trauma-related disorder, can present in a myriad of ways, from depression and suicidality to interpersonal problems and substance abuse. In particular, we often encounter:

- Loss of trust in self or others

- Loss of faith/belief (especially religious)

- Loss of meaning or purpose in life

- Fatalism and nihilism

- Spiritual/existential crisis

- Doubt, confusion, and questioning about morality

- Complicated grief

- Resentment and blame

- Loss of caring

- Feeling "haunted" by the past

- Sense of betrayal

- Difficulty forgiving

- Self-condemnation

The existential, humanistic underpinnings of TFACT make it well suited to all these issues.

How TFACT Helps with Moral Injury

Our work with moral injury begins, as you'd expect, with lots of normalizing and validating of the client's emotional and cognitive reactions—especially the shame and guilt that usually predominates—followed by defusion, acceptance, and self-compassion.

Clients often ruminate excessively on many of the themes above: *Things like this shouldn't happen! The world shouldn't be like this! Why do bad things happen to good people? How can God allow this? How could I have done that? Why didn't I speak up or do something? What does that say about me?* Thus, when leading into defusion, we might say:

Therapist: The human mind is a sense-making machine. It tries to make sense of everything—to map it all out, so there's a clear path for us to follow. And if the mind can't do that, it goes a bit haywire; it goes round and round in circles, trying to fit all the pieces together, put everything in the right place. But the problem is, life is often messy, confusing, chaotic. Bad things happen. Things we never expected to have to deal with. Bad things can happen to good people. And good people can do bad things. And people can do bad things and get away with it. And people can do good things and suffer for it. And our minds find that hard to compute. It doesn't fit with the way we want the world to be. The sense-making machine doesn't like that—so round and round it goes.

Following this, we can help the client interrupt such rumination, as covered in chapter eleven. However, we don't want to dismiss or ignore these thoughts, so we explore them as below.

Stuck Not Broken

Clients often think their morality has been irreparably damaged. So the classic ACT saying, "People aren't broken; they just get stuck," is very relevant:

Therapist: Your moral compass isn't broken. The fact you're suffering so much tells you that it's still there and working; if it wasn't, you wouldn't be having all this pain—you wouldn't care about what had happened. What's happened is, you're getting hooked by all these thoughts and feelings, and they're acting like a blindfold, so you can't see the compass. But when you unhook, it's like lifting up the blindfold; you'll be able to see the compass.

Client: You reckon?

Therapist: Well, can we do an experiment to find out? Would you be willing to do an exercise right now—to see if you can lift the blindfold and see the compass?

We could now take the client through a values-clarification exercise. For example, we could help the client contact their emotional pain, and then explore: "What does this pain tell you really matters to you? What it does remind you that you want to stand for, or against?" much as we do in the Scrunching Emotions exercise, in chapter twenty-four.

Grief, Forgiveness, and Compassion for Others

With moral injury (as with many other trauma-related concerns), there are often issues of blame, resentment, and complicated grief. In response, we help clients to grieve healthily, practice forgiving, and develop compassion for themselves and others (see chapter thirty-one).

Meaning and Locus of Control

Existential themes are often at the core of clients' struggles with moral injury. The two existential issues that clients most commonly grapple with are:

- Amid the vastness of time and space, we are small, insignificant, and powerless.

- Life is inherently meaningless.

Working with values, we address both these themes. We give our lives meaning through connecting with and acting on our values. And the antidote to insignificance and powerlessness is committed action: operating within our locus of control. We focus on what we *can* do, what we *can* influence, what we *can* contribute through acting on our values. We can't alter the past, but we can contribute to life in the present, and play our role in making the world a better place. And if we ourselves have done wrong, although we can't change what happened, we can atone for it, make amends. How? By putting our moral values into play—in our relationships, our work, or other domains that matter.

Religion and Spirituality

In addition to therapy, many clients find it useful to talk to a priest, chaplain, rabbi, or Imam or to revisit religious or spiritual texts that have previously inspired them. However, some turn away from their religious and spiritual ideology—and this too is a perfectly valid reaction.

It's often useful to explore clients' religious, philosophical, and spiritual beliefs as they relate to the themes we've discussed in this chapter. We want to encourage a flexible perspective on these beliefs: are they helping the client to adapt, heal, and grow—or the opposite? If the opposite, we can explore the differences between "rules" and "values," and then help clients apply the three strategies for defusion from rigid rules, covered in chapter eleven.

Takeaway

Moral pain is a normal reaction when one's moral principles are violated. When clients respond to that pain inflexibly—with fusion, avoidance, and unworkable action—moral injury results. As an existential, humanistic therapy, TFACT is well equipped to handle all aspects of moral injury—including the existential questions so often raised.

CHAPTER TWENTY-SIX

Suicidality

Suicidality—a term that includes thinking about, planning, threatening, or attempting suicide—is a daunting issue for practitioners. It's a huge topic, and we only have space to touch on it briefly, so if you want to know more, I recommend you read the *Clinical Manual for Assessment and Treatment of Suicidal Patients* by Chiles, Strosahl, and Roberts (2018). In this brief but excellent textbook (from which this chapter draws heavily), the authors talk about "the three 'I's of suicidality." This refers to three self-limiting perspectives clients have of their pain:

Intolerable: I can't tolerate this pain any longer.

Interminable: This pain is always there and never going to end.

Inescapable: Everything that gives me short-term relief from pain only creates more problems or makes life worse in the long term.

From the perspective of the thee "I"s, life seems unbearable, and if clients are unable to come up with effective solutions to reduce their suffering, suicide offers an escape. Thus, beneath suicidality, we usually find a potent combination of cognitive fusion, experiential avoidance, and ineffective problem solving.

Risk Assessment

Every practitioner working with trauma should know how to conduct a suicide risk assessment. (That topic is beyond the scope of this book, so if you lack skills or knowledge in this area, start by reading the paper "Scientizing and Routinizing the Assessment of Suicidality in Outpatient Practice" by Joiner et al., 1999. The authors suggest a risk assessment based on seven domains: previous suicidal behavior; nature of current suicidal symptoms; current life stressors; general symptomatic presentation, including a mood of despair or hopelessness; impulsivity and lack of self-control; various other predispositions; and protective factors.) If your client is at significant risk of suicide, you should follow the guidelines recommended by your professional organization and workplace. In addition to (but not in place of) those guidelines, this chapter gives you some ideas for using TFACT.

Strategies for Addressing Suicidality

Suicidal behavior is multifactorial in origin, and all core ACT processes are relevant and useful in undermining it. Dropping anchor is a good first-line skill. Four other strategies likely to help are:

- defusing from hopelessness and suicidal ideation

- using values to find reasons to live

- practicing acceptance and self-compassion to handle pain

- pursuing committed action with an emphasis on problem solving

Defusing from Hopelessness and Suicidal Ideation

Yes, you guessed it: to defuse from hopelessness and suicidal ideation, we again return to the strategy of *notice, name, normalize, purpose, workability*.

NOTICE, NAME, NORMALIZE

When noticing and naming thoughts, we may refer to the client's "suicidal thoughts" or "problem-solving thoughts" or "your mind trying to figure out how to end the pain"—or we may invite clients to come up with their own names, such as "death thoughts" or the "topping myself" theme. To normalize them, it's useful to quote the statistics on suicidality (Chiles et al., 2018), as follows:

Therapist: You know, research shows that one in two people become actively suicidal at some point in their life, for a period of two weeks or more. Think about that statistic for a moment: one in two, one in two of your friends, your family, the people on your street, the people at your work, the staff in your local supermarket...

PURPOSE

Next we look at the purpose of suicidal ideation: it's a form of problem solving. We may ask, "What problem is so painful that you're trying to kill yourself as a way to solve it?" Whatever the client answers, we can reply, "That is an immensely painful problem. And your mind is trying to solve it and stop your pain. And suicide is one possible solution."

In other words, we acknowledge that suicidality is an understandable response to the three "I"s. Consider for a moment: if you were in great pain, which you truly perceived as intolerable, interminable, and inescapable, would you think about killing yourself? If not, you are in the minority. Most people would at least consider it. And in that moment where someone thinks, *I could kill myself and all this pain would be gone*, there will usually be an immediate sense of relief. To quote the famous philosopher Friedrich Nietzsche, "The thought of suicide is a great consolation: by means of it one gets through many a dark night."

In line with this, we might say to a client, "Right now, your pain seems unbearable, never-ending, and inescapable; almost anyone in your shoes would have suicidal thoughts. Your mind is a problem-solving machine—and every time it generates these thoughts, it's doing its job—it's trying to solve your problems and save you from pain." This reframe is enormously helpful for clients racked with guilt or anxiety over their suicidal thoughts ("Why do I have these thoughts?" "It's against God's will," "It means I don't love my children"); it facilitates acceptance, defusion, and self-compassion.

In addition to experiential avoidance, there are often other reinforcers for suicidality. So we may prompt the client: "I'm wondering—do you think your mind may be trying to help you in other ways?"

Compassionate exploration frequently uncovers reinforcers such as:

- overt avoidance (i.e., escape from difficult situations)

- diminished responsibility (i.e., others expect less of you)

- gaining attention, care, support, help, or forgiveness from others

- distraction from other painful issues

- punishing, hurting, or getting revenge on someone (e.g., a caregiver)

- preventing abandonment (e.g., by a partner)

- escaping or reducing punishment

- fitting in with or belonging to a group

- identifying with an idol or a hero

As these are clarified, we validate them: "So again, this is your mind trying to help you do/get/ avoid these things."

WORKABILITY

The final step, after validating the reinforcers identified above, is to explore workability:

Therapist: So when your mind starts getting into the "kill myself" theme, there are some real short-term benefits of going along with those thoughts, letting them guide you. But how does that work in the long term, when it comes to things you really want to do with your life, like A and B and C?

The letters A, B, C represent the client's values and values-based goals. If you don't yet have this information, you can use the generic phrase "building a better life"—then clarify values, as discussed below.

Take Your Pick of Strategies

The next step is to bring in any of the defusion strategies we've covered. The methods in chapter eleven for disrupting rumination and worrying are especially useful for suicidal ideation.

Using Values to Find Reasons to Live

Values can help clients find reasons to live even though life seems unbearable. A good question is, "What has stopped you from killing yourself so far?" Often clients will mention a beloved cat or dog, their children, their parents, or their partner; we can then explore those relationships and tease out the client's values. Here are three examples:

Therapist: What has stopped you from killing yourself so far?

Client: My dog, Mira.

Therapist: Mira?

Client: Yeah. She's the only one who loves me.

Therapist: What sort of dog is she?

Client: A Doberman.

Therapist: Have you got a photo of her?

Client: Yeah. Here. (*holds up a picture on her phone screen*)

Therapist: She's beautiful. How old?

Client: Three.

Therapist: So even though you're in all this pain, you're staying alive because you care about Mira. What do you most like doing with her?

    (*The therapist now goes into the Connect and Reflect exercise.*)

Therapist: What has stopped you from killing yourself so far?

Client: I wouldn't want to dump that on my kids.

Therapist: Why not?

Client: Because it would mess them up.

Therapist: So even though you're in all this pain, you're staying alive because you care about your kids?

Therapist: What has stopped you from killing yourself so far?

Client: Because I'm such a loser, I'd probably just screw it up.

Therapist: And then what would happen?

Client: I'd end up in a wheelchair or something.

Therapist: So life would be even worse than it is now?

Client: Yeah.

Therapist: So notice this—somewhere inside you, amid all that pain, there's a part of you that's looking out for you, trying to protect you—a part that cares about you enough that it wants to prevent your life from getting even worse than it already is.

From here, we can move on to other values-clarification strategies. The values and values-based goals we help clients discover then become both "reasons to live" and aids to defusion: "So there's a caring part of you—that really cares about things like D and E and F—and then there's this 'kill your-self' theme that shows up. And there's a choice to make: if you want to build a better life, which one are you going to use as a guide?"

Practicing Acceptance and Self-Compassion to Handle Pain

Every suicidal client is suffering intensely. So one of our top priorities is to help them learn how to make room for their pain, respond with kindness, and soothe themselves. This reduces their suffering and undermines the experiential avoidance that's always at the core of suicidality. Of course, some clients will resist this work, especially if fused with rules such as "I don't deserve to live" or "I don't deserve kindness" or "I deserve to suffer"; and again, we respond to these as discussed in chapter fourteen.

Pursuing Committed Action with an Emphasis on Problem Solving

Most suicidal clients either lack problem-solving skills or are not applying them. As mentioned in chapter sixteen, we help clients either to develop these skills or—if they already have them—to apply them more effectively. We may explain, "Your mind is a problem-solving machine. But at the moment, it's so overwhelmed by all your pain and suffering, it keeps going back to the same old solution: kill yourself and stop the pain. So to get through this, and start building a better life (even though your mind says that's impossible), we're going to need to ramp up your problem-solving skills, so you can come up with solutions that actually help you build a life rather than end it. Can we spend a bit of time on this, right now?"

Chronic Suicidality and Relapse

In addition to all the above, committed action for chronically suicidal clients will usually require ongoing training in the following skills:

- seeking social support

- self-care

- crisis coping

- impulse control

- interpersonal effectiveness (e.g., assertiveness, communication, negotiation, conflict resolution)

Relapse plans such as the one in chapter thirty-two are also essential.

Takeaway

As long as clients perceive their pain as intolerable, interminable, and inescapable, suicidality is likely. But TFACT does not go "on hold" until suicidality ceases. Rather, suicidal behavior becomes the central focus, and we bring all the core ACT processes to bear upon it.

CHAPTER TWENTY-SEVEN

Finding the Treasure

At the core of all mindfulness practices is the process ACT calls "contacting the present moment." In earlier sessions, I've emphasized this as a way to reduce suffering—through dropping anchor, mindful body scans, and so on. However, we can also use it to enhance pleasure and fulfilment in life, through mindfully appreciating meaningful or pleasurable moments. After all, even amid great suffering, there are times when life gives us what we want—but all too often, we "miss out" on the potential pleasure or satisfaction of these experiences; lost in our thoughts, we don't notice them; or operating on auto-pilot, we take them for granted.

Introducing Mindful Appreciation

If we introduce mindful appreciation too early in therapy, it can easily backfire or rub clients the wrong way, for two good reasons. First, it's hard to appreciate anything when you're emotionally numb or deeply fused with your suffering. Second, it may come across as similar to "positive thinking" memes: "Be grateful for what you have," "Count your blessings," "Stop and smell the roses."

Another problem occurs when clients are still fused with the agenda of emotional control: trying hard to avoid unwanted feelings, and craving or clinging to pleasant ones, in the service of their number one goal—to "feel good." They are likely to recruit these new skills in that same agenda—in which case, they'll soon complain that "it isn't working." So, for example, if clients complain of feeling numb, empty, flat, or continually in a low mood, it's not advisable to leap into mindful savoring exercises too early; usually we need to work first with acceptance and self-compassion and mindfulness of the body.

However, later in therapy, when clients are living by their values, willingly making room for their feelings, and being kind to themselves, it's a different story. We may introduce mindful appreciation like this:

Therapist: We've done a lot of work unhooking from difficult thoughts, making room for painful feelings, being kind to yourself, living your values, dropping anchor, and so on...and I'm thinking it may be time to look at something a bit different.

Client: Like what?

Therapist:	Well, there's so much pain and suffering in your life, so many problems and difficulties. And the thing is, amid all that pain, there are often little, precious moments you can treasure. And most of us don't even realize these things are there—because we're on autopilot, or lost in our thoughts, or struggling with our feelings. So there's a skill we can use to spot those treasures, and appreciate them—because when we do that, it really adds to our life.
Client:	I'm not sure what you mean.
Therapist:	Well, for example—you mentioned your sister has been quite supportive. Was there ever a moment where you really strongly felt that she was there for you?
Client:	Yeah, at the funeral. I was a blubbering mess. And she (*tearing up*)...she held me... she just held me, for ages, and I sobbed all over her, and she kept holding me and stroking my back. (*tear runs down her cheek; face looks soft and warm*)
Therapist:	So you really felt her...love, kindness...? (*Client nods.*) That's the kind of thing I'm talking about—moments when there's something going on, amid all the pain, that we can appreciate.
Client:	Yeah, well—there aren't many of those.
Therapist:	Sure, that may well be the case, but I wonder if you're open to doing a couple of short exercises today, to see if *just maybe* you can discover some things in your life you perhaps take for granted, or don't get much satisfaction from, and see what it's like when you tune in to those experiences and actively appreciate them.
Client:	Okay. I'll give it a shot.

Note the therapist's language above; there is no suggestion that this is about getting rid of or distracting from pain. It's about appreciating precious moments "amid all that pain" because it "adds to our life." With some clients we may need to be more explicit: "This isn't a way to control your feelings; it's about increasing satisfaction in life by appreciating aspects that we normally miss out on."

We also explain:

Therapist:	Most people find that the more caught up they are in their thoughts and feelings, the harder it is to enjoy life's simple pleasures—like eating, drinking, hanging out with a friend. Have you experienced that? (*Therapist gets the client to describe one or two times when this has happened.*) So when we do something in a distracted, disengaged, or unfocused way, we don't find it satisfying—whether it's playing a game or eating a meal or listening to music...whatever. But if we can unhook from our thoughts and feelings, and engage in what we're doing, it's much more satisfying.

Brief Exercises

To help clients appreciate their present moment experience, we can encourage them to do various activities mindfully in session: eating a piece of chocolate; sipping cold water; listening to music of their choice; examining a beautiful ornament; or even leaving the office and going for a walk, to take in the sights and sounds of the neighborhood. Here's the general introduction:

> Therapist: So the challenge here is to really pay attention to everything that you do, and everything that happens—as if you're a curious scientist who has never encountered something like this.
>
> Client: Okay.
>
> Therapist: And as we do this, all sorts of thoughts and feelings will likely arise, and they can easily hook your attention, pull it away from the task. So the aim is to focus fully on the activity. And whenever you notice your attention has wandered off, take a moment to note what hooked you, then gently refocus.
>
> Client: Got it.

My two favorite exercises for this purpose are Notice Your Hand and Mindful Eating. The former involves a five-minute mindful exploration of the front and back of one hand—noticing the shapes, colors, textures, movements, and so on. (For a detailed description of the exercise and how to debrief it, see *ACT Made Simple*, 2nd edition, pages 194–197 [Harris, 2019]; for an audio recording, see Extra Bits.) Most people initially expect this exercise will be boring, tiring, and difficult to do—but, by the end, find they are appreciative of their hand's great complexity and the invaluable role it plays in their life.

For eating exercises, both therapist and client have a small morsel of food, which they both eat mindfully. Again, most people expect this to be boring or difficult—yet find themselves astonished by the amount of taste in one small morsel. Jon Kabat-Zinn (1982) popularized the use of raisins, but of course, we can use any food for this exercise. Below is a basic script; as always, please modify and improvise around it. Allow around three to five seconds between instructions.

Mindful Eating

Throughout this exercise, all sorts of thoughts and feelings will arise. Let them come and stay and go in their own good time and keep your attention on the activity. And if at any point you realize your attention has wandered, briefly note what distracted you, then refocus on eating.

> *Begin by looking at this raisin as if you're a curious scientist who has never seen such a thing before. Notice the shape, the color, the different shades, the contours, the tiny pit where the stalk was once attached.*
>
> *Notice the weight of it in your hand and the feel of the skin against your fingers: its texture and temperature.*

Raise it to your nose and inhale...and notice the aroma.

Raise it to your lips and pause for a moment before biting into it; and notice what's happening inside your mouth: the salivation...the urge to bite...

Now slowly bite it in half, noticing how your teeth cut the skin, sinking into the flesh...and keep hold of one half, and let the other half drop onto your tongue...and notice the sweetness.

Now let that half-raisin rest on your tongue...and notice the urge to chew...to swallow...

And ever so slowly, starting to chew...noticing the taste...and the texture.

Noticing the movement of your jaws...the sounds of chewing...the flesh of the raisin breaking down...

Notice how your tongue shapes the food...and your urge to swallow it...

And now, as slowly as possible, swallowing...and noticing the sound and movement in your throat...

And notice how the taste gradually disappears...and how your tongue cleans your teeth.

And notice your urge to eat the remaining half.

So now I'm going to stop talking, and in silence, let's both eat the remaining halves of our raisins in exactly the same way.

Debriefing and Homework

After any mindful appreciation exercise, useful questions to ask include:

- What did you notice?

- How did that differ from the way you normally do this?

- What did you get out of it?

- What thoughts and feelings hooked you? Were you able to unhook and refocus?

- How can you apply this to other activities in your life?

With prompting, clients usually report awe or wonder or interest, pleasure or satisfaction, a sense of intense engagement or absorption; and how this all disappears when they get hooked by thoughts and feelings; and how it returns when they unhook and refocus. We then explore the relevance to areas of life clients wish to improve, such as relationships: What happens when they pay attention fully? What happens when they get hooked and tune out?

For homework, we encourage such exercises several times daily. Clients can invent their own or we can make suggestions, as in the extracts below from the "Life Appreciation Worksheet" (see Extra Bits):

Savoring Pleasurable Activities

Every day pick a simple pleasurable activity—ideally one you take for granted or do on autopilot—and see if you can extract every ounce of pleasure out of it. This might include hugging a loved one, stroking your cat, walking your dog, playing with your kids, drinking a cool glass of water or a warm cup of tea, eating your lunch or dinner, listening to your favorite music, having a hot bath or shower, walking in the park—you name it. (Don't try this with activities that actually require you to get lost in your thoughts, such as reading a book or doing crossword puzzles.) As you do this activity, use your five senses to be fully present: notice what you can see, hear, touch, taste, and smell—and savor every aspect of it.

Appreciating People

Each day, pick one person, and notice their face as if you've never seen it before: the color of their eyes, teeth, and hair; the pattern of the wrinkles in their skin; and the manner in which they move, walk, and talk. Notice their facial expressions, body language, and tone of voice. See if you can read their emotions and tune in to what they are feeling. When they talk to you, pay attention as if they are the most fascinating speaker you've ever heard and you've paid a million dollars for the privilege of listening. And very importantly: notice what happens because of this more mindful interaction.

EXTRA BIT In *Trauma-Focused ACT: The Extra Bits*, chapter twenty-seven, you'll find an audio recording of Notice Your Hand and a "Life Appreciation Worksheet."

Takeaway

We usually bring in mindful appreciation somewhat later in therapy, because early on it can easily fail, backfire, or be recruited for emotional control. And it's something that's very relevant to all of us because we all tend to take life for granted, go through the day on autopilot. When we mindfully appreciate what we have, life is so much richer and more fulfilling.

CHAPTER TWENTY-EIGHT

Building Better Relationships

Rainer Maria Rilke, a famous poet and novelist, wrote, "For one human being to love another human being: that is perhaps the most difficult task that has been given to us, the ultimate, the final problem and proof, the work for which all other work is merely preparation."

He wasn't wrong! Even when life is going relatively well, close, intimate relationships are fraught with challenges. But in the aftermath of trauma, these difficulties are massively amplified. So let's take a look at how TFACT can help. I've chunked this chapter into four sections:

- Understanding what goes wrong in relationships

- Applying TFACT to any relationship issue

- Developing relationship skills

- Addressing issues of trust

Understanding What Goes Wrong in Relationships

The chances are, with almost every client, interpersonal issues of one sort or another will arise. Avoidance behaviors in particular—drug or alcohol abuse, self-harming, social withdrawal, and so on—often have a huge negative impact on relationships. In addition, we often see:

- conflict, hostility, aggression

- withdrawal, disconnection, avoidance of intimacy

- possessiveness, jealousy

- excessive seeking of support, reassurance, or approval

- passivity, compliance, submissiveness

- deceit, dishonesty, manipulation

And the list goes on; almost any fused or avoidant behavior will impact negatively on relationships once it becomes excessive. Naturally, when working with any interpersonal issue, we want to know about the context: What's the history of the relationship? What makes it better? What makes it worse? What are the strengths and weakness of both parties? How does each party contribute to the issue?

Fruitful areas to explore are:

A. What does the client want from this relationship? What are their needs and desires?

B. What does the client find most threatening in this relationship? What is the other person saying or doing at those times?

C. What does the client want the other person to start or stop doing? What strategies has the client tried to achieve that? And what were the results?

D. What does the client want to contribute to the relationship? What sort of person do they want to be? What values do they want to live by? How do they want to treat the other person?

E. Which of their own behaviors does the client see as helpful or unhelpful? Which of their own behaviors would they like to stop or reduce? Which behaviors would they like to start or do more of?

Give and Take

Understandably, many clients are focused on what they want to *get* from the relationship and how they want *the other person* to change. Often, they haven't thought about what they want to contribute, what values they want to live by, or how they might want to change their own behavior. So it's essential we raise and explore this, because healthy relationships require both giving and taking.

Some clients are excessively focused on giving to or pleasing others—and are not looking after themselves—and this obviously isn't healthy. So we help them explore values such as self-care, self-compassion, self-support, courage, independence, and assertiveness. However, if clients are excessively focused on their own needs, to the detriment of others—well, that isn't healthy either. In such cases, we can help connect them with values such as caring, giving, fairness, gratitude, and so on.

Validation and Psychoeducation

Functional analysis (chapter seventeen) offers a simple way to understand and validate any problematic interpersonal behavior. Once we know the antecedents (situations, cognitions, emotions) that trigger it, and the consequences that reinforce it (avoidance of something unwanted, or access to something desired), we can say, "It makes perfect sense that you would do this." Validating the behavior does not mean we agree with it, or it's justified, or there's no need to change it. It only means that it's understandable: a normal and natural response given the client's life history and current circumstances.

With many clients these problematic behaviors (or functionally similar ones) go way back in time, to early childhood—where their main functions were keeping the child safe or helping them get their needs met in abusive or neglectful relationships. And this is where attachment theory comes in.

Attachment Theory

Experiencing childhood trauma frequently has a negative impact on clients' relationships in later life. Attachment theory helps us to understand how and why this happens. In chapter fourteen, the section "Attachment Theory in a Nutshell" covers the main points of the theory. We can repeat that section almost word-for-word to our clients to introduce the main concepts, adding, "The reason I'm talking about this is that our attachment style acts as a sort of guide for the relationships we form in later life. So if we know a bit about it, that can help us to understand why we do what we do in our relationships."

To work with attachment theory, we don't need an in-depth history of the client's childhood; the broad strokes are more than enough. Indeed, some clients can't remember their childhood or refuse to talk about it—and that's absolutely fine; we can still look at their attachment style knowing nothing about the past history that shaped it.

ATTACHMENT STYLES

The descriptions below of different attachment styles and their possible impact on relationships are extracts from the "Attachment Styles" handout (see Extra Bits), a simple way to explore this complex subject.

Secure Attachment

The caregiver mostly responds positively, consistently, and reliably to the child's "bids," so the child feels secure in the relationship. This creates a model for positive, healthy, intimate relationships in later life.

Attitude: "I love you, I care about you, and I'm okay with that. I can handle a bit of tension or conflict in the relationship because I know that's part and parcel of a loving relationship."

Anxious-Preoccupied Attachment

The caregiver is very inconsistent. Often they respond positively to the child's bids—but equally often, they ignore them. So the child is insecure, anxious, and very uncertain about whether their needs will be met or not. In later life, this often leads to yearning for attention in relationships and clinginess, possessiveness, or jealousy.

Attitude: "I'm worried you might not love me, or you might leave me, and I don't know if I can rely on you. I really need *to know for sure* that you love me, and you won't leave me."

Dismissive-Avoidant Attachment

The caregiver rarely responds positively to the child's bids; most of the time they are distant and disengaged and ignore the child's needs. In response, the child is emotionally distant, comes to expect that their needs won't be met, and often gives up trying. As adults, they tend to avoid seeking nurture, closeness, or caring in relationships and are therefore often lonely. In fact, often they prefer to avoid relationships altogether.

Attitude: "I don't want to care about you deeply or get too close to you—because if I do, I'll only end up disappointed, hurt, or lonely."

Disorganized Attachment

The caregiver rarely responds to bids positively. Most of the time, they respond with aggression or hostility. As a result, the child is confused and doesn't know how to get their needs met. When around their caregivers, these children often appear wary, anxious, or dazed. As adults, they find it hard to trust; they are fearful of being hurt, and closeness brings high levels of anxiety. They have difficulty forming relationships, and the ones they have are often brief.

Attitude: "I don't know what I want. Getting close to you scares me. At times I want to love you; at times I want to leave you."

ATTACHMENT STYLES CAN CHANGE

We may have different styles of attachment in different relationships; for example, we may be secure with one parent but anxious-preoccupied with the other. Also, our attachment styles may change throughout our lives, either from being in different relationships or through actively working on our behavior in therapy or coaching.

We can share the "Attachment Styles" handout with clients and explore, for this specific relationship:

- Which of these styles seems closest to your own?

- How does that play out in the relationship?

From there, it's often useful to focus on two common areas of difficulty: threats and needs. (Clients may not relate to the terms "threat" or "threatening," so consider alternatives like "difficult," "scary," or "stressful.") We want to find out:

- What does the client find threatening in this relationship?

- What needs does the client find it hard to meet in this relationship?

- What difficult cognitions and emotions show up when the client feels threatened or their needs aren't being met?

- What does the client do in response to those cognitions and emotions, and how does that behavior affect the relationship?

WHY INCLUDE ATTACHMENT THEORY?

We don't have to bring in attachment theory, but it can be useful for three reasons: First, it raises self-awareness (and can then be used for noticing and naming: "Aha! Here's my anxious attachment showing up").

Second, it helps clients be more accepting of, forgiving of, and compassionate toward themselves because they realize they do not choose these emotional and cognitive reactions; rather, these reactions result from childhood events that were outside their control. Similarly, the behaviors they do (in response to those antecedents) make perfect sense; these behaviors have, in the past, served to protect the client or meet their needs in difficult situations.

Finally, it helps clients understand behaviors they find odd or confusing in themselves; it answers their questions like "Why do I keep doing this?" For example, many clients desire intimacy and closeness, yet as a relationship deepens, they withdraw physically or emotionally, or they push the other person away in various ways (e.g., overworking, having affairs, becoming hypercritical). We help them see that because of their past history, they find intimacy and closeness threatening, so naturally, as a relationship deepens, they become increasingly anxious. Their behaviors help them avoid the threat (of intimacy) by creating distance and disconnection. (Of course, we can do all of this without ever mentioning attachment theory, but it does add an extra layer of understanding.)

THREE CAUTIONS

Three potential problems can occur when we explicitly focus on attachment theory. One is that sessions can become too analytical and intellectual. A little bit of insight-oriented work is useful, but generally, it's wise to keep discussions on attachment short and sweet (clients can read up on it later, if interested) and quickly segue into practical skill building. Understanding and insight play only small roles in behavioral change; the bulk of the work involves learning new ways of responding to difficult thoughts and feelings and experimenting with new patterns of behavior.

A second problem is that some clients think, *Well, if that's my attachment style, that means I can't change.* So we are clear with *all* clients that even when these patterns of behavior are long established and deeply entrenched, they are still changeable; it requires work, for sure, but it's definitely doable.

Third: clients may suddenly recognize the destructive effects of their own behavior on their children—triggering anxiety and harsh self-judgment. However, if handled well, these reactions are good opportunities for growth. Acceptance, defusion, and self-compassion are good first-line responses. We can then explore the client's values and translate them into new patterns of action, in line with the sort of caregiver they really want to be. (The Scrunching Emotions exercise, chapter twenty-four, is often helpful.)

Applying TFACT to Any Relationship Issue

There are four main ways we can use TFACT to help clients with relationship issues:

1. to take care of themselves and better handle the painful thoughts and feelings that inevitably show up when relationships are unsatisfactory;

2. to change what they say and do in their relationships in order to reduce damage and get better results;

3. to influence the other person's behavior *constructively*, in ways that are *healthy* for the relationship (e.g., through assertiveness and good communication); and

4. to end a relationship or develop a new one.

Practical Tip

When a client complains about difficulties in several relationships, the first step is to narrow the focus. We ask them to pick just one relationship, we listen compassionately to their difficulties within it, we validate their concerns and frustrations, and then we establish behavioral goals:

Therapist: There are a lot of problems in this relationship, and you're suffering. So there are basically four things we can work on here to help improve things. *(Therapist briefly runs through the four options above.)* Which of these would suit you best?

Sometimes practitioners are reluctant to run through these options; they feel uncomfortable or think it's too directive. But if your client just keeps venting about all the problems in the relationship, and this fills up the session so they're not developing psychological flexibility or learning new interpersonal skills, you will need to make room for your discomfort and actively establish some clear goals, or you won't get anywhere.

The Tools We Need

Whatever the client's relationship issues—attachment related or not—we now have all the tools we need to:

- instigate and reinforce any new interpersonal behavior (chapter sixteen)

- undermine any problematic interpersonal behavior (chapter seventeen)

- overcome psychological barriers to change and maintain new behaviors over time (chapter eighteen)

- overcome avoidance of intimacy through compassionate, flexible exposure (chapter twenty)

- increase satisfaction and deepen connection in relationships through mindful appreciation of others (chapter twenty-seven)

- handle the painful cognitions and emotions inevitable in all relationships using dropping anchor, defusion, acceptance, self-compassion, and self-as-context skills

And, in addition to all the above, there's the choice point. As illustrated below, we can use it to quickly map out any interpersonal issue (attachment related or not).

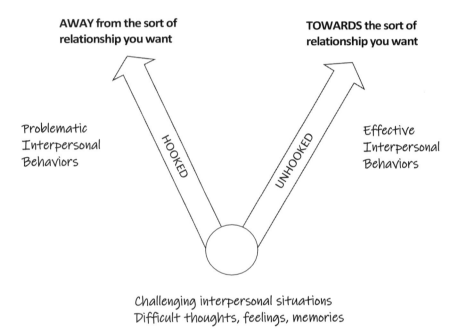

As with other issues, when using the choice point, we usually start at the bottom: we identify a difficult interpersonal situation and the thoughts, feelings, memories, or urges that show up. Then:

Therapist: What we want to do next is get a sense of what you say and do when this stuff (*pointing to the bottom*) shows up—and whether those things are towards moves, that help build the sort of relationship you want, or away moves, that make it worse.

Next, we look at the adaptive functions of the client's problematic interpersonal behaviors: how they have helped to protect the client or meet their needs in various ways, both recently and in the past. (As mentioned earlier, this is especially important when working with complex trauma because these behaviors often started in childhood as ways to survive abuse or neglect.)

Finally, we complete the towards arrow with new interpersonal behaviors (values-based goals and actions) to help clients build the sorts of relationships they want. The challenge formula often comes in handy during this work.

The Challenge Formula

The challenge formula is useful for any type of relationship—with partners, children, parents, friends, co-workers, and so on. The three options are:

A. Leave the relationship.

B. Stay, and live by your values; do what you can to improve the relationship while effectively handling the pain that's inevitable.

C. Stay, and do things that don't help or make it worse.

When we compassionately and respectfully present this formula, most clients choose option b. However, sometimes they choose option a, in which case, we help them leave the relationship, acting mindfully on their values. Usually this warrants a lot of acceptance and self-compassion, followed by work on grieving and forgiving (chapter thirty-one). Of course, if the client is unwilling to leave, at least for the time being, then b and c are the only alternatives.

Only rarely do clients choose option c. This almost always indicates high experiential avoidance and fusion with hopelessness. In such cases, we acknowledge and validate that choice and work on developing TFACT skills (including lots of self-compassion) until the client has enough psychological flexibility to choose option a or b.

But what if a client says, "I just don't know whether to stay or leave"? This is a sticky situation and, to address it effectively, I recommend my worksheet for dilemmas (see Extra Bits). In the meantime, until the dilemma is resolved, we can suggest, "So perhaps one day you *will* decide to leave, but until that day comes, you are still in the relationship. And every day you remain, you have two options: b or c. So each morning, when you wake up, ask yourself: which option will I choose for today? Or, if you can't choose for an entire day, then just choose for half a day, or even just for the next hour. Ask yourself, *For the next sixty minutes, which option do I choose?* And when that time is up, choose again."

Note: obviously different strategies are necessary when the relationship involves abuse or violence, but that's beyond the scope of this book.

But It's Not My Fault! They Need to Change!

Some clients will initially react negatively to the idea of looking at their own interpersonal behavior. They may say things like, "But it's him. He's the problem, not me! Why should I have to change?" or "She needs to change first. If she'd just stop doing XYZ, it'd be fine," or "They need to accept me the way I am!"

In such cases, we first validate their reactions, then explore the issue of control. For example:

Therapist: You are right. Their behavior is creating problems for you—and if they would just change their behavior, it would be so much easier for you. So would you be interested in learning how to make that happen? (*Client agrees.*) Great, so we can't actually *control* other people, but we can influence how they behave. And the way we do that is through our own words and our actions.

Client: I've already tried that. Nothing works.

Therapist: That sounds very frustrating. I'd be feeling the same way if I were in your shoes. However, it's a good place to start. Let's recap everything you've tried that *hasn't* worked—so we can be sure to look at some new strategies that you haven't yet tried.

Next, we return to workability. We elicit all the strategies the client has used to try resolving the relationship issue(s). We validate and normalize them, then encourage the client to look at them in terms of their effects on the relationship: are they making it better or worse? Then we summarize: "So you've worked hard at this relationship, and most of the strategies you've used are extremely common— things we all tend to say and do to try to influence others. And sometimes these things *do* work, in the short term, to meet your needs—but long term, they're not building the relationship you want. Would you be open to trying something different?"

If the client answers no, we can revisit the challenge formula and clarify, with great compassion, "I totally get your reluctance to do that, and I'll certainly honor your wishes. I just want us both to be clear though—what you're choosing is option c: stay in the relationship and do things that don't help or make it worse."

If the client answers yes to trying something different, the door is now open to teaching new skills such as assertiveness, communication, and negotiation. However, it's important to explain, "These are *influencing* skills. They are ways to *influence* the behavior of others, not to *control* it. They hugely increase the chances of getting what you want—or stopping what you don't want—but they don't guarantee it. They are not magic, so there will be times they won't achieve what you're hoping for, which is obviously upsetting. So another part of our work here is learning how to handle the pain that shows up for you at those times when these skills *don't* give you what you want."

Developing Relationship Skills

As a rule of thumb, the more complex and numerous the relationship issues are, the greater the need for training in interpersonal skills. We should be able to teach clients the following basic relationship skills:

- Assertiveness—including how to say no, make requests, express genuine opinions, and set boundaries

- Effective communication—including words, facial expressions, tone of voice, physical posture

- Giving and receiving feedback—both positive and negative

- Negotiating, compromising, and reciprocity

- Conflict resolution—including how to apologize and make reparations

- Developing empathy and compassion for others, to see things from their point of view and imagine how they might think and feel

- Reinforcing desired behavior when it occurs (e.g., through actively noticing it and showing appreciation or gratitude)

Note that these are all basic therapy skills (hardly surprising, given the central importance of building a strong relationship), so we should all be somewhat familiar with them. Unfortunately, we don't have room to go through them here, but you'll find them in my self-help book on ACT for relationship issues, which is appropriately titled *ACT with Love*, and also in the textbook *Acceptance and Commitment Therapy for Borderline Personality Disorder* by Patricia Zurita Ona (2019).

Arguably the best way to develop these skills is through active role-play in session. Initially the client plays the role of the other party, while the therapist plays the role of the client and demonstrates the new skill. They then swap roles: the therapist now plays the other party, while the client plays themselves and experiments with the new skill. The therapist then gives feedback, the client reflects on what they discovered, and then they try it again. And so on, and so on, until the client gets the hang of it.

And of course, learning new skills is challenging, so we help clients bring in values for motivation, overcome HARD barriers, and practice self-compassion when things go poorly.

Addressing Issues of Trust

If we have been badly hurt, threatened, betrayed, or abused by others, often we find it hard to trust again. We easily fuse with the rule "Don't trust or you'll get hurt!" The problem is, without trust, we can't build deep and meaningful relationships. So to help clients address this issue, we can revisit the three strategies for rigid rule following (chapter eleven):

1. defuse from the rule,

2. discover the underlying values and explore flexible ways of living them, and

3. make room for pain and be kind to yourself.

Let's quickly run through these.

Defusion from the Rule "Don't Trust!"

Once again, we can turn to the strategy of *notice, name, normalize, purpose, workability*. It's usually easy to notice and name the rules clients are fusing with: "I can't trust XYZ, because if I do, bad things will happen and I'll get hurt." We normalize such rules: we all have them to various extents, and their purpose is to keep us safe. In terms of workability, following such a rule has a big short-term payoff: it reduces anxiety and fear of getting hurt, and it gives a sense of security and self-protection. So we want to validate those benefits: "When the people around you are dangerous or unreliable, following this rule keeps you safe. In the past, it has protected you."

We then compassionately explore the costs of *rigidly* following this rule today: loneliness and isolation; lack of intimacy, connection, or depth in close relationships; or ongoing conflict due to checking on, interrogating, or disbelieving others. Sometimes this will lead to an exchange like this:

Client: So are you telling me to just trust everyone?

Therapist: No. Not at all. That would be a recipe for getting hurt, abused, and betrayed. I'm inviting you to consider the possibility that maybe there's another way to use this rule. Rather than see it as a law that you must always obey, no matter what, you could see it as a piece of advice that's useful to follow strictly in some situations, but helpful to bend in others.

At this point, we usually need to do some psychoeducation on the difference between "blind trust" and "mindful trust" (Harris, 2009b).

BLIND TRUST AND MINDFUL TRUST

"Blind trust" means trusting someone completely, without taking the time to assess whether they are deserving of your trust or not. "Mindful trust," on the other hand, means carefully observing the behavior of another person before deciding whether to trust them—and continuing to observe carefully if and when we do start trusting. We may encourage clients to look out for five factors:

- Is this person considerate? (Do they consider and respect your feelings, wishes, needs, and opinions?)

- Is this person sincere? (Do they mean what they say?)

- Is this person reliable? (Do they follow through on the things they say they will do?)

- Is this person responsible? (Do they consider the consequences of their actions? If they make mistakes or disappoint, do they own up to it, apologize, and atone?)

- Is this person competent? (Are they able to do what they say they will do?)

We can suggest clients get to know someone slowly; take their time. Experiment with small actions of trust, carefully observing how the other person behaves: do they tend to be considerate, sincere, reliable, responsible, and competent?

Over time, they can experiment with larger acts of trusting (another example of graded exposure) while continuing to carefully track the consequences. Obviously, no one is perfect in all these five areas; at times we are all lacking, but these qualities at least give some basis for cautious trusting. And if there's little or no sign of such qualities—that's a big red flag *not* to trust.

Discover Underlying Values and Flexibly Apply Them

Underneath the rule "Do not trust," we usually find a value such as self-protection. So we help clients flexibly act in self-protective ways while also living their values of being trusting. We can draw a Venn diagram with two overlapping circles, one labeled "trust," the other "self-protection." In the outer area of one circle are behaviors that are trusting but not self-protective; in the outer area of the other are behaviors that are self-protective but not trusting. And in the overlapping central area go behaviors both self-protective and trusting. We can then explore when, where, how, and to what extent to draw upon behaviors from that overlapping area, in the service of building meaningful relationships. And again, graded exposure: small acts of trust initially, building up gradually over time.

The fact is, any act of trusting involves some risk. If you want absolute certainty that you will never get hurt in a significant relationship, the only way to ensure that is to avoid significant relationships. And if that's what a client genuinely chooses, we would respect that. However, so far I've never heard of a psychologically flexible person choosing that option; when people say they'd rather be alone than risk being hurt, that's almost certainly fusion and avoidance doing the talking. In such cases, we could work on building psychological flexibility in other areas of life—then revisit relationships later.

Make Room for Pain and Respond with Kindness

Trusting again, after previous violations, will generate many uncomfortable thoughts, feelings, and memories. So if close, meaningful relationships are important to the client, are they willing to make room for the inevitable pain involved? For all that anxiety and uncertainty? All those fears of being hurt, betrayed, or disappointed?

While we have a lot of control over the actions of trust, we have no control over the feelings. Feelings of trust are hard to describe: a sense of security, comfort, confidence, safety, and calmness. So if you've been hurt or abused in previous significant relationships, feelings of trust will be few and far between when you're forming new ones, whereas feelings of anxiety, doubt, insecurity, and vulnerability will be plentiful.

Over time, if the other person continues behaving in a trustworthy manner, then maybe the feelings of trust will eventually arise. But this is not something we can control. So, the two questions for our clients are (1) in the service of building relationships, are you willing to make room for these inevitable difficult thoughts and feelings? and (2) can you acknowledge how painful and difficult and scary this is—and treat yourself kindly?

EXTRA BIT In chapter twenty-eight you'll find the "Attachment Styles" handout and the "Difficult Dilemmas" worksheet.

Takeaway

TFACT is well-suited for any relationship issue, and attachment theory is often a useful addition. While psychological flexibility helps build better relationships (we get along better with others when we are present, open, and living by our values), clients often need additional training in interpersonal skills. Trust issues are common in clients with a history of trauma, and an important part of our work is to distinguish blind trust from mindful trust.

And, well done. You've made it to the end of part three of the book, which covers the bulk of our work in TFACT: helping our clients live meaningful lives in the present. In part four, we'll focus on healing the past, which, needless to say, is hugely important when working with trauma.

PART FOUR

Healing the Past

CHAPTER TWENTY-NINE

Supporting the "Younger You"

Many adults initially find it hard to be compassionate to themselves as they are today. They often find it easier to imagine being compassionate to a childhood version of themselves. Thus, TFACT often uses "inner child imagery and rescripting" as a pathway to self-compassion. In these exercises, you revisit a painful childhood memory, and you imagine yourself as the adult you are today going back in time to comfort and soothe the "younger you"—the child you were back then. Your aim is to empathize with, validate, and support the "younger you"; to be there in a kind and protective way, and help them understand what was going on at the time.

Practical Tip

Although I'm using it here, I recommend you don't use the phrase "inner child" with clients, for two good reasons. One, it's often associated with "new age" practices or nonscientific models of therapy. Two, we often work with memories from teenage or young adult years, as opposed to childhood.

Inner Child Imagery and Rescripting

In the big, wide world of TFACT, there are many variations on inner child imagery and rescripting, so please modify the script below as desired. To set these exercises up safely, make sure clients have good dropping anchor skills (in case of adverse reactions) and practice graded exposure: start with less challenging memories and gradually work up to more difficult ones. Also, clearly establish that there is an "adult you"—the person you are today—and a "younger you"—the child, teenager, or younger adult you were back then, in the memory. (For ease, I'll just use the word "child" in the rest of the chapter.) Always have your client look through the eyes of their adult self—and from that perspective, see the child. This is so important. We don't ask the client to imagine they *are* the child, because that could easily plunge them into a world of fusion. Keep the client identifying with the adult—always seeing the child through the adult's eyes.

Make It Interactive

We talk freely with our client throughout these exercises. We continually check in and ask the client what the child is doing and saying, how the child looks, how the child is responding. And the things the adult says to the child should not slavishly follow the generic script below. Rather, we help the client come up with their own words and gestures toward the child. Some clients struggle to think of supportive, caring words or actions—especially if they come from backgrounds where they themselves never had such experiences. If so, we can be as directive as necessary, actively coaching the adult in what to say and do to support the child.

Clients often fuse with "It's my fault" or "I should have stopped it," especially when dealing with childhood sexual abuse. During inner child work, an alternative self-compassionate narrative often spontaneously shows up; the client, without coaching from us, tells the child, "It wasn't your fault." But if this doesn't happen spontaneously, we prompt it: "Is she still holding on tightly to 'It's my fault'? What is it like for that child to go through life holding on to that judgment? Is there something you might like to say or do to help her unhook?"

If necessary, we then coach the client to speak and act compassionately, to recognize and meet the physical, emotional, and psychological needs of the child. For example, we may advise the adult to pass on important bits of psychoeducation to the child: why they froze up or why they experienced pleasure even though they hated what was happening.

In the Compassion for the Younger You exercise, below, the instructions basically involve asking the child if there's anything they need or want from you and providing it for them; offering your kindness, compassion, and support; letting them know you'll always be here to help them; and giving them a gift of some sort. A sample script follows.

Compassion for the Younger You

You are about to do an exercise in imagination. Some people imagine with vivid, colorful pictures, much like those on a TV screen; others imagine with vague, fuzzy, unclear pictures; while others imagine without using pictures at all, relying more on words and ideas. However you imagine is just fine.

You're going to imagine traveling back in time to visit a younger version of yourself, at some point in your life when you were struggling, and the people around you were for one reason or another unable to give you the care and support you needed. This could be when you were a child, or more recently as a teenager or young adult.

Find a comfortable position and drop anchor: acknowledge what's going on in your inner world... connect with your body, moving, stretching, breathing...engage in the world around you...noticing what you can see and hear and smell and touch.

Now either close your eyes or fix them on a spot, and allow yourself to imagine.

Imagine yourself getting into a time machine. I'm not going to describe it—imagine it however you like: a portal, a bright light, a mechanical apparatus, or just a vague sense of something you can't even see.

And once inside it, imagine yourself traveling back in time to visit your younger self. Find the "younger you" at some point in their life when they are struggling—and the adults around them are not providing the care and support they need.

Now step out of the time machine and establish contact with the younger you. Take a good look at this child (*or teenager or young adult*) and get a sense of what they are going through. Are they crying? Are they angry or frightened? Are they feeling guilty or ashamed? What does this young person really need: love, kindness, understanding, forgiveness, acceptance?

In a kind, calm, and gentle voice, tell this younger you that you know what has happened, that you know what they've been through, that you know how much they are hurting.

Tell this younger you that they got through this difficult patch in their life and it is now a distant memory.

Tell this younger you that you are here, that you know how much this truly hurts and you want to help in any way you can.

Ask this young person if there's anything they need or want from you—and whatever they ask for, provide it. If they ask you to take them somewhere special, go ahead and do it. Offer a hug, a kiss, words of kindness, or a gift of some sort. This is an exercise in imagination, so you can give them anything they want—even if in the real world it would be impossible. If this younger you doesn't know what they want or doesn't trust you, then let them know that's fine; they don't need to say or do anything.

Tell this young person anything you think they need to hear to help them understand what has happened—and to help them put an end to self-blaming.

Tell them that you are here for them, that you care, and you'll do whatever you can to help them get through this.

Continue to radiate caring and kindness toward this younger you in any way you can think of: through words, gestures, deeds—or if you prefer, through magic or telepathy.

Once you have a sense that this younger you has accepted your caring and kindness, it's time to bid farewell. Give them a gift of some sort to symbolize the connection between you. (*The therapist makes suggestions if the client is stuck—a toy or teddy bear for a younger child; for someone older, perhaps an item of clothing, a book, a magical object, or anything else that springs to mind.*)

Say goodbye and let them know that you'll come back to visit again.

Then get in your time machine and come back to the present.

And now, let's drop anchor...

Unpack the Exercise

When unpacking the exercise, we may ask:

- What was that like; what did you get out of it or learn from it?

- What words would you use to describe the way you treated the "younger you"?

- How can you apply this to your life today?

- What can you say and do for yourself when you are hurting just like that child was?

The idea with these questions is to translate self-compassion into practical words and deeds the client can say or do throughout the day. Many clients benefit from repeating this exercise as a homework task, working with different memories.

EXTRA BIT Download *Trauma-Focused ACT: The Extra Bits* from the "Free Resources" page on http://www.ImLearningACT.com. In chapter twenty-eight you'll find a script for a "younger you" exercise (one version among many).

Takeaway

"Younger you" exercises are an important tool in our armory against shame, self-blame, and worthlessness. They are especially useful with clients who initially resist self-compassion, because they often find it easier to be compassionate toward a younger version of themselves.

CHAPTER THIRTY

Exposure to Memories

As mentioned earlier, we tend to leave formal exposure to traumatic memories until late in therapy, for the simple reason that it's often unnecessary. In earlier sessions, there's been plenty of *informal* exposure to memories: noticing and naming them; acknowledging them while dropping anchor; interacting with them through inner child work; and responding to them with self-compassion. This, in combination with all the other work on values, defusion, acceptance, self-as-context, and self-soothing, is enough for many clients to get on with their lives and respond flexibly when difficult memories arise.

However, if the client is still responding inflexibly to difficult memories (i.e., getting hooked, doing away moves), then formal exposure is warranted. But before we start, it's essential for the client to understand that the aim is *not* to reduce anxiety or eliminate the memory; it's to help them stay present and act effectively when these memories surface, so they can live their values and pursue their goals. The Horror Movie metaphor in chapter seven conveys this well. (And if clients *are* fixated on eliminating memories, we return to creative hopelessness.)

Considerations for Formal Exposure

Before commencing formal exposure, there are a number of practicalities to consider: how to ensure a safe experience for the client, how to prepare ahead for the likelihood of fusion, and how to monitor responses during the procedure. Let's quickly take a look at each of these topics.

Setting Up Safely

Before beginning formal exposure, we check off every item on this list:

1. You've established a clear, nonverbal safety signal.

2. The client has good dropping anchor skills.

3. The client has at least basic skills in defusion, acceptance, and self-compassion.

4. The client can take the observer perspective (self-as-context).

5. Values-based goals are the motivation for exposure.

6. The client understands the purpose and intended outcomes.

7. The client has chosen a specific memory to work with.

Practical Tip

If the client has so many painful memories that they can't settle on one, we can list them all on a sheet of paper, flip a coin above it, then work with whichever one the coin lands on. Alternatively, we can write them all on small strips of paper, put them into a bag, shuffle them around, and draw one out at random.

Preempting the Mind and Writing Thoughts Down

Fusion is likely to arise during this process, especially with harsh self-judgment and self-blame, so it's often useful to revisit the strategies of preempting the mind and writing thoughts down: "What unhelpful things do you think your mind might say as we do this?" "Can we write those thoughts down, so we're ready for them if they show up?" Then, when fusion arises, we can point to the written words: "There it is. We guessed your mind was going to say that. So do we need to address this—or can we carry on?" Usually, the client defuses rapidly and chooses to continue.

Tracking Responses and Moving with the TIMES

When all the above is in place, we can undertake exposure, as described in chapter twenty, ensuring that we always keep the client within their window of flexibility. We start and end each session with at least one or two minutes of dropping anchor and use the three scales of presence, willingness, and control over physical actions (CPA) to track the client's responses. Throughout exposure, we repeatedly connect clients with their values; every few minutes we ask questions such as "And what's this work in the service of?" "And what values are you living right now, as we do this?" "And take a moment to connect with why you're doing this challenging task."

We also "move with the TIMES" (thoughts, images, memories, emotions, sensations). So if an intense, overwhelming emotion shows up, we shift focus from the memory to the emotion. Then, once the client scores seven or above for presence, willingness, and CPA, we return to the memory. Similarly, if clients fuse or dissociation seems imminent, we drop anchor, defuse, and then return to the memory.

Case Example: Extract from a Session with Beth

Beth is a forty-five-year-old ambulance driver and paramedic with two young daughters. She is currently not working due to PTSD she developed following her attendance at a car accident in which a baby and a toddler died. All seven points on the checklist above have been addressed.

Beth's motivations for exposure are "loving, caring for, and being present with my girls" and "going back to work, so I can get back to helping and looking after people." Beth has predicted that self-judgmental thoughts are likely to arise: *I'm pathetic, I should be over this, I'm letting everyone down, I should be able to deal with this by myself.* She has written these on a piece of paper, which rests on the couch beside her. The exchange below follows two minutes of dropping anchor:

Therapist:	So what's showing up for you now?
Client:	I'm really scared. I'm really terrified that you're not going to be able to help me.
Therapist:	Yeah. So...do you notice that in your body anywhere in particular?
Client:	I feel...yeah. I feel kind of numb and weak.
Therapist:	Where do you feel that most in your body right now?
Client:	You know I kind of feel something here. I don't even know what it is, but I just feel like I have no, no movement in my body. No...no strength.
Therapist:	Okay. So can I just ask you to drop anchor again? Push your feet into the floor, sit up straight. (*Client does so.*) And can I get you to just push your fingertips really firmly together there? (*Client does so.*) And see if you can feel that all the way up your arms. Can you feel your elbows?
Client:	Yeah.
	(*Dropping anchor continues for another minute. Then the therapist asks for scores on presence and CPA; Beth scores eight and nine.*)
Therapist:	So are you willing to have this anxiety, in order to do something that matters?
Client:	Yes.
Therapist:	How much, zero to ten?
Client:	Eight.
Therapist:	Great. And as we continue, anytime you're getting overwhelmed, or locked up, or shutting down, I'll get you to run through this drill, okay?
Client:	Okay.

Therapist:	So I'm going to ask you to tell me about the accident—but let's not plunge right into the most awful part of it. Let's lead into it gradually. So maybe start with you responding to the call. And talk me through it as if it's happening now. So who's driving the ambulance?
Client:	Yep, I'm driving.
Therapist:	Okay so you're driving, and how do you hear about the accident?
Client:	Well, we heard the dispatcher, and we were closest to the scene; I think we were ten minutes away—so siren on.

(The client has slipped into speaking in the past tense—"we were"—so the therapist now steers her to speak in the present tense—"you are driving." This is to keep the memory immediate, as if happening now.)

Therapist:	Okay, so you are driving, and you're ten minutes away. Can you tell me what you hear on the call, as if it's happening now?
Client:	Uh yeah, well they're saying it's an accident on the interstate. Just routine. Doesn't seem like a big deal.

(For the next two minutes, the therapist elicits details about the drive to the scene of the accident. Beth says the traffic conditions are good. She describes her fellow paramedic, Dave, as reliable, with a good sense of humor, and says they work together well. She says they are both a bit annoyed because it's near the end of the shift and they want to go home. Suddenly Beth goes pale and tenses up.)

Therapist:	What just happened?
Client:	Blood.
Therapist:	You saw blood? Okay—so your mind has pulled you ahead—can we rewind the memory, back to where you're driving? Is that okay?
Client:	Yep. Yep.
Therapist:	Just push those feet into the floor. Push those hands together. Just look around the room. It's you and me, working together, here and now. Are we okay to keep going?
Client:	*(nodding)* Yeah.

(Beth is very obviously moving, engaging, responsive, and willing to continue, so the therapist doesn't formally obtain scores for presence, willingness, or CPA. For the next few minutes, the therapist "advances" the memory—prompting Beth to describe how

events unfolded, moment by moment, with as much sensory detail as possible: what she can see, hear, touch, and smell. Soon she reaches a more disturbing part of the memory.)

Client: The traffic is backed up so we know it's ahead. You know, people are rubbernecking, slowing down. Um, and the truck, it's kind of come across the road, from the opposite side, right?

(Beth is now breathing rapidly, very tense, very pale. The therapist helps her drop anchor, then checks scores: CPA eight, presence eight, willingness seven.)

Therapist: So...okay to keep going?

Client: Yeah, yeah...I just. You know, I think of those kids on the road and that they're never going to...you know... *(tearing up, voice shaking)*...and it makes it really hard to even be with my girls.

Therapist: Yes, it's horrific. It's just...for me just hearing the story from you...it's horrifying.

Client: It is. It is. And I can't even be with my kids without thinking about this. I mean...

(The therapist now moves briefly into acceptance and self-compassion: Beth notices and names her feelings and does a ninety-second version of the Kind Hands exercise. Then the therapist asks for more detail. Beth says it's a large white truck, and it's "corkscrewed on itself." Sixty feet in front of the truck, there's an overturned green sedan, lying upside down on its roof. The windows are smashed, a door is open...)

Client: And I'm kind of coming toward it. I'm driving toward it.

Therapist: So again, those feet on the floor, noticing your breath, noticing you're here with me and we're talking about a memory. And let's bring in that noticing and naming stuff. Can you say, I'm noticing a memory of...

Client: I'm noticing a memory of...the truck and the sedan...on the road.

Therapist: Okay. And a quick check-in: what's showing up for you?

(Beth reports feeling "sick in the stomach," "tightness in the throat," and a "sense of impending doom." The therapist helps her NAME and drop anchor.)

Therapist: Now just...how in control are you of your arms and legs right now?

Client: I'm good. Nine.

Therapist: And you're here with me—present?

Client: Yep. Nine.

Therapist:	And the memory is here too?
Client:	Yep.
Therapist:	So there's you and me here, working together, with this memory. And I'm curious, what's your mind saying about all this—about what we're doing?
Client:	The same old stuff. *Why am I being so pathetic? I've been trained for this. I should be able to suck it up, get on with it.*
Therapist:	Yeah, it doesn't stop that theme for long, does it? (*Therapist points to the list of self-judgmental thoughts Beth wrote down earlier.*) So do we need to address that—or can you just let it chatter away?
Client:	It's not too loud. We can leave it.
Therapist:	Okay to carry on?
Client:	Yeah.

Over the next ten minutes, the same process is repeated. Prompted by the therapist, Beth talks through the memory, moment by moment. The ambulance screeches to a halt. Beth switches off the engine. The siren stops. Dave gets out first, slams the door, runs off. A few seconds later, Beth gets out from the other door. She runs to the overturned car. Dave is there, ahead of her. There's a mechanical smell—fumes, burned rubber. Debris all over the road.

The therapist frequently pauses and asks Beth to pause and check in: to notice what thoughts and feelings are showing up and give scores for presence, willingness, and CPA. They segue into defusion, acceptance, self-compassion, or dropping anchor as required—and once the scores are seven or above, they continue advancing through the memory.

When Beth reaches the worst part, where she first sees the dead baby, she goes pale, hyperventilates, stops talking. Her presence score drops to four and CPA to three, and it takes three minutes of dropping anchor to get them back to seven. After this, the therapist introduces a brief "values break."

Taking Values Breaks

Exposure sessions typically go for twenty to forty minutes, but they can be shorter or longer, and if at any point the client wants to stop, that's fine. If the client seems to be getting tired or overwhelmed or starts to dissociate, we help them drop anchor and then take a quick "values break," to help them connect more deeply with the values-based goals motivating this challenging work. Here's the values break with Beth, mentioned above:

Therapist:	Just remind me about your kids. They're ten and seven, right?

Client:	Yeah. Dawn and Sarah.
Therapist:	Okay. And what are some of the cutest things they do?
Client:	Oh, like just you know...millions of things, every day. You know in the last couple of weeks as well, they've just been super helpful and you know, lots of "I love you" and doing sweet little things. I mean I'm so worried that they are being affected by this you know, 'cause I'm kind of...I'm not there really and they know it. (*Tearing up.*) Um...they know it...
Therapist:	Are you getting pulled into that stuff again? (*Therapist points to the page of self-judgmental thoughts.*)
Client:	Yeah. Yeah. Yeah.
Therapist:	Just come back to telling me some of the cute things that they do.
Client:	So Sasha, my eldest, she loves baking and making cupcakes and stuff like that.
Therapist:	Yeah? What's the most recent thing she's made you?
Client:	Oh she makes little lemon tart things all the time. She's just super beautiful. She's so kind, yeah.
Therapist:	What are you feeling right now as you kind of share this with me?
Client:	Oh I just want to be with them. I just want to hug them.
Therapist:	So that's a big part of what this work is about, right? You and your kids...and being there for them... Being loving and caring and present...
Client:	Right.
Therapist:	So can we carry on? Or you've had enough for today?
Client:	We can carry on.

Checking In for Impulses to Move

During a check-in, in addition to noticing thoughts and feelings, and scoring presence, willingness, and CPA, we can ask about urges or impulses to move, stretch, or change position. These often show up at various points, and if so, we can invite the client to mindfully follow through on them. Here's an example from about ten minutes into the session with Beth:

Therapist:	I'm wondering—as we do this work, sometimes people feel the need to move in particular ways. Are you feeling an urge to stretch or move in any particular way?

Client: Yeah, do you mind if I sit—I want to sit differently. (*Beth lifts her legs and sits cross-legged on the couch.*)

Therapist: Crossed legs is better for you?

Client: I prefer that, yeah, I just...

Therapist: Is there a...you know, is there a particular stretch you might like to do? Are you tensing up anywhere?

Client: Yeah, I just feel this kind of neck thing.

Therapist: Do you want to do a bit of neck stretching?

Client: Yep. (*Beth stretches her neck.*)

Continuing the Session

The session with Beth continues for another fifteen minutes. Bit by bit, she describes the rest of the memory—the severely injured mother, the second dead child, the procedures she followed, and so on. And all the while, the therapist helps her respond flexibly, from all three points on the triflex, working with the core processes until her scores reach seven or above. Next the therapist suggests summarizing the memory:

Therapist: So, is it okay if we go through that again, but a lot faster this time? The idea is to see if you can distill it to about sixty to ninety seconds, still covering all the main points—but just like a brief summary. And the idea is to talk it through, and see if you can stay present, and allow your feelings, and from time to time, stretch or move—make sure you've got control of your arms and legs.

Beth follows the instructions. She talks through the memory from start to end, and it takes about ninety seconds. The therapist is fully prepared to intervene, but it isn't necessary. Beth's voice is shaky, but she finds it easier to talk than the first time around, and is much less distressed as she does so. At the end, her scores are all seven or above.

The therapist then asks her to do the same again. This time she describes the memory in a calmer, more fluent voice, and it takes about seventy-five seconds. At the end, her scores are all eight or above. The therapist suggests this is a good place to stop, and Beth agrees. They finish up with a two-minute combination of dropping anchor and self-compassion.

The exposure session has taken just under thirty minutes, which includes two minutes of dropping anchor at the start, and another two at the end. This leaves ten minutes to debrief and discuss homework. For homework, we generally recommend two things:

- If this memory or a similar one appears, the client is to respond as they practiced. They notice and name it, make room for their thoughts and feelings, connect with their body, take control of their actions, and engage in what they are doing.

- If the client has been avoiding important values-base activities in order to avoid triggering this memory (or similar ones), they now resume those activities (following an exposure hierarchy, if desired).

Many Ways of Working with Memories

If you wish to use EMDR or prolonged exposure (PE) as an addition or alternative to the TFACT procedures above, that's fine; however, tweaking is needed to ensure the models don't clash. Most importantly, keep the aim of exposure ACT-congruent: to enable flexible, effective, values-based behavior in response to painful memories. Also, reduce the emphasis on lowering anxiety or distress. This is especially important when it comes to the SUDS. As you know, in TFACT we don't use the SUDS, but in both EMDR and PE it's a central tool. So if you're bringing procedures from those models into a TFACT framework, and you intend to keep using SUDS, you want to place much more importance on scores for presence, willingness, and CPA than you do on the SUDS. And when the SUDS drops, you might say, "Enjoy that when it happens; it often does. But keep in mind, that's a bonus—not the main aim." (If the client seems confused, revisit the values-based goals motivating the exposure.) Another option is to drop the SUDS altogether—just stick to scores for presence, willingness, and CPA.

Finally, the diagram below summarizes many ways we can work with memories in TFACT—all of which involve exposure. We've covered most of them in this book.

Dropping anchor: Acknowledge inner experience, connect with body; engage in what you're doing

Self-compassion: Acknowledging the memory and how much it hurts, making room for the pain, and responding to yourself with kindness

Noticing & naming:
I'm noticing/having a memory of...
Putting the memory into a historical narrative (e.g., *Noticing a memory of my father beating me*)

Values: What does this memory tell you really matters to you? What does it tell you about what you want to stand for—or against?

Self-as-context: Observing memories from the perspective of the "noticing self"

Acceptance: "Physicalize" the memory—imagine it as an object: shape, color, size, temperature, movement, weight, etc. Locate where it is in the body or "place it" in the room.

Acceptance: "Sitting with" the memory and making room for it—as well as for all the thoughts and feelings that go with it

Defusion: "Leaves on a Stream"—placing visual memories onto the leaves

Mindful physical movement: Stretching, walking, drinking, moving, changing postures, moving head and arms, tapping feet, pressing palms together, etc.

"Deconstructing" the memory: Mindfully noticing and naming the various "components" of it. This includes images, sounds, smells, tastes, and sensations "within" the memory, and all the thoughts, images, memories, emotions, and sensations that show up in connection with the memory. Segue into acceptance of each "component."

MEMORIES

Artwork: Drawing/painting/sculpting the memory

Exposure through writing: Write a detailed sensory step-by-step description of the memory.

Nightmare rescripting: Transcribe the memory that recurs inside the nightmare, but change one significant detail, such as the ending.

Values and posttraumatic growth: Write about ways you have grown as a result of the events in the memory. Write a letter to yourself from the future describing how you recovered and turned your life around.

Compassionate self-touch: Kind self-touch in the presence of the memory (e.g., hugging yourself, laying a hand on your heart or over the pain, massaging your temples)

Formal exposure: Mindfully describing the memory, and responding flexibly to it

"Inner Child" work: Visualize/imagine the adult self going back in time to help the younger self. The adult self can console, comfort, support, advise, counsel, intervene, and help the younger self understand what happened and why.

Body-memory connection: Explore mindfully what happens in different parts of the body when the memory is present: sensations, postures, actions, movements, feelings, urges. Explore new responses to these body events (e.g., self-touch, self-compassion, physical movement, breathing differently)

Extending the memory: Include positive or neutral events that happened immediately before or after, and re-run the memory with these incorporated (especially identifying strengths)

Exposure with an imaginary TV or computer screen: It's safest to leave this to late in therapy, after other techniques have been used. Visualize the memory on a screen and play around with zooming in and out of different parts; altering contrast, color, sharpness, brightness, volume, and sound; noticing the background; or adding nonjudgmental, factually descriptive subtitles. Or look at the image as if you are a cinematographer and note details like shadows, lighting, colors, and textures.

Summary of Methods for Working with Memories

Takeaway

Formal, organized exposure to traumatic memories is often unnecessary. But if and when it *is* necessary, we use the same core processes we would with any other repertoire-narrowing stimuli. First, we help clients drop anchor. Then we help them dance around the triflex—being present, opening up, doing what matters—to broaden their window of flexibility.

CHAPTER THIRTY-ONE

Grieving and Forgiving

Trauma always involves significant loss. People may lose their loved ones through death or separation; their physical health; their freedom or independence; their sense of security or trust; their roles; their community; their childhood; their basic rights to be loved, respected, and cared for; and so much more. Given all these losses, it's no surprise we are often working with grief.

What Is Grief?

Many people talk about grief as if it is synonymous with sadness; but grief is not an emotion. Grief is a psychological process of reacting to any significant loss. During a grieving process, we may feel a wide range of emotions, from sadness and anxiety to anger and guilt, as well as physical reactions such as sleep disturbance, fatigue, lethargy, apathy, and changes in appetite.

Stages of Grief

The famous "five stages of grief" are denial, anger, bargaining, depression, and acceptance. When Elisabeth Kübler-Ross described these stages, she was referring to death and dying, but they can apply to any type of major loss. As Kübler-Ross often stated, there's no fixed order to these stages, and not everyone goes through them all. Nor are they discrete and well-defined; rather they tend to ebb and flow and blend into one another—and they often seem to end, then start again.

Although contemporary models of grief counseling no longer use Kübler-Ross's framework, the stages she described are very common, and your clients are likely to experience at least some of them. And because these stages are now so well-known, it's good to be aware of them, in case your clients wish to discuss them.

"Denial" means a refusal or inability to acknowledge the reality of the situation: unwillingness to talk or think about it; trying to pretend it's not happening; a sense of being numb or "shut down"; or walking around in a daze, feeling like it's not real—it's a bad dream.

"Anger" refers to anything from resentment and indignation to fury and outrage, or a strong sense of unfairness or injustice. You might get angry with yourself, or others, or life itself, and frequently this spills over into blame.

"Bargaining" means that you are trying to strike deals to alter reality. You might ask God for a reprieve or ask a surgeon to guarantee a successful operation. Often there's a whole lot of wishful thinking and fantasizing about alternative realities: "If only this had happened"; "If only I hadn't done that."

"Depression" has nothing to do with the clinical disorder of the same name. This unfortunate choice of word refers to emotions such as sadness, sorrow, fear, anxiety, and uncertainty: all normal, natural human reactions to loss.

"Acceptance" means making peace with our new reality instead of struggling with it or avoiding it. This frees us up to invest our energy in gradually rebuilding our life.

Many Ways to Grieve

Probably one of the most useful things we can convey to clients is that there is no "right way" to grieve. There are no "right things" to do; no "right feelings" to have; no "right amount of time" to grieve for. Everyone finds their own unique way of grieving, and that will be hugely influenced by factors such as family history, cultural background, and religious or spiritual affiliations.

There are ideas "out there" that you should feel this, or you shouldn't feel that; or you *should* cry, or you *shouldn't* cry—and so on. And the truth is there is no right or wrong way to feel when you're grieving. Some people feel angry. Others feel sad. Some feel guilty. Others feel numb. Some people even feel relief. And as with all emotions, they change like the weather: they rise and they fall; they come and they go.

Everyone is free to grieve in their own way, to feel what they feel and to grieve for as long or as short as they wish. One of the biggest myths about grief is that if it goes on for too long, it's pathological; that there should be a certain duration to it, and beyond that, there's something wrong. But if you're a parent and you've lost a young child, it's not uncommon to experience periods of grieving for the rest of your life—on and off, at different times and places.

The Act of Grieving

TFACT lends itself beautifully to the grieving process. Initially, our focus is on helping clients to drop anchor amid the huge waves of emotional pain that hit them again and again, normalizing their pain as a natural reaction to loss, and fostering acceptance and self-compassion. Later, we explore values: What do they want to stand for in the face of all this pain, tragedy, and suffering? How do they want to treat themselves and others as they go through this?

And then we help them translate these values into action: adjusting to their loss and rebuilding their lives, one small step at a time. This will vary enormously from person to person. We need to explore: What is workable for this unique client at this time? Do they need to slow down, take time out from their daily routine—to rest and recuperate? Or do they need to do the opposite: reengage in life, reach out to and connect with others?

The metaphor of "taking a stand" is often helpful:

Therapist: There's a massive reality gap here; a huge chasm between the reality you want and the reality you've got. And most of us, at least initially—we kind of get crushed by that reality gap; or we run from it, hide from it, with, you know, all the usual suspects: drugs, alcohol, distraction. But what we're talking about here is turning toward this huge gaping hole—and standing for something.

And it's totally up to you what you stand for—whether that's courage or honesty or compassion or love or...you know, there's no right or wrong...it's just about being who you want to be, in the face of this. So, suppose I bump into you, five years from now, and I ask you, "What did you stand for, back then, five years ago, in the face of that huge reality gap? How did you treat yourself and the people you love?" What would you want to answer?

When we help clients to live their values in the face of a huge loss, it empowers them. They discover they don't have to give up on life; even with its gaping holes, they can embrace it. And after they've reached that point, we can help them to "find the treasure" (i.e., use their mindfulness skills to notice, appreciate, and savor those moments or aspects of life that are meaningful, enjoyable, or inspiring).

This is not about "positive thinking," seeing "the glass as half full," finding the "silver lining in every cloud." And it's not about ignoring or distracting from the pain. It's about recognizing that in the midst of your pain and suffering, there are aspects of life you can treasure. You can savor that glass of cold water that quenches your thirst. You can appreciate acts of kindness, caring, and support. You can step out and marvel at the sunset. While this doesn't alter the past or get rid of your pain, it does help you connect with the richness and fullness of life in this moment.

Complicated Grief

Grief is a normal psychological process of coming to terms with a loss, accepting it, and adjusting to and reengaging in life. "Complicated grief" is a pathological process where normal grieving is interrupted by cognitive fusion and experiential avoidance.

Clients may fuse with narratives such as "Life's not worth living," "I can never get over this," "It would be dishonorable of me to get on with my life," or "I don't deserve to get over this; I'm such a bad person."

The other aspect of complicated grief is experiential avoidance. In a typical grieving process, we expect painful emotions, and our aim in TFACT is to open up and make room for them; allow them to come and stay and go in their own good time. But if we're high in experiential avoidance and we're not willing to have those painful feelings, then what happens? Well, all the usual suspects: drugs, alcohol, social withdrawal, interpersonal conflict—all the various strategies that humans use to fight with or run from painful emotions.

So fusion and avoidance lead to unworkable action. And at times this can result in seemingly contradictory patterns of behavior. For example, after the death of their child, a parent may avoid anything or anyone that reminds them of the loss, such as friends or family with children of a similar age; yet at the same time, they may preserve the child's bedroom exactly as it was and spend large amounts of time in there, reliving the past.

Basically, then, the greater the client's fusion and experiential avoidance, the more likely is complicated grief. And we target this with all the core processes: defusion, acceptance, present moment, values, committed action, self as context, and especially self-compassion. For more on this topic, you may appreciate my self-help book on ACT for grief and loss. In the UK, Australia, and New Zealand it's called *The Reality Slap* (2nd edition; Harris, 2020); in the US, it's titled *When Life Hits Hard*.

Resentment and Forgiving

Many clients get consumed by resentment: dwelling, with anger and bitterness, on past events. There are several powerful metaphors that relate to this. In Buddhism, they say resentment is like holding on to a red-hot coal to throw it at somebody else. (A friend of mine, who works with teenage boys, changed this to "Resentment is like holding a squishy dog shit, to throw it at someone else.") In Hinduism, they say resentment is like burning down your house to get rid of a rat. And in Alcoholics Anonymous, they say resentment is like swallowing poison and hoping the other person dies.

These metaphors all convey the same message: you are the one getting most hurt by resentment. Sure, from time to time, in the grip of it, you may act out and hurt others; but you're the one who's getting hurt on a daily basis. It may be that the events that happened to you are now years or decades in the past. But in the grip of resentment, you experience them over and over, each time painfully scolded by the injustice and unfairness of the world. So it's a painful and life-draining process, which doesn't alter the past or help you heal.

It's often helpful to mention the origin of the word:

Therapist:	Did you know the word "resentment" comes from the French word *ressentir*, which means "to feel again"?
Client:	Err, no.
Therapist:	(*playfully*) Well, don't say you didn't learn anything in these sessions. (*Client chuckles.*) So basically, your mind hooks you and drags you back into the past—reliving all the old hurts and wounds and the bad stuff—so you get to feel it, over and over, getting angry about all the events that happened. And of course, that's completely natural. We all do it. But the problem is, it sucks the life out of you.
Client:	(*sadly*) Yeah. It does.

The antidote to resentment is forgiving. (I use the verb "forgiving" rather the noun "forgiveness" because it's an ongoing activity. At times, we're forgiving, and at other times, we aren't.) Unfortunately, many clients think forgiving means "letting them get away with it" or saying what happened didn't matter. So we explain:

Therapist: "Forgiving," at least as we use the word in TFACT, means giving yourself back what life was like before resentment took over. So it's something you do for yourself. You don't do it for anyone else; it's just for you. To give you peace of mind. And help you live a better life, moving forward.

When working with our clients, or practicing this ourselves, the first step in forgiving is getting present. Our minds try to pull us back into the past. But life is happening here, right now. So it's about unhooking ourselves from all that past-oriented cognition and coming back to the present. Dropping anchor (chapter eight) and Getting Out of the River (chapter eleven) are both useful practices for this.

The next step is making room for that pain and practicing self-compassion.

And the third step is returning to our values, asking ourselves, "That was in the past; from here onward what do I want to be about? What do I want to do with my time left on this planet? What sort of future do I want to build?"

(Are you getting a sense of déjà vu, here? Because TFACT is transdiagnostic, the same overarching processes—be present, open up, do what matters—apply to just about every trauma-related issue we encounter.)

Self-Forgiving

Have you ever beaten yourself up for doing something you now regret? Or for not doing something you "should" have done? Ever gotten hooked by "Why did I do that?" "Why *didn't* I do that?" "How could I have been so stupid?" "How could I have let that happen?"

Sure, you have. We all beat ourselves up over this stuff. But often our clients take this to extremes of self-blame, self-criticism, and self-hatred. They may blame and judge themselves for acts of violence, such as shooting an innocent person in a war zone; or for doing destructive things under the influence of drugs and alcohol; or for neglecting their children; or for "freezing" instead of fighting; or a million and one other things.

Self-forgiving is arguably a "subset" of self-compassion. It involves defusing from harsh self-judgment, acknowledging how painful it is that those things happened, and treating yourself with kindness and understanding. And it's important to connect with the values underneath all that harsh self-judgment. We may say, "You know, the fact that your mind is beating you up and giving you such a hard time over this… What does that tell you about the sort of person you really want to be, deep inside? What does that tell you really matters to you?"

For example, if a client is beating themself up over neglecting or hurting their loved ones, that suggests values of being loving and caring. And if they're blaming themself because they didn't report, stop, or address something, that points to values of courage, assertiveness, and justice. We may point out, "If you didn't have those values, you wouldn't be giving yourself such a hard time about this."

Forgiving Others

The TFACT take on forgiving is very liberating. You don't have to say or do anything to the other person—which is good, because they may be dead, oblivious, or in denial; or you may not even know who they are. And you don't have to "let them get away with it"; with this approach, you can practice forgiving yet still take the wrongdoer to court and prosecute them.

Sometimes clients read self-help books that assert, "To recover from your past, you must forgive those who hurt you." But there is no scientific validity to those claims. When it comes to trauma, it may be impossible to forgive the people who have hurt, harmed, betrayed, or abused you. So if a client says things like "I know I *should* forgive them," we help them defuse:

Therapist:	Notice your mind laying down the law. This is *your* life. It's about what *you* want to do, not what your mind says you *should* do. If it's important to you to forgive them, if that's what matters deep in your heart—we can work on that. But if you don't want to or you're not ready to, that's fine; you certainly don't *have to*.

I think of forgiving others in terms of two different stages—the second being significantly harder than the first. Let's take a look at them.

STAGE ONE

The first stage in forgiving others is outlined in the worksheet below (which you can find in Extra Bits).

How to Forgive Others

When I get hooked by blame, judgment, or resentment toward the person(s) who hurt me, and pulled into reliving what they did, the effect that has on me is

_____

At times, when hooked by those thoughts, feelings, and memories, I have done things that made my life worse, such as

_____

And what that has cost me is _____

So for my own health and well-being, I choose to practice unhooking from blame, judgment, and resentment. The methods I will use are

_____

And when difficult memories arise, I will acknowledge the pain and be kind to myself, as follows:

_____

I will also reflect regularly on the following:

- What they did to hurt me. It gave rise to much pain and suffering.

- It was not okay. I will not forget it.

- If I knew them inside out, knew their whole life history, I would understand why they did this. But I will never know for sure why they did what they did—and I don't need to.

- The fact is, we all screw up, make mistakes, and do things that hurt others.

- The fact is, we all at times get hooked by thoughts and feelings and pulled into destructive patterns of behavior.

- The person(s) who did this is/are imperfect and fallible, prone to human weakness and error—just as I am.

- The person(s) who did this gets/get hooked by their own thoughts and feelings and pulled into destructive patterns of behavior—just as I do.

- They did what they did, and I can't change that, but I can unhook from my judgments and my blaming and practice self-compassion; and in the interest of building a better life for myself, I will continue to do so.

STAGE TWO

Stage two involves communicating with the person(s) who hurt you—in your imagination, rather than real life—letting them know that you forgive them, and extending kindness toward them. This commonly involves either visualization, meditation, or writing a letter (which you don't send). Loving-Kindness Meditation is a powerful way of doing this work. If you read the full script in Extra Bits, you'll see that the final part of this practice involves thinking of someone who is a source of suffering in your life, recognizing that they are a fallible human being who hurts and suffers much like you, and sending out warmth and kindness toward them. If you introduce this practice, I recommend clients begin with some "less difficult people," and over time, build up their compassion muscles until they're ready to attempt this with someone who hurt them badly.

EXTRA BIT   Download *Trauma-Focused ACT: The Extra Bits* from the "Free Resources" page on http://www.ImLearningACT.com. In chapter thirty-one, you'll find a script for Loving-Kindness Meditation and a worksheet on forgiving.

Takeaway

Grieving and forgiving are important aspects of working with trauma, for which we utilize all the core ACT processes. Grieving is a normal psychological process of coming to terms with loss, but it becomes complicated when fusion and experiential avoidance predominate. Forgiving, in TFACT, means freeing yourself from the burden of resentment. Self-compassion plays a central role in both grieving and forgiving.

We've covered the first two interweaving strands of TFACT: living in the present and healing the past. So you now have a solid foundation of skills, strategies, and tools for treating clients with trauma-related disorders. Next we'll turn to the third strand of TFACT: building the future.

PART FIVE

Building the Future

CHAPTER THIRTY-TWO

The Path Ahead

While the main emphasis of ACT is living in the here and now—acting on our values and mindfully engaging in what we do—throughout therapy, we repeatedly look to the future. This begins on the very first session, when we ask questions like "What will you be doing differently if our work is successful?" And it continues every time we help clients to set goals, create action plans, anticipate obstacles, prepare contingency plans, or ask questions like "Will that take you toward or away from the life you want?"

So although I've placed "Building the Future" as the final section of the book, it's by no means the final stage in therapy. Forward thinking, looking ahead, and planning for the future come into every session—even if only to agree upon homework tasks for the forthcoming week. However, as we near the end of therapy, "building the future" tends to take center stage: sessions increasingly focus on goal setting, action planning, problem solving, anticipating obstacles, overcoming barriers, maintaining motivation, and sustaining new behaviors. So let's do a quick review of all these topics, and then we'll look at posttraumatic growth.

Values, Goals, Actions, and Obstacles

Throughout therapy, we encourage clients to develop the skill of goal setting, which we hope they'll actively use for the rest of their lives. And the more challenging the goal is, the greater the need to chunk it into easier, smaller goals—which are ideally SMART: Specific, Motivated by values, Adaptive, Realistic, Time-framed. We follow this with action planning: What actions are needed to achieve this goal? And what's plan B, if plan A fails?

The HARD barriers—Hooked, Avoiding discomfort, Remoteness from values, and Doubtful goals—are likely to arise repeatedly, so we help clients prepare for them: get them ready to unhook, open up, connect with their values, and set SMART goals, as needed. Useful questions include:

- How's your mind going to try to talk you out of this? How will you unhook from that?

- What difficult thoughts and feelings are likely show up? How will you make room for them?

- What can motivate you to persist?

The Willingness and Action Plan (see Extra Bits) brings all the above elements together, so it's particularly useful in later sessions.

Maintaining Change and Handling Setbacks

As Mark Twain said, "Habit is habit, and not to be flung out of the window by any man, but coaxed downstairs a step at a time." We all know how easy it is to fall back into old ways, so we can encourage clients to use the Seven Rs: Reminders, Records, Rewards, Routines, Relationships, Reflection, and Restructuring the environment.

In addition, we can help clients defuse from perfectionistic ideas and unrealistic expectations. We all go offtrack at times, no matter how much therapy or personal development we do. This is just as true for practitioners as for clients—an aspect of our common humanity. At times we will give up on our goals, lose touch with our values, or fall back into old self-defeating patterns of behavior—and we will hurt and suffer when that happens. Our default setting at these times is to pull out a big stick and start beating ourselves up. But if beating ourselves up were a good way to change behavior, wouldn't we be perfect by now?

So we help our clients expect and prepare for these setbacks: to drop anchor, acknowledge their pain, and respond with kindness; then come back to their values and start again. We will all need to do this many thousands of times, for the rest of our lives. (As I say to clients, "We get to improve our behavior, but we don't get to be perfect.")

Specific Plans: Safety, Relapse Prevention, and Crisis Coping

It's often useful to plan ahead for recurrences of problematic behavior, to predict what might trigger it and prepare a contingency plan, such as a safety plan for suicidality, a relapse-prevention plan for addiction, or a crisis-coping plan for stressful events. For this, the choice point comes in very handy, as illustrated on the next page.

Professional Help (Names and contact numbers):

Friends & Family Help: (Names and contact numbers):

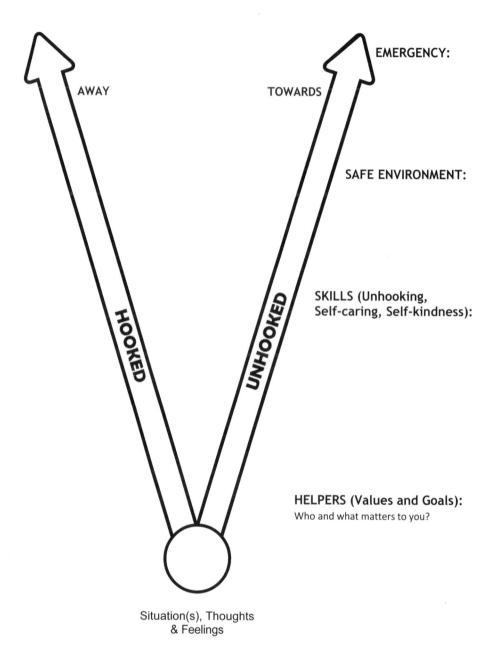

EMERGENCY:

AWAY   TOWARDS

SAFE ENVIRONMENT:

SKILLS (Unhooking,
Self-caring, Self-kindness):

HOOKED   UNHOOKED

HELPERS (Values and Goals):
Who and what matters to you?

Situation(s), Thoughts
& Feelings

Safety, Relapse Prevention, and Crisis-Coping Plan

At the top of the sheet we write in names and contact numbers of professional sources of help (e.g., doctor, therapist, hospital, crisis line, support service) and names and contact numbers of friends, family, and others (e.g., a neighbor or sponsor) whom the client can talk to or ask for help.

At the bottom of the choice point, we write in likely antecedents for suicidality (or relapse or crisis). This includes situations, cognitions, emotions, memories, sensations, and urges.

On the away arrow we write in problematic behaviors (both overt and covert) to look out for. For example, in a typical safety plan, away moves might include suicidal ideation, suicide threats, suicide planning, and suicide attempts. In a relapse-prevention plan, the away moves would be the addictive behaviors in question (e.g., taking drugs, drinking, gambling) or ideation about doing them.

On the towards arrow, there are four sections. At the very bottom: HELPERS (often called "reasons to live" in safety plans, or "reasons to abstain" in relapse prevention). Here we write in values and values-congruent goals; important people, activities, and domains of life; and important beliefs or ideas that motivate towards moves.

In the middle: SKILLS. Here we write in useful mindfulness skills (e.g., defusion, acceptance), self-compassion skills (e.g., kind self-talk, kind self-touch), and self-care skills (e.g., self-soothing, assertiveness, problem solving). And as therapy progresses, we add in the new skills developed.

Near the top: SAFE ENVIRONMENT. Here we document what to bring into or remove from the environment to make it safer. For example, a client may remove drugs, alcohol, guns, or poisons, or bring in a friend, a pet, or self-help resources such as books and recordings. Sometimes the client will need to leave the environment—in which case we specify safer environments to move to.

At the top: EMERGENCY. Here we write emergency contacts, in case all else fails: names, numbers, and locations (e.g., crisis line, hospital emergency department, or a reliable support person).

Anticipating Further Trauma

Some clients are at risk of exposure to further traumatic events, either through their employment (e.g., emergency services), or because they are in difficult situations they can't simply leave (e.g., prison), or due to ongoing systemic problems like racism. In such cases, we revisit the challenge formula.

Option one is to leave. If the client *can* leave the difficult situation (e.g., by changing career), we help them explore the pros and cons, after which they may choose to leave.

If the client can't or won't leave the situation, then we help them implement option two: live by your values, do whatever you can to improve things, and make room for the pain that's inevitable. This includes actively reaching out to supportive others and using all their TFACT skills—especially self-compassion—to take care of themselves as best as they can in such difficult circumstances.

Ending Therapy

Our final session with a client usually focuses heavily on building the future, including much of the content above. We recap the three overarching TFACT skills—*be present, open up, do what matters*—and we explore: How will the client apply these skills going forward? What areas of life do they intend to explore and expand? What long-term goals are they aiming for?

And we again want to highlight the inevitable recurrence of HARD barriers, and ensure clients are adequately prepared to handle them. (Remember, "forewarned is forearmed.")

We also explore reactions to ending therapy. These vary enormously, and the entire range of emotions may arise—in ourselves as well as in our clients. Whatever a client's reaction, we want to normalize and validate it (our own, too), bringing in acceptance, self-compassion, and defusion as required. Self-doubt and feelings of anxiety are incredibly common—"I might relapse," "I don't know if I can keep it up," "I'm scared of doing it alone." So yet again, we reframe this as "your mind and body trying to protect you." And of course, we let clients know that if they ever want to return, the door is open.

Posttraumatic Growth

Psychologists Richard Tedeschi and Lawrence Calhoun (1996) popularized the term "posttraumatic growth." They interviewed survivors of trauma to see what sort of long-term outcomes they had, and they discovered, to their surprise, that many people went on to develop and grow in positive, life-enhancing ways.

For example, many survivors developed a much greater appreciation for life. Prior to their trauma, they were taking life for granted, but afterward, they started to truly appreciate and be grateful for the opportunities life afforded them. Many also reported changes in their sense of priority. They were more attuned to what was important and meaningful. They gave priority to people they loved and activities that fulfilled them—rather than all that "time-wasting stuff" that easily fills up our lives.

Many reported developing warmer, closer relationships. They were better at empathizing; better at having deeper, more intimate connections. And many developed a greater sense of personal strength, more courage or self-confidence, new life directions, and new paths for spiritual growth.

Posttraumatic growth is different from "resilience," which means bouncing back to your previous point—back to where you were before the trauma happened. Posttraumatic growth goes way beyond that. It involves profound personal development and an increased ability to actively create and appreciate a meaningful, fulfilling life. While some clients spontaneously report these changes, often we need to gently prompt them. Useful questions include:

- What has been most meaningful or valuable to you in the work we've done here?

- Which new skills have been most useful?

- What are the most positive changes you've noticed in how you do things?

- How have you grown or developed?

- What differences have you noticed in your relationships?

Of course, we don't have to leave such discussions to the end of therapy—but if we haven't already explored them, we definitely want to do so in the final session.

EXTRA BIT Download *Trauma-Focused ACT: The Extra Bits* from the "Free Resources" page on http://www.ImLearningACT.com. In chapter thirty-two, you'll find (a) a printable Relapse-Prevention Plan and (b) the Willingness and Action Plan.

Takeaway

We can't know for sure what the future holds, but we can to some extent predict it, prepare for it, and influence it through the actions we take in the present. So throughout therapy, we encourage clients to "build the future" through a variety of methods, from goal setting and action planning to preparing for obstacles and setbacks.

With TFACT, we're hoping to help clients not just recover, but experience posttraumatic growth. Obviously, this won't happen with everyone; to expect that is unrealistic. But it's an outcome well worth aiming for.

CHAPTER THIRTY-THREE

TFACT as a Brief Intervention

Most clients end therapy quickly. For example, in one eye-opening study from 2005, researchers tracked data from 9,600 clients and found that 85% ended treatment by the fifth session (Brown & Jones, 2005). The same study showed that the most common number of sessions a client had (i.e., the "modal number") was…*just one*!

This is just one example from a large body of research that shows around 30 to 40% of clients end therapy quickly, without consulting their therapist, and most average only four to six sessions. (For sure, some clients *do* prefer long-term therapy—but they are a small minority.) Aside from these sobering statistics, the fact is, our clients are suffering, and they want relief. So the sooner we can provide it, the better. Hence our challenge: How can we optimize client outcomes in as short a time frame as possible? How can we help them reduce their suffering and build meaningful lives—before they drop out of therapy?

For in-depth answers to these questions, I recommend you investigate "focused acceptance and commitment therapy," better known as FACT: a brief intervention model pioneered by Kirk Strosahl and Patricia Robinson. (Start with their excellent textbook, coauthored with Thomas Gustavsson: *Brief Interventions for Radical Change* [Strosahl et al., 2012].) FACT is useful for anyone who wishes to do ACT more efficiently—especially practitioners in time-limited settings, such as primary care, short inpatient stays, school or university counseling, prisons, employee assistance programs, and crisis intervention services. I won't attempt to cover the whole FACT model in this chapter, but I will draw from it to give you some ideas.

The Brief Intervention Mindset

When doing TFACT as a brief intervention, we start from the assumption that rapid change is possible—even for clients with long-standing problems. This is a pragmatic assumption; if it turns out to be wrong—well, at least we tried. But if we start from the opposite assumption, that rapid change is not possible—and because of this, we move much more slowly than we need to, and therefore the client drops out of therapy before developing any practical skills—then clearly we've done them a disservice.

The First Session

A key assumption is that the first session is the most important—because for a significant number of clients, it will be the only one they have. The FACT mantra goes, "Assume one session, hope for six." In other words, when we see this new client for the first time, we *hope* they'll return for at least six sessions, but we are prepared for the possibility they won't.

Working from this assumption, we don't use the entire first session for assessment; we need to free up time for active intervention. In each session (including the first) we aim to do at least one brief intervention from at least one point on the triflex: something that helps the client develop a core TFACT skill, which they can immediately take away, practice, and utilize. And if the client returns for a second session, we can then complete the assessment (if we really need to). We would make this explicit as part of informed consent:

> *Therapist:*   The idea here is that we work together as a team. We have about thirty minutes in total, and we really want to use that time effectively, to do something practical, like develop a new skill or strategy that you can take away and use.

We know the client has come to see us—a huge act of trust—because they want our help, so we don't spend several sessions "building rapport" before starting active intervention. We assume rapport is already there, and the alliance will strengthen as we help the client develop TFACT skills.

What Can We Do in Just Ten Minutes?

Get into the habit of asking yourself, *What practical skill can my client learn in this session, to take home and use straight away?* Here are some things we can do in under ten minutes:

- Teach dropping anchor

- Clarify some values (e.g., connect and reflect)

- Set a goal and create an action plan (e.g., the bull's eye)

- Teach a defusion skill (e.g., *I'm having the thought that…*)

- Teach an acceptance skill (e.g., physicalizing an emotion)

- Teach a self-compassion skill (e.g., kind hands)

- Teach a self-as-context skill (e.g., leaves on a stream)

With a bit of creativity, you can do almost every exercise, skill, or practice in this book within five to ten minutes. So for a thirty-minute session, allocate at least ten minutes to experiential exercises or skills training. (But for a fifty-minute session, allocate at least twenty minutes for this.)

The idea is to give clients one "piece" of the model on each visit. For example, on session one, we might just give them dropping anchor; on session two, some defusion; session three, some values, and so on. Think of a domino effect: a small change in a positive direction can have powerful ripple effects in other areas, and a versatile skill like dropping anchor can be usefully applied to many different problems.

How Do We Find Ten Minutes?

To ensure we have at least ten minutes, we need to (a) focus on one specific problem and (b) shorten other things that eat up therapy time.

To focus on a specific problem, we may say, "Could you pick just one main problem or issue for today's session? I know there are many, but if we try to cover them all, we'll run out of time without achieving anything useful. So let's focus on one, and once you have a strategy and a skill that you can use to deal with it better, if there's time, we can move on to another."

To shorten other things that eat up therapy time, consider these options:

- Cut back on psychoeducation.

- Keep metaphors brief, and use them sparingly.

- Reduce time spent "talking about ACT"—describing ACT processes and how they can theoretically help—and instead, actively practice new skills in session.

- Create a Brief Intervention Toolkit you can easily dip into (see Extra Bits).

- Shorten creative hopelessness (see Extra Bits).

- Make your initial assessment shorter. Consider: do you really need *all* that information?

- Take less history. Practitioners often gather a huge amount of information that plays little or no role in terms of intervention.

But My Clients Want to Talk!

Our clients, just like us, want to be seen, heard, understood, validated. Thus, in many models, the idea is that the client talks in depth and at length about their trauma, while the therapist listens compassionately and validates their feelings. This is often called "processing the trauma."

In a brief intervention approach, we attend mindfully and bear witness compassionately—seeing our clients as rainbows, not roadblocks—and we do a whole lot more. When we are truly present and compassionate, most clients feel heard, understood, and validated quite quickly; it doesn't take *an entire session*. And we continue holding that Rogerian stance even as we move into building skills.

So if a client wants to keep talking, but we haven't yet introduced a practical skill they'll be able to take home and apply, and we are now running out of time—then for the benefit of the client, we need to take the reins and get the session on track. (And uncomfortable though this may be, if we don't do it, we're doing our client a disservice.) I've experimented with different ways of doing this and found the following five-step formula works well, as long as it's delivered with genuine compassion and respect:

1. We first validate the client's suffering.

2. Then we say, "I would like to know more, but we have limited time…"

3. Then we apologize: "I'm sorry if this seems rude…"

4. Then we ask permission: "Given our limited time, would it be okay if we moved on to something practical…"

5. We give a rationale: "…because I really want you to leave here today with something useful—a skill/technique/strategy that you can use after the session, to help deal with this."

For example:

Therapist: What you're going through is really tough, really difficult…and I hate to interrupt, but is it okay if I press pause for a moment? My mind's telling me that you'll think I'm rude or uncaring and you'll be upset with me… But I notice we only have ten minutes left of our session… And I'd really like to use that remaining time to do something practical, to help you to deal with all these painful memories and feelings. So is it okay if we switch modes?

EXTRA BIT   Download *Trauma-Focused ACT: The Extra Bits* from the "Free Resources" page on http://www.ImLearningACT.com. In chapter thirty-three, you'll find (a) How to Do Creative Hopelessness Briefly and (b) How to Create a Brief Intervention Toolkit.

Takeaway

TFACT is very suitable for brief therapy with trauma. The key is to think in terms of simple, easy-to-teach skills that we can run through in ten minutes or less. If we can introduce a client to even one TFACT skill in a session—and encourage them to take it away and practice it—we're doing something useful.

CHAPTER THIRTY-FOUR

Parting Words

So here we are in the final chapter, and what a journey it's been. (At least it has for me; hope it has for you too.) We'll finish off with a few parting comments and an inspiring poem.

Failure Is Inevitable

Here's my guarantee: as you practice TFACT, you're going to experience failure. There will be clients who don't react the way you expected or hoped they would, techniques that fail or backfire, and sessions where everything you try just doesn't work. And of course, this isn't just TFACT; it's true for every model of therapy. No model works for everyone. Whatever approach you use, some clients will love it, and some will hate it, and most will be somewhere in between.

And here's another guarantee: you'll make lots of mistakes. (If I were to type out transcripts of all the mistakes I've made doing TFACT, the resulting book would be several times the size of this one.) And making mistakes is painful. But they hurt a whole lot more when our harsh, judgmental minds start playing the "I'm a lousy therapist" theme: *I can't do this, That was a disaster, I suck, This bloody TFACT stuff doesn't work!* and so on.

We can't stop our minds from saying these things, but we can notice, name, and unhook from the "lousy therapist" theme, make room for our painful feelings, and be kind to ourselves. And we can acknowledge that our work is challenging; that it's impossible to have good outcomes with every client; that there's no such thing as a perfect practitioner, and at times we will all make mistakes.

We can then reflect on the session and reframe it as "a learning experience." After all, no matter what happened, no matter how badly it went, there's always something we can learn from it. Where did we get stuck? Did we ourselves become fused or avoidant in session? Did we omit parts of the model? Did we get so focused on technique that we forgot about the therapeutic relationship? Did we hold back, go too slow, when the client was ready to move forward? Did our own fusion or avoidance stop us from doing the necessary exposure or other challenging experiential work? Or did we perhaps move too quickly, when the client wasn't ready?

It's also important to consider: Were there any moments in the session—even if fleeting—where the client *did* respond flexibly? Any moments where they were present, open, or doing what matters? If so, what was different in those moments?

More simply, we ask ourselves three questions:

- What worked?

- What didn't work?

- What could we do more of, less of, or differently next time around?

Self-Care

Working with trauma is often stressful, and many therapists at times suffer from vicarious trauma, compassion fatigue, moral injury, or burnout. So it's important that we apply ACT to ourselves: defusing from unhelpful thoughts, making room for painful emotions, and holding ourselves kindly; living our values both at work and outside it; investing in our relationships; and looking after our physical health through exercise, nutrition, leisure, and sleep.

Of course, it's much easier to say all that than to do it. But here's one practical tip that can really help: create your own ultra-brief self-compassion ritual—even if it's just one minute long—that you do after every client. For example, at the end of a session, after the client has left, you could take one minute to drop anchor, acknowledge your thoughts and feelings, place a kind hand over your heart, and say something supportive to yourself. Also try a longer version at the very end of your work day; you can use this as a "transition ritual" to help leave work behind and return to your home with a fresh mindset.

The Joy and the Sorrow

At times our work is fulfilling, inspiring, and uplifting. And at other times it is distressing and disheartening. We don't get the highs without the lows. When we care deeply about our clients, naturally we experience joy when we can help them—and sorrow when we can't. Because of this, I always end my TFACT workshops by reading a poem from *The Prophet*, by Kahlil Gibran, and I've decided to end this textbook the same way. This poem, "Joy and Sorrow," is often read aloud at funerals because it cuts right to the heart of the human condition. So, leaving you with the wise words below, I'll say farewell and wish you all the best for your ongoing journey with TFACT.

Joy and Sorrow

Your joy is your sorrow unmasked.

And the selfsame well from which your laughter rises was oftentimes filled with your tears.

And how else can it be?

The deeper that sorrow carves into your being, the more joy you can contain.

Is not the cup that holds your wine the very cup that was burned in the potter's oven?

And is not the lute that soothes your spirit, the very wood that was hollowed with knives?

When you are joyous, look deep into your heart and you shall find it is only that which has given you sorrow that is giving you joy.

When you are sorrowful look again in your heart, and you shall see that in truth you are weeping for that which has been your delight.

Some of you say, "Joy is greater than sorrow," and others say, "Nay, sorrow is the greater."

But I say unto you, they are inseparable.

Together they come, and when one sits alone with you at your board, remember that the other is asleep upon your bed.

Acknowledgments

First and foremost, several Olympic-size swimming pools of gratitude for my beloved Natasha, for all her love and support and advice and ideas, and for cheering me on during the many times I wanted to give up (as well as giving me multiple life-saving doses of salted caramel Lindt chocolate at all the right times).

Also, as usual, a bazillion buckets of deepest gratitude to Steve Hayes, the originator of ACT—and to his co-creators, Kelly Wilson and Kirk Strosahl. All three have been endless sources of knowledge and inspiration. And along with that, many thanks to Sonja Batten, Robyn Walser, Patricia Robinson, and Victoria Follette, pioneers of ACT with trauma, and John Forsyth, Georg Eifert, and Mike Twohig, pioneers of ACT with anxiety disorders; I have learned so much from all of them.

I am also very thankful to the larger ACT community; many ideas within these pages have developed from discussions in the ACT Made Simple Facebook group, the ACBS email list, and the forums of my online courses. And I'm particularly grateful to Patricia Zurita Ona, who strongly encouraged me to write this book when I kept hesitating, and Claudette Foley, who reminded me of some really important aspects of this work.

Next, many mega-doses of thanks to the entire team at New Harbinger—including Catherine Meyer, Matt McKay, Clancy Drake, Erin Anderson, Analis Souza, Karen Hathaway, Lisa Gunther, Leyza Yardley, Cassie Stossel, Michele Waters, Madison Davis, Vicraj Gill, Amy Shoup, and Caleb Beckwith—for all the hard work, care, and attention they have invested in this book.

Editors are always the unsung heroes of successful books, so here's my loud chorus of appreciation to the heroic editorial efforts of Rona Bernstein (whom I was delighted to work with again after her brilliant work on the second edition of *ACT Made Simple*).

And last but definitely not least, a gargantuan grail of gratitude to Michael Brekelmans, for his continual support and encouragement to move in new directions, and his huge help and influence in creating new and better training materials.

Resources

Free Resources

In addition to *Trauma-Focused ACT: The Extra Bits*, there's a huge treasure trove of free materials—including audio recordings, e-books, handouts and worksheets, YouTube videos, book chapters, articles, blogs, and published studies—available on the "Free Resources" page of http://www.ImLearningACT.com. There, you can also sign up for my quarterly newsletter, where I distribute new free resources as I create them.

Books by Russ Harris

ACT Made Simple, 2nd edition (New Harbinger, 2019)

The world's best-selling textbook on ACT, with over 100,000 copies sold, and translations into 20 languages. A classic in the field of psychotherapy literature. (The second edition has over 50% new material.)

The Happiness Trap (Exisle Publishing, 2007)

The world's best-selling self-help book on ACT, aimed at everyone and anyone. Over one million copies sold, and published in 30 languages.

The Illustrated Happiness Trap—by Russ Harris and Bev Aisbett (Shambhala Publications, 2014)

A fun, comic-book version of the original—especially for teenagers and adults who are not into reading. (It's alternatively titled *The Happiness Trap Pocketbook* in the UK and Australia.)

The Reality Slap, 2nd edition (Exisle Publishing, 2020)

An ACT-based self-help book for grief, loss, and crisis, with a major emphasis on self-compassion. (The second edition has more than 50% new material.)

When Life Hits Hard (New Harbinger, 2021)

This is the same book as *The Reality Slap* (second edition), mentioned above. Because it has over 50% new material, the US publishers decided to change the title and release it as a new book.

The Confidence Gap (Exisle Publishing, 2011)

A self-help book that looks at confidence, success, and performance from an ACT perspective; especially suitable for life coaching, executive coaching, and sports and business performance.

ACT with Love (New Harbinger, 2009)

A popular self-help book on the use of ACT for common relationship issues. (By the way, you may have noticed my other three self-help books all have rhyming titles—*The Happiness Trap*, *The Reality Slap*, *The Confidence Gap*—but this one doesn't. I wanted to call it *The Relationship Crap*, but the publishers wouldn't let me.)

Getting Unstuck in ACT (New Harbinger, 2013)

The first advanced-level textbook on ACT. This does not cover the basics; it assumes you know them. Instead, it focuses on common sticking points for both clients and therapists.

ACT Questions & Answers (New Harbinger, 2018)

Also known as "Everything you wanted to know about ACT but were afraid to ask!" This is another advanced-level textbook, in an easy-to-read Q&A format. It covers all those tricky, sticky questions about problems not covered in most textbooks.

The Weight Escape—by Joe Ciarrochi, Ann Bailey, and Russ Harris (Shambhala Publications, 2014)

A self-help book on the ACT approach to fitness, weight loss, and self-acceptance with any size body.

Online Training—Public and Professional

In case you don't make it to appendix B, I want to mention this here: I have created a range of online training courses in ACT, from beginner to advanced level, covering everything from trauma, depression, and anxiety disorders to adolescents, grief and loss, and brief interventions. They are available at http://www.ImLearningACT.com. And if you would like to go further with TFACT, this is the course to choose:

Trauma-Focused ACT: Online Training

This advanced-level course—which includes many videos of therapy sessions—is intensely practical, with a strong emphasis on skills development. You'll discover a treasure trove of methods to increase your knowledge and skill level with TFACT, so you can help your clients rapidly progress to posttraumatic growth.

The Happiness Trap Online: 8-Week Program

This is a personal-growth program for well-being and vitality, inspired by and adapted from the book *The Happiness Trap*. It's a beautifully filmed and very entertaining online course, developed for the general public—suitable for pretty much everyone. We've also designed a version of the program that therapists can use with clients as an adjunct to their therapy sessions. Find out more at http://www.TheHappinessTrap.com.

MP3s

I have three albums of MP3s that you can purchase from https://www.actmindfully.com.au: Mindfulness Skills Volume 1, Mindfulness Skills Volume 2, and Exercises and Meditations from *The Reality Slap*.

ACT Companion: Smartphone App

Australian psychologist Anthony Berrick created this excellent app for use as an adjunct to therapy. It's loaded with cool ACT tools, including the choice point, and contains over two hours of audio recordings—some with my voice, some with Anthony's.

Values Cards

I've created a pack of full-color values cards containing simple descriptions of values accompanied by delightful cartoons. More specifically, they're "values, goals, and barriers" cards; there are extra cards for goal setting, action planning, and dealing with barriers such as values conflicts, fusion, and so on. In Australia, you can purchase these at https://www.actmindfully.com.au. For orders outside Australia, go to https://www.edgarpsych.co.uk/shop.

Facebook Group

The ACT Made Simple Facebook group is a huge online community where you can share resources, ask questions, discuss struggles and successes, get the latest updates and free materials from me, and so much more. Just go to Facebook and search for "ACT Made Simple."

Further Training

Live Workshops in Australia

I run live workshops around Australia throughout the year. You can find details at https://www.act-mindfully.com.au. (Unfortunately, I rarely make it overseas because of the long travel times and horrendous jet lag—but hey, if you live outside Australia, you can attend my online trainings, described below.)

Online Courses

I offer a range of online courses in ACT, where you can interact with me directly via the forum, watch videos of therapy sessions, and access a stack of specially designed audio, visual, and text-based training materials. The scope is continually expanding; at the time of writing it includes the following courses:

- Trauma-Focused ACT

- ACT for Beginners

- ACT for Depression and Anxiety Disorders

- ACT for Adolescents

- ACT as a Brief Intervention

- ACT for Grief and Loss

- ACT for Complex Cases

- ACT for Chronic Pain

For more information go to http://www.ImLearningACT.com.

ACBS Website

The mothership organization of ACT and RFT (relational frame theory) is ACBS: Association for Contextual Behavioral Science. The ACBS website is truly vast, and in addition to many free resources, you can find details on ACT trainings, workshops, courses, and conferences worldwide. You can also join numerous forums and special interest groups, find an ACT supervisor, find an ACT therapist, and much, much more. Go to https://www.contextualscience.org.

References

Arch, J. J., & Craske, M. G. (2011). Addressing relapse in cognitive behavioral therapy for panic disorder: Methods for optimizing long-term treatment outcomes. *Cognitive and Behavioral Practice*, *18*(3), 306–315.

Boals, A., & Murrell, A. R. (2016). I am > trauma: Experimentally reducing event centrality and PTSD symptoms in a clinical trial. *Journal of Loss and Trauma*, *21*(6), 471–483.

Boals, A., Steward, J. M., & Schuettler, D. (2010). Advancing our understanding of posttraumatic growth by considering event centrality. *Journal of Loss and Trauma*, *15*(6), 518–533.

Bowlby, J. (1969). *Attachment and loss*. Basic Books.

Brown, G. S., & Jones, E. R. (2005). Implementation of a feedback system in a managed care environment: What are patients teaching us? *Journal of Clinical Psychology*, *61*, 187–198.

Chawla N., & Ostafin, B. (2007). Experiential avoidance as a functional dimensional approach to psychopathology: An empirical review. *Journal of Clinical Psychology*, *63*(9), 871–890.

Chiles, J. A., Strosahl, K. D., & Roberts, L. W. (2018). *The suicidal patient: Principles of assessment, treatment, and case management* (2nd ed.). American Psychiatric Association.

Ciarrocchi, J., Bailey, A., & Harris, R. (2013). *The weight escape: How to stop dieting and start living*. Penguin Books Australia.

Craske, M. G., Treanor, M., Conway, C. C., Zbozinek, T., & Vervliet, B. (2014). Maximizing exposure therapy: An inhibitory learning approach. *Behaviour Research and Therapy*, *58*, 10–23.

Eifert, G., & Forsyth, J. (2005). *Acceptance and commitment therapy for anxiety disorders: A practitioner's treatment guide to using mindfulness, acceptance, and values-based behavior change strategies*. New Harbinger.

Gloster, A. T., Walder, N., Levin, M. E., Twohig, M. P., & Karekla, M. (2020). The empirical status of acceptance and commitment therapy: A review of meta-analyses. *Journal of Contextual Behavioral Science*, *18*, 181–192.

Harris, R. (2007). *The happiness trap: Stop struggling, start living*. Exisle Publishing.

Harris, R. (2009a). *ACT made simple: An easy-to-read primer on acceptance and commitment therapy*. New Harbinger.

Harris, R. (2009b). *ACT with love: Stop struggling, reconcile differences, and strengthen your relationship with acceptance and commitment therapy*. New Harbinger.

Harris, R. (2011). *The confidence gap: A guide to overcoming fear and self-doubt*. Penguin Books Australia.

Harris, R. (2012). *The reality slap: Finding peace and fulfillment when life hurts*. Exisle Publishing.

Harris, R. (2013). *Getting unstuck in ACT: A clinician's guide to overcoming common obstacles in acceptance and commitment therapy*. New Harbinger.

Harris, R. (2015). *ACT for Trauma* [Online training program]. http://www.ImLearningACT.com

Harris, R. (2018). *ACT questions and answers: A practitioner's guide to 150 common sticking points in acceptance and commitment therapy*. New Harbinger.

Harris, R. (2019). *ACT made simple: An easy-to-read primer on acceptance and commitment therapy* (2nd ed.). New Harbinger.

Harris, R. (2020). *The reality slap: How to survive and thrive when life hits hard*. (2nd ed.). Exisle Publishing.

Harris, R., & Aisbett, B. (2014). *The illustrated happiness trap: How to stop struggling and start living*. Shambhala Publications.

Hayes, S. C., Strosahl, K. D., & Wilson, K. G. (1999). *Acceptance and commitment therapy: An experiential approach to behavior change*. Guilford Press.

Joiner, T. E., Jr., Walker, R. L., Rudd, M. D., & Jobes, D. A. (1999). Scientizing and routinizing the assessment of suicidality in outpatient practice. *Professional Psychology: Research and Practice*, 30(5), 447–453.

Kabat-Zinn, J. (1982). An outpatient program in behavioral medicine for chronic pain patients based on the practice of mindfulness meditation. *General Hospital Psychiatry*, 4, 33–47.

Kashdan, T., Breen, W., & Julian, T. (2010). Everyday strivings in war veterans with post-traumatic stress disorder: Suffering from a hyper-focus on avoidance and emotion regulation. *Behavior therapy*, 41, 350–63. https://doi.org/10.1016/j.beth.2009.09.003

Kashdan, T. B., & Kane, J. Q. (2011). Post-traumatic distress and the presence of post-traumatic growth and meaning in life: Experiential avoidance as a moderator. *Personality and Individual Differences*, 50(1), 84–89.

Lang, A. J., Schnurr, P. P., Jain, S., He, F., Walser, R. D., Bolton, E., Benedek, D. M., Norman, S. B., Sylvers, P., Flashman, L., Strauss, J., Raman, R., & Chard, K. M. (2017). Randomized controlled trial of acceptance and commitment therapy for distress and impairment in OEF/OIF/OND veterans. *Psychological Trauma: Theory, Research, Practice, and Policy*, 9(Suppl 1), 74–84.

Lindahl, J., Fisher, N., Cooper, D., Rosen, R., & Britton, W. (2017). The varieties of contemplative experience: A mixed-methods study of meditation-related challenges in Western Buddhists. *PLoS One, 12*(5), e0176239.

Luoma, J. B., Kohlenberg, B. S., Hayes, S. C., & Fletcher, L. (2012). Slow and steady wins the race: A randomized clinical trial of acceptance and commitment therapy targeting shame in substance use disorders. *Journal of Consulting and Clinical Psychology, 80*(1), 43–53.

Luoma, J. B., & LeJeune, J. T. (2020). Incorporating affective science into ACT to treat highly self-critical and shame prone clients. In M. E. Levin, M. P. Twohig, & J. Kraft (Eds.), *Innovations in ACT* (pp. 110–123). New Harbinger.

Marlatt, A., Gordon, J. (1985). *Relapse prevention: Maintenance strategies in the treatment of addictive behaviors*. Guilford Press.

Masters, W., & Johnson, V.E. (1966). *Human sexual response*. Little, Brown and Company.

Neff, K. (2003). Self-compassion: An alternative conceptualization of a healthy attitude toward oneself. *Self and Identity, 2*(2), 85–101.

Porges, S. W. (1995). Orienting in a defensive world: Mammalian modifications of our evolutionary heritage. A polyvagal theory. *Psychophysiology, 32*, 301–318.

Prochaska, J. O., & DiClemente, C. C. (1983). Stages and processes of self-change of smoking: Toward an integrative model of change. *Journal of Consulting and Clinical Psychology, 51*(3), 390–395.

Strosahl, K., Robinson, P., & Gustavsson, T. (2012). *Brief interventions for radical change: Principles and practice of focused acceptance and commitment therapy*. New Harbinger.

Tedeschi, R. G., & Calhoun, L. G. (1996). The posttraumatic growth inventory: Measuring the positive legacy of trauma. *Journal of Traumatic Stress, 9*, 455–471.

Tirch, D., Schoendorff, B., & Silberstein, L. R. (2014). *The ACT practitioner's guide to the science of compassion: Tools for fostering psychological flexibility*. New Harbinger.

Tol, A. W., Leku, M. R., Lakin, D. P., Carswell, K., Augustinavicius, J., Adaku, A., Au, T. M., Brown, F. L., Bryant, R. L., Garcia-Moreno, C., Musci, R. J., Ventevogel, P., White, R. G., & van Ommeren, M. (2020, February 1). Guided self-help to reduce psychological distress in South Sudanese female refugees in Uganda: A cluster randomised trial. *The Lancet, 8*(2), E254-E263.

Wells, A. (2009). *Metacognitive therapy for anxiety and depression*. Guilford Press.

Wilson, K. G., & DuFrene, T. (2009). *Mindfulness for two: An acceptance and commitment therapy approach to mindfulness in psychotherapy*. New Harbinger.

Zurita Ona, P. (2019). *Acceptance and commitment therapy for borderline personality disorder: A flexible treatment plan for clients with emotion dysregulation*. New Harbinger.

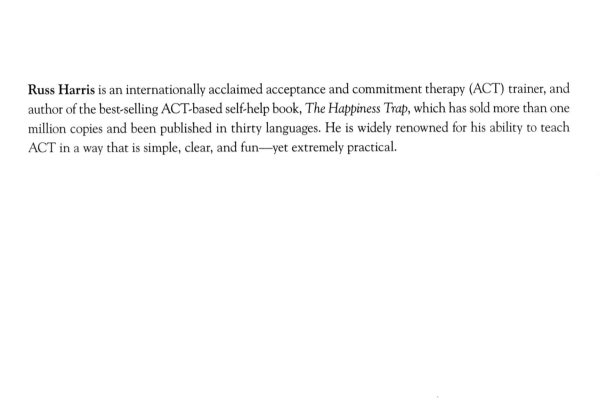

Russ Harris is an internationally acclaimed acceptance and commitment therapy (ACT) trainer, and author of the best-selling ACT-based self-help book, *The Happiness Trap*, which has sold more than one million copies and been published in thirty languages. He is widely renowned for his ability to teach ACT in a way that is simple, clear, and fun—yet extremely practical.

Index

FROM OUR PUBLISHER—

As the publisher at New Harbinger and a clinical psychologist since 1978, I know that emotional problems are best helped with evidence-based therapies. These are the treatments derived from scientific research (randomized controlled trials) that show what works. Whether these treatments are delivered by trained clinicians or found in a self-help book, they are designed to provide you with proven strategies to overcome your problem.

Therapies that aren't evidence-based—whether offered by clinicians or in books—are much less likely to help. In fact, therapies that aren't guided by science may not help you at all. That's why this New Harbinger book is based on scientific evidence that the treatment can relieve emotional pain.

This is important: if this book isn't enough, and you need the help of a skilled therapist, use the following resources to find a clinician trained in the evidence-based protocols appropriate for your problem. And if you need more support—a community that understands what you're going through and can show you ways to cope—resources for that are provided below, as well.

Real help is available for the problems you have been struggling with. The skills you can learn from evidence-based therapies will change your life.

Matthew McKay, PhD
Publisher, New Harbinger Publications

If you need a therapist, the following organization can help you find a therapist trained in acceptance and commitment therapy (ACT).

Association for Contextual Behavioral Science (ACBS)
please visit www.contextualscience.org and click on *Find an ACT Therapist*.

For additional support for patients, family, and friends, please contact the following:

National Center for PTSD
visit www.ptsd.va.gov

Anxiety and Depression Association of American (ADAA)
Please visit www.adaa.org

National Suicide Prevention Lifeline
Call 24 hours a day 1-800-273-TALK (8255)
or visit www.suicidepreventionlifeline.org

MORE BOOKS from NEW HARBINGER PUBLICATIONS

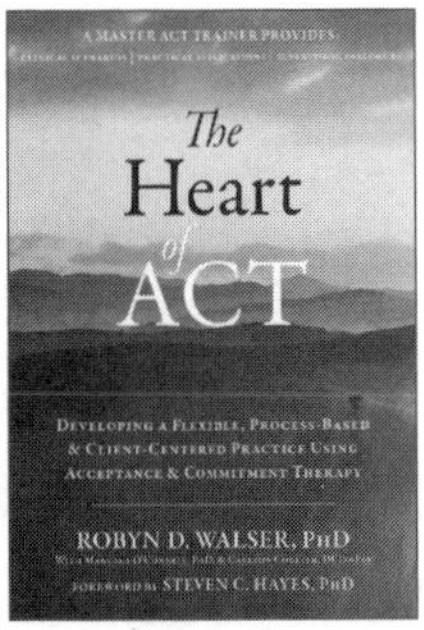

THE HEART OF ACT

Developing a Flexible, Process-Based, and Client-Centered Practice Using Acceptance and Commitment Therapy

978-1684030392 / US $49.95

CONTEXT PRESS
An Imprint of New Harbinger Publications

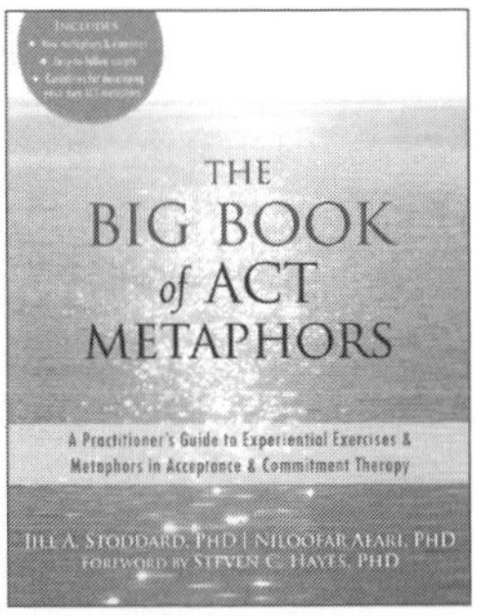

THE BIG BOOK OF ACT METAPHORS

A Practitioner's Guide to Experiential Exercises and Metaphors in Acceptance and Commitment Therapy

978-1608825295 / US $59.95

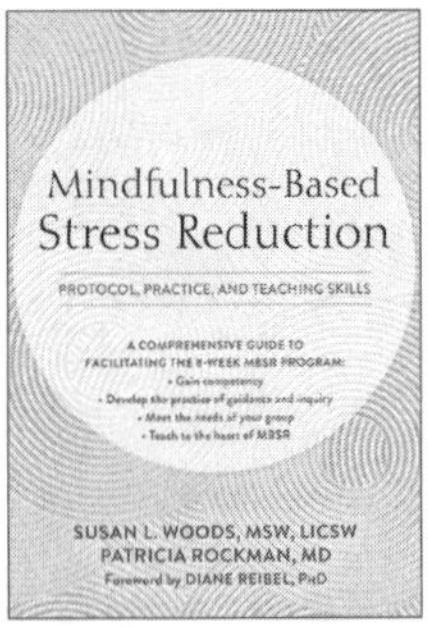

MINDFULNESS-BASED STRESS REDUCTION

Protocol, Practice, and Teaching Skills

978-1684035601 / US $59.95

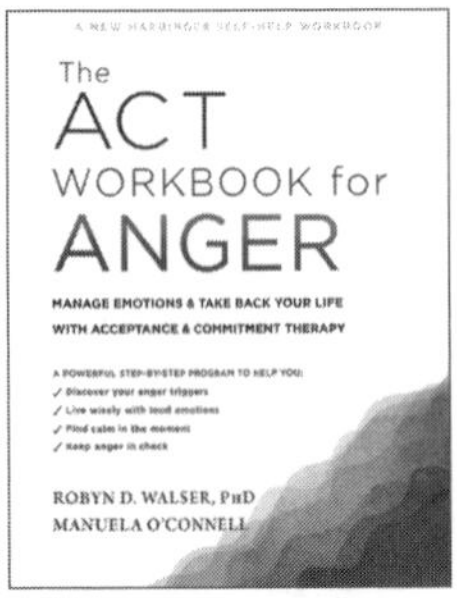

THE ACT WORKBOOK FOR ANGER

Manage Emotions and Take Back Your Life with Acceptance and Commitment Therapy

978-16840653-0 / US $21.95

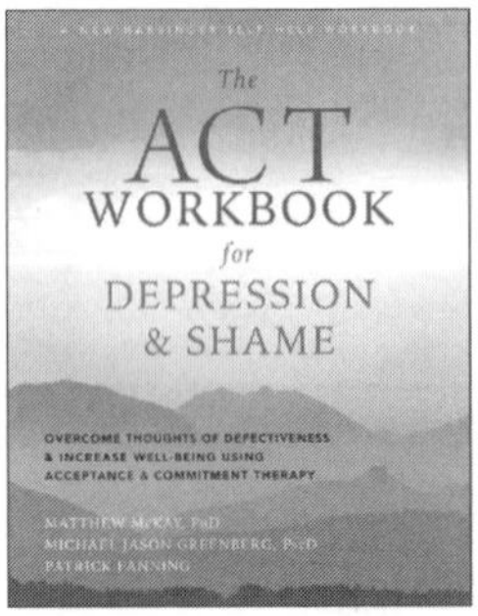

THE ACT WORKBOOK FOR DEPRESSION AND SHAME

Overcome Thoughts of Defectiveness and Increase Well-Being Using Acceptance and Commitment Therapy

978-1684035540 / US $22.95

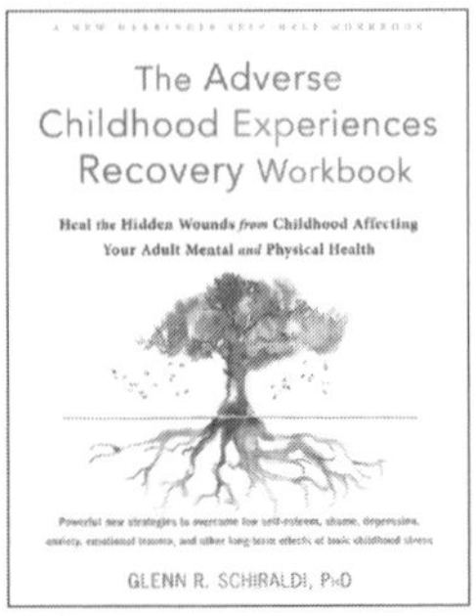

THE ADVERSE CHILDHOOD EXPERIENCES RECOVERY WORKBOOK

Heal the Hidden Wounds from Childhood Affecting Your Adult Mental and Physical Health

978-1684036646 / US $24.95

newharbingerpublications
1-800-748-6273 / newharbinger.com

(VISA, MC, AMEX / prices subject to change without notice)
Follow Us

Don't miss out on new books in the subjects that interest you.
Sign up for our Book Alerts at **newharbinger.com/bookalerts**